POEMS O

Tennyson

RIVERSIDE EDITIONS

RIVERSIDE EDITIONS

UNDER THE GENERAL EDITORSHIP OF

Gordon N. Ray

POEMS OF

Tennyson

SELECTED WITH AN INTRODUCTION AND NOTES BY

Jerome Hamilton Buckley

HARVARD UNIVERSITY

HOUGHTON MIFFLIN COMPANY

BOSTON

CONTENTS

INTRODUCTION

by Jerome Hamilton Buckley

THE significance of *In Memoriam* far transcends the approval of Prince Albert. Yet it was fitting that one November night of 1850 the Prince, who did admire the poem, should come to Tennyson in a dream and kiss him encouragingly upon the cheek — and altogether characteristic that the poet still dreaming should remark to himself with a thoroughly English embarrassment, "Very kind, but very German." For the next morning Tennyson was to receive a letter from the Queen offering him (largely on the strength of the elegy) the post of Poet Laureate as successor to Wordsworth. Such official recognition, though quite unexpected, was singularly appropriate insofar as *In Memoriam* was already a great public document and its author was to remain the most representative poet of his age, the one most sensitive to the hopes and fears and spiritual dilemmas of Victorian England.

But as the dreamer's guarded response to the royal patronage was both grateful and uneasy, so the poet's relation to his world was forever in some sort ambiguous. Tennyson surely desired as artist to achieve public communication, far less for his own advancement than in conscious fulfilment of a responsibility; he often chose to comment directly, though sometimes ill-advisedly, on issues of immediate social concern; and he habitually drew upon forms and images familiar to a general culture and seldom upon a private or unduly recondite symbolism. Yet he sought also to preserve his independence of judgment, to maintain an aesthetic distance from his public, and even to accomplish through his poetry an ordering of his own most intimate experience, an expression and at the same time a concealment or rather objectification of his lifelong struggle toward "self-reverence, self-knowledge, self-control."

Finding his personal lyrics frequently more intense than his public verses, a good many modern critics (indebted especially to Harold Nicolson's brilliant though incomplete interpretation) have drawn a ready distinction between the timeless poet who sang with an ineffable melancholy of the individual man's everlasting aloneness and the Victorian bard who spoke to one time only of ideas and sentiments that once were timely. But the distinction is essentially false and misleading. We may properly regard "The Charge of the Light Brigade," on the one hand, as a curious gloss on the particular conduct or misconduct of the war in the Crimea; and we may rightly value "Tears, Idle Tears," on the other hand, as a personal meditation on the universal death-in-life. Yet we should remember that much of Tennyson's best and most enduring work is neither wholly topical nor wholly remote from the concerns of the nineteenth century. Professor Whitehead as philosopher had good warrant to deem *In Memoriam* a most important reflection of the Victorian mind; and T. S. Eliot as poet had no less reason to consider it the product of a unique sensibility, "the concentrated diary of a man confessing himself." For the overall design of the elegy and much of the poignancy of its separate parts depend upon the close interplay of idea and emotion, the impact upon the lonely self of new knowledge growing from more to more in a troublous and changeful society. Similarly "The Two Voices," *Maud,* the *Idylls of the King,* and many a shorter poem are at once both private and public; each represents an attempt to effect a harmony between the poet's inner experience and his conviction that no man — and so no artist — can live in selfish isolation from mankind. But distrustful alike of a too subjective impulse and of too peremptory demands from the world without, Tennyson himself often remained aloof and disengaged, like the hero of *The Princess* uncertain as to which ultimately was the reality, unable to "know / The shadow from the substance." Yet, even in his confusions, his shifting attitudes towards the self or society, he held fast to one firm commitment. Whether lyrist or bard, throughout a long career he remained the serious and strenuously dedicated poet.

*   *   *   *

Tennyson's dedication to poetry began with his boyhood in Lincolnshire, where he was born in August of 1809. While still a child, he learned the uses of a controlled and "measured language." Before he was old enough to write them down, he had found in his own singsong incantations a discipline and a harmony but fitfully present in his own home. For his life in the rectory at Somersby, though happy in many essential respects, was shadowed always by the unpredictable behavior of his father, a spurned elder son whose aggrieved sense of dispossession expressed itself variously in a morbid self-pity, in a wilful disregard of his eleven children alternating with an overanxious solicitude, in sudden angry recriminations, and even on occasion in outbursts of physical violence. Nonetheless, to this unstable man he owed not only his constitutional melancholia but also his first delight in classical literature and his precocious command of the arts of rhetoric.

Composed in part to please his father, in part perhaps to escape him, and in part surely to exercise his own verbal talents, Tennyson's earliest extant verses are exuberantly derivative from his wide if scattered reading. His "Translation from Claudian's Proserpine," for example, which dates from his twelfth or thirteenth year, is clearly indebted in style to Pope's Homer. *The Devil and the Lady,* a blank-verse play concerning an aged necromancer's efforts to avoid being cuckolded by his volatile young wife, vigorously imitates as much of an Elizabethan gusto of speech as a remarkable boy of fourteen could master. "Armageddon," written when the poet was about fifteen, is often self-consciously Miltonic — yet personal in substance, since it records in a strange and sometimes powerful dream-vision Tennyson's own recurrent experience of dissociation and mystical communion. And the pieces in *Poems by Two Brothers* (the volume, published when Alfred was seventeen, to which his brothers Charles and Frederick also contributed) freely echo the fashionable Romantics, especially Tom Moore and the Byronic Byron, not from any particular sympathy with popular modes but in the declared hope of meeting the public taste. As a release from unresolved private tensions, most of such early work, except a very few poems like "Armageddon," is intentionally quite objective. Meanwhile, however, apart from the actual making of verses, Tennyson's sensibility during his apprenticeship was gradually defining itself less in determined revolt from the disorders of Somersby than in quiet response to the peace of its lawns and gardens, the long lonely stretches of moorland, and the great ebb-and-flow of the not-far-distant sea, physical realities which, remembered with nostalgia or terror, were one day to become presences and images in his most assured and disciplined art.

During his residence at Cambridge (1828–1831) poetry was both his defense and his distinction. It offered him, as a restless and unhappy youth already somewhat isolated from his fellows by temperament and rustic manner, the opportunity of self-appraisal and escape, the occasion to explore such moods as animate "Supposed Confessions," "Recollections of the Arabian Nights," and the more oblique "Mariana." And before long it brought him some attention and acclaim, especially from the earnest and gifted young men of Trinity known as the Cambridge Apostles. When his "Timbuctoo," based in part on the early "Armageddon," received the Chancellor's Medal in 1829, "Apostolic" faith in his genius seemed more than justified. Tennyson — acknowledged as the Apollo of the Apostles and, by virtue of his athletic prowess, as their Hercules — was to be the awakener of a new Albion, the poet-prophet of the good society to come. Tennyson for his part responded to many of their enthusiasms, shared (as "The Poet" testifies) something of their Shelleyan moral-aesthetic, and pondered with them the conflicts he had already privately faced between life and art, social purpose and poetic design, engagement and detachment, the endless debate variously conceived, developed or resolved in "The Lady of Shalott," "The Lotos-Eaters," "The Hesperides," and "The Palace of Art." Among the Apostles he found also a reflection of his own religious doubts, his distrust of dogma, and at the same time a confirmation of his reliance upon direct intuitions of meaning, the rediscovery of spiritual values through the sort of personal experience that ultimately would give him both as man and artist his only real certainty.

But more decisive than any attitude or theory as an influence on his character and work was the actual presence of Arthur Henry Hallam, the most articulate and discerning of the Apostles and the one readiest to understand and encourage the poet's dedication. From Hallam in particular Tennyson gained a renewed confidence, a sense of mission and direction, which helped sustain him through the dark months of 1831 when his father's death forced him to abandon his university career and to assume responsibility for the troubled household at Somersby. Despite the cool reception that greeted his *Poems* published late in the following year, his commitment to poetry and so to an object in living remained almost unshaken. His first true crisis of feeling arose neither from the innumerable family problems thrust upon him nor from the hostility of harsh reviewers. It was not until the report of Hallam's sudden death reached him in October of 1833 that he was driven seriously to question the worth of life itself; and even then he turned immediately to his poetry as his first and last resource, his means of confronting and asserting his own death-wish, his mortal fear, and his essential will to accept and survive.

Written within a few weeks of Hallam's death to express "the need of going forward," "Ulysses" dramatized the hope that man's reason for being might lie in his everlasting aspiration, his desire "to follow knowledge" across the endlessly receding horizon. But "The Two Voices" of the same period asked with a more characteristic despondency whether "knowledge" of itself could ever furnish sufficient motive for the human struggle:

> Forerun thy peers, thy time, and let
> Thy feet, millenniums hence, be set
> In midst of knowledge, dream'd not yet.
>
> Thou hast not gain'd a real height,
> Nor art thou nearer to the light,
> Because the scale is infinite.

> 'T were better not to breathe or speak
> Than cry for strength, remaining weak,
> And seem to find, but still to seek.

To such argument the soul in debate with itself could at length oppose the "heat of inward evidence," its own intuitions, its reasons beyond reason, beyond knowing. Yet "knowledge" remained a central concern, a challenge and a menace, to Tennyson throughout the 1830's. The so-called "years of silence," when in retreat he refused to publish his verses, were in fact years of inquiry and self-examination, of the soliloquies in the dark night that eventually appeared as *In Memoriam*. At Cambridge with its pre-eminence in the natural sciences he had come to think of knowledge as scientific demonstration — "For knowledge is of things we see." He had shown a greater receptivity than the other Apostles to the method and intention of the new inductive scientists, for as a poet he himself had had from the beginning a strong empirical bias, a preference in his verse for microscopic accuracy of detail and precision of image. Now in retirement, seeking a necessary self-justification, he strove to look upon the world in the perspective of such knowledge. In a new astronomy, which charted the course of "blindly" running stars and speculated on the death of the sun, he saw a threat to all sense of human purpose and volition. And from the unorthodox theory of uniformitarian change propounded by Charles Lyell's *Principles of Geology*, he deduced the disquieting notion of human evolution, which Lyell himself was reluctant to make explicit. Though first of all an elegy to his friend, *In Memoriam*, which distilled his thought and emotion, became by extension a lament for modern man living in a universe of changeless change, compelled to demand if humanity were but an accident of Nature and if human history were no more than a cruel delusion:

> And he, shall he,

> Man, her last work, who seem'd so fair,
> Such splendid purpose in his eyes,
> Who roll'd the psalm to wintry skies,
> Who built him fanes of fruitless prayer,

> Who trusted God was love indeed
> And love Creation's final law —
> Tho' Nature, red in tooth and claw
> With ravine, shriek'd against his creed —

> Who loved, who suffer'd countless ills,
> Who battled for the True, the Just,

> Be blown about the desert dust,
> Or seal'd within the iron hills?

To so large a question science unaided could have no answer. The wider man's knowledge, the "more of reverence" he required, the stronger faith; for faith alone, "Believing where we cannot prove," could affirm truth, continuity, and value. And faith properly tested by denial, strengthened indeed by "honest doubt," was itself a hard-won fact of human experience. In the climactic ninety-fifth lyric of the elegy Tennyson described a moment of revelation, an "epiphany," when, transcending time as in the vision of "Armageddon," he achieved release from the deathful self and came with certitude "on that which is," the essence of the eternal and the real, the abiding at the heart of change. Though it passed understanding, the reverence for life so recovered could now assimilate and interpret both science and history:

> The love that rose on stronger wings,
>   Unpalsied when he met with Death,
>   Is comrade to the lesser faith
> That sees the course of human things. . . .
>
>   I see in part
>   That all, as in some piece of art,
>   Is toil coöperant to an end.

So persuaded that mankind's struggle might in general have pattern and meaning and his own deepest hopes some valid sanction, Tennyson was at last prepared to accept with confidence the conditions of his world, to return to his kind, to "take what fruit may be / Of sorrow under human skies." If the resolution of his grief was ultimately personal, it had been accomplished only by facing and laying "the spectres of the mind," by meeting the negations of a scientific age; and as such it would be broadly comprehensible to a whole Victorian generation.

Though not published until 1850, *In Memoriam* was substantially complete by 1842 when Tennyson issued two volumes of verse: one consisting mostly of old poems revised and reshaped, the other of new ones — a few like "Break, Break, Break" relating directly to his personal crisis and a number attempting more objectively to appraise contemporary customs and attitudes with the sanguine "lesser faith" he had attained. Among the latter, "Locksley Hall" proved immediately popular as the sketch of a young man's conversion from a morbid Byronism to a naïve acceptance of the early-Victorian gospel of activity and aspiration:

Not in vain the distance beacons. Forward, forward let us range,
Let the great world spin for ever down the ringing grooves of change.

But despite his hero's ebullient rhetoric proclaiming the idea of progress, Tennyson himself was still at heart eager for stability and nos-
talgic for a lost order. His political verses accordingly, prompted by
a deep mistrust of violence, counseled respect for a long tradition
wherein freedom had grown by organic process from precedent to
precedent. And the descriptive poems he later called "English Idyls,"
though at times touching lightly on current unrest, focused attention
upon the manners of a semi-rural society as yet for the most part rela-
tively unhurried and secure. Indeed, of all the genres in which he now
practiced a fastidious craftsmanship, he found the domestic idyl most
congenial. For the idyl, as he conceived it, was essentially a static
"little picture" to be elaborated in close detail with a gentle humor
and as much sentiment or sentimentality as he cared to indulge; demanding calm considerate vision, it imposed its mood upon the poet.
Though in the main quite alien to the taste of the twentieth century,
his many exercises in the form thus served a distinct purpose in his
own development and, incidentally, proved at the time attractive to
his ever-widening circle of admirers.

As a "medley," *The Princess* of 1847–51 mingled the idyllic mode
and the mock-heroic in curious proportions with which (as the epilogue suggests) perhaps no one could be wholly satisfied. At all events,
most of the Victorians who approved the "solemn close" deplored the
initial levity of the action, whereas, I should think, the modern reader,
who might commend the burlesque with all its epical hyperbole, must
lament the orotund gravity of the conclusion. The poet's intentions
and his methods are indeed consciously ambiguous. His subject apparently concerns the rights of women in general and female educa-
tion in particular — a timely Victorian issue; but he translates his
theme from its place in a real present to an indeterminate setting in
a pseudo-medieval past; and within the framework of his fantasy he
seems undecided whether to attack or defend the feminist cause.
Actually he identifies his feelings only with those of the Prince, whose
"weird seizures" conveniently detach him at crucial moments from the
outward events of the plot. Like the Prince he is preoccupied less
with the problem of feminism than with the character and conduct of
Princess Ida, who, to be sure, has the attributes of Amazonian womanhood but who also — and more importantly — is the imperious muse,
the pride and intellect of poetry, walled off, like the soul in "The
Palace of Art," from human life and love. The mock-epic style allows
Tennyson to measure both the strength and the weakness of the Prin-

cess with a disengaged irony and at the same time to establish a context for the singing or reading of the exquisitely shaped blank-verse lyrics in which his own emotion reaches its fullest expression. To these the Princess responds according to her limited capacity until she has achieved humility and understanding; "Tears, Idle Tears," she hears with disdain; but "Come Down, O Maid," which accompanies her humanization, an idyl within an idyl, she reads with "luminous eyes" and trembling lips. The Prince's final address is necessarily serious, for it marks the triumph of love and the defeat of a cold aestheticism.

Tennyson's career as poet was less than half over in 1850 when he at last published *In Memoriam*, attained the personal security of marriage, and accepted the post of Laureate, which brought formal acknowledgment of his place in Victorian culture. Thereafter in the long years ahead he was frequently expected to assume the role of national bard and oracle. But, despite the pressures laid upon him, he persisted in following first of all the dictate of his own dedicated imagination. When stirred by a public event, he could write occasional verse, like his "Ode on the Death of the Duke of Wellington," which memorably celebrated the general sentiment. Yet when his private feeling ran counter to common prejudice, he would make no concession to the latter. *Maud*, for example, his first longer poem to appear after his appointment as Laureate, offended readers and reviewers alike by its assault on the canting materialism of the "wretchedest age since Time began." Though the hero who delivers the indictment is clearly unbalanced, there is nonetheless method in his madness, the sharp realization that a ruthlessly self-seeking economic individualism may destroy all true individuality. The hero's growth through love is accomplished only in defiance of a false convention. And his ultimate recovery after complete frustration depends on nothing less than social cataclysm; whatever its merits as a crusade, the Crimean war to which he looks for renewal seems at least less dishonest than the war of trade, and it imposes on society, for the moment at any rate, the fearful need of co-operation. Wrenched from this grim setting, the passionate lyrics of *Maud* eventually won wide popularity; but the intention of the "monodrama" as a whole remained quite foreign — and scarcely intelligible — to the greater part of Tennyson's mid-Victorian audience.

The *Idylls of the King*, on the other hand, published in 1859 and augmented, revised and arranged over the years until 1888, carried his public fame to its highest peak. But in the attacks leveled against the poem by George Meredith, Swinburne and others began the total reaction from Tennyson's poetry which continued into the early twentieth century. Even in the revival of interest in Tennyson, few critics have attempted satisfactory reappraisal of the *Idylls;* Harold Nicolson in 1923 could not bring himself to discuss the work; more recently W. H. Auden has complained that Tennyson had no talent whatsoever for epic forms; and Professor P. F. Baum, who has at least considered the narratives, is studiously hostile to all but the poet's calculated craftsmanship. Yet the *Idylls* taken singly repay close analysis, and as a sequence they represent the most sustained effort of any Victorian poet to deal with the moral problem of a society in crisis. It is mistaken, I think, to object either that Tennyson has deserted his own time or that he has misrepresented the middle ages. For the Idylls, conceived as romance and developed with allegory and symbol, are not to be judged in terms of epic realism. Despite derivation from Malory and other medieval sources and despite parallels to Victorian culture, they create a world which never was, and is not now, and yet remains as an ideal beyond all the social betrayals that would destroy it; they depict the enchanted city described by Merlin to Gareth,

> the city . . . built
> To music, therefore never built at all,
> And therefore built for ever.

In origin and end a supernatural figure ("From the great deep to the great deep he goes"), King Arthur is less a man than a symbol; he is the soul of the city, the right that must be accepted on faith and cannot be fully proved or "known," the voice of civic duty to be ignored only at the peril of the civilization itself. Guinevere, on the contrary, who lives the life of passion, is essentially a human being, both in her pride and beauty and in her tragic remorse; but she is also the Queen whose conduct must be exemplary, and her guilty love for Lancelot, the more demoralizing because concealed, thus sanctions the perfidy that at last in grosser forms undermines the fellowship and common trust of the whole Arthurian order. Across the later *Idylls*, particularly "The Holy Grail" of 1869 and "The Last Tournament" of 1871, falls the shadow of social doom and the implicit judgment of Tennyson's more and more insistent idealism. Except to a very few, the Grail quest proves to be no sacred enterprise but rather a retreat from responsibility, an effort to achieve the consolations of religion without transcending the creed and practice of self-interest. And the story of Tristram, reworked with new cogency, is no longer (as in Wagner) a hymn to love eternal but the tale of a selfish opportunist exploiting the confusion of a decadent society. To the dismay of some readers, Tennyson has drastically reconstituted his materials, has imposed on old legends what he liked to call a "modern frame." But only by doing so could he give poetic form to his vision. The *Idylls*, especially the darker ones, gain their force and continued relevance from the intensity of the poet's growing disillusion with the courses of an atomistic modern world.

Though *Enoch Arden and Other Poems*, a resounding best-seller in 1864, represented one of several returns to the domestic sentimentalism of the 'forties, Tennyson's work thereafter was largely directed, like the *Idylls of the King*, towards an analysis of social forces or devoted to a lyrical expression of his own warm responses to books and men and his deepened faith in the validity of a personal idealism. His plays, *Harold, Queen Mary*, and *Becket*, which absorbed much of his time and energy throughout the 'seventies, sought to dramatize the condition of England at periods of historic change and crisis; but the demand for dramatic realism fettered his imagination and left him unable to explore the broader significance of his central themes. "Locksley Hall Sixty Years After" (1886), on the other hand, was too sketchily developed as a dramatic monologue to provide an adequate vehicle for his more direct assault on the intellectual and social temper of the late Victorians; the opinions of the aged speaker, though not without foundation in fact, remained splenetic and hysterical, expository and general, unrelated to the particulars of one man's experience. Appearing as it did not long after Tennyson's acceptance of a barony, the poem seemed to represent the poet's complete repudiation of the society that had honored him. Tennyson, however, who still revered the best traditions of his culture, had grown steadily more independent of both praise and blame. Like his own Tiresias, unheeded or misunderstood, he felt it incumbent upon him to communicate his sense of threatening disaster.

Tennyson continued to write and publish his verses until his death in 1892. And by no means all of his later work was darkened by prophetic forebodings. "To Virgil," for instance, paid moving tribute to the "lord of language" who from the beginning had been his great exemplar, while "Merlin and the Gleam" recorded in final retrospect the steadfastness of his own poetic dedication. Perhaps most acceptant of all, and the ultimate guide to his personal vision, was "The Ancient Sage," in which an aged seer, explaining to a skeptical young poet the need of a philosophic and psychological sanction for all art, describes the intimations of reality he has received since childhood:

> "for oft
> On me, when boy, there came what then I call'd,
> Who knew no books and no philosophies,
> In my boy-phrase, 'The Passion of the Past.'

The first gray streak of earliest summer-dawn,
The last long stripe of waning crimson gloom,
As if the late and early were but one —
A height, a broken grange, a grove, a flower
Had murmurs, 'Lost and gone, and lost and gone!'
A breath, a whisper — some divine farewell —
Desolate sweetness — far and far away —
What had he loved, what had he lost, the boy?
I know not, and I speak of what has been.

    "And more, my son! for more than once when I
Sat all alone, revolving in myself
The word that is the symbol of myself,
The mortal limit of the Self was loosed,
And passed into the Nameless, as a cloud
Melts into heaven. I touch'd my limbs, the limbs
Were strange, not mine — and yet no shade of doubt,
But utter clearness, and thro' loss of self
The gain of such large life as match'd with ours
Were sun to spark — unshadowable in words,
Themselves but shadows of a shadow-world."

Such lines, almost too private for articulation, represent far more than
the sage's apologia, for they suggest what essentially lay beyond words,
the nostalgia, the yearning, and the mystic intuition that had sustained
Tennyson himself through a long life of poetry.

       *   *   *   *

IN HIS stimulating essay on *In Memoriam* T. S. Eliot assures us that
Tennyson, by virtue of his "abundance, variety and complete competence," must be adjudged "a great poet." The present volume is
designed to furnish ample evidence to substantiate so positive an ap-
praisal. Though his strength depends in part on his long-continued
productivity, Tennyson like most other major writers clearly gains by
selection. To be sure, even his failures — his too sweet domestic
idyls, his too harsh and ill-tempered political verses, the contrived
lady's-book portraits of his early period, the stony sermons and peev-
ish diatribes of his later years — served to exercise his verbal talents
or to release his personal emotions and so remain of some interest to
the student of prosody or the biographer. But undue attention to such
pieces has all too often confused both Victorian and modern estimates
of his best accomplishment. To emphasize what seems to me the best,
I have deliberately avoided many of the shorter poems once held up
to easy ridicule, and I have excluded a number of others, higher in

quality, as either too limited in their local color or else too close in manner and matter to the ones I have selected. Among the longer works also omitted, the plays perhaps merit some consideration — especially *The Devil and the Lady* as an amazing exhibit of juvenile exuberance and *Becket* as proof that the mature poet had some real sense of dramatic situation; yet none of the plays gives adequate scope to Tennyson's essential gifts: his mastery of mood and atmosphere, his lyric cry, his skill at recovering the passion of the past and at picturing the moment of insight and illumination. *The Princess* and the *Idylls of the King*, on the other hand, are here represented with unusual fulness since each contributes significantly to our understanding of his poetic development. My purpose indeed has been to suggest not only Tennyson's power but also the course of his growth as artist, and I have therefore drawn upon his poetry of all periods from the "Armageddon" of his boyhood to the posthumously published "Death of Œnone." The reader may thus relate any given poem he regards of particular intrinsic worth to the context of the poet's total sensibility.

No responsible critic, however ill disposed he may be in general towards Tennyson, has refused to concede him a remarkable technical virtuosity, an almost overpowering control of the resources of the English language. The pages that follow demonstrate his command of nearly all the traditional verse forms and his constant experiment with new ones, his familiarity with the colors of rhetoric, his certain feeling for verbal sound and texture and his ability to achieve variation within fixed meters. They evince, too, his concern with many poetic genres: the lyric, the idyl, the ode, the ballad, the epigram, the epistle, the debate, the dream vision, the monologue, the monodrama, the mock epic, the narrative, the character, the confessional. And they reveal an impressive range of styles from the rough dialect of the "Northern Farmer" to the Horatian urbanity of the letters to F. D. Maurice and Edward Lear, from the relaxed colloquialism of "Will Waterproof" to the ornate involution of some of the *Idylls*, from the assured satiric thrust of "The New Timon and the Poets" to the lonely naked voice that rises from the darker sections of *In Memoriam*. Such diversity should make us hesitate to speak, as some literary historians have spoken, of the Tennysonian mode, as if Tennyson had but one manner of speech and one point of view; and it should help us to understand how during his long career, moving from form to form, he perpetually outdistanced the host of his imitators and eluded the many parodists who sought to reduce him to a single gesture.

But despite his endowment as artificer, or perhaps because of it, Tennyson was often perplexed by the difficulties of finding a subject matter commensurate with his craftsmanship. Matthew Arnold demanded of every great poet the capacity of the ancients to delineate a great action rather than the will of the moderns to find self-expression. But Tennyson in this respect belongs essentially with the moderns, with the major Romantics before him and with the representative poets of our own century. Like the Romantics he was devoted first of all not to a general "criticism of life" but to an interpretation of private and personal experience, which might or might not lead to conclusions of broader relevance. And like our contemporaries he was obliged as artist to seek for himself sustaining values in the wastelands of the modern world where all things seemed relative, transient and inconclusive. His poetry deals typically not with the great action seen as an object in itself but with the search through situation and symbol for meaning and the sudden illuminating discovery of purpose. Any reasonably full selection of his verse should indicate his awareness of themes and issues still significant to the modern reader: the moral implications of an amoral science, the need for faith and the necessity of doubt, the isolation of the individual and the extent to which the self must find social fulfilment. This edition, though it attempts to illustrate his entire thematic range, lays particular and rather uncommon stress on the poems in which Tennyson throughout his life, mindful of his own dedication, examined the nature of poetry and the role of the poet. For these poems, especially, reflect the struggles and triumphs of his sensibility and by extension the plight and achievement of every modern artist.

ACKNOWLEDGMENTS

THE passage from "Armageddon" with which this edition opens and the sonnet "She took the dappled partridge" are reprinted from Tennyson's *Unpublished Early Poems* (1931) with the gracious permission of the editor, Sir Charles Tennyson, and by arrangement with the publishers, Macmillan and Company, Limited, London, and St. Martin's Press, Incorporated, New York. The five poems preceding "Crossing the Bar" at the close of this volume are drawn from *The Death of Œnone, Akbar's Dream, and Other Poems*, published by the Macmillan Company immediately after Tennyson's death in 1892. All the other poems follow, with a few changes, the text of the Cambridge Tennyson, edited with notes by W. J. Rolfe and published by the Houghton Mifflin Company.

Like all students of Tennyson, I am indebted to Sir Charles for the admirable full-scale biography of his grandfather, which supplements and corrects the monumental source-book known as the *Memoir,* issued by the poet's son, Hallam Lord Tennyson. In preparing this edition I am especially grateful for the co-operation of Dr. Henry Thoma of Houghton Mifflin and the encouragement of my wife, Elizabeth. And since the Laureate Edition was dedicated "To the Queen," I may perhaps not inappropriately inscribe my part in the present work to my own Victoria.

BIBLIOGRAPHY

Auden, W. H., "Introduction," *A Selection from the Poems of Alfred, Lord Tennyson*. New York, 1944.

Baker, A. E., *A Concordance to the Poetical and Dramatic Works. . . .* New York, 1914.

Baum, Paull F., "Alfred, Lord Tennyson" in F. E. Faverty, ed., *The Victorian Poets: A Guide to Research*. Cambridge, Mass., 1956.

Baum, Paull F., *Tennyson Sixty Years After*. Chapel Hill, 1948.

Bradley, A. C., *A Commentary on Tennyson's In Memoriam*. London, 1930.

Buckley, Jerome H., *The Victorian Temper*. Cambridge, Mass., 1951.

Bush, Douglas, "Introduction," *Tennyson: Selected Poetry*. New York, 1951.

Bush, Douglas, *Mythology and the Romantic Tradition*. Cambridge, Mass., 1937.

Carr, Arthur J., "Tennyson as a Modern Poet," *University of Toronto Quarterly*, XIX (1950), 361–382.

Eliot, T. S., "In Memoriam," *Essays Ancient and Modern*. New York, 1936.

Johnson, E. D. H., *The Alien Vision of Victorian Poetry*. Princeton, 1952.

Langbaum, Robert, *The Poetry of Experience*. New York, 1957.

Masterman, C. F. G., *Tennyson as a Religious Teacher*. London, 1900.

Mattes, Eleanor B., *In Memoriam: the Way of a Soul*. New York, 1951.

Motter, T. H. V., *The Writings of Arthur Hallam*. New York, 1943.

Nicolson, Harold, *Tennyson: Aspects of his Life, Character and Poetry*. New York, 1923.

Paden, W. D., *Tennyson in Egypt: a Study of the Imagery in his Earlier Work*. Lawrence, Kansas, 1942.

Priestley, F. E. L., "Tennyson's *Idylls*," *University of Toronto Quarterly*, XIX (1949), 35–49.

Shannon, Edgar F., Jr., *Tennyson and the Reviewers*. Cambridge, Mass., 1952.

Stevenson, Lionel, *Darwin among the Poets*. Chicago, 1932.

Tennyson, Sir Charles, *Alfred Tennyson*. New York, 1949.

Tennyson, Sir Charles, ed., *The Devil and the Lady*. London, 1930.

Tennyson, Hallam Lord, *Alfred Lord Tennyson: A Memoir*. 2 vols. New York, 1897.

POEMS OF

Tennyson

NOTE

The following poems are arranged, as far as possible or practicable, in the approximate order of composition. The date in roman type after each selection is that of first publication. A date in italics indicates the time, as far as the present editor can determine, at which the poem was written. An asterisk accompanying the date or dates signifies an entry on the piece in the appended "Notes."

From ARMAGEDDON

II

THE rustling of white wings! The bright descent
Of a young seraph! and he stood beside me
In the wide foldings of his argent robes
There on the ridge, and look'd into my face
With his unutterable shining eyes,
So that with hasty motion I did veil
My vision with both hands, and saw before me
Such coloured spots as dance before the eyes
Of those that gaze upon the noonday sun.
    "O Son of Man, why stand you here alone   10
Upon the mountain, knowing not the things
Which will be, and the gathering of the nations
Unto the mighty battle of the Lord?
Thy sense is clogg'd with dull Mortality,
Thy spirit fetter'd with the bond of clay —
Open thine eyes and see!"
                           I look'd, but not
Upon his face, for it was wonderful
With its exceeding brightness, and the light
Of the great Angel Mind that look'd from out
The starry glowing of his restless eyes.   20
I felt my soul grow godlike, and my spirit
With supernatural excitation bound
Within me, and my mental eye grew large
With such a vast circumference of thought,
That, in my vanity, I seem'd to stand
Upon the outward verge and bound alone
Of God's omniscience. Each failing sense,
As with a momentary flash of light,
Grew thrillingly distinct and keen. I saw
The smallest grain that dappled the dark Earth,   30
The indistinctest atom in deep air,
The Moon's white cities, and the opal width
Of her small, glowing lakes, her silver heights
Unvisited with dew of vagrant cloud,
And the unsounded, undescended depth
Of her black hollows. Nay — the hum of men
Or other things talking in unknown tongues,
And notes of busy Life in distant worlds,
Beat, like a far wave, on my anxious ear.

1

I wondered with deep wonder at myself: 40
My mind seem'd wing'd with knowledge and the strength
Of holy musings and immense Ideas,
Even to Infinitude. All sense of Time
And Being and Place was swallowed up and lost
Within a victory of boundless thought.
I was a part of the Unchangeable,
A scintillation of Eternal Mind,
Remix'd and burning with its parent fire.
Yea! in that hour I could have fallen down
Before my own strong soul and worshipp'd it.   50
   Highly and holily the Angel look'd.
Immeasurable Solicitude and Awe,
And solemn Adoration and high Faith,
Were trac'd on his imperishable front —
Then with a mournful and ineffable smile,
Which but to look on for a moment fill'd
My eyes with irresistible sweet tears,
In accents of majestic melody,
Like a swollen river's gushings in still night
Mingled with floating music, thus he spoke.   60

III

"O Everlasting God, and thou not less
The Everlasting Man (since that great spirit
Which permeates and informs thine inward sense,
Though limited in action, capable
Of the extreme of knowledge — whether join'd
Unto thee in conception or confin'd
From former wanderings in other shapes
I know not — deathless as its God's own life,
Burns on with inextinguishable strength),
O Lords of Earth and Tyrannies of Hell,   70
And thrones of Heaven, whose triple pride shall clash
In the annihilating anarchy
Of unimaginable war, a day
Of darkness riseth on ye, a thick day,
Pall'd with dun wreaths of dusky fight, a day
Of many thunders and confuséd noise,
Of bloody grapplings in the interval
Of the opposéd Battle, a great day
Of wonderful revealings and vast sights
And inconceivable visions, such as yet   80
Have never shone into the heart of Man —
THE DAY of the Lord God!" . . .

1824? (1931)*

ODE TO MEMORY

I

Thou who stealest fire,
From the fountains of the past,
To glorify the present, O, haste,
      Visit my low desire!
Strengthen me, enlighten me!
I faint in this obscurity,
Thou dewy dawn of memory.

II

Come not as thou camest of late,
   Flinging the gloom of yesternight
On the white day, but robed in soften'd light   10
         Of orient state.
Whilome thou camest with the morning mist,
   Even as a maid, whose stately brow
The dew-impearled winds of dawn have kiss'd,
         When she, as thou,
Stays on her floating locks the lovely freight
Of overflowing blooms, and earliest shoots
Of orient green, giving safe pledge of fruits,
   Which in wintertide shall star
The black earth with brilliance rare.   20

III

Whilome thou camest with the morning mist,
   And with the evening cloud,
Showering thy gleaned wealth into my open breast;
Those peerless flowers which in the rudest wind
         Never grow sere,
When rooted in the garden of the mind,
   Because they are the earliest of the year.
         Nor was the night thy shroud.
In sweet dreams softer than unbroken rest
Thou leddest by the hand thine infant Hope.   30
The eddying of her garments caught from thee
The light of thy great presence; and the cope
   Of the half-attain'd futurity,
      Tho' deep not fathomless,
Was cloven with the million stars which tremble
O'er the deep mind of dauntless infancy.
Small thought was there of life's distress;

For sure she deem'd no mist of earth could dull
Those spirit-thrilling eyes so keen and beautiful;
Sure she was nigher to heaven's spheres,   40
Listening the lordly music flowing from
      The illimitable years.
   O, strengthen me, enlighten me!
   I faint in this obscurity,
   Thou dewy dawn of memory.

            IV

Come forth, I charge thee, arise,
Thou of the many tongues, the myriad eyes!
Thou comest not with shows of flaunting vines
     Unto mine inner eye,
     Divinest Memory!   50
  Thou wert not nursed by the waterfall
Which ever sounds and shines
  A pillar of white light upon the wall
Of purple cliffs, aloof descried:
Come from the woods that belt the gray hillside,
  The seven elms, the poplars four
  That stand beside my father's door,
And chiefly from the brook that loves
To purl o'er matted cress and ribbed sand,
Or dimple in the dark of rushy coves,   60
Drawing into his narrow earthen urn,
   In every elbow and turn,
The filter'd tribute of the rough woodland;
   O, hither lead thy feet!
Pour round mine ears the livelong bleat
Of the thick-fleeced sheep from wattled folds,
   Upon the ridged wolds,
When the first matin-song hath waken'd loud
Over the dark dewy earth forlorn,
What time the amber morn   70
Forth gushes from beneath a low-hung cloud.

            V

Large dowries doth the raptured eye
  To the young spirit present
    When first she is wed,
     And like a bride of old
    In triumph led,
      With music and sweet showers
      Of festal flowers,

Unto the dwelling she must sway.
Well hast thou done, great artist Memory
    In setting round thy first experiment   80
        With royal framework of wrought gold;
Needs must thou dearly love thy first essay,
And foremost in thy various gallery
    Place it, where sweetest sunlight falls
    Upon the storied walls;
            For the discovery
And newness of thine art so pleased thee
That all which thou hast drawn of fairest
Or boldest since but lightly weighs   90
With thee unto the love thou bearest
The first-born of thy genius. Artist-like,
Ever retiring thou dost gaze
On the prime labor of thine early days,
No matter what the sketch might be:
Whether the high field on the bushless pike,
Or even a sand-built ridge
Of heaped hills that mound the sea,
Overblown with murmurs harsh,
Or even a lowly cottage whence we see   100
Stretch'd wide and wild the waste enormous marsh,
Where from the frequent bridge,
Like emblems of infinity,
The trenched waters run from sky to sky;
Or a garden bower'd close
With plaited alleys of the trailing rose,
Long alleys falling down to twilight grots,
Or opening upon level plots
Of crowned lilies, standing near
Purple-spiked lavender: 110
Whither in after life retired
From brawling storms,
From weary wind,
With youthful fancy re-inspired,
We may hold converse with all forms
Of the many-sided mind,
And those whom passion hath not blinded,
Subtle-thoughted, myriad-minded.

My friend, with you to live alone
Were how much better than to own   120
A crown, a sceptre, and a throne!

O, strengthen me, enlighten me!
I faint in this obscurity,
Thou dewy dawn of memory.
1826 ? (1830) *

SONG

I

A SPIRIT haunts the year's last hours
Dwelling amid these yellowing bowers.
To himself he talks;
For at eventide, listening earnestly,
At his work you may hear him sob and sigh
In the walks;
Earthward he boweth the heavy stalks
Of the mouldering flowers.
Heavily hangs the broad sunflower
Over its grave i' the earth so chilly;   10
Heavily hangs the hollyhock,
Heavily hangs the tiger-lily.

II

The air is damp, and hush'd, and close,
As a sick man's room when he taketh repose
An hour before death;
My very heart faints and my whole soul grieves
At the moist rich smell of the rotting leaves,
And the breath
Of the fading edges of box beneath,
And the year's last rose.   20
Heavily hangs the broad sunflower
Over its grave i' the earth so chilly;
Heavily hangs the hollyhock,
Heavily hangs the tiger-lily.

1830

THE MYSTIC

ANGELS have talked with him, and showed him thrones:
Ye knew him not; he was not one of ye,
Ye scorned him with an undiscerning scorn:
Ye could not read the marvel in his eye,

The still serene abstraction: he hath felt
The vanities of after and before;
Albeit, his spirit and his secret heart
The stern experiences of converse lives,
The linkéd woes of many a fiery change
Had purified, and chastened, and made free.   10
Always there stood before him, night and day,
Of wayward vary-colored circumstance
The imperishable presences serene,
Colossal, without form, or sense, or sound,
Dim shadows but unwaning presences
Fourfacéd to four corners of the sky:
And yet again, three shadows, fronting one,
One forward, one respectant, three but one;
And yet again, again and evermore,
For the two first were not, but only seemed.   20
One shadow in the midst of a great light,
One reflex from eternity on time,
One mighty countenance of perfect calm,
Awful with most invariable eyes.
For him the silent congregated hours,
Daughters of time, divinely tall, beneath
Severe and youthful brows, with shining eyes
Smiling a godlike smile (the innocent light
Of earliest youth pierced through and through with all
Keen knowledges of low-embowéd eld)   30
Upheld, and ever hold aloft the cloud
Which droops low-hung on either gate of life,
Both birth and death: he in the centre fixt,
Saw far on each side through the grated gates
Most pale and clear and lovely distances.
He often lying broad awake, and yet
Remaining from the body, and apart
In intellect and power and will, hath heard
Time flowing in the middle of the night,
And all things creeping to a day of doom.   40
How could ye know him? Ye were yet within
The narrower circle: he had wellnigh reached
The last, which with a region of white flame,
Pure without heat, into a larger air
Upburning, and an ether of black blue,
Investeth and ingirds all other lives.

1830*

SUPPOSED CONFESSIONS

OF A SECOND-RATE SENSITIVE MIND

O GOD! my God! have mercy now.
I faint, I fall. Men say that Thou
Didst die for me, for such as *me*,
Patient of ill, and death, and scorn,
And that my sin was as a thorn
Among the thorns that girt Thy brow,
Wounding Thy soul. — That even now,
In this extremest misery
Of ignorance, I should require
A sign! and if a bolt of fire   10
Would rive the slumbrous summer noon
While I do pray to Thee alone,
Think my belief would stronger grow!
Is not my human pride brought low?
The boastings of my spirit still?
The joy I had in my free-will
All cold, and dead, and corpse-like grown?
And what is left to me but Thou,
And faith in Thee? Men pass me by;
Christians with happy countenances —   20
And children all seem full of Thee!
And women smile with saint-like glances
Like Thine own mother's when she bow'd
Above Thee, on that happy morn
When angels spake to men aloud,
And Thou and peace to earth were born.
Good-will to me as well as all —
I one of them; my brothers they;
Brothers in Christ — a world of peace
And confidence, day after day;   30
And trust and hope till things should cease,
And then one Heaven receive us all.

How sweet to have a common faith!
To hold a common scorn of death!
And at a burial to hear
The creaking cords which wound and eat
Into my human heart, whene'er
Earth goes to earth, with grief, not fear,
With hopeful grief, were passing sweet!

Thrice happy state again to be   40
The trustful infant on the knee,
Who lets his rosy fingers play
About his mother's neck, and knows
Nothing beyond his mother's eyes!
They comfort him by night and day;
They light his little life alway;
He hath no thought of coming woes;
He hath no care of life or death;
Scarce outward signs of joy arise,
Because the Spirit of happiness   50
And perfect rest so inward is;
And loveth so his innocent heart,
Her temple and her place of birth,
Where she would ever wish to dwell,
Life of the fountain there, beneath
Its salient spirngs, and far apart,
Hating to wander out on earth,
Or breathe into the hollow air,
Whose chillness would make visible
Her subtil, warm, and golden breath,   60
Which mixing with the infant's blood,
Fulfils him with beatitude.
O, sure it is a special care
Of God, to fortify from doubt,
To arm in proof, and guard about
With triple-mailed trust, and clear
Delight, the infant's dawning year.

Would that my gloomed fancy were
As thine, my mother, when with brows
Propt on thy knees, my hands upheld   70
In thine, I listen'd to thy vows,
For me outpour'd in holiest prayer —
For me unworthy! — and beheld
Thy mild deep eyes upraised, that knew
The beauty and repose of faith,
And the clear spirit shining thro'.
O, wherefore do we grow awry
From roots which strike so deep? why dare
Paths in the desert? Could not I
Bow myself down, where thou hast knelt,   80
To the earth — until the ice would melt
Here, and I feel as thou hast felt?
What devil had the heart to scathe
Flowers thou hadst rear'd — to brush the dew

From thine own lily, when thy grave
Was deep, my mother, in the clay?
Myself? Is it thus? Myself? Had I
So little love for thee? But why
Prevail'd not thy pure prayers? Why pray
To one who heeds not, who can save   90
But will not? Great in faith, and strong
Against the grief of circumstance,
Wert thou, and yet unheard. What if
Thou pleadest still, and seest me drive
Thro' utter dark a full-sail'd skiff,
Unpiloted i' the echoing dance
Of reboant whirlwinds, stooping low
Unto the death, not sunk! I know
At matins and at evensong,
That thou, if thou wert yet alive,   100
In deep and daily prayers wouldst strive
To reconcile me with thy God.
Albeit, my hope is gray, and cold
At heart, thou wouldest murmur still —
"Bring this lamb back into Thy fold,
My Lord, if so it be Thy will."
Wouldst tell me I must brook the rod
And chastisement of human pride;
That pride, the sin of devils, stood
Betwixt me and the light of God;   110
That hitherto I had defied
And had rejected God — that grace
Would drop from His o'er-brimming love,
As manna on my wilderness,
If I would pray — that God would move
And strike the hard, hard rock, and thence,
Sweet in their utmost bitterness,
Would issue tears of penitence
Which would keep green hope's life. Alas!
I think that pride hath now no place   120
Nor sojourn in me. I am void,
Dark, formless, utterly destroyed.

Why not believe then? Why not yet
Anchor thy frailty there, where man
Hath moor'd and rested? Ask the sea
At midnight, when the crisp slope waves
After a tempest rib and fret
The broad-imbased beach, why he

Slumbers not like a mountain tarn?
Wherefore his ridges are not curls   130
And ripples of an inland mere?
Wherefore he moaneth thus, nor can
Draw down into his vexed pools
All that blue heaven which hues and paves
The other? I am too forlorn,
Too shaken: my own weakness fools
My judgment, and my spirit whirls,
Moved from beneath with doubt and fear.

"Yet," said I, in my morn of youth,
The unsunn'd freshness of my strength,   140
When I went forth in quest of truth,
"It is man's privilege to doubt,
If so be that from doubt at length
Truth may stand forth unmoved of change,
An image with profulgent brows
And perfect limbs, as from the storm
Of running fires and fluid range
Of lawless airs, at last stood out
This excellence and solid form
Of constant beauty. For the ox   150
Feeds in the herb, and sleeps, or fills
The horned valleys all about,
And hollows of the fringed hills
In summer heats, with placid lows
Unfearing, till his own blood flows
About his hoof. And in the flocks
The lamb rejoiceth in the year,
And raceth freely with his fere,
And answers to his mother's calls
From the flower'd furrow. In a time   160
Of which he wots not, run short pains
Thro' his warm heart; and then, from whence
He knows not, on his light there falls
A shadow; and his native slope,
Where he was wont to leap and climb,
Floats from his sick and filmed eyes,
And something in the darkness draws
His forehead earthward, and he dies.
Shall man live thus, in joy and hope
As a young lamb, who cannot dream,   170
Living, but that he shall live on?
Shall we not look into the laws

Of life and death, and things that seem,
And things that be, and analyze
Our double nature, and compare
All creeds till we have found the one,
If one there be?" Ay me! I fear
All may not doubt, but everywhere
Some must clasp idols. Yet, my God,
Whom call I idol? Let Thy dove   180
Shadow me over, and my sins
Be unremember'd, and Thy love
Enlighten me. O, teach me yet
Somewhat before the heavy clod
Weighs on me, and the busy fret
Of that sharp-headed worm begins
In the gross blackness underneath.

O weary life! O weary death!
O spirit and heart made desolate!
O damned vacillating state!   190
1830*

THE DYING SWAN

I

THE plain was grassy, wild and bare,
Wide, wild, and open to the air,
Which had built up everywhere
  An under-roof of doleful gray.
With an inner voice the river ran,
Adown it floated a dying swan,
   And loudly did lament.
  It was the middle of the day.
Ever the weary wind went on,
  And took the reed-tops as it went.   10

II

Some blue peaks in the distance rose,
And white against the cold-white sky
Shone out their crowning snows.
  One willow over the river wept,
And shook the wave as the wind did sigh;
Above in the wind was the swallow,
  Chasing itself at its own wild will,

And far thro' the marish green and still
  The tangled water-courses slept,
Shot over with purple, and green, and yellow.   20

III

The wild swan's death-hymn took the soul
Of that waste place with joy
Hidden in sorrow. At first to the ear
The warble was low, and full and clear;
And floating about the under-sky,
Prevailing in weakness, the coronach stole
Sometimes afar, and sometimes anear;
But anon her awful jubilant voice,
With a music strange and manifold,
Flow'd forth on a carol free and bold;   30
As when a mighty people rejoice
With shawms, and with cymbals, and harps of gold,
And the tumult of their acclaim is roll'd
Thro' the open gates of the city afar,
To the shepherd who watcheth the evening star.
And the creeping mosses and clambering weeds,
And the willow-branches hoar and dank,
And the wavy swell of the soughing reeds,
And the wave-worn horns of the echoing bank,
And the silvery marish-flowers that throng   40
The desolate creeks and pools among,
Were flooded over with eddying song.
1830

THE KRAKEN

BELOW the thunders of the upper deep,
Far, far beneath in the abysmal sea,
His ancient, dreamless, uninvaded sleep
The Kraken sleepeth: faintest sunlights flee
About his shadowy sides; above him swell
Huge sponges of millennial growth and height;
And far away into the sickly light,
From many a wondrous grot and secret cell
Unnumber'd and enormous polypi
Winnow with giant arms the slumbering green.   10
There hath he lain for ages, and will lie

Battening upon huge sea-worms in his sleep,
Until the latter fire shall heat the deep;
Then once by man and angels to be seen,
In roaring he shall rise and on the surface die.
1830*

RECOLLECTIONS OF THE ARABIAN NIGHTS

WHEN the breeze of a joyful dawn blew free
In the silken sail of infancy,
The tide of time flow'd back with me,
   The forward-flowing tide of time;
And many a sheeny summer-morn,
Adown the Tigris I was borne,
By Bagdat's shrines of fretted gold,
High-walled gardens green and old;
True Mussulman was I and sworn,
   For it was in the golden prime   10
     Of good Haroun Alraschid.

Anight my shallop, rustling thro'
The low and bloomed foliage, drove
The fragrant, glistening deeps, and clove
The citron-shadows in the blue;
By garden porches on the brim,
The costly doors flung open wide,
Gold glittering thro' lamplight dim,
And broider'd sofas on each side.
   In sooth it was a goodly time,   20
   For it was in the golden prime
     Of good Haroun Alraschid.

Often, where clear-stemm'd platans guard
The outlet, did I turn away
The boat-head down a broad canal
From the main river sluiced, where all
The sloping of the moonlit sward
Was damask-work, and deep inlay
Of braided blooms unmown, which crept
Adown to where the water slept.   30
   A goodly place, a goodly time,
   For it was in the golden prime
     Of good Haroun Alraschid.

A motion from the river won
Ridged the smooth level, bearing on
My shallop thro' the star-strown calm,
Until another night in night
I enter'd, from the clearer light,
Imbower'd vaults of pillar'd palm,
Imprisoning sweets, which, as they clomb   40
Heavenward, were stay'd beneath the dome
    Of hollow boughs. A goodly time,
    For it was in the golden prime
      Of good Haroun Alraschid.

Still onward; and the clear canal
Is rounded to as clear a lake.
From the green rivage many a fall
Of diamond rillets musical,
Thro' little crystal arches low
Down from the central fountain's flow   50
Fallen silver-chiming, seemed to shake
The sparkling flints beneath the prow.
    A goodly place, a goodly time,
    For it was in the golden prime
      Of good Haroun Alraschid.

Above thro' many a bowery turn
A walk with vari-colored shells
Wander'd engrain'd. On either side
All round about the fragrant marge
From fluted vase, and brazen urn   60
In order, eastern flowers large,
Some dropping low their crimson bells
Half-closed, and others studded wide
    With disks and tiars, fed the time
    With odor in the golden prime
      Of good Haroun Alraschid.

Far off, and where the lemon grove
In closest coverture upsprung,
The living airs of middle night
Died round the bulbul as he sung;   70
Not he, but something which possess'd
The darkness of the world, delight,
Life, anguish, death, immortal love,
Ceasing not, mingled, unrepress'd,

Apart from place, withholding time,
But flattering the golden prime
   Of good Haroun Alraschid.

Black the garden-bowers and grots
Slumber'd; the solemn palms were ranged
Above, unwoo'd of summer wind;   80
A sudden splendor from behind
Flush'd all the leaves with rich gold-green,
And, flowing rapidly between
Their interspaces, counterchanged
The level lake with diamond-plots
   Of dark and bright. A lovely time,
   For it was in the golden prime
      Of good Haroun Alraschid.

Dark-blue the deep sphere overhead,
Distinct with vivid stars inlaid,   90
Grew darker from that under-flame;
So, leaping lightly from the boat,
With silver anchor left afloat,
In marvel whence that glory came
Upon me, as in sleep I sank
In cool soft turf upon the bank,
   Entranced with that place and time,
   So worthy of the golden prime
      Of good Haroun Alraschid.

Thence thro' the garden I was drawn —   100
A realm of pleasance, many a mound,
And many a shadow-chequer'd lawn
Full of the city's stilly sound,
And deep myrrh-thickets blowing round
The stately cedar, tamarisks,
Thick rosaries of scented thorn,
Tall orient shrubs, and obelisks
   Graven with emblems of the time,
   In honor of the golden prime
      Of good Haroun Alraschid.   110

With dazed vision unawares
From the long alley's latticed shade
Emerged, I came upon the great
Pavillion of the Caliphat.
Right to the carven cedarn doors,

Flung inward over spangled floors,
Broad-based flights of marble stairs
Ran up with golden balustrade,
   After the fashion of the time,
   And humor of the golden prime   120
      Of good Haroun Alraschid.

The fourscore windows all alight
As with the quintessence of flame,
A million tapers flaring bright
From twisted silvers look'd to shame
The hollow-vaulted dark, and stream'd
Upon the mooned domes aloof
In inmost Bagdat, till there seem'd
Hundreds of crescents on the roof
   Of night new-risen, that marvellous time   130
   To celebrate the golden prime
      Of good Haroun Alraschid.

Then stole I up, and trancedly
Gazed on the Persian girl alone,
Serene with argent-lidded eyes
Amorous, and lashes like to rays
Of darkness, and a brow of pearl
Tressed with redolent ebony,
In many a dark delicious curl,
Flowing beneath her rose-hued zone;   140
   The sweetest lady of the time,
   Well worthy of the golden prime
      Of good Haroun Alraschid.

Six columns, three on either side,
Pure silver, underpropt a rich
Throne of the massive ore, from which
Down-droop'd, in many a floating fold,
Engarlanded and diaper'd
With inwrought flowers, a cloth of gold.
Thereon, his deep eye laughter-stirr'd   150
With merriment of kingly pride,
   Sole star of all that place and time,
   I saw him — in his golden prime,
     THE GOOD HAROUN ALRASCHID.

1830*

MARIANA

"Mariana in the moated grange."
Measure for Measure.

WITH blackest moss the flower-plots
  Were thickly crusted, one and all;
The rusted nails fell from the knots
  That held the pear to the gable-wall.
The broken sheds look'd sad and strange:
  Unlifted was the clinking latch;
  Weeded and worn the ancient thatch
Upon the lonely moated grange.
    She only said, "My life is dreary,
      He cometh not," she said;   10
    She said, "I am aweary, aweary,
      I would that I were dead!"

Her tears fell with the dews at even;
  Her tears fell ere the dews were dried;
She could not look on the sweet heaven,
  Either at morn or eventide.
After the flitting of the bats,
  When thickest dark did trance the sky,
  She drew her casement-curtain by,
And glanced athwart the glooming flats.   20
    She only said, "The night is dreary,
      He cometh not," she said;
    She said, "I am aweary, aweary,
      I would that I were dead!"

Upon the middle of the night,
  Waking she heard the night-fowl crow;
The cock sung out an hour ere light;
  From the dark fen the oxen's low
Came to her; without hope of change,
  In sleep she seem'd to walk forlorn,   30
  Till cold winds woke the gray-eyed morn
About the lonely moated grange.
    She only said, "The day is dreary,
      He cometh not," she said;
    She said, "I am aweary, aweary,
      I would that I were dead!"

About a stone-cast from the wall
　　A sluice with blacken'd waters slept,
And o'er it many, round and small,
　　The cluster'd marish-mosses crept.　　　40
Hard by a poplar shook alway,
　　All silver-green with gnarled bark:
For leagues no other tree did mark
The level waste, the rounding gray.
　　　　She only said, "My life is dreary,
　　　　　　He cometh not," she said;
　　　　She said, "I am aweary, aweary,
　　　　　　I would that I were dead!"

And ever when the moon was low,
　　And the shrill winds were up and away,　　50
In the white curtain, to and fro,
　　She saw the gusty shadow sway.
But when the moon was very low,
　　And wild winds bound within their cell,
　　The shadow of the poplar fell
Upon her bed, across her brow.
　　　　She only said, "The night is dreary,
　　　　　　He cometh not," she said;
　　　　She said, "I am aweary, aweary,
　　　　　　I would that I were dead!"　　　60

All day within the dreamy house,
　　The doors upon their hinges creak'd;
The blue fly sung in the pane; the mouse
　　Behind the mouldering wainscot shriek'd,
Or from the crevice peer'd about.
　　Old faces glimmer'd thro' the doors,
　　Old footsteps trod the upper floors,
Old voices called her from without.
　　　　She only said, "My life is dreary,
　　　　　　He cometh not," she said;　　　70
　　　　She said, "I am aweary, aweary,
　　　　　　I would that I were dead!"

The sparrow's chirrup on the roof,
　　The slow clock ticking, and the sound
Which to the wooing wind aloof
　　The poplar made, did all confound
Her sense; but most she loathed the hour
　　When the thick-moted sunbeam lay

Athwart the chambers, and the day
Was sloping toward his western bower. 80
Then said she, "I am very dreary,
He will not come," she said;
She wept, "I am aweary, aweary,
O God, that I were dead!"

1830

SONNET

SHE took the dappled partridge fleckt with blood,
And in her hand the drooping pheasant bare,
And by his feet she held the woolly hare,
And like a master-painting where she stood,
Lookt some new goddess of an English wood.
Nor could I find an imperfection there,
Nor blame the wanton act that showed so fair —
To me whatever freak she plays is good.
Hers is the fairest Life that breathes with breath,
And *their* still plumes and azure eyelids closed 10
Made quiet Death so beautiful to see
That Death lent grace to Life and Life to Death
And in one image Life and Death reposed,
To make my love an Immortality.

1830 ? (1931)

THE SLEEPING BEAUTY

I

YEAR after year unto her feet,
She lying on her couch alone,
Across the purple coverlet
The maiden's jet-black hair has grown,
On either side her tranced form
Forth streaming from a braid of pearl;
The slumbrous light is rich and warm,
And moves not on the rounded curl.

II

The silk star-broider'd coverlid
Unto her limbs itself doth mould 10

Languidly ever; and, amid
    Her full black ringlets downward roll'd,
Glows forth each softly-shadow'd arm
    With bracelets of the diamond bright.
Her constant beauty doth inform
    Stillness with love, and day with light.

III

She sleeps; her breathings are not heard
    In palace chambers far apart.
The fragrant tresses are not stirr'd
    That lie upon her charmed heart.   20
She sleeps; on either hand upswells
    The gold-fringed pillow lightly prest;
She sleeps, nor dreams, but ever dwells
    A perfect form in perfect rest.

1830, 1842*

A CHARACTER

WITH a half-glance upon the sky
At night he said, "The wanderings
Of this most intricate Universe
Teach me the nothingness of things;"
Yet could not all creation pierce
Beyond the bottom of his eye.

He spake of beauty: that the dull
Saw no divinity in grass,
Life in dead stones, or spirit in air;
Then looking as 't were in a glass,   10
He smooth'd his chin and sleek'd his hair,
And said the earth was beautiful.

He spake of virtue: not the gods
More purely when they wish to charm
Pallas and Juno sitting by;
And with a sweeping of the arm,
And a lack-lustre dead-blue eye,
Devolved his rounded periods.

Most delicately hour by hour
He canvass'd human mysteries,   20

And trod on silk, as if the winds
Blew his own praises in his eyes,
And stood aloof from other minds
In impotence of fancied power.

With lips depress'd as he were meek,
Himself unto himself he sold:
Upon himself himself did feed;
Quiet, dispassionate, and cold,
And other than his form of creed,
With chisell'd features clear and sleek.
1830*

THE POET

THE poet in a golden clime was born,
    With golden stars above;
Dower'd with the hate of hate, the scorn of scorn,
    The love of love.

He saw thro' life and death, thro' good and ill,
    He saw thro' his own soul.
The marvel of the everlasting will,
    An open scroll,

Before him lay; with echoing feet he threaded
    The secretest walks of fame: 10
The viewless arrows of his thoughts were headed
    And wing'd with flame,

Like Indian reeds blown from his silver tongue,
    And of so fierce a flight,
From Calpe unto Caucasus they sung,
    Filling with light

And vagrant melodies the winds which bore
    Them earthward till they lit;
Then, like the arrow-seeds of the field flower,
    The fruitful wit   20

Cleaving took root, and springing forth anew
    Where'er they fell, behold,
Like to the mother plant in semblance, grew
    A flower all gold,

And bravely furnish'd all abroad to fling
    The winged shafts of truth,
To throng with stately blooms the breathing spring
    Of Hope and Youth.

So many minds did gird their orbs with beams,
    Tho' one did fling the fire;   30
Heaven flow'd upon the soul in many dreams
    Of high desire.

Thus truth was multiplied on truth, the world
    Like one great garden show'd,
And thro' the wreaths of floating dark upcurl'd,
    Rare sunrise flow'd.

And Freedom rear'd in that august sunrise
    Her beautiful bold brow,
When rites and forms before his burning eyes
    Melted like snow.   40

There was no blood upon her maiden robes
    Sunn'd by those orient skies;
But round about the circles of the globes
    Of her keen eyes

And in her raiment's hem was traced in flame
    WISDOM, a name to shake
All evil dreams of power — a sacred name.
    And when she spake,

Her words did gather thunder as they ran,
    And as the lightning to the thunder   50
Which follows it, riving the spirit of man,
    Making earth wonder,

So was their meaning to her words. No sword
    Of wrath her right arm whirl'd,
But one poor poet's scroll, and with *his* word
    She shook the world.

1830

SIR LAUNCELOT AND QUEEN GUINEVERE

A FRAGMENT

LIKE souls that balance joy and pain,
With tears and smiles from heaven again
The maiden Spring upon the plain
Came in a sunlit fall of rain.
    In crystal vapor everywhere
Blue isles of heaven laugh'd between,
And far, in forest-deeps unseen,
The topmost elm-tree gather'd green
    From draughts of balmy air.

Sometimes the linnet piped his song;   10
Sometimes the throstle whistled strong;
Sometimes the sparhawk, wheel'd along,
Hush'd all the groves from fear of wrong;
    By grassy capes with fuller sound
In curves the yellowing river ran,
And drooping chestnut-buds began
To spread into the perfect fan,
    Above the teeming ground.

Then, in the boyhood of the year,
Sir Launcelot and Queen Guinevere   20
Rode thro' the coverts of the deer,
With blissful treble ringing clear.
    She seem'd a part of joyous Spring;
A gown of grass-green silk she wore,
Buckled with golden clasps before;
A light-green tuft of plumes she bore
    Closed in a golden ring.

Now on some twisted ivy-net,
Now by some tinkling rivulet,
In mosses mixt with violet   30
Her cream-white mule his pastern set;
    And fleeter now she skimm'd the plains
Than she whose elfin prancer springs
By night to eery warblings,
When all the glimmering moorland rings
    With jingling bridle-reins.

As she fled fast thro' sun and shade,
The happy winds upon her play'd,
Blowing the ringlet from the braid.
She look'd so lovely, as she sway'd   40
    The rein with dainty finger-tips,
A man had given all other bliss,
And all his worldly worth for this,
To waste his whole heart in one kiss
    Upon her perfect lips.

1830 (1842) *

THE LADY OF SHALOTT

PART I

On either side the river lie
Long fields of barley and of rye,
That clothe the wold and meet the sky;
And thro' the field the road runs by
    To many-tower'd Camelot;
And up and down the people go,
Gazing where the lilies blow
Round an island there below,
    The island of Shalott.

Willows whiten, aspens quiver,   10
Little breezes dusk and shiver
Thro' the wave that runs for ever
By the island in the river
    Flowing down to Camelot.
Four gray walls, and four gray towers,
Overlook a space of flowers,
And the silent isle imbowers
    The Lady of Shalott.

By the margin, willow-veil'd,
Slide the heavy barges trail'd   20
By slow horses; and unhail'd
The shallop flitteth silken-sail'd
    Skimming down to Camelot:
But who hath seen her wave her hand?
Or at the casement seen her stand?
Or is she known in all the land,
    The Lady of Shalott?

Only reapers, reaping early
In among the bearded barley,
Hear a song that echoes cheerly   30
From the river winding clearly,
     Down to tower'd Camelot;
And by the moon the reaper weary,
Piling sheaves in uplands airy,
Listening, whispers " 'T is the fairy
     Lady of Shalott."

PART II

There she weaves by night and day
A magic web with colors gay.
She has heard a whisper say,
A curse is on her if she stay   40
     To look down to Camelot.
She knows not what the curse may be,
And so she weaveth steadily,
And little other care hath she,
     The Lady of Shalott.

And moving thro' a mirror clear
That hangs before her all the year,
Shadows of the world appear.
There she sees the highway near
     Winding down to Camelot;   50
There the river eddy whirls,
And there the surly village-churls,
And the red cloaks of market girls,
     Pass onward from Shalott.

Sometimes a troop of damsels glad,
An abbot on an ambling pad,
Sometimes a curly shepherd-lad,
Or long-hair'd page in crimson clad,
     Goes by to tower'd Camelot;
And sometimes thro' the mirror blue   60
The knights come riding two and two:
She hath no loyal knight and true,
     The Lady of Shalott.

But in her web she still delights
To weave the mirror's magic sights,
For often thro' the silent nights
A funeral, with plumes and lights

And music, went to Camelot;
Or when the moon was overhead,
Came two young lovers lately wed: 70
"I am half sick of shadows," said
      The Lady of Shalott.

PART III

A bow-shot from her bower-eaves,
He rode between the barley-sheaves.
The sun came dazzling thro' the leaves,
And flamed upon the brazen greaves
      Of bold Sir Lancelot.
A red-cross knight for ever kneel'd
To a lady in his shield,
That sparkled on the yellow field,   80
      Beside remote Shalott.

The gemmy bridle glitter'd free,
Like to some branch of stars we see
Hung in the golden Galaxy.
The bridle bells rang merrily
      As he rode down to Camelot;

And from his blazon'd baldric slung
A mighty silver bugle hung,
And as he rode his armor rung,
      Beside remote Shalott.   90

All in the blue unclouded weather
Thick-jewell'd shone the saddle-leather,
The helmet and the helmet-feather
Burn'd like one burning flame together,
      As he rode down to Camelot;
As often thro' the purple night,
Below the starry clusters bright,
Some bearded meteor, trailing light,
      Moves over still Shalott.

His broad clear brow in sunlight glow'd;   100
On burnish'd hooves his war-horse trode;
From underneath his helmet flow'd
His coal-black curls as on he rode,
      As he rode down to Camelot.
From the bank and from the river

He flash'd into the crystal mirror,
"Tirra lirra," by the river
     Sang Sir Lancelot.

She left the web, she left the loom,
She made three paces thro' the room,   110
She saw the water-lily bloom,
She saw the helmet and the plume,
     She look'd down to Camelot.
Out flew the web and floated wide;
The mirror crack'd from side to side;
"The curse is come upon me," cried
     The Lady of Shalott.

PART IV

In the stormy east-wind straining,
The pale yellow woods were waning,
The broad stream in his banks complaining,   120
Heavily the low sky raining
     Over tower'd Camelot;
Down she came and found a boat
Beneath a willow left afloat,
And round about the prow she wrote
     The Lady of Shalott.

And down the river's dim expanse
Like some bold seër in a trance,
Seeing all his own mischance —
With a glassy countenance   130
     Did she look to Camelot.
And at the closing of the day
She loosed the chain, and down she lay;
The broad stream bore her far away,
     The Lady of Shalott.

Lying, robed in snowy white
That loosely flew to left and right —
The leaves upon her falling light —
Thro' the noises of the night
     She floated down to Camelot;   140
And as the boat-head wound along
The willowy hills and fields among,
They heard her singing her last song,
     The Lady of Shalott.

Heard a carol, mournful, holy,
Chanted loudly, chanted lowly,
Till her blood was frozen slowly,
And her eyes were darken'd wholly,
  Turn'd to tower'd Camelot.
For ere she reach'd upon the tide   150
The first house by the water-side,
Singing in her song she died,
  The Lady of Shalott.

Under tower and balcony,
By garden-wall and gallery,
A gleaming shape she floated by,
Dead-pale between the houses high,
  Silent into Camelot.
Out upon the wharfs they came,
Knight and burgher, lord and dame,   160
And round the prow they read her name,
  The Lady of Shalott.

Who is this? and what is here?
And in the lighted palace near
Died the sound of royal cheer;
And they cross'd themselves for fear,
  All the knights at Camelot:
But Lancelot mused a little space;
He said, "She has a lovely face;
God in his mercy lend her grace,   170
  The Lady of Shalott."

1832, 1842°

MARIANA IN THE SOUTH

WITH one black shadow at its feet,
 The house thro' all the level shines,
Close-latticed to the brooding heat,
 And silent in its dusty vines;
A faint-blue ridge upon the right,
 An empty river-bed before,
 And shallows on a distant shore,
In glaring sand and inlets bright.
  But "Ave Mary," made she moan,

And "Ave Mary," night and morn,   10
And "Ah," she sang, "to be all alone,
　To live forgotten, and love forlorn."

She, as her carol sadder grew,
　From brow and bosom slowly down
Thro' rosy taper fingers drew
　Her streaming curls of deepest brown
To left and right, and made appear
　Still-lighted in a secret shrine
　Her melancholy eyes divine,
The home of woe without a tear.   20
　　And "Ave Mary," was her moan,
　　　"Madonna, sad is night and morn,"
　　And "Ah," she sang, "to be all alone,
　　　To live forgotten, and love forlorn."

Till all the crimson changed, and past
　Into deep orange o'er the sea,
Low on her knees herself she cast,
　Before Our Lady murmur'd she;
Complaining, "Mother, give me grace
　To help me of my weary load."   30
And on the liquid mirror glow'd
The clear perfection of her face.
　　"Is this the form," she made her moan,
　　　"That won his praises night and morn?"
　　And "Ah," she said, "but I wake alone,
　　　I sleep forgotten, I wake forlorn."

Nor bird would sing, nor lamb would bleat,
　Nor any cloud would cross the vault,
But day increased from heat to heat,
　On stony drought and steaming salt;   40
Till now at noon she slept again,
　And seem'd knee-deep in mountain grass,
　And heard her native breezes pass,
And runlets babbling down the glen.
　　She breathed in sleep a lower moan,
　　　And murmuring, as at night and morn,
　　She thought, "My spirit is here alone,
　　　Walks forgotten, and is forlorn."

Dreaming, she knew it was a dream;
　She felt he was and was not there.   50

She woke; the babble of the stream
  Fell, and, without, the steady glare
Shrank one sick willow sere and small.
  The river-bed was dusty-white;
  And all the furnace of the light
Struck up against the blinding wall.
    She whisper'd, with a stifled moan
      More inward than at night or morn,
    "Sweet Mother, let me not here alone
      Live forgotten and die forlorn."   60

And, rising, from her bosom drew
  Old letters, breathing of her worth,
For "Love," they said, "must needs be true,
  To what is loveliest upon earth."
An image seem'd to pass the door,
  To look at her with slight, and say
  "But now thy beauty flows away,
So be alone for evermore."
    "O cruel heart," she changed her tone,
      "And cruel love, whose end is scorn,   70
    Is this the end, to be left alone,
      To live forgotten, and die forlorn?"

But sometimes in the falling day
  An image seem'd to pass the door,
To look into her eyes and say,
  "But thou shalt be alone no more."
And flaming downward over all
  From heat to heat the day decreased,
  And slowly rounded to the east
The one black shadow from the wall.   80
    "The day to night," she made her moan,
      "The day to night, the night to morn,
    And day and night I am left alone
      To live forgotten, and love forlorn."

At eve a dry cicala sung,
  There came a sound as of the sea;
Backward the lattice-blind she flung,
  And lean'd upon the balcony.
There all in spaces rosy-bright
    Large Hesper glitter'd on her tears,   90
    And deepening thro' the silent spheres
Heaven over heaven rose the night.

And weeping then she made her moan,
"The night comes on that knows not morn,
When I shall cease to be all alone,
To live forgotten, and love forlorn."

1832, 1842

ŒNONE

THERE lies a vale in Ida, lovelier
Than all the valleys of Ionian hills.
The swimming vapor slopes athwart the glen,
Puts forth an arm, and creeps from pine to pine,
And loiters, slowly drawn. On either hand
The lawns and meadow-ledges midway down
Hang rich in flowers, and far below them roars
The long brook falling thro' the cloven ravine
In cataract after cataract to the sea.
Behind the valley topmost Gargarus   10
Stands up and takes the morning; but in front
The gorges, opening wide apart, reveal
Troas and Ilion's column'd citadel,
The crown of Troas.
                         Hither came at noon
Mournful Œnone, wandering forlorn
Of Paris, once her playmate on the hills.
Her cheek had lost the rose, and round her neck
Floated her hair or seem'd to float in rest.
She, leaning on a fragment twined with vine,
Sang to the stillness, till the mountain shade   20
Sloped downward to her seat from the upper cliff.

"O mother Ida, many-fountain'd Ida,
Dear mother Ida, harken ere I die.
For now the noonday quiet holds the hill;
The grasshopper is silent in the grass;
The lizard, with his shadow on the stone,
Rests like a shadow, and the winds are dead.
The purple flower droops, the golden bee
Is lily-cradled; I alone awake.
My eyes are full of tears, my heart of love,   30
My heart is breaking, and my eyes are dim,
And I am all aweary of my life.

"O mother Ida, many-fountain'd Ida,
Dear mother Ida, harken ere I die.
Hear me, O earth, hear me, O hills, O caves
That house the cold crown'd snake! O mountain brooks,
I am the daughter of a River-God,
Hear me, for I will speak, and build up all
My sorrow with my song, as yonder walls
Rose slowly to a music slowly breathed,   40
A cloud that gather'd shape; for it may be
That, while I speak of it, a little while
My heart may wander from its deeper woe.

"O mother Ida, many-fountain'd Ida,
Dear mother Ida, harken ere I die.
I waited underneath the dawning hills;
Aloft the mountain lawn was dewy-dark,
And dewy dark aloft the mountain pine.
Beautiful Paris, evil-hearted Paris,
Leading a jet-black goat white-horn'd, white-hooved,   50
Came up from reedy Simois all alone.

"O mother Ida, harken ere I die.
Far-off the torrent call'd me from the cleft;
Far up the solitary morning smote
The streaks of virgin snow. With downdropt eyes
I sat alone; white-breasted like a star
Fronting the dawn he moved; a leopard skin
Droop'd from his shoulder, but his sunny hair
Cluster'd about his temples like a God's;
And his cheeks brighten'd as the foam-bow brightens   60
When the wind blows the foam, and all my heart
Went forth to embrace him coming ere he came.

"Dear mother Ida, harken ere I die.
He smiled, and opening out his milk-white palm
Disclosed a fruit of pure Hesperian gold,
That smelt ambrosially, and while I look'd
And listen'd, the full-flowing river of speech
Came down upon my heart:
                  " 'My own Œnone,
Beautiful-brow'd Œnone, my own soul,
Behold this fruit, whose gleaming rind ingraven   70
"For the most fair," would seem to award it thine,
As lovelier than whatever Oread haunt
The knolls of Ida, loveliest in all grace
Of movement, and the charm of married brows.'

"Dear mother Ida, harken ere I die.
He prest the blossom of his lips to mine,
And added, 'This was cast upon the board,
When all the full-faced presence of the Gods
Ranged in the halls of Peleus; whereupon
Rose feud, with question unto whom 't were due;   80
But light-foot Iris brought it yester-eve,
Delivering, that to me, by common voice
Elected umpire, Herè comes to-day,
Pallas and Aphrodite, claiming each
This meed of fairest. Thou, within the cave
Behind yon whispering tuft of oldest pine,
Mayst well behold them unbeheld, unheard
Hear all, and see thy Paris judge of Gods.'

"Dear mother Ida, harken ere I die.
It was the deep midnoon; one silvery cloud   90
Had lost his way between the piny sides
Of this long glen. Then to the bower they came,
Naked they came to that smooth-swarded bower,
And at their feet the crocus brake like fire,
Violet, amaracus, and asphodel,
Lotos and lilies; and a wind arose,
And overhead the wandering ivy and vine,
This way and that, in many a wild festoon
Ran riot, garlanding the gnarled boughs
With bunch and berry and flower thro' and thro'.   100

"O mother Ida, harken ere I die.
On the tree-tops a crested peacock lit,
And o'er him flow'd a golden cloud, and lean'd
Upon him, slowly dropping fragrant dew.
Then first I heard the voice of her to whom
Coming thro' heaven, like a light that grows
Larger and clearer, with one mind the Gods
Rise up for reverence. She to Paris made
Proffer of royal power, ample rule
Unquestion'd, overflowing revenue   110
Wherewith to embellish state, 'from many a vale
And river-sunder'd champaign clothed with corn,
Or labor'd mine undrainable of ore.
Honor,' she said, 'and homage, tax and toll,
From many an inland town and haven large,
Mast-throng'd beneath her shadowing citadel
In glassy bays among her tallest towers.'

"O mother Ida, harken ere I die.
Still she spake on and still she spake of power,
'Which in all action is the end of all;
Power fitted to the season; wisdom-bred
And throned of wisdom — from all neighbor crowns
Alliance and allegiance, till thy hand
Fail from the sceptre-staff. Such boon from me,
From me, heaven's queen, Paris, to thee king-born,
A shepherd all thy life, but yet king-born.
Should come most welcome, seeing men, in power
Only, are likest Gods, who have attain'd
Rest in a happy place and quiet seats
Above the thunder, with undying bliss
In knowledge of their own supremacy.'   120

    130

    "Dear mother Ida, harken ere I die.
She ceased, and Paris held the costly fruit
Out at arm's-length, so much the thought of power
Flatter'd his spirit; but Pallas where she stood
Somewhat apart, her clear and bared limbs
O'erthwarted with the brazen-headed spear
Upon her pearly shoulder leaning cold,
The while, above, her full and earnest eye
Over her snow-cold breast and angry cheek
Kept watch, waiting decision, made reply: 140

    " 'Self-reverence, self-knowledge, self-control,
These three alone lead life to sovereign power.
Yet not for power (power of herself
Would come uncall'd for) but to live by law,
Acting the law we live by without fear;
And, because right is right, to follow right
Were wisdom in the scorn of consequence.'

    "Dear mother Ida, harken ere I die.
Again she said: 'I woo thee not with gifts.   150
Sequel of guerdon could not alter me
To fairer. Judge thou me by what I am,
So shalt thou find me fairest.
                 Yet, indeed,
If gazing on divinity disrobed
Thy mortal eyes are frail to judge of fair,
Unbias'd by self-profit, O, rest thee sure
That I shall love thee well and cleave to thee,
So that my vigor, wedded to thy blood,

Shall strike within thy pulses, like a God's,
To push thee forward thro' a life of shocks,   160
Dangers, and deeds, until endurance grow
Sinew'd with action, and the full-grown will,
Circled thro' all experiences, pure law,
Commeasure perfect freedom.'
              "Here she ceas'd,
And Paris ponder'd, and I cried, 'O Paris,
Give it to Pallas!' but he heard me not,
Or hearing would not hear me, woe is me!

   "O mother Ida, many-fountain'd Ida,
Dear mother Ida, harken ere I die.
Idalian Aphrodite beautiful,   170
Fresh as the foam, new-bathed in Paphian wells,
With rosy slender fingers backward drew
From her warm brows and bosom her deep hair
Ambrosial, golden round her lucid throat
And shoulder; from the violets her light foot
Shone rosy-white, and o'er her rounded form
Between the shadows of the vine-bunches
Floated the glowing sunlights, as she moved.

   "Dear mother Ida, harken ere I die.
She with a subtle smile in her mild eyes,   180
The herald of her triumph, drawing nigh
Half-whisper'd in his ear, 'I promise thee
The fairest and most loving wife in Greece.'
She spoke and laugh'd; I shut my sight for fear;
But when I look'd, Paris had raised his arm,
And I beheld great Herè's angry eyes,
As she withdrew into the golden cloud,
And I was left alone within the bower;
And from that time to this I am alone,
And I shall be alone until I die.   190

   "Yet, mother Ida, harken ere I die.
Fairest — why fairest wife? am I not fair?
My love hath told me so a thousand times.
Methinks I must be fair, for yesterday,
When I past by, a wild and wanton pard,
Eyed like the evening star, with playful tail
Crouch'd fawning in the weed. Most loving is she?
Ah me, my mountain shepherd, that my arms
Were wound about thee, and my hot lips prest

Close, close to thine in that quick-falling dew   200
Of fruitful kisses, thick as autumn rains
Flash in the pools of whirling Simois!

    "O mother, hear me yet before I die.
They came, they cut away my tallest pines,
My tall dark pines, that plumed the craggy ledge
High over the blue gorge, and all between
The snowy peak and snow-white cataract
Foster'd the callow eaglet — from beneath
Whose thick mysterious boughs in the dark morn
The panther's roar came muffled, while I sat   210
Low in the valley. Never, never more
Shall lone Œnone see the morning mist
Sweep thro' them; never see them overlaid
With narrow moonlit slips of silver cloud,
Between the loud stream and the trembling stars.

"O mother, hear me yet before I die.
I wish that somewhere in the ruin'd folds,
Among the fragments tumbled from the glens,
Or the dry thickets, I could meet with her
The Abominable, that uninvited came   220
Into the fair Peleïan banquet-hall,
And cast the golden fruit upon the board,
And bred this change; that I might speak my mind,
And tell her to her face how much I hate
Her presence, hated both of Gods and men.

    "O mother, hear me yet before I die.
Hath he not sworn his love a thousand times,
In this green valley, under this green hill,
Even on this hand, and sitting on this stone?
Seal'd it with kisses? water'd it with tears?   230
O happy tears, and how unlike to these!
O happy heaven, how canst thou see my face?
O happy earth, how canst thou bear my weight?
O death, death, death, thou ever-floating cloud,
There are enough unhappy on this earth,
Pass by the happy souls, that love to live;
I pray thee, pass before my light of life,
And shadow all my soul, that I may die.
Thou weighest heavy on the heart within,
Weigh heavy on my eyelids; let me die.   240

"O mother, hear me yet before I die.
I will not die alone, for fiery thoughts
Do shape themselves within me, more and more,
Whereof I catch the issue, as I hear
Dead sounds at night come from the inmost hills,
Like footsteps upon wool. I dimly see
My far-off doubtful purpose, as a mother
Conjectures of the features of her child
Ere it is born. Her child! — a shudder comes
Across me: never child be born of me,   250
Unblest, to vex me with his father's eyes!

"O mother, hear me yet before I die.
Hear me, O earth. I will not die alone,
Lest their shrill happy laughter come to me
Walking the cold and starless road of death
Uncomforted, leaving my ancient love
With the Greek woman. I will rise and go
Down into Troy, and ere the stars come forth
Talk with the wild Cassandra, for she says
A fire dances before her, and a sound   260
Rings ever in her ears of armed men.
What this may be I know not, but I know
That, wheresoe'er I am by night and day,
All earth and air seem only burning fire."

1832, 1842*

TO ——

WITH THE FOLLOWING POEM

I SEND you here a sort of allegory —
For you will understand it — of a soul,
A sinful soul possess'd of many gifts,
A spacious garden full of flowering weeds,
A glorious devil, large in heart and brain,
That did love beauty only — beauty seen
In all varieties of mould and mind —
And knowledge for its beauty; or if good,
Good only for its beauty, seeing not
That Beauty, Good, and Knowledge are three sisters   10

That doat upon each other, friends to man,
Living together under the same roof,
And never can be sunder'd without tears.
And he that shuts Love out, in turn shall be
Shut out from Love, and on her threshold lie
Howling in outer darkness. Not for this
Was common clay ta'en from the common earth
Moulded by God, and temper'd with the tears
Of angels to the perfect shape of man.
      1832*

THE PALACE OF ART

I BUILT my soul a lordly pleasure-house,
      Wherein at ease for aye to dwell.
I said, "O Soul, make merry and carouse,
      Dear soul, for all is well."

A huge crag-platform, smooth as burnish'd brass,
      I chose. The ranged ramparts bright
From level meadow-bases of deep grass
      Suddenly scaled the light.

Thereon I built it firm. Of ledge or shelf
      The rock rose clear, or winding stair.
My soul would live alone unto herself
      In her high palace there.

And "while the world runs round and round," I said,
      "Reign thou apart, a quiet king,
Still as, while Saturn whirls, his steadfast shade
      Sleeps on his luminous ring."

To which my soul made answer readily:
      "Trust me, in bliss I shall abide
In this great mansion, that is built for me,
      So royal-rich and wide."   20
      .   .   .   .
Four courts I made, East, West and South and North,
      In each a squared lawn, wherefrom
The golden gorge of dragons spouted forth
      A flood of fountain-foam.

And round the cool green courts there ran a row
  Of cloisters, branch'd like mighty woods,
Echoing all night to that sonorous flow
  Of spouted fountain-floods;

And round the roofs a gilded gallery
  That lent broad verge to distant lands,   30
Far as the wild swan wings, to where the sky
  Dipt down to sea and sands.

From those four jets four currents in one swell
  Across the mountain stream'd below
In misty folds, that floating as they fell
  Lit up a torrent-bow.

And high on every peak a statue seem'd
  To hang on tiptoe, tossing up
A cloud of incense of all odor steam'd
  From out a golden cup.   40

So that she thought, "And who shall gaze upon
  My palace with unblinded eyes,
While this great bow will waver in the sun,
  And that sweet incense rise?"

For that sweet incense rose and never fail'd,
  And, while day sank or mounted higher,
The light aerial gallery, golden-rail'd,
  Burnt like a fringe of fire.

Likewise the deep-set windows, stain'd and traced,
  Would seem slow-flaming crimson fires   50
From shadow'd grots of arches interlaced,
  And tipt with frost-like spires.

. . . .

Full of long-sounding corridors it was,
  That over-vaulted grateful gloom,
Thro' which the livelong day my soul did pass,
  Well-pleased, from room to room.

Full of great rooms and small the palace stood,
  All various, each a perfect whole
From living Nature, fit for every mood
  And change of my still soul.   60

For some were hung with arras green and blue,
    Showing a gaudy summer-morn,
Where with puff'd cheek the belted hunter blew
    His wreathed bugle-horn.

One seem'd all dark and red — a tract of sand,
    And some one pacing there alone,
Who paced for ever in a glimmering land,
    Lit with a low large moon.

One show'd an iron coast and angry waves,
    You seem'd to hear them climb and fall   70
And roar rock-thwarted under bellowing caves,
    Beneath the windy wall.

And one, a full-fed river winding slow
    By herds upon an endless plain,
The ragged rims of thunder brooding low,
    With shadow-streaks of rain.

And one, the reapers at their sultry toil.
    In front they bound the sheaves. Behind
Were realms of upland, prodigal in oil,
    And hoary to the wind.   80

And one a foreground black with stones and slags;
    Beyond, a line of heights; and higher
All barr'd with long white cloud the scornful crags;
    And highest, snow and fire.

And one, an English home — gray twilight pour'd
    On dewy pastures, dewy trees,
Softer than sleep — all things in order stored,
    A haunt of ancient Peace.

Nor these alone, but every landscape fair,
    As fit for every mood of mind,   90
Or gay, or grave, or sweet, or stern, was there,
    Not less than truth design'd.

. . . .

Or the maid-mother by a crucifix,
    In tracts of pasture sunny-warm,
Beneath branch-work of costly sardonyx
    Sat smiling, babe in arm.

Or in a clear-wall'd city on the sea,
　　Near gilded organ-pipes, her hair
Wound with white roses, slept Saint Cecily;
　　An angel look'd at her.　　　　　　　　　　**100**

Or thronging all one porch of Paradise
　　A group of Houris bow'd to see
The dying Islamite, with hands and eyes
　　That said, We wait for thee.

Or mythic Uther's deeply-wounded son
　　In some fair space of sloping greens
Lay, dozing in the vale of Avalon,
　　And watch'd by weeping queens.

Or hollowing one hand against his ear,
　　To list a foot-fall, ere he saw　　　　　　**110**
The wood-nymph, stay'd the Ausonian king to hear
　　Of wisdom and of law.

Or over hills with peaky tops engrail'd,
　　And many a tract of palm and rice,
The throne of Indian Cama slowly sail'd
　　A summer fann'd with spice.

Or sweet Europa's mantle blew unclasp'd,
　　From off her shoulder backward borne;
From one hand droop'd a crocus; one hand grasp'd
　　The mild bull's golden horn.　　　　　　　**120**

Or else flush'd Ganymede, his rosy thigh
　　Half-buried in the eagle's down,
Sole as a flying star shot thro' the sky
　　Above the pillar'd town.

Nor these alone; but every legend fair
　　Which the supreme Caucasian mind
Carved out of Nature for itself was there,
　　Not less than life design'd.

. . . .
Then in the towers I placed great bells that swung,
　　Moved of themselves, with silver sound;　　**130**
And with choice paintings of wise men I hung
　　The royal dais round.

For there was Milton like a seraph strong,
    Beside him Shakespeare bland and mild;
And there the world-worn Dante grasp'd his song,
    And somewhat grimly smiled.

And there the Ionian father of the rest;
    A million wrinkles carved his skin;
A hundred winters snow'd upon his breast,
    From cheek and throat and chin.   140

Above, the fair hall-ceiling stately-set
    Many an arch high up did lift,
And angels rising and descending met
    With interchange of gift.

Below was all mosaic choicely plann'd
    With cycles of the human tale
Of this wide world, the times of every land
    So wrought they will not fail.

The people here, a beast of burden slow,
    Toil'd onward, prick'd with goads and stings;   150
Here play'd, a tiger, rolling to and fro
    The heads and crowns of kings;

Here rose, an athlete, strong to break or bind
    All force in bonds that might endure,
And here once more like some sick man declined,
    And trusted any cure.

But over these she trod; and those great bells
    Began to chime. She took her throne;
She sat betwixt the shining oriels,
    To sing her songs alone.   160

And thro' the topmost oriels' colored flame
    Two godlike faces gazed below;
Plato the wise, and large-brow'd Verulam,
    The first of those who know.

And all those names that in their motion were
    Full-welling fountain-heads of change,
Betwixt the slender shafts were blazon'd fair
    In diverse raiment strange;

Thro' which the lights, rose, amber, emerald, blue,
    Flush'd in her temples and her eyes,   170
And from her lips, as morn from Memnon, drew
    Rivers of melodies.

No nightingale delighteth to prolong
    Her low preamble all alone,
More than my soul to hear her echo'd song
    Throb thro' the ribbed stone;

Singing and murmuring in her feastful mirth,
    Joying to feel herself alive,
Lord over Nature, lord of the visible earth,
    Lord of the senses five;   180

Communing with herself: "All these are mine,
    And let the world have peace or wars,
'T is one to me." She — when young night divine
    Crown'd dying day with stars,

Making sweet close of his delicious toils —
    Lit light in wreaths and anadems,
And pure quintessences of precious oils
    In hollow'd moons of gems,

To mimic heaven; and clapt her hands and cried,
    "I marvel if my still delight   190
In this great house so royal-rich and wide
    Be flatter'd to the height.

"O all things fair to sate my various eyes!
    O shapes and hues that please me well!
O silent faces of the Great and Wise,
    My Gods, with whom I dwell!

"O Godlike isolation which art mine,
    I can but count thee perfect gain,
What time I watch the darkening droves of swine
    That range on yonder plain.   200

"In filthy sloughs they roll a prurient skin,
    They graze and wallow, breed and sleep;
And oft some brainless devil enters in,
    And drives them to the deep."

Then of the moral instinct would she prate
    And of the rising from the dead,
As hers by right of full-accomplish'd Fate;
    And at the last she said:

"I take possession of man's mind and deed.
    I care not what the sects may brawl.   210
I sit as God holding no form of creed,
    But contemplating all."

. . . .

Full oft the riddle of the painful earth
    Flash'd thro' her as she sat alone,
Yet not the less held she her solemn mirth,
    And intellectual throne.

And so she throve and prosper'd; so three years
    She prosper'd; on the fourth she fell,
Like Herod, when the shout was in his ears,
    Struck thro' with pangs of hell.   220

Lest she should fail and perish utterly,
    God, before whom ever lie bare
The abysmal deeps of personality,
    Plagued her with sore despair.

When she would think, where'er she turn'd her sight
    The airy hand confusion wrought,
Wrote, "Mene, mene," and divided quite
    The kingdom of her thought.

Deep dread and loathing of her solitude
    Fell on her, from which mood was born   230
Scorn of herself; again, from out that mood
    Laughter at her self-scorn.

"What! is not this my place of strength," she said,
    "My spacious mansion built for me,
Whereof the strong foundation-stones were laid
    Since my first memory?"

But in dark corners of her palace stood
    Uncertain shapes; and unawares
On white-eyed phantasms weeping tears of blood,
    And horrible nightmares,   240

And hollow shades enclosing hearts of flame,
    And, with dim fretted foreheads all,
On corpses three-months-old at noon she came,
    That stood against the wall.

A spot of dull stagnation, without light
    Or power of movement, seem'd my soul,
Mid onward-sloping motions infinite
    Making for one sure goal;

A still salt pool, lock'd in with bars of sand,
    Left on the shore, that hears all night   250
The plunging seas draw backward from the land
    Their moon-led waters white;

A star that with the choral starry dance
    Join'd not, but stood, and standing saw
The hollow orb of moving Circumstance
    Roll'd round by one fix'd law.

Back on herself her serpent pride had curl'd.
    "No voice," she shriek'd in that lone hall,
"No voice breaks thro' the stillness of this world;
    One deep, deep silence all!"   260

She, mouldering with the dull earth's mouldering sod,
    Inwrapt tenfold in slothful shame,
Lay there exiled from eternal God,
    Lost to her place and name;

And death and life she hated equally,
    And nothing saw, for her despair,
But dreadful time, dreadful eternity,
    No comfort anywhere;

Remaining utterly confused with fears,
    And ever worse with growing time,   270
And ever unrelieved by dismal tears,
    And all alone in crime.

Shut up as in a crumbling tomb, girt round
    With blackness as a solid wall,
Far off she seem'd to hear the dully sound
    Of human footsteps fall:

As in strange lands a traveller walking slow,
    In doubt and great perplexity,
A little before moonrise hears the low
      Moan of an unknown sea;   280

And knows not if it be thunder, or a sound
    Of rocks thrown down, or one deep cry
Of great wild beasts; then thinketh, "I have found
      A new land, but I die."

She howl'd aloud, "I am on fire within.
    There comes no murmur of reply.
What is it that will take away my sin,
      And save me lest I die?"

So when four years were wholly finished,
    She threw her royal robes away.   290
"Make me a cottage in the vale," she said,
    "Where I may mourn and pray.

"Yet pull not down my palace towers, that are
    So lightly, beautifully built;
Perchance I may return with others there
      When I have purged my guilt."

1832, 1842*

THE HESPERIDES

"Hesperus and his daughters three,
That sing about the golden tree."

Comus.

THE North-wind fall'n, in the new-starréd night
Zidonian Hanno, voyaging beyond
The hoary promontory of Soloë
Past Thymiaterion, in calméd bays,
Between the southern and the western Horn,
Heard neither warbling of the nightingale,
Nor melody of the Libyan lotus flute
Blown seaward from the shore; but from a slope
That ran bloom-bright into the Atlantic blue,
Beneath a highland leaning down a weight   10

Of cliffs, and zoned below with cedar shade,
Came voices, like the voices in a dream,
Continuous, till he reached the outer sea.

SONG

I

The golden apple, the golden apple, the hallowed fruit,
Guard it well, guard it warily,
Singing airily,
Standing about the charméd root.
Round about all is mute,
As the snow-field on the mountain-peaks,
As the sand-field at the mountain-foot.   20
Crocodiles in briny creeks
Sleep and stir not: all is mute.
If ye sing not, if ye make false measure,
We shall lose eternal pleasure,
Worth eternal want of rest.
Laugh not loudly: watch the treasure
Of the wisdom of the West.
In a corner wisdom whispers. Five and three
(Let it not be preached abroad) make an awful mystery.
For the blossom unto threefold music bloweth;   30
Evermore it is born anew;
And the sap to threefold music floweth,
From the root
Drawn in the dark,
Up to the fruit,
Creeping under the fragrant bark,
Liquid gold, honeysweet, thro' and thro'.
Keen-eyed Sisters, singing airily,
Looking warily
Every way,   40
Guard the apple night and day,
Lest one from the East come and take it away.

II

Father Hesper, Father Hesper, watch, watch, ever and aye,
Looking under silver hair with a silver eye.
Father, twinkle not thy steadfast sight;
Kingdoms lapse, and climates change, and races die;
Honor comes with mystery;
Hoarded wisdom brings delight.
Number, tell them over and number

How many the mystic fruit-tree holds   50
Lest the red-combed dragon slumber
Rolled together in purple folds.
Look to him, father, lest he wink, and the golden apple be stol'n away,
For his ancient heart is drunk with overwatchings night and day,
Round about the hallowed fruit-tree curled —
Sing away, sing aloud evermore in the wind, without stop,
Lest his scaléd eyelid drop,
For he is older than the world.
If he waken, we waken,
Rapidly levelling eager eyes.   60
If he sleep, we sleep,
Dropping the eyelid over the eyes.
If the golden apple be taken,
The world will be overwise.
Five links, a golden chain, are we,
Hesper, the dragon, and sisters three,
Bound about the golden tree.

III

Father Hesper, Father Hesper, watch, watch, night and day,
Lest the old wound of the world be healéd,
The glory unsealéd,   70
The golden apple stolén away,
And the ancient secret revealéd.
Look from west to east along:
Father, old Himala weakens, Caucasus is bold and strong.
Wandering waters unto wandering waters call;
Let them clash together, foam and fall.
Out of watchings, out of wiles,
Comes the bliss of secret smiles.
All things are not told to all.
Half-round the mantling night is drawn,   80
Purple fringéd with even and dawn.
Hesper hateth Phosphor, evening hateth morn.

IV

Every flower and every fruit the redolent breath
Of this warm sea-wind ripeneth,
Arching the billow in his sleep;
But the land-wind wandereth,
Broken by the highland-steep,
Two streams upon the violet deep;
For the western sun and the western star,
And the low west-wind, breathing afar,   90

The end of day and beginning of night
Make the apple holy and bright;
Holy and bright, round and full, bright and blest,
Mellowed in a land of rest;
Watch it warily day and night;
All good things are in the west.
Till mid noon the cool east light
Is shut out by the round of the tall hillbrow.
But when the full-faced sunset yellowly
Stays on the flowering arch of the bough,   100
The luscious fruitage clustereth mellowly,
Golden-kernelled, golden-cored,
Sunset-ripened above on the tree.
The world is wasted with fire and sword,
But the apple of gold hangs over the sea
Five links, a golden chain are we,
Hesper, the dragon, and sisters three,
Daughters three,
Bound about
All round about   110
The gnarléd bole of the charméd tree.
The golden apple, the golden apple, the hallowed fruit,
Guard it well, guard it warily,
Watch it warily,
Singing airily,
Standing about the charméd root.
1832*

THE LOTOS-EATERS

"Courage!" he said, and pointed toward the land,
"This mounting wave will roll us shoreward soon."
In the afternoon they came unto a land
In which it seemed always afternoon.
All round the coast the languid air did swoon,
Breathing like one that hath a weary dream.
Full-faced above the valley stood the moon;
And, like a downward smoke, the slender stream
Along the cliff to fall and pause and fall did seem.

A land of streams! some, like a downward smoke,   10
Slow-dropping veils of thinnest lawn, did go;

And some thro' wavering lights and shadows broke,
Rolling a slumbrous sheet of foam below.
They saw the gleaming river seaward flow
From the inner land; far off, three mountain-tops,
Three silent pinnacles of aged snow,
Stood sunset-flush'd; and, dew'd with showery drops,
Up-clomb the shadowy pine above the woven copse.

The charmed sunset linger'd low adown
In the red West; thro' mountain clefts the dale   20
Was seen far inland, and the yellow down
Border'd with palm, and many a winding vale
And meadow, set with slender galingale;
A land where all things always seem'd the same!
And round about the keel with faces pale,
Dark faces pale against that rosy flame,
The mild-eyed melancholy Lotos-eaters came.

Branches they bore of that enchanted stem,
Laden with flower and fruit, whereof they gave
To each, but whoso did receive of them   30
And taste, to him the gushing of the wave
Far far away did seem to mourn and rave
On alien shores; and if his fellow spake,
His voice was thin, as voices from the grave;
And deep-asleep he seem'd, yet all awake,
And music in his ears his beating heart did make.

They sat them down upon the yellow sand,
Between the sun and moon upon the shore;
And sweet it was to dream of Fatherland,
Of child, and wife, and slave; but evermore   40
Most weary seem'd the sea, weary the oar,
Weary the wandering fields of barren foam.
Then some one said, "We will return no more;"
And all at once they sang, "Our island home
Is far beyond the wave; we will no longer roam."

CHORIC SONG

I

THERE is sweet music here that softer falls
Than petals from blown roses on the grass,
Or night-dews on still waters between walls
Of shadowy granite, in a gleaming pass;

Music that gentlier on the spirit lies,
Than tired eyelids upon tired eyes;
Music that brings sweet sleep down from the blissful skies.
Here are cool mosses deep,
And thro' the moss the ivies creep,
And in the stream the long-leaved flowers weep,
And from the craggy ledge the poppy hangs in sleep.　　　　10

II

Why are we weigh'd upon with heaviness,
And utterly consumed with sharp distress,
While all things else have rest from weariness?
All things have rest: why should we toil alone,
We only toil, who are the first of things,
And make perpetual moan,
Still from one sorrow to another thrown;
Nor ever fold our wings,
And cease from wanderings,　　　　20
Nor steep our brows in slumber's holy balm;
Nor harken what the inner spirit sings,
"There is no joy but calm!" —
Why should we only toil, the roof and crown of things?

III

Lo! in the middle of the wood,
The folded leaf is woo'd from out the bud
With winds upon the branch, and there
Grows green and broad, and takes no care,
Sun-steep'd at noon, and in the moon
Nightly dew-fed; and turning yellow　　　　30
Falls, and floats adown the air.
Lo! sweeten'd with the summer light,
The full-juiced apple, waxing over-mellow,
Drops in a silent autumn night.
All its allotted length of days
The flower ripens in its place,
Ripens and fades, and falls, and hath no toil,
Fast-rooted in the fruitful soil.

IV

Hateful is the dark-blue sky,
Vaulted o'er the dark-blue sea.　　　　40
Death is the end of life; ah, why
Should life all labor be?
Let us alone. Time driveth onward fast,

And in a little while our lips are dumb.
Let us alone. What is it that will last?
All things are taken from us, and become
Portions and parcels of the dreadful past.
Let us alone. What pleasure can we have
To war with evil? Is there any peace
In ever climbing up the climbing wave?   50
All things have rest, and ripen toward the grave
In silence — ripen, fall, and cease:
Give us long rest or death, dark death, or dreamful ease.

V

How sweet it were, hearing the downward stream,
With half-shut eyes ever to seem
Falling asleep in a half-dream!
To dream and dream, like yonder amber light,
Which will not leave the myrrh-bush on the height;
To hear each other's whisper'd speech;
Eating the Lotos day by day,   60
To watch the crisping ripples on the beach,
And tender curving lines of creamy spray;
To lend our hearts and spirits wholly
To the influence of mild-minded melancholy;
To muse and brood and live again in memory,
With those old faces of our infancy
Heap'd over with a mound of grass,
Two handfuls of white dust, shut in an urn of brass!

VI

Dear is the memory of our wedded lives,
And dear the last embraces of our wives   70
And their warm tears; but all hath suffer'd change;
For surely now our household hearths are cold,
Our sons inherit us, our looks are strange,
And we should come like ghosts to trouble joy.
Or else the island princes over-bold
Have eat our substance, and the minstrel sings
Before them of the ten years' war in Troy,
And our great deeds, as half-forgotten things.
Is there confusion in the little isle?
Let what is broken so remain.   80
The Gods are hard to reconcile;
'T is hard to settle order once again.
There *is* confusion worse than death,
Trouble on trouble, pain on pain,

Long labor unto aged breath,
Sore task to hearts worn out by many wars
And eyes grown dim with gazing on the pilot-stars.

VII

But, propt on beds of amaranth and moly,
How sweet — while warm airs lull us, blowing lowly —
With half-dropt eyelid still,   90
Beneath a heaven dark and holy,
To watch the long bright river drawing slowly
His waters from the purple hill —
To hear the dewy echoes calling
From cave to cave thro' the thick-twined vine —
To watch the emerald-color'd water falling
Thro' many a woven acanthus-wreath divine!
Only to hear and see the far-off sparkling brine,
Only to hear were sweet, stretch'd out beneath the pine.

VIII

The Lotos blooms below the barren peak,   100
The Lotos blows by every winding creek;
All day the wind breathes low with mellower tone;
Thro' every hollow cave and alley lone
Round and round the spicy downs the yellow Lotos-dust is blown.
We have had enough of action, and of motion we,
Roll'd to starboard, roll'd to larboard, when the surge was seething
        free,
Where the wallowing monster spouted his foam-fountains in the sea.
Let us swear an oath, and keep it with an equal mind,
In the hollow Lotos-land to live and lie reclined
On the hills like Gods together, careless of mankind.   110
For they lie beside their nectar, and the bolts are hurl'd
Far below them in the valleys, and the clouds are lightly curl'd
Round their golden houses, girdled with the gleaming world;
Where they smile in secret, looking over wasted lands,
Blight and famine, plague and earthquake, roaring deeps and fiery
        sands,
Clanging fights, and flaming towns, and sinking ships, and praying
        hands.
But they smile, they find a music centred in a doleful song
Steaming up, a lamentation and an ancient tale of wrong,
Like a tale of little meaning tho' the words are strong;
Chanted from an ill-used race of men that cleave the soil,   120
Sow the seed, and reap the harvest with enduring toil,

Storing yearly little dues of wheat, and wine and oil;
Till they perish and they suffer — some, 't is whisper'd — down in
    hell
Suffer endless anguish, others in Elysian valleys dwell,
Resting weary limbs at last on beds of asphodel.
Surely, surely, slumber is more sweet than toil, the shore
Than labor in the deep mid-ocean, wind and wave and oar;
O, rest ye, brother mariners, we will not wander more.
1832, 1842*

A DREAM OF FAIR WOMEN

I READ, before my eyelids dropt their shade,
    "*The Legend of Good Women*," long ago
Sung by the morning star of song, who made
        His music heard below;

Dan Chaucer, the first warbler, whose sweet breath
    Preluded those melodious bursts that fill
The spacious times of great Elizabeth
        With sounds that echo still.

And, for a while, the knowledge of his art
    Held me above the subject, as strong gales   10
Hold swollen clouds from raining, tho' my heart,
        Brimful of those wild tales,

Charged both mine eyes with tears. In every land
    I saw, wherever light illumineth,
Beauty and anguish walking hand in hand
        The downward slope to death.

Those far-renowned brides of ancient song
    Peopled the hollow dark, like burning stars,
And I heard sounds of insult, shame, and wrong,
        And trumpets blown for wars;   20

And clattering flints batter'd with clanging hoofs;
    And I saw crowds in column'd sanctuaries,
And forms that pass'd at windows and on roofs
        Of marble palaces;

Corpses across the threshold, heroes tall
  Dislodging pinnacle and parapet
Upon the tortoise creeping to the wall,
    Lances in ambush set;

And high shrine-doors burst thro' with heated blasts
  That run before the fluttering tongues of fire; 30
White surf wind-scatter'd over sails and masts,
    And ever climbing higher;

Squadrons and squares of men in brazen plates,
  Scaffolds, still sheets of water, divers woes,
Ranges of glimmering vaults with iron grates,
    And hush'd seraglios.

So shape chased shape as swift as, when to land
  Bluster the winds and tides the selfsame way,
Crisp foam-flakes scud along the level sand,
    Torn from the fringe of spray. 40

I started once, or seem'd to start in pain,
  Resolved on noble things, and strove to speak,
As when a great thought strikes along the brain
    And flushes all the cheek.

And once my arm was lifted to hew down
  A cavalier from off his saddle-bow,
That bore a lady from a leaguer'd town;
    And then, I know not how,

All those sharp fancies, by down-lapsing thought
  Stream'd onward, lost their edges, and did creep 50
Roll'd on each other, rounded, smooth'd, and brought
    Into the gulfs of sleep.

At last methought that I had wander'd far
  In an old wood; fresh-wash'd in coolest dew
The maiden splendors of the morning star
    Shook in the steadfast blue.

Enormous elm-tree boles did stoop and lean
  Upon the dusky brushwood underneath
Their broad curved branches, fledged with clearest green,
    New from its silken sheath. 60

The dim red Morn had died, her journey done,
   And with dead lips smiled at the twilight plain,
Half-fallen across the threshold of the sun,
     Never to rise again.

There was no motion in the dumb dead air,
   Not any song of bird or sound of rill;
Gross darkness of the inner sepulchre
     Is not so deadly still

As that wide forest. Growths of jasmine turn'd
   Their humid arms festooning tree to tree,   70
And at the root thro' lush green grasses burn'd
     The red anemone.

I knew the flowers, I knew the leaves, I knew
   The tearful glimmer of the languid dawn
On those long, rank, dark wood-walks drench'd in dew,
     Leading from lawn to lawn.

The smell of violets, hidden in the green,
   Pour'd back into my empty soul and frame
The times when I remember to have been
     Joyful and free from blame.   80

And from within me a clear undertone
   Thrill'd thro' mine ears in that unblissful clime,
"Pass freely thro'; the wood is all thine own
     Until the end of time."

At length I saw a lady within call,
   Stiller than chisell'd marble, standing there;
A daughter of the gods, divinely tall,
     And most divinely fair.

Her loveliness with shame and with surprise
   Froze my swift speech; she turning on my face   90
The star-like sorrows of immortal eyes,
     Spoke slowly in her place:

"I had great beauty; ask thou not my name:
   No one can be more wise than destiny.
Many drew swords and died. Where'er I came
     I brought calamity."

"No marvel, sovereign lady: in fair field
   Myself for such a face had boldly died,"
I answer'd free; and turning I appeal'd
     To one that stood beside.   **100**

But she, with sick and scornful looks averse,
   To her full height her stately stature draws;
"My youth," she said, "was blasted with a curse:
     This woman was the cause.

"I was cut off from hope in that sad place
   Which men call'd Aulis in those iron years:
My father held his hand upon his face;
     I, blinded with my tears,

"Still strove to speak: my voice was thick with sighs
   As in a dream. Dimly I could descry   **110**
The stern black-bearded kings with wolfish eyes,
     Waiting to see me die.

"The high masts flicker'd as they lay afloat;
   The crowds, the temples, waver'd, and the shore;
The bright death quiver'd at the victim's throat —
     Touch'd — and I knew no more."

Whereto the other with a downward brow:
   "I would the white cold heavy-plunging foam,
Whirl'd by the wind, had roll'd me deep below,
     Then when I left my home."   **120**

Her slow full words sank thro' the silence drear,
   As thunder-drops fall on a sleeping sea:
Sudden I heard a voice that cried, "Come here,
     That I may look on thee."

I turning saw, throned on a flowery rise,
   One sitting on a crimson scarf unroll'd;
A queen, with swarthy cheeks and bold black eyes,
     Brow-bound with burning gold.

She, flashing forth a haughty smile, began:
   "I govern'd men by change, and so I sway'd   **130**
All moods. 'T is long since I have seen a man.
     Once, like the moon, I made

"The ever-shifting currents of the blood
　According to my humor ebb and flow.
I have no men to govern in this wood:
　　That makes my only woe.

"Nay — yet it chafes me that I could not bend
　One will; nor tame and tutor with mine eye
That dull cold-blooded Cæsar. Prythee, friend,
　　Where is Mark Antony?　　　　　　　　140

"The man, my lover, with whom I rode sublime
　On Fortune's neck; we sat as God by God:
The Nilus would have risen before his time
　　And flooded at our nod.

"We drank the Libyan Sun to sleep, and lit
　Lamps which out-burn'd Canopus. O, my life
In Egypt! O, the dalliance and the wit,
　　The flattery and the strife,

"And the wild kiss, when fresh from war's alarms,
　My Hercules, my Roman Antony,　　　　　150
My mailed Bacchus leapt into my arms,
　　Contented there to die!

"And there he died: and when I heard my name
　Sigh'd forth with life I would not brook my fear
Of the other; with a worm I balk'd his fame.
　　What else was left? look here!" —

With that she tore her robe apart, and half
　The polish'd argent of her breast to sight
Laid bare. Thereto she pointed with a laugh,
　　Showing the aspick's bite. —　　　　　　160

"I died a Queen. The Roman soldier found
　Me lying dead, my crown about my brows,
A name for ever! — lying robed and crown'd,
　　Worthy a Roman spouse."

Her warbling voice, a lyre of widest range
　Struck by all passion, did fall down and glance
From tone to tone, and glided thro' all change
　　Of liveliest utterance.

When she made pause I knew not for delight;
  Because with sudden motion from the ground   170
She raised her piercing orbs, and fill'd with light
  The interval of sound.

Still with their fires Love tipt his keenest darts;
  As once they drew into two burning rings
All beams of love, melting the mighty hearts
  Of captains and of kings.

Slowly my sense undazzled. Then I heard
  A noise of some one coming thro' the lawn,
And singing clearer than the crested bird
  That claps his wings at dawn: 180

"The torrent brooks of hallow'd Israel
  From craggy hollows pouring, late and soon,
Sound all night long, in falling thro' the dell,
  Far-heard beneath the moon.

"The balmy moon of blessed Israel
  Floods all the deep-blue gloom with beams divine;
All night the splinter'd crags that wall the dell
  With spires of silver shine."

As one that museth where broad sunshine laves
  The lawn by some cathedral, thro' the door   190
Hearing the holy organ rolling waves
  Of sound on roof and floor

Within, and anthem sung, is charm'd and tied
  To where he stands, — so stood I, when that flow
Of music left the lips of her that died
  To save her father's vow;

The daughter of the warrior Gileadite,
  A maiden pure; as when she went along
From Mizpeh's tower'd gate with welcome light,
  With timbrel and with song.   200

My words leapt forth: "Heaven heads the count of crimes
  With that wild oath." She render'd answer high:
"Not so, nor once alone; a thousand times
  I would be born and die.

"Single I grew, like some green plant, whose root
   Creeps to the garden water-pipes beneath,
Feeding the flower; but ere my flower to fruit
   Changed, I was ripe for death.

"My God, my land, my father — these did move
   Me from my bliss of life that Nature gave,   210
Lower'd softly with a threefold cord of love
   Down to a silent grave.

"And I went mourning, 'No fair Hebrew boy
   Shall smile away my maiden blame among
The Hebrew mothers' — emptied of all joy,
   Leaving the dance and song,

"Leaving the olive-gardens far below,
   Leaving the promise of my bridal bower,
The valleys of grape-loaded vines that glow
   Beneath the battled tower.   220

"The light white cloud swam over us. Anon
   We heard the lion roaring from his den;
We saw the large white stars rise one by one,
   Or, from the darken'd glen,

"Saw God divide the night with flying flame,
   And thunder on the everlasting hills.
I heard Him, for He spake, and grief became
   A solemn scorn of ills.

"When the next moon was roll'd into the sky,
   Strength came to me that equall'd my desire.   230
How beautiful a thing it was to die
   For God and for my sire!

"It comforts me in this one thought to dwell,
   That I subdued me to my father's will;
Because the kiss he gave me, ere I fell,
   Sweetens the spirit still.

"Moreover it is written that my race
   Hew'd Ammon, hip and thigh, from Aroer
On Arnon unto Minneth." Here her face
   Glow'd, as I look'd at her.   240

She lock'd her lips; she left me where I stood:
    "Glory to God," she sang, and past afar,
Thridding the sombre boskage of the wood,
      Toward the morning-star.

Losing her carol I stood pensively,
    As one that from a casement leans his head,
When midnight bells cease ringing suddenly,
      And the old year is dead.

"Alas! alas!" a low voice, full of care,
    Murmur'd beside me: "Turn and look on me;   250
I am that Rosamond, whom men call fair,
      If what I was I be.

"Would I had been some maiden coarse and poor!
    O me, that I should ever see the light!
Those dragon eyes of anger'd Eleanor
      Do hunt me, day and night."

She ceased in tears, fallen from hope and trust;
    To whom the Egyptian: "O, you tamely died!
You should have clung to Fulvia's waist, and thrust
      The dagger thro' her side."   260

With that sharp sound the white dawn's creeping beams,
    Stolen to my brain, dissolved the mystery
Of folded sleep. The captain of my dreams
      Ruled in the eastern sky.

Morn broaden'd on the borders of the dark
    Ere I saw her who clasp'd in her last trance
Her murder'd father's head, or Joan of Arc,
      A light of ancient France;

Or her who knew that Love can vanquish Death,
    Who kneeling, with one arm about her king,   270
Drew forth the poison with her balmy breath,
      Sweet as new buds in spring.

No memory labors longer from the deep
    Gold-mines of thought to lift the hidden ore
That glimpses, moving up, than I from sleep
      To gather and tell o'er

Each little sound and sight. With what dull pain
　Compass'd, how eagerly I sought to strike
Into that wondrous track of dreams again!
　　But no two dreams are like.　　　　　　　　280

As when a soul laments, which hath been blest,
　Desiring what is mingled with past years,
In yearnings that can never be exprest
　　By signs or groans or tears;

Because all words, tho' cull'd with choicest art,
　Failing to give the bitter of the sweet,
Wither beneath the palate, and the heart
　　Faints, faded by its heat.

1832, 1842*

TO —

As when with downcast eyes we muse and brood,
And ebb into a former life, or seem
To lapse far back in some confused dream
To states of mystical similitude,
If one but speaks or hems or stirs his chair,
Ever the wonder waxeth more and more,
So that we say, "All this hath been before,
All this hath been, I know not when or where;"
So, friend, when first I look'd upon your face,
Our thought gave answer each to each, so true —　　10
Opposed mirrors each reflecting each —
That, tho' I knew not in what time or place,
Methought that I had often met with you,
And either lived in either's heart and speech.

1832*

TO CHRISTOPHER NORTH

You did late review my lays,
　Crusty Christopher;
You did mingle blame and praise,
　Rusty Chrstopher.

When I learnt from whom it came,
I forgave you all the blame,
   Musty Christopher;
I could *not* forgive the praise,
   Fusty Christopher.

1832*

TO J. S.

THE wind that beats the mountain blows
   More softly round the open wold,
And gently comes the world to those
   That are cast in gentle mould.

And me this knowledge bolder made,
   Or else I had not dared to flow
In these words toward you, and invade
   Even with a verse your holy woe.

'T is strange that those we lean on most,
   Those in whose laps our limbs are nursed,   10
Fall into shadow, soonest lost;
   Those we love first are taken first.

God gives us love. Something to love
   He lends us; but, when love is grown
To ripeness, that on which it throve
   Falls off, and love is left alone.

This is the curse of time. Alas!
   In grief I am not all unlearn'd;
Once thro' mine own doors Death did pass;
   One went who never hath return'd.   20

He will not smile — not speak to me
   Once more. Two years his chair is seen
Empty before us. That was he
   Without whose life I had not been.

Your loss is rarer; for this star
   Rose with you thro' a little arc
Of heaven, nor having wander'd far
   Shot on the sudden into dark.

I knew your brother; his mute dust
    I honor and his living worth;   30
A man more pure and bold and just
    Was never born into the earth.

I have not look'd upon you nigh
    Since that dear soul hath fallen asleep.
Great Nature is more wise than I;
    I will not tell you not to weep.

And tho' mine own eyes fill with dew,
    Drawn from the spirit thro' the brain,
I will not even preach to you,
    "Weep, weeping dulls the inward pain."   40

Let Grief be her own mistress still.
    She loveth her own anguish deep
More than much pleasure. Let her will
    Be done — to weep or not to weep.

I will not say, "God's ordinance
    Of death is blown in every wind;"
For that is not a common chance
    That takes away a noble mind.

His memory long will live alone
    In all our hearts, as mournful light   50
That broods above the fallen sun,
    And dwells in heaven half the night.

Vain solace! Memory standing near
    Cast down her eyes, and in her throat
Her voice seem'd distant, and a tear
    Dropt on the letters as I wrote.

I wrote I know not what. In truth,
    How *should* I soothe you any way,
Who miss the brother of your youth?
    Yet something I did wish to say;   60

For he too was a friend to me.
    Both are my friends, and my true breast
Bleedeth for both; yet it may be
    That only silence suiteth best.

Words weaker than your grief would make
  Grief more. 'T were better I should cease
Although myself could almost take
  The place of him that sleeps in peace.

Sleep sweetly, tender heart, in peace;
  Sleep, holy spirit, blessed soul,   70
While the stars burn, the moons increase,
  And the great ages onward roll.

Sleep till the end, true soul and sweet.
  Nothing comes to thee new or strange.
Sleep full of rest from head to feet;
  Lie still, dry dust, secure of change.

1832*

ULYSSES

It little profits that an idle king,
By this still hearth, among these barren crags,
Match'd with an aged wife, I mete and dole
Unequal laws unto a savage race,
That hoard, and sleep, and feed, and know not me.
I cannot rest from travel; I will drink
Life to the lees. All times I have enjoy'd
Greatly, have suffer'd greatly, both with those
That loved me, and alone; on shore, and when
Thro' scudding drifts the rainy Hyades   10
Vext the dim sea. I am become a name;
For always roaming with a hungry heart
Much have I seen and known, — cities of men
And manners, climates, councils, governments,
Myself not least, but honor'd of them all, —
And drunk delight of battle with my peers,
Far on the ringing plains of windy Troy.
I am a part of all that I have met;
Yet all experience is an arch wherethro'
Gleams that untravell'd world whose margin fades   20
For ever and for ever when I move.
How dull it is to pause, to make an end,
To rust unburnish'd, not to shine in use!
As tho' to breathe were life! Life piled on life
Were all too little, and of one to me
Little remains; but every hour is saved

From that eternal silence, something more,
A bringer of new things; and vile it were
For some three suns to store and hoard myself,
And this gray spirit yearning in desire   30
To follow knowledge like a sinking star,
Beyond the utmost bound of human thought.

   This is my son, mine own Telemachus,
To whom I leave the sceptre and the isle, —
Well-loved of me, discerning to fulfil
This labor, by slow prudence to make mild
A rugged people, and thro' soft degrees
Subdue them to the useful and the good.
Most blameless is he, centred in the sphere
Of common duties, decent not to fail   40
In offices of tenderness, and pay
Meet adoration to my household gods,
When I am gone. He works his work, I mine.

   There lies the port; the vessel puffs her sail;
There gloom the dark, broad seas. My mariners,
Souls that have toil'd, and wrought, and thought with me, —
That ever with a frolic welcome took
The thunder and the sunshine, and opposed
Free hearts, free foreheads, — you and I are old;
Old age hath yet his honor and his toil.   50
Death closes all; but something ere the end,
Some work of noble note, may yet be done,
Not unbecoming men that strove with Gods.
The lights begin to twinkle from the rocks;
The long day wanes; the slow moon climbs; the deep
Moans round with many voices. Come, my friends.
'T is not too late to seek a newer world.
Push off, and sitting well in order smite
The sounding furrows; for my purpose holds
To sail beyond the sunset, and the baths   60
Of all the western stars, until I die.
It may be that the gulfs will wash us down;
It may be we shall touch the Happy Isles,
And see the great Achilles, whom we knew.
Tho' much is taken, much abides; and tho'
We are not now that strength which in old days
Moved earth and heaven, that which we are, we are, —
One equal temper of heroic hearts,
Made weak by time and fate, but strong in will
To strive, to seek, to find, and not to yield.   70

1833 (1842) *

TITHONUS

THE woods decay, the woods decay and fall,
The vapors weep their burthen to the ground,
Man comes and tills the field and lies beneath,
And after many a summer dies the swan.
Me only cruel immortality
Consumes; I wither slowly in thine arms,
Here at the quiet limit of the world,
A white-hair'd shadow roaming like a dream
The ever-silent spaces of the East,
Far-folded mists, and gleaming halls of morn.   10
   Alas! for this gray shadow, once a man —
So glorious in his beauty and thy choice,
Who madest him thy chosen, that he seem'd
To his great heart none other than a God!
I ask'd thee, "Give me immortality."
Then didst thou grant mine asking with a smile,
Like wealthy men who care not how they give.
But thy strong Hours indignant work'd their wills,
And beat me down and marr'd and wasted me,
And tho' they could not end me, left me maim'd   20
To dwell in presence of immortal youth,
Immortal age beside immortal youth,
And all I was in ashes. Can thy love,
Thy beauty, make amends, tho' even now,
Close over us, the silver star, thy guide,
Shines in those tremulous eyes that fill with tears
To hear me? Let me go; take back thy gift.
Why should a man desire in any way
To vary from the kindly race of men,
Or pass beyond the goal of ordinance   30
Where all should pause, as is most meet for all?
   A soft air fans the cloud apart; there comes
A glimpse of that dark world where I was born.
Once more the old mysterious glimmer steals
From thy pure brows, and from thy shoulders pure,
And bosom beating with a heart renew'd.
Thy cheek begins to redden thro' the gloom,
Thy sweet eyes brighten slowly close to mine.
Ere yet they blind the stars, and the wild team
Which love thee, yearning for thy yoke, arise,   40
And shake the darkness from their loosen'd manes,

And beat the twilight into flakes of fire.
Lo! ever thus thou growest beautiful
In silence, then before thine answer given
Departest, and thy tears are on my cheek.
Why wilt thou ever scare me with thy tears,
And make me tremble lest a saying learnt,
In days far-off, on that dark earth, be true?
"The Gods themselves cannot recall their gifts."
Ay me! ay me! with what another heart   50
In days far-off, and with what other eyes
I used to watch — if I be he that watch'd —
The lucid outline forming round thee; saw
The dim curls kindle into sunny rings;
Changed with thy mystic change, and felt my blood
Glow with the glow that slowly crimson'd all
Thy presence and thy portals, while I lay,
Mouth, forehead, eyelids, growing dewy-warm
With kisses balmier than half-opening buds
Of April, and could hear the lips that kiss'd   60
Whispering I knew not what of wild and sweet,
Like that strange song I heard Apollo sing,
While Ilion like a mist rose into towers.
Yet hold me not for ever in thine East;
How can my nature longer mix with thine?
Coldly thy rosy shadows bathe me, cold
Are all thy lights, and cold my wrinkled feet
Upon thy glimmering thresholds, when the steam
Floats up from those dim fields about the homes
Of happy men that have the power to die,   70
And grassy barrows of the happier dead.
Release me, and restore me to the ground.
Thou seest all things, thou wilt see my grave;
Thou wilt renew thy beauty morn by morn,
I earth in earth forget these empty courts,
And thee returning on thy silver wheels.

1833 f. (1860) *

THE TWO VOICES

A STILL small voice spake unto me,
"Thou art so full of misery,
Were it not better not to be?"

Then to the still small voice I said:
"Let me not cast in endless shade
What is so wonderfully made."

To which the voice did urge reply:
"To-day I saw the dragon-fly
Come from the wells where he did lie.

"An inner impulse rent the veil   10
Of his old husk; from head to tail
Came out clear plates of sapphire mail.

"He dried his wings; like gauze they grew;
Thro' crofts and pastures wet with dew
A living flash of light he flew."

I said: "When first the world began,
Young Nature thro' five cycles ran,
And in the sixth she moulded man.

"She gave him mind, the lordliest
Proportion, and, above the rest,   20
Dominion in the head and breast."

Thereto the silent voice replied:
"Self-blinded are you by your pride;
Look up thro' night; the world is wide.

"This truth within thy mind rehearse,
That in a boundless universe
Is boundless better, boundless worse.

"Think you this mould of hopes and fears
Could find no statelier than his peers
In yonder hundred million spheres?"   30

It spake, moreover, in my mind:
"Tho' thou wert scatter'd to the wind,
Yet is there plenty of the kind."

Then did my response clearer fall:
"No compound of this earthly ball
Is like another, all in all."

To which he answer'd scoffingly:
"Good soul! suppose I grant it thee,
Who'll weep for thy deficiency?

"Or will one beam be less intense,   40
When thy peculiar difference
Is cancell'd in the world of sense?"

I would have said, "Thou canst not know,"
But my full heart, that work'd below,
Rain'd thro' my sight its overflow.

Again the voice spake unto me:
"Thou art so steep'd in misery,
Surely 't were better not to be.

"Thine anguish will not let thee sleep,
Nor any train of reason keep;   50
Thou canst not think, but thou wilt weep."

I said: "The years with change advance;
If I make dark my countenance,
I shut my life from happier chance.

"Some turn this sickness yet might take,
Even yet." But he: "What drug can make
A wither'd palsy cease to shake?"

I wept: "Tho' I should die, I know
That all about the thorn will blow
In tufts of rosy-tinted snow;   60

"And men, thro' novel spheres of thought
Still moving after truth long sought,
Will learn new things when I am not."

"Yet," said the secret voice, "some time,
Sooner or later, will gray prime
Make thy grass hoar with early rime.

"Not less swift souls that yearn for light,
Rapt after heaven's starry flight,
Would sweep the tracts of day and night.

"Not less the bee would range her cells,   70
The furzy prickle fire the dells,
The foxglove cluster dappled bells."

I said that "all the years invent;
Each month is various to present
The world with some development.

"Were this not well, to bide mine hour,
Tho' watching from a ruin'd tower
How grows the day of human power?"

"The highest-mounted mind," he said,
"Still sees the sacred morning spread   80
The silent summit overhead.

"Will thirty seasons render plain
Those lonely lights that still remain,
Just breaking over land and main?

"Or make that morn, from his cold crown
And crystal silence creeping down,
Flood with full daylight glebe and town?

"Forerun thy peers, thy time, and let
Thy feet, millenniums hence, be set
In midst of knowledge, dream'd not yet.   90

"Thou hast not gain'd a real height,
Nor art thou nearer to the light,
Because the scale is infinite.

" 'T were better not to breathe or speak,
Than cry for strength, remaining weak,
And seem to find, but still to seek.

"Moreover, but to seem to find
Asks what thou lackest, thought resign'd,
A healthy frame, a quiet mind."

I said: "When I am gone away,   100
'He dared not tarry,' men will say,
Doing dishonor to my clay."

"This is more vile," he made reply,
"To breathe and loathe, to live and sigh,
Than once from dread of pain to die.

"Sick art thou — a divided will
Still heaping on the fear of ill
The fear of men, a coward still.

"Do men love thee? Art thou so bound
To men that how thy name may sound   110
Will vex thee lying underground?

"The memory of the wither'd leaf
In endless time is scarce more brief
Than of the garner'd autumn-sheaf.

"Go, vexed spirit, sleep in trust;
The right ear that is fill'd with dust
Hears little of the false or just."

"Hard task, to pluck resolve," I cried,
"From emptiness and the waste wide
Of that abyss, or scornful pride!   120

"Nay — rather yet that I could raise
One hope that warm'd me in the days
While still I yearn'd for human praise.

"When, wide in soul and bold of tongue,
Among the tents I paused and sung,
The distant battle flash'd and rung.

"I sung the joyful Pæan clear,
And, sitting, burnish'd without fear
The brand, the buckler, and the spear —

"Waiting to strive a happy strife,   130
To war with falsehood to the knife,
And not to lose the good of life —

"Some hidden principle to move,
To put together, part and prove,
And mete the bounds of hate and love —

"As far as might be, to carve out
Free space for every human doubt,
That the whole mind might orb about —

"To search thro' all I felt or saw,
The springs of life, the depths of awe,   140
And reach the law within the law;

"At least, not rotting like a weed,
But, having sown some generous seed,
Fruitful of further thought and deed,

"To pass, when Life her light withdraws,
Not void of righteous self-applause,
Nor in a merely selfish cause —

"In some good cause, not in mine own,
To perish, wept for, honor'd, known,
And like a warrior overthrown;   150

"Whose eyes are dim with glorious tears,
When, soil'd with noble dust, he hears
His country's war-song thrill his ears:

"Then dying of a mortal stroke,
What time the foeman's line is broke,
And all the war is roll'd in smoke."

"Yea!" said the voice, "thy dream was good,
While thou abodest in the bud.
It was the stirring of the blood.

"If Nature put not forth her power   160
About the opening of the flower,
Who is it that could live an hour?

"Then comes the check, the change, the fall,
Pain rises up, old pleasures pall.
There is one remedy for all.

"Yet hadst thou, thro' enduring pain,
Link'd month to month with such a chain
Of knitted purport, all were vain.

"Thou hadst not between death and birth
Dissolved the riddle of the earth.   170
So were thy labor little worth.

"That men with knowledge merely play'd,
I told thee — hardly nigher made,
Tho' scaling slow from grade to grade;

"Much less this dreamer, deaf and blind,
Named man, may hope some truth to find,
That bears relation to the mind.

"For every worm beneath the moon
Draws different threads, and late and soon
Spins, toiling out his own cocoon.   180

"Cry, faint not: either Truth is born
Beyond the polar gleam forlorn,
Or in the gateways of the morn.

"Cry, faint not, climb: the summits slope
Beyond the furthest flights of hope,
Wrapt in dense cloud from base to cope.

"Sometimes a little corner shines,
As over rainy mist inclines
A gleaming crag with belts of pines.

"I will go forward, sayest thou,   190
I shall not fail to find her now.
Look up, the fold is on her brow.

"If straight thy track, or if oblique,
Thou know'st not. Shadows thou dost strike,
Embracing cloud, Ixion-like;

"And owning but a little more
Than beasts, abidest lame and poor,
Calling thyself a little lower

"Than angels. Cease to wail and brawl!
Why inch by inch to darkness crawl?   200
There is one remedy for all."

"O dull, one-sided voice," said I,
"Wilt thou make everything a lie,
To flatter me that I may die?

"I know that age to age succeeds,
Blowing a noise of tongues and deeds,
A dust of systems and of creeds.

"I cannot hide that some have striven,
Achieving calm, to whom was given
The joy that mixes man with Heaven;   210

"Who, rowing hard against the stream,
Saw distant gates of Eden gleam,
And did not dream it was a dream;

"But heard, by secret transport led,
Even in the charnels of the dead,
The murmur of the fountain-head —

"Which did accomplish their desire,
Bore and forebore, and did not tire,
Like Stephen, an unquenched fire.

"He heeded not reviling tones,   220
Nor sold his heart to idle moans,
Tho' cursed and scorn'd, and bruised with stones;

"But looking upward, full of grace,
He pray'd, and from a happy place
God's glory smote him on the face."

The sullen answer slid betwixt:
"Not that the grounds of hope were fix'd,
The elements were kindlier mix'd."

I said: "I toil beneath the curse,
But, knowing not the universe,
I fear to slide from bad to worse;   230

"And that, in seeking to undo
One riddle, and to find the true,
I knit a hundred others new;

"Or that this anguish fleeting hence,
Unmanacled from bonds of sense,
Be fix'd and frozen to permanence:

"For I go, weak from suffering here;
Naked I go, and void of cheer:
What is it that I may not fear?   240

"Consider well," the voice replied,
"His face, that two hours since hath died;
Wilt thou find passion, pain or pride?

"Will he obey when one commands?
Or answer should one press his hands?
He answers not, nor understands.

"His palms are folded on his breast;
There is no other thing express'd
But long disquiet merged in rest.

"His lips are very mild and meek;   250
Tho' one should smite him on the cheek,
And on the mouth, he will not speak.

"His little daughter, whose sweet face
He kiss'd, taking his last embrace,
Becomes dishonor to her race —

"His sons grow up that bear his name,
Some grow to honor, some to shame, —
But he is chill to praise or blame.

"He will not hear the north-wind rave,
Nor, moaning, household shelter crave   260
From winter rains that beat his grave.

"High up the vapors fold and swim;
About him broods the twilight dim;
The place he knew forgetteth him."

"If all be dark, vague voice," I said,
"These things are wrapt in doubt and dread,
Nor canst thou show the dead are dead.

"The sap dries up: the plant declines.
A deeper tale my heart divines.
Know I not death? the outward signs?   270

"I found him when my years were few;
A shadow on the graves I knew,
And darkness in the village yew.

"From grave to grave the shadow crept;
In her still place the morning wept;
Touch'd by his feet the daisy slept.

"The simple senses crown'd his head:
'Omega! thou art Lord,' they said,
'We find no motion in the dead!'

"Why, if man rot in dreamless ease,   280
Should that plain fact, as taught by these,
Not make him sure that he shall cease?

"Who forged that other influence,
That heat of inward evidence,
By which he doubts against the sense?

"He owns the fatal gift of eyes,
That read his spirit blindly wise,
Not simple as a thing that dies.

"Here sits he shaping wings to fly;
His heart forebodes a mystery;   290
He names the name Eternity.

"That type of Perfect in his mind
In Nature can he nowhere find.
He sows himself on every wind.

"He seems to hear a Heavenly Friend,
And thro' thick veils to apprehend
A labor working to an end.

"The end and the beginning vex
His reason: many things perplex,
With motions, checks, and counterchecks.   300

"He knows a baseness in his blood
At such strange war with something good,
He may not do the thing he would.

"Heaven opens inward, chasms yawn,
Vast images in glimmering dawn,
Half shown, are broken and withdrawn.

"Ah! sure within him and without,
Could his dark wisdom find it out,
There must be answer to his doubt,

"But thou canst answer not again.   310
With thine own weapon art thou slain,
Or thou wilt answer but in vain.

"The doubt would rest, I dare not solve.
In the same circle we revolve.
Assurance only breeds resolve."

As when a billow, blown against,
Falls back, the voice with which I fenced
A little ceased, but recommenced:

"Where wert thou when thy father play'd
In his free field, and pastime made,   320
A merry boy in sun and shade?

"A merry boy they call'd him then,
He sat upon the knees of men
In days that never come again;

"Before the little ducts began
To feed thy bones with lime, and ran
Their course, till thou wert also man:

"Who took a wife, who rear'd his race,
Whose wrinkles gather'd on his face,
Whose troubles number with his days;   330

"A life of nothings, nothing worth,
From that first nothing ere his birth
To that last nothing under earth!"

"These words," I said, "are like the rest;
No certain clearness, but at best
A vague suspicion of the breast:

"But if I grant, thou mightst defend
The thesis which thy words intend —
That to begin implies to end;

"Yet how should I for certain hold,   340
Because my memory is so cold,
That I first was in human mould?

"I cannot make this matter plain,
But I would shoot, howe'er in vain,
A random arrow from the brain.

"It may be that no life is found,
Which only to one engine bound
Falls off, but cycles always round.

"As old mythologies relate,
Some draught of Lethe might await   350
The slipping thro' from state to state;

"As here we find in trances, men
Forget the dream that happens then,
Until they fall in trance again;

"So might we, if our state were such
As one before, remember much,
For those two likes might meet and touch.

"But, if I lapsed from nobler place,
Some legend of a fallen race
Alone might hint of my disgrace;   360

"Some vague emotion of delight
In gazing up an Alpine height,
Some yearning toward the lamps of night;

"Or if thro' lower lives I came —
Tho' all experience past became
Consolidate in mind and frame —

"I might forget my weaker lot;
For is not our first year forgot?
The haunts of memory echo not.

"And men, whose reason long was blind,
From cells of madness unconfined,   370
Oft lose whole years of darker mind.

"Much more, if first I floated free,
As naked essence, must I be
Incompetent of memory;

"For memory dealing but with time,
And he with matter, could she climb
Beyond her own material prime?

"Moreover, something is or seems,
That touches me with mystic gleams,   380
Like glimpses of forgotten dreams —

"Of something felt, like something here;
Of something done, I know not where;
Such as no language may declare."

The still voice laugh'd. "I talk," said he,
"Not with thy dreams. Suffice it thee
Thy pain is a reality."

"But thou," said I, "hast missed thy mark,
Who sought'st to wreck my mortal ark,
By making all the horizon dark.   390

"Why not set forth, if I should do
This rashness, that which might ensue
With this old soul in organs new?

"Whatever crazy sorrow saith,
No life that breathes with human breath
Has ever truly long'd for death.

" 'T is life, whereof our nerves are scant,
O, life, not death, for which we pant;
More life, and fuller, that I want."

I ceased, and sat as one forlorn.   400
Then said the voice, in quiet scorn,
"Behold, it is the Sabbath morn."

And I arose, and I released
The casement, and the light increased
With freshness in the dawning east.

Like soften'd airs that blowing steal,
When meres begin to uncongeal,
The sweet church bells began to peal.

On to God's house the people prest;
Passing the place where each must rest,   410
Each enter'd like a welcome guest.

One walk'd between his wife and child,
With measured footfall firm and mild,
And now and then he gravely smiled.

The prudent partner of his blood
Lean'd on him, faithful, gentle, good,
Wearing the rose of womanhood.

And in their double love secure,
The little maiden walk'd demure,
Pacing with downward eyelids pure.   420

These three made unity so sweet,
My frozen heart began to beat,
Remembering its ancient heat.

I blest them, and they wander'd on;
I spoke, but answer came there none;
The dull and bitter voice was gone.

A second voice was at mine ear,
A little whisper silver-clear,
A murmur, "Be of better cheer."

As from some blissful neighborhood,   430
A notice faintly understood,
"I see the end, and know the good."

A little hint to solace woe,
A hint, a whisper breathing low,
"I may not speak of what I know."

Like an Æolian harp that wakes
No certain air, but overtakes
Far thought with music that it makes;

Such seem'd the whisper at my side:
"What is it thou knowest, sweet voice?" I cried.   440
"A hidden hope," the voice replied;

So heavenly-toned, that in that hour
From out my sullen heart a power
Broke, like the rainbow from the shower,

To feel, altho' no tongue can prove,
That every cloud that spreads above
And veileth love, itself is love.

And forth into the fields I went,
And Nature's living motion lent
The pulse of hope to discontent.   450

I wonder'd at the bounteous hours,
The slow result of winter showers;
You scarce could see the grass for flowers.

I wonder'd, while I paced along;
The woods were fill'd so full with song,
There seem'd no room for sense of wrong;

And all so variously wrought,
I marvell'd how the mind was brought
To anchor by one gloomy thought;

And wherefore rather I made choice   460
To commune with that barren voice,
Than him that said, "Rejoice! Rejoice!"
1833 (1842) *

"BREAK, BREAK, BREAK"

Break, break, break,
    On thy cold gray stones, O Sea!
And I would that my tongue could utter
    The thoughts that arise in me.

O, well for the fisherman's boy,
    That he shouts with his sister at play!
O, well for the sailor lad,
    That he sings in his boat on the bay!

And the stately ships go on
    To their haven under the hill;   10
But O for the touch of a vanish'd hand,
    And the sound of a voice that is still!

Break, break, break,
    At the foot of thy crags, O Sea!
But the tender grace of a day that is dead
    Will never come back to me.
1834? (1842)

"YOU ASK ME WHY"

You ask me, why, tho' ill at ease,
    Within this region I subsist,
    Whose spirits falter in the mist,
And languish for the purple seas.

It is the land that freemen till,
    That sober-suited Freedom chose,
    The land, where girt with friends or foes
A man may speak the thing he will;

A land of settled government,
  A land of just and old renown,
  Where Freedom slowly broadens down   10
From precedent to precedent;

Where faction seldom gathers head,
  But, by degrees to fullness wrought,
  The strength of some diffusive thought
Hath time and space to work and spread.

Should banded unions persecute
  Opinion, and induce a time
  When single thought is civil crime,
And individual freedom mute,   20

Tho' power should make from land to land
  The name of Britain trebly great —
  Tho' every channel of the State
Should fill and choke with golden sand —

Yet waft me from the harbor-mouth,
  Wild wind! I seek a warmer sky,
  And I will see before I die
The palms and temples of the South.
  1834 (1842)

"OF OLD SAT FREEDOM ON THE HEIGHTS"

OF old sat Freedom on the heights,
  The thunders breaking at her feet;
Above her shook the starry lights;
  She heard the torrents meet.

There in her place she did rejoice,
  Self-gather'd in her prophet-mind,
But fragments of her mighty voice
  Came rolling on the wind.

Then stept she down thro' town and field
  To mingle with the human race,   10
And part by part to men reveal'd
  The fullness of her face —

Grave mother of majestic works,
   From her isle-altar gazing down,
Who, Godlike, grasps the triple forks,
   And, king-like, wears the crown.

Her open eyes desire the truth.
   The wisdom of a thousand years
Is in them. May perpetual youth
   Keep dry their light from tears;   20

That her fair form may stand and shine,
   Make bright our days and light our dreams,
Turning to scorn with lips divine
   The falsehood of extremes!

1834 (1842)

"LOVE THOU THY LAND"

Love thou thy land, with love far-brought
   From out the storied past, and used
   Within the present, but transfused
Thro' future time by power of thought;

True love turn'd round on fixed poles,
   Love, that endures not sordid ends,
   For English natures, freemen, friends,
Thy brothers and immortal souls.

But pamper not a hasty time,
   Nor feed with crude imaginings   10
   The herd, wild hearts and feeble wings
That every sophister can lime.

Deliver not the tasks of might
   To weakness, neither hide the ray
   From those, not blind, who wait for day,
Tho' sitting girt with doubtful light.

Make knowledge circle with the winds;
   But let her herald, Reverence, fly
   Before her to whatever sky
Bear seed of men and growth of minds.   20

Watch what main-currents draw the years;
    Cut Prejudice against the grain.
    But gentle words are always gain;
Regard the weakness of thy peers.

Nor toil for title, place, or touch
    Of pension, neither count on praise —
    It grows to guerdon after-days.
Nor deal in watch-words overmuch;

Not clinging to some ancient saw,
    Not master'd by some modern term,   30
    Not swift nor slow to change, but firm;
And in its season bring the law,

That from Discussion's lip may fall
    With Life that, working strongly, binds —
    Set in all lights by many minds,
To close the interests of all.

For Nature also, cold and warm,
    And moist and dry, devising long,
    Thro' many agents making strong,
Matures the individual form.   40

Meet is it changes should control
    Our being, lest we rust in ease.
    We all are changed by still degrees,
All but the basis of the soul.

So let the change which comes be free
    To ingroove itself with that which flies,
    And work, a joint of state, that plies
Its office, moved with sympathy.

A saying hard to shape in act;
    For all the past of Time reveals   50
    A bridal dawn of thunder-peals,
Wherever Thought hath wedded Fact.

Even now we hear with inward strife
    A motion toiling in the gloom —
    The Spirit of the years to come
Yearning to mix himself with Life.

A slow-develop'd strength awaits
   Completion in a painful school;
   Phantoms of other forms of rule,
New Majesties of mighty States —   60

The warders of the growing hour,
   But vague in vapor, hard to mark;
   And round them sea and air are dark
With great contrivances of Power.

Of many changes, aptly join'd,
   Is bodied forth the second whole.
   Regard gradation, lest the soul
Of Discord race the rising wind;

A wind to puff your idol-fires,
   And heap their ashes on the head;   70
   To shame the boast so often made,
That we are wiser than our sires.

O, yet, if Nature's evil star
   Drive men in manhood, as in youth,
   To follow flying steps of Truth
Across the brazen bridge of war —

If New and Old, disastrous feud,
   Must ever shock, like armed foes,
   And this be true, till Time shall close,
That Principles are rain'd in blood;   80

Not yet the wise of heart would cease
   To hold his hope thro' shame and guilt,
   But with his hand against the hilt,
Would pace the troubled land, like Peace;

Not less, tho' dogs of Faction bay,
   Would serve his kind in deed and word,
   Certain, if knowledge bring the sword,
That knowledge takes the sword away —

Would love the gleams of good that broke
   From either side, nor veil his eyes;   90
   And if some dreadful need should rise
Would strike, and firmly, and one stroke.

To-morrow yet would reap to-day,
   As we bear blossom of the dead;
   Earn well the thrifty months, nor wed
Raw Haste, half-sister to Delay.

1834 (1842)

ST. AGNES' EVE

DEEP on the convent-roof the snows
   Are sparkling to the moon;
My breath to heaven like vapor goes;
   May my soul follow soon!
The shadows of the convent-towers
   Slant down the snowy sward,
Still creeping with the creeping hours
   That lead me to my Lord.
Make Thou my spirit pure and clear
   As are the frosty skies,   10
Or this first snowdrop of the year
   That in my bosom lies.

As these white robes are soil'd and dark,
   To yonder shining ground;
As this pale taper's earthly spark,
   To yonder argent round;
So shows my soul before the Lamb,
   My spirit before Thee;
So in mine earthly house I am,
   To that I hope to be.   20
Break up the heavens, O Lord! and far,
   Thro' all yon starlight keen,
Draw me, thy bride, a glittering star,
   In raiment white and clean.

He lifts me to the golden doors;
   The flashes come and go;
All heaven bursts her starry floors,
   And strows her lights below,
And deepens on and up! the gates
   Roll back, and far within   30
For me the Heavenly Bridegroom waits,
   To make me pure of sin.

The Sabbaths of Eternity,
   One Sabbath deep and wide —
A light upon the shining sea —
   The Bridegroom with his bride!
1834 (1837) *

"MOVE EASTWARD, HAPPY EARTH"

Move eastward, happy earth, and leave
   Yon orange sunset waning slow;
From fringes of the faded eve,
   O happy planet, eastward go,
Till over thy dark shoulder glow
   Thy silver sister-world, and rise
   To glass herself in dewy eyes
That watch me from the glen below.

Ah, bear me with thee, smoothly borne,
   Dip forward under starry light,   10
And move me to my marriage-morn,
   And round again to happy night.
1836 (1842) *

A FAREWELL

Flow down, cold rivulet, to the sea,
   Thy tribute wave deliver;
No more by thee my steps shall be,
   For ever and for ever.

Flow, softly flow, by lawn and lea,
   A rivulet, then a river;
Nowhere by thee my steps shall be,
   For ever and for ever.

But here will sigh thine alder-tree,
   And here thine aspen shiver;   10
And here by thee will hum the bee,
   For ever and for ever.

A thousand suns will stream on thee,
    A thousand moons will quiver;
But not by thee my steps shall be,
    For ever and for ever.

1837 (1842)*

THE EPIC

At Francis Allen's on the Christmas-eve, —
The game of forfeits done — the girls all kiss'd
Beneath the sacred bush and past away —
The parson Holmes, the poet Everard Hall,
The host, and I sat round the wassail-bowl,
Then half-way ebb'd; and there we held a talk,
How all the old honor had from Christmas gone,
Or gone or dwindled down to some odd games
In some odd nooks like this; till I, tired out
With cutting eights that day upon the pond,   10
Where, three times slipping from the outer edge,
I bump'd the ice into three several stars,
Fell in a doze; and half-awake I heard
The parson taking wide and wider sweeps,
Now harping on the church-commissioners,
Now hawking at geology and schism;
Until I woke, and found him settled down
Upon the general decay of faith
Right thro' the world: "at home was little left,
And none abroad; there was no anchor, none,   20
To hold by." Francis, laughing, clapt his hand
On Everard's shoulder, with "I hold by him."
"And I," quoth Everard, "by the wassail-bowl."
"Why yes," I said, "we knew your gift that way
At college; but another which you had —
I mean of verse (for so we held it then),
What came of that?" "You know," said Frank, "he burnt
His epic, his King Arthur, some twelve books" —
And then to me demanding why: "O, sir,
He thought that nothing new was said, or else   30
Something so said 't was nothing — that a truth
Looks freshest in the fashion of the day;
God knows; he has a mint of reasons; ask.
It pleased *me* well enough." "Nay, nay," said Hall,

"Why take the style of those heroic times?
For nature brings not back the mastodon,
Nor we those times; and why should any man
Remodel models? these twelve books of mine
Were faint Homeric echoes, nothing-worth,
Mere chaff and draff, much better burnt." "But I,"   40
Said Francis, "pick'd the eleventh from this hearth,
And have it; keep a thing, its use will come.
I hoard it as a sugar-plum for Holmes."
He laugh'd, and I, tho' sleepy, like a horse
That hears the corn-bin open, prick'd my ears;
For I remember'd Everard's college fame
When we were Freshmen. Then at my request
He brought it; and the poet, little urged,
But with some prelude of disparagement,
Read, mouthing out his hollow oes and aes,   50
Deep-chested music, and to this result.

[Here follows "Morte d' Arthur," ll. 170–440 of "The Passing of Arthur," pp. 464–470, below. Then "The Epic" continues.]

Here ended Hall, and our last light, that long
Had wink'd and threaten'd darkness, flared and fell;
At which the parson, sent to sleep with sound,
And waked with silence, grunted "Good!" but we
Sat rapt: it was the tone with which he read —
Perhaps some modern touches here and there
Redeem'd it from the charge of nothingness —
Or else we loved the man, and prized his work;
I know not; but we sitting, as I said,   60
The cock crew loud, as at that time of year
The lusty bird takes every hour for dawn.
Then Francis, muttering, like a man ill-used,
"There now — that's nothing!" drew a little back,
And drove his heel into the smoulder'd log,
That sent a blast of sparkles up the flue.
And so to bed, where yet in sleep I seem'd
To sail with Arthur under looming shores,
Point after point; till on to dawn, when dreams
Begin to feel the truth and stir of day,   70
To me, methought, who waited with the crowd,
There came a bark that, blowing forward, bore
King Arthur, like a modern gentleman
Of stateliest port; and all the people cried,
"Arthur is come again: he cannot die."

Then those that stood upon the hills behind
Repeated — "Come again, and thrice as fair;"
And, further inland, voices echoed — "Come
With all good things, and war shall be no more."
At this a hundred bells began to peal,⁣   80
That with the sound I woke, and heard indeed
The clear church-bells ring in the Christmas morn.

1838 (1842) *

AUDLEY COURT

"THE Bull, the Fleece are cramm'd, and not a room
For love or money. Let us picnic there
At Audley Court."
                    I spoke, while Audley feast
Humm'd like a hive all round the narrow quay,
To Francis, with a basket on his arm,
To Francis just alighted from the boat
And breathing of the sea. "With all my heart,"
Said Francis. Then we shoulder'd thro' the swarm,
And rounded by the stillness of the beach
To where the bay runs up its latest horn.   10
    We left the dying ebb that faintly lipp'd
The flat red granite; so by many a sweep
Of meadow smooth from aftermath we reach'd
The griffin-guarded gates, and pass'd thro' all
The pillar'd dusk of sounding sycamores,
And cross'd the garden to the gardener's lodge,
With all its casements bedded, and its walls
And chimneys muffled in the leafy vine.
    There, on a slope of orchard, Francis laid
A damask napkin wrought with horse and hound,   20
Brought out a dusky loaf that smelt of home,
And, half-cut-down, a pasty costly-made,
Where quail and pigeon, lark and leveret lay,
Like fossils of the rock, with golden yolks
Imbedded and injellied; last, with these,
A flask of cider from his father's vats,
Prime, which I knew; and so we sat and eat
And talk'd old matters over, — who was dead,
Who married, who was like to be, and how
The races went, and who would rent the hall;   30

Then touch'd upon the game, how scarce it was
This season; glancing thence, discuss'd the farm,
The four-field system, and the price of grain;
And struck upon the corn-laws, where we split,
And came again together on the king
With heated faces; till he laugh'd aloud,
And, while the blackbird on the pippin hung
To hear him, clapt his hand in mine and sang:

   "O, who would fight and march and countermarch,
Be shot for sixpence in a battle-field,   **40**
And shovell'd up into some bloody trench
Where no one knows? but let me live my life.

   "O, who would cast and balance at a desk,
Perch'd like a crow upon a three-legg'd stool,
Till all his juice is dried, and all his joints
Are full of chalk? but let me live my life.

   "Who'd serve the state? for if I carved my name
Upon the cliffs that guard my native land,
I might as well have traced it in the sands;
The sea wastes all; but let me live my life.   **50**

   "O, who would love? I woo'd a woman once,
But she was sharper than an eastern wind,
And all my heart turn'd from her, as a thorn
Turns from the sea; but let me live my life."

   He sang his song, and I replied with mine.
I found it in a volume, all of songs,
Knock'd down to me, when old Sir Robert's pride,
His books — the more the pity, so I said —
Came to the hammer here in March — and this —
I set the words, and added names I knew: **60**

   "Sleep, Ellen Aubrey, sleep, and dream of me:
Sleep, Ellen, folded in thy sister's arm,
And sleeping, haply dream her arm is mine.

   "Sleep, Ellen, folded in Emilia's arm:
Emilia, fairer than all else but thou,
For thou art fairer than all else that is.

   "Sleep, breathing health and peace upon her breast;
Sleep, breathing love and trust against her lip.
I go to-night; I come to-morrow morn.

"I go, but I return; I would I were   **70**
The pilot of the darkness and the dream.
Sleep, Ellen Aubrey, love, and dream of me."

   So sang we each to either, Francis Hale,
The farmer's son, who lived across the bay,
My friend; and I, that having wherewithal,

And in the fallow leisure of my life
A rolling stone of here and everywhere,
Did what I would. But ere the night we rose
And saunter'd home beneath a moon that, just
In crescent, dimly rain'd about the leaf   80
Twilights of airy silver, till we reach'd
The limit of the hills; and as we sank
From rock to rock upon the glooming quay,
The town was hush'd beneath us; lower down
The bay was oily calm; the harbor-buoy,
Sole star of phosphorescence in the calm,
With one green sparkle ever and anon
Dipt by itself, and we were glad at heart.

1838? (1842)*

LOVE AND DUTY

OF love that never found his earthly close,
What sequel? Streaming eyes and breaking hearts?
Or all the same as if he had not been?
    Not so. Shall Error in the round of time
Still father Truth? O, shall the braggart shout
For some blind glimpse of freedom work itself
Thro' madness, hated by the wise, to law,
System, and empire? Sin itself be found
The cloudy porch oft opening on the sun?
And only he, this wonder, dead, become   10
Mere highway dust? or year by year alone
Sit brooding in the ruins of a life,
Nightmare of youth, the spectre of himself?
    If this were thus, if this, indeed, were all,
Better the narrow brain, the stony heart,
The staring eye glazed o'er with sapless days,
The long mechanic pacings to and fro,
The set gray life, and apathetic end.
But am I not the nobler thro' thy love?
O, three times less unworthy! likewise thou   20
Art more thro' Love, and greater than thy years,
The sun will run his orbit, and the moon
Her circle. Wait, and Love himself will bring
The drooping flower of knowledge changed to fruit
Of wisdom. Wait; my faith is large in Time.

And that which shapes it to some perfect end.
    Will some one say, Then why not ill for good?
Why took ye not your pastime? To that man
My work shall answer, since I knew the right
And did it; for a man is not as God,   30
But then most Godlike being most a man. —
So let me think 't is well for thee and me —
Ill-fated that I am, what lot is mine
Whose foresight preaches peace, my heart so slow
To feel it! For how hard it seem'd to me,
When eyes, love-languid thro' half tears would dwell
One earnest, earnest moment upon mine,
Then not to dare to see! when thy low voice,
Faltering, would break its syllables, to keep
My own full-tuned, — hold passion in a leash,   40
And not leap forth and fall about thy neck,
And on thy bosom — deep desired relief! —
Rain out the heavy mist of tears, that weigh'd
Upon my brain, my senses, and my soul!
    For Love himself took part against himself
To warn us off, and Duty loved of Love —
O, this world's curse — beloved but hated — came
Like Death betwixt thy dear embrace and mine,
And crying, "Who is this? behold thy bride,"
She push'd me from thee.
                 If the sense is hard   50
To alien ears, I did not speak to these —
No, not to thee, but to thyself in me.
Hard is my doom and thine; thou knowest it all.
    Could Love part thus? was it not well to speak,
To have spoken once? It could not but be well.
The slow sweet hours that bring us all things good,
The slow sad hours that bring us all things ill,
And all good things from evil, brought the night
In which we sat together and alone,
And to the want that hollow'd all the heart   60
Gave utterance by the yearning of an eye,
That burn'd upon its object thro' such tears
As flow but once a life.
               The trance gave way
To those caresses, when a hundred times
In that last kiss, which never was the last,
Farewell, like endless welcome, lived and died.
Then follow'd counsel, comfort, and the words
That make a man feel strong in speaking truth;

Till now the dark was worn, and overhead
The lights of sunset and of sunrise mix'd   70
In that brief night, the summer night, that paused
Among her stars to hear us, stars that hung
Love-charm'd to listen; all the wheels of Time
Spun round in station, but the end had come.
    O, then, like those who clench their nerves to rush
Upon their dissolution, we two rose,
There — closing like an individual life —
In one blind cry of passion and of pain,
Like bitter accusation even to death,
Caught up the whole of love and utter'd it,   80
And bade adieu for ever.
                      Live — yet live —
Shall sharpest pathos blight us, knowing all
Life needs for life is possible to will? —
Live happy; tend thy flowers; be tended by
My blessing! Should my Shadow cross thy thoughts
Too sadly for their peace, remand it thou
For calmer hours to Memory's darkest hold,
If not to be forgotten — not at once —
Not all forgotten. Should it cross thy dreams,
O, might it come like one that looks content,   90
With quiet eyes unfaithful to the truth,
And point thee forward to a distant light,
Or seem to lift a burthen from thy heart
And leave thee freer, till thou wake refresh'd
Then when the first low matin-chirp hath grown
Full quire, and morning driven her plow of pearl
Far furrowing into light the mounded rack,
Beyond the fair green field and eastern sea.
1840? (1842)*

WILL WATERPROOF'S LYRICAL MONOLOGUE

MADE AT THE COCK

O PLUMP head-waiter at The Cock,
    To which I most resort,
How goes the time? 'T is five o'clock.
    Go fetch a pint of port;
But let it not be such as that

You set before chance-comers,
But such whose father-grape grew fat
On Lusitanian summers.

No vain libation to the Muse,
But may she still be kind,   10
And whisper lovely words, and use
Her influence on the mind,
To make me write my random rhymes,
Ere they be half-forgotten;
Nor add and alter, many times,
Till all be ripe and rotten.

I pledge her, and she comes and dips
Her laurel in the wine,
And lays it thrice upon my lips,
These favor'd lips of mine;   20
Until the charm have power to make
New life-blood warm the bosom,
And barren commonplaces break
In full and kindly blossom.

I pledge her silent at the board;
Her gradual fingers steal
And touch upon the master-chord
Of all I felt and feel.
Old wishes, ghosts of broken plans,
And phantom hopes assemble;   30
And that child's heart within the man's
Begins to move and tremble.

Thro' many an hour of summer suns,
By many pleasant ways,
Against its fountain upward runs
The current of my days.
I kiss the lips I once have kiss'd;
The gaslight wavers dimmer;
And softly, thro' a vinous mist,
My college friendships glimmer.   40

I grow in worth and wit and sense,
Unboding critic-pen,
Or that eternal want of pence
Which vexes public men,
Who hold their hands to all, and cry

For that which all deny them —
Who sweep the crossings, wet or dry,
    And all the world go by them.

Ah! yet, tho' all the world forsake,
    Tho' fortune clip my wings,
I will not cramp my heart, nor take   50
    Half-views of men and things.
Let Whig and Tory stir their blood;
    There must be stormy weather;
But for some true result of good
    All parties work together.

Let there be thistles, there are grapes;
    If old things, there are new;
Ten thousand broken lights and shapes,
    Yet glimpses of the true.   60
Let raffs be rife in prose and rhyme,
    We lack not rhymes and reasons,
As on this whirligig of Time
    We circle with the seasons.

This earth is rich in man and maid,
    With fair horizons bound;
This whole wide earth of light and shade
    Comes out a perfect round.
High over roaring Temple-bar,
    And set in heaven's third story,   70
I look at all things as they are,
    But thro' a kind of glory.

———————

Head-waiter, honor'd by the guest
    Half-mused, or reeling ripe,
The pint you brought me was the best
    That ever came from pipe.
But tho' the port surpasses praise,
    My nerves have dealt with stiffer.
Is there some magic in the place?
    Or do my peptics differ?   80

For since I came to live and learn,
    No pint of white or red
Had ever half the power to turn

This wheel within my head,
Which bears a season'd brain about,
    Unsubject to confusion,
Tho' soak'd and saturate, out and out,
    Thro' every convolution.

For I am of a numerous house,
    With many kinsmen gay,   90

Where long and largely we carouse
    As who shall say me nay?
Each month, a birthday coming on,
    We drink, defying trouble,
Or sometimes two would meet in one
    And then we drank it double;

Whether the vintage, yet unkept,
    Had relish fiery-new,
Or elbow-deep in sawdust slept,
    As old as Waterloo,   100
Or, stow'd when classic Canning died,
    In musty bins and chambers,
Had cast upon its crusty side
    The gloom of ten Decembers.

The Muse, the jolly Muse, it is!
    She answer'd to my call;
She changes with that mood or this,
    Is all-in-all to all;
She lit the spark within my throat,
    To make my blood run quicker,   110
Used all her fiery will, and smote
    Her life into the liquor.

And hence this halo lives about
    The waiter's hands, that reach
To each his perfect pint of stout,
    His proper chop to each.
He looks not like the common breed
    That with the napkin dally;
I think he came, like Ganymede,
    From some delightful valley.   120

The Cock was of a larger egg
    Than modern poultry drop,

Stept forward on a firmer leg,
    And cramm'd a plumper crop,
Upon an ampler dunghill trod,
    Crow'd lustier late and early,
Sipt wine from silver, praising God,
    And raked in golden barley.

A private life was all his joy,
    Till in a court he saw   130
A something-pottle-bodied boy
    That knuckled at the taw.
He stoop'd and clutch'd him, fair and good,
    Flew over roof and casement;
His brothers of the weather stood
    Stock-still for sheer amazement.

But he, by farmstead, thorpe, and spire,
    And follow'd with acclaims,
A sign to many a staring shire,
    Came crowing over Thames.   140
Right down by smoky Paul's they bore,
    Till, where the street grows straiter,
One fix'd for ever at the door,
    And one became head-waiter.

––––––––

But whither would my fancy go?
    How out of place she makes
The violet of a legend blow
    Among the chops and steaks!
'T is but a steward of the can,
    One shade more plump than common;   150
As just and mere a serving-man
    As any born of woman.

I ranged too high: what draws me down
    Into the common day?
Is it the weight of that half-crown
    Which I shall have to pay?
For, something duller than at first,
    Nor wholly comfortable,
I sit, my empty glass reversed,
    And thrumming on the table: 160

Half fearful that, with self at strife,
    I take myself to task,
Lest of the fulness of my life
    I leave an empty flask;
For I had hope, by something rare,
    To prove myself a poet,
But, while I plan and plan, my hair
    Is gray before I know it.

So fares it since the years began,
    Till they be gather'd up;   **170**
The truth, that flies the flowing can,
    Will haunt the vacant cup;
And others' follies teach us not,
    Nor much their wisdom teaches;
And most, of sterling worth, is what
    Our own experience preaches.

Ah, let the rusty theme alone!
    We know not what we know.
But for my pleasant hour, 't is gone;
    'T is gone, and let it go.   **180**
'T is gone: a thousand such have slipt
    Away from my embraces,
And fallen into the dusty crypt
    Of darken'd forms and faces.

Go, therefore, thou! thy betters went
    Long since, and came no more;
With peals of genial clamor sent
    From many a tavern-door,
With twisted quirks and happy hits,
    From misty men of letters;   **190**
The tavern-hours of mighty wits, —
    Thine elders and thy betters;

Hours when the Poet's words and looks
    Had yet their native glow,
Nor yet the fear of little books
    Had made him talk for show;
But, all his vast heart sherris-warm'd,
    He flash'd his random speeches,
Ere days that deal in ana swarm'd
    His literary leeches.   **200**

So mix for ever with the past,
    Like all good things on earth!
For should I prize thee, couldst thou last,
    At half thy real worth?
I hold it good, good things should pass;
    With time I will not quarrel;
It is but yonder empty glass
    That makes me maudlin-moral.

———————

Head-waiter of the chop-house here,
    To which I most resort,   210
I too must part; I hold thee dear
    For this good pint of port.
For this, thou shalt from all things suck
    Marrow of mirth and laughter;
And wheresoe'er thou move, good luck
    Shall fling her old shoe after.

But thou wilt never move from hence,
    The sphere thy fate allots;
Thy latter days increased with pence
    Go down among the pots;   220
Thou battenest by the greasy gleam
    In haunts of hungry sinners,
Old boxes, larded with the steam
    Of thirty thousand dinners.

We fret, we fume, would shift our skins,
    Would quarrel with our lot;
Thy care is, under polish'd tins,
    To serve the hot-and-hot;
To come and go, and come again,
    Returning like the pewit,   230
And watch'd by silent gentlemen,
    That trifle with the cruet.

Live long, ere from thy topmost head
    The thick-set hazel dies;
Long, ere the hateful crow shall tread
    The corners of thine eyes;
    Live long, nor feel in head or chest
    Our changeful equinoxes,

Till mellow Death, like some late guest,
    Shall call thee from the boxes.

But when he calls, and thou shalt cease
    To pace the gritted floor,
And, laying down an unctuous lease
    Of life, shalt earn no more,
No carved cross-bones, the types of Death,
    Shall show thee past to heaven,
But carved cross-pipes, and, underneath,
    A pint-pot neatly graven.

1840? (1842) *

LOCKSLEY HALL

COMRADES, leave me here a little, while as yet 't is early morn;
Leave me here, and when you want me, sound upon the bugle-horn.

'T is the place, and all around it, as of old, the curlews call,
Dreary gleams about the moorland flying over Locksley Hall;

Locksley Hall, that in the distance overlooks the sandy tracts,
And the hollow ocean-ridges roaring into cataracts.

Many a night from yonder ivied casement, ere I went to rest,
Did I look on great Orion sloping slowly to the west.

Many a night I saw the Pleiads, rising thro' the mellow shade,
Glitter like a swarm of fireflies tangled in a silver braid.

10

Here about the beach I wander'd, nourishing a youth sublime
With the fairy tales of science, and the long result of time;

When the centuries behind me like a fruitful land reposed;
When I clung to all the present for the promise that it closed;

When I dipt into the future far as human eye could see,
Saw the vision of the world and all the wonder that would be. —

In the spring a fuller crimson comes upon the robin's breast;
In the spring the wanton lapwing gets himself another crest;

In the spring a livelier iris changes on the burnish'd dove;
In the spring a young man's fancy lightly turns to thoughts of love. 20

Then her cheek was pale and thinner than should be for one so young,
And her eyes on all my motions with a mute observance hung.

And I said, "My cousin Amy, speak, and speak the truth to me,
Trust me, cousin, all the current of my being sets to thee."

On her pallid cheek and forehead came a color and a light,
As I have seen the rosy red flushing in the northern night.

And she turn'd — her bosom shaken with a sudden storm of sighs —
All the spirit deeply dawning in the dark of hazel eyes —

Saying, "I have hid my feelings, fearing they should do me wrong,"
Saying, "Dost thou love me, cousin?" weeping, "I have loved thee
    long."   30

Love took up the glass of Time, and turn'd it in his glowing hands;
Every moment, lightly shaken, ran itself in golden sands.

Love took up the harp of Life, and smote on all the chords with might;
Smote the chord of Self, that, trembling, past in music out of sight.

Many a morning on the moorland did we hear the copses ring,
And her whisper throng'd my pulses with the fulness of the spring.

Many an evening by the waters did we watch the stately ships,
And our spirits rush'd together at the touching of the lips.

O my cousin, shallow-hearted! O my Amy, mine no more!
O the dreary, dreary moorland! O the barren, barren shore!   40

Falser than all fancy fathoms, falser than all songs have sung,
Puppet to a father's threat, and servile to a shrewish tongue!

Is it well to wish thee happy? — having known me — to decline
On a range of lower feelings and a narrower heart than mine!

Yet it shall be; thou shalt lower to his level day by day,
What is fine within thee growing coarse to sympathize with clay.

As the husband is, the wife is; thou art mated with a clown,
And the grossness of his nature will have weight to drag thee down.

He will hold thee, when his passion shall have spent its novel force,
Something better than his dog, a little dearer than his horse.   50

What is this? his eyes are heavy; think not they are glazed with wine.
Go to him, it is thy duty; kiss him, take his hand in thine.

It may be my lord is weary, that his brain is overwrought;
Soothe him with thy finer fancies, touch him with thy lighter thought.

He will answer to the purpose, easy things to understand —
Better thou wert dead before me, tho' I slew thee with my hand!

Better thou and I were lying, hidden from the heart's disgrace,
Roll'd in one another's arms, and silent in a last embrace.

Cursed be the social wants that sin against the strength of youth!
Cursed be the social lies that warp us from the living truth!   60

Cursed be the sickly forms that err from honest Nature's rule!
Cursed be the gold that gilds the straiten'd forehead of the fool!

Well — 't is well that I should bluster! — Hadst thou less unworthy
        proved —
Would to God — for I had loved thee more than ever wife was loved.

Am I mad, that I should cherish that which bears but bitter fruit?
I will pluck it from my bosom, tho' my heart be at the root.

Never, tho' my mortal summers to such length of years should come
As the many-winter'd crow that leads the clanging rookery home.

Where is comfort? in division of the records of the mind?
Can I part her from herself, and love her, as I knew her, kind?   70

I remember one that perish'd; sweetly did she speak and move;
Such a one do I remember, whom to look at was to love.

Can I think of her as dead, and love her for the love she bore?
No — she never loved me truly; love is love for evermore.

Comfort? comfort scorn'd of devils! this is truth the poet sings,
That a sorrow's crown of sorrow is remembering happier things.

Drug thy memories, lest thou learn it, lest thy heart be put to proof,
In the dead unhappy night, and when the rain is on the roof.

Like a dog, he hunts in dreams, and thou art staring at the wall,
Where the dying night-lamp flickers, and the shadows rise and fall.   80

Then a hand shall pass before thee, pointing to his drunken sleep,
To thy widow'd marriage-pillows, to the tears that thou wilt weep.

Thou shalt hear the "Never, never," whisper'd by the phantom years,
And a song from out the distance in the ringing of thine ears;

And an eye shall vex thee, looking ancient kindness on thy pain.
Turn thee, turn thee on thy pillow; get thee to thy rest again.

Nay, but Nature brings thee solace; for a tender voice will cry.
'T is a purer life than thine, a lip to drain thy trouble dry.

Baby lips will laugh me down; my latest rival brings thee rest.
Baby fingers, waxen touches, press me from the mother's breast.   90

O, the child too clothes the father with a dearness not his due.
Half is thine and half is his; it will be worthy of the two.

O, I see thee old and formal, fitted to thy petty part,
With a little hoard of maxims preaching down a daughter's heart.

"They were dangerous guides the feelings — she herself was not
        exempt —
Truly, she herself had suffer'd" — Perish in thy self-contempt!

Overlive it — lower yet — be happy! wherefore should I care?
I myself must mix with action, lest I wither by despair.

What is that which I should turn to, lighting upon days like these?
Every door is barr'd with gold, and opens but to golden keys.   100

Every gate is throng'd with suitors, all the markets overflow.
I have but an angry fancy; what is that which I should do?

I had been content to perish, falling on the foeman's ground,
When the ranks are roll'd in vapor, and the winds are laid with sound.

But the jingling of the guinea helps the hurt that Honor feels,
And the nations do but murmur, snarling at each other's heels.

Can I but relive in sadness? I will turn that earlier page.
Hide me from my deep emotion, O thou wondrous Mother-Age!

Make me feel the wild pulsation that I felt before the strife,
When I heard my days before me, and the tumult of my life;   110

Yearning for the large excitement that the coming years would yield,
Eager-hearted as a boy when first he leaves his father's field,

And at night along the dusky highway near and nearer drawn,
Sees in heaven the light of London flaring like a dreary dawn;

And his spirit leaps within him to be gone before him then,
Underneath the light he looks at, in among the throngs of men;

Men, my brothers, men the workers, ever reaping something new;
That which they have done but earnest of the things that they shall do.

For I dipt into the future, far as human eye could see,
Saw the Vision of the world, and all the wonder that would be;   120

Saw the heavens fill with commerce, argosies of magic sails,
Pilots of the purple twilight, dropping down with costly bales;

Heard the heavens fill with shouting, and there rain'd a ghastly dew
From the nations' airy navies grappling in the central blue;

Far along the world-wide whisper of the south-wind rushing warm,
With the standards of the peoples plunging thro' the thunder-storm;

Till the war-drum throbb'd no longer, and the battle-flags were furl'd
In the Parliament of man, the Federation of the world.

There the common sense of most shall hold a fretful realm in awe,
And the kindly earth shall slumber, lapt in universal law.   130

So I triumph'd ere my passion sweeping thro' me left me dry,
Left me with the palsied heart, and left me with the jaundiced eye;

Eye, to which all order festers, all things here are out of joint.
Science moves, but slowly, slowly, creeping on from point to point;

Slowly comes a hungry people, as a lion, creeping nigher,
Glares at one that nods and winks behind a slowly-dying fire.

Yet I doubt not thro' the ages one increasing purpose runs,
And the thoughts of men are widen'd with the process of the suns.

What is that to him that reaps not harvest of his youthful joys,
Tho' the deep heart of existence beat for ever like a boy's? 140

Knowledge comes, but wisdom lingers, and I linger on the shore,
And the individual withers, and the world is more and more.

Knowledge comes, but wisdom lingers, and he bears a laden breast,
Full of sad experience, moving toward the stillness of his rest.

Hark, my merry comrades call me, sounding on the bugle-horn,
They to whom my foolish passion were a target for their scorn.

Shall it not be scorn to me to harp on such a moulder'd string?
I am shamed thro' all my nature to have loved so slight a thing.

Weakness to be wroth with weakness! woman's pleasure, woman's
    pain —
Nature made them blinder motions bounded in a shallower brain. 150

Woman is the lesser man, and all thy passions, match'd with mine,
Are as moonlight unto sunlight, and as water unto wine —

Here at least, where nature sickens, nothing. Ah, for some retreat
Deep in yonder shining Orient, where my life began to beat,

Where in wild Mahratta-battle fell my father evil-starr'd; —
I was left a trampled orphan, and a selfish uncle's ward.

Or to burst all links of habit — there to wander far away,
On from island unto island at the gateways of the day.

Larger constellations burning, mellow moons and happy skies,
Breadths of tropic shade and palms in cluster, knots of Paradise. 160

Never comes the trader, never floats an European flag,
Slides the bird o'er lustrous woodland, swings the trailer from the
    crag;

Droops the heavy-blossom'd bower, hangs the heavy-fruited tree —
Summer isles of Eden lying in dark-purple spheres of sea.

There methinks would be enjoyment more than in this march of mind,
In the steamship, in the railway, in the thoughts that shake mankind.

There the passions cramp'd no longer shall have scope and breathing
 space;
I will take some savage woman, she shall rear my dusky race.

Iron-jointed, supple-sinew'd, they shall dive, and they shall run,
Catch the wild goat by the hair, and hurl their lances in the sun;   170

Whistle back the parrot's call and leap the rainbows of the brooks,
Not with blinded eyesight poring over miserable books —

Fool, again the dream, the fancy! but I *know* my words are wild,
But I count the gray barbarian lower than the Christian child.

I, to herd with narrow foreheads, vacant of our glorious gains,
Like a beast with lower pleasures, like a beast with lower pains!

Mated with a squalid savage — what to me were sun or clime?
I the heir of all the ages, in the foremost files of time —

I that rather held it better men should perish one by one,
Than that earth should stand at gaze like Joshua's moon in Ajalon!

Not in vain the distance beacons. Forward, forward let us range,   181
Let the great world spin for ever down the ringing grooves of change.

Thro' the shadow of the globe we sweep into the younger day;
Better fifty years of Europe than a cycle of Cathay.

Mother-Age, — for mine I knew not, — help me as when life begun;
Rift the hills, and roll the waters, flash the lightnings, weigh the sun.

O, I see the crescent promise of my spirit hath not set.
Ancient founts of inspiration well thro' all my fancy yet.

Howsoever these things be, a long farewell to Locksley Hall!
Now for me the woods may wither, now for me the roof-tree fall.   190

Comes a vapor from the margin, blackening over heath and holt,
Cramming all the blast before it, in its breast a thunderbolt.

Let it fall on Locksley Hall, with rain or hail, or fire or snow;
For the mighty wind arises, roaring seaward, and I go.

1842°

THE VISION OF SIN

I

I HAD a vision when the night was late;
A youth came riding toward a palace-gate.
He rode a horse with wings, that would have flown,
But that his heavy rider kept him down.
And from the palace came a child of sin,
And took him by the curls, and led him in,
Where sat a company with heated eyes,
Expecting when a fountain should arise.
A sleepy light upon their brows and lips —
As when the sun, a crescent of eclipse,   10
Dreams over lake and lawn, and isles and capes —
Suffused them, sitting, lying, languid shapes,
By heaps of gourds, and skins of wine, and piles of grapes.

II

Then methought I heard a mellow sound,
Gathering up from all the lower ground;
Narrowing in to where they sat assembled,
Low voluptuous music winding trembled,
Woven in circles. They that heard it sigh'd,
Panted hand-in-hand with faces pale,
Swung themselves, and in low tones replied;   20
Till the fountain spouted, showering wide
Sleet of diamond-drift and pearly hail.
Then the music touch'd the gates and died,
Rose again from where it seem'd to fail,
Storm'd in orbs of song, a growing gale;
Till thronging in and in, to where they waited,
As 't were a hundred-throated nightingale,
The strong tempestuous treble throbb'd and palpitated;
Ran into its giddiest whirl of sound,
Caught the sparkles, and in circles,   30
Purple gauzes, golden hazes, liquid mazes,
Flung the torrent rainbow round.
Then they started from their places,
Moved with violence, changed in hue,
Caught each other with wild grimaces,
Half-invisible to the view,
Wheeling with precipitate paces
To the melody, till they flew,

Hair and eyes and limbs and faces,
Twisted hard in fierce embraces,   40
Like to Furies, like to Graces,
Dash'd together in blinding dew;
Till, kill'd with some luxurious agony,
The nerve-dissolving melody
Flutter'd headlong from the sky.

III

And then I look'd up toward a mountain-tract,
That girt the region with high cliff and lawn.
I saw that every morning, far withdrawn
Beyond the darkness and the cataract,
God made Himself an awful rose of dawn,   50
Unheeded; and detaching, fold by fold,
From those still heights, and, slowly drawing near,
A vapor heavy, hueless, formless, cold,
Came floating on for many a month and year,
Unheeded; and I thought I would have spoken,
And warn'd that madman ere it grew too late,
But, as in dreams, I could not. Mine was broken,
When that cold vapor touch'd the palace-gate,
And link'd again. I saw within my head
A gray and gap-tooth'd man as lean as death,   60
Who slowly rode across a wither'd heath,
And lighted at a ruin'd inn, and said:

IV

"Wrinkled ostler, grim and thin!
    Here is custom come your way;
Take my brute, and lead him in,
    Stuff his ribs with mouldy hay.

"Bitter barmaid, waning fast!
    See that sheets are on my bed.
What! the flower of life is past;
    It is long before you wed.   70

"Slip-shod waiter, lank and sour,
    At the Dragon on the heath!
Let us have a quiet hour,
    Let us hob-and-nob with Death.

"I am old, but let me drink;
    Bring me spices, bring me wine;

I remember, when I think,
 That my youth was half divine.

"Wine is good for shrivell'd lips,
 When a blanket wraps the day,   80
When the rotten woodland drips,
 And the leaf is stamp'd in clay.

"Sit thee down, and have no shame,
 Cheek by jowl, and knee by knee;
What care I for any name?
 What for order or degree?

"Let me screw thee up a peg;
 Let me loose thy tongue with wine;
Callest thou that thing a leg?
 Which is thinnest? thine or mine? 90

"Thou shalt not be saved by works,
 Thou hast been a sinner too;
Ruin'd trunks on wither'd forks,
 Empty scarecrows, I and you!

"Fill the cup and fill the can,
 Have a rouse before the morn;
Every moment dies a man,
 Every moment one is born.

"We are men of ruin'd blood;
 Therefore comes it we are wise. 100
Fish are we that love the mud,
 Rising to no fancy-flies.

"Name and fame! to fly sublime
 Thro' the courts, the camps, the schools,
Is to be the ball of Time,
 Bandied by the hands of fools.

"Friendship! — to be two in one —
 Let the canting liar pack!
Well I know, when I am gone,
 How she mouths behind my back. 110

"Virtue! — to be good and just —
 Every heart, when sifted well,

Is a clot of warmer dust,
   Mix'd with cunning sparks of hell.

"O, we two as well can look
   Whited thought and cleanly life
As the priest, above his book
   Leering at his neighbor's wife.

"Fill the cup and fill the can,
   Have a rouse before the morn: 120
Every moment dies a man,
   Every moment one is born.

"Drink, and let the parties rave;
   They are fill'd with idle spleen,
Rising, falling, like a wave,
   For they know not what they mean.

"He that roars for liberty
   Faster binds a tyrant's power,
And the tyrant's cruel glee
   Forces on the freer hour.   130

"Fill the can and fill the cup;
   All the windy ways of men
Are but dust that rises up,
   And is lightly laid again.

"Greet her with applausive breath,
   Freedom, gaily doth she tread;
In her right a civic wreath,
   In her left a human head.

"No, I love not what is new;
   She is of an ancient house,   140
And I think we know the hue
   Of that cap upon her brows.

"Let her go! her thirst she slakes
   Where the bloody conduit runs,
Then her sweetest meal she makes
   On the first-born of her sons.

"Drink to lofty hopes that cool, —
   Visions of a perfect State;

Drink we, last, the public fool,
    Frantic love and frantic hate.   150

"Chant me now some wicked stave,
    Till thy drooping courage rise,
And the glow-worm of the grave
    Glimmer in thy rheumy eyes.

"Fear not thou to loose thy tongue,
    Set thy hoary fancies free;
What is loathsome to the young
    Savors well to thee and me.

"Change, reverting to the years,
    When thy nerves could understand   160
What there is in loving tears,
    And the warmth of hand in hand.

"Tell me tales of thy first love —
    April hopes, the fools of chance —
Till the graves begin to move,
    And the dead begin to dance.

"Fill the can and fill the cup;
    All the windy ways of men
Are but dust that rises up,
    And is lightly laid again.   170

"Trooping from their mouldy dens
    The chap-fallen circle spreads —
Welcome, fellow-citizens,
    Hollow hearts and empty heads!

"You are bones, and what of that?
    Every face, however full,
Padded round with flesh and fat,
    Is but modell'd on a skull.

"Death is king, and Vivat Rex!
    Tread a measure on the stones,   180
Madam — if I know your sex
    From the fashion of your bones.

"No, I cannot praise the fire
    In your eye — nor yet your lip;

All the more do I admire
　　Joints of cunning workmanship.

"Lo! God's likeness — the ground-plan —
　　Neither modell'd, glazed, nor framed;
Buss me, thou rough sketch of man,
　　Far too naked to be shamed! 　　　　　　　190

"Drink to Fortune, drink to Chance,
　　While we keep a little breath!
Drink to heavy Ignorance!
　　Hob-and-nob with brother Death!

"Thou art mazed, the night is long,
　　And the longer night is near —
What! I am not all as wrong
　　As a bitter jest is dear.

"Youthful hopes, by scores, to all,
　　When the locks are crisp and curl'd; 　　　200
Unto me my maudlin gall
　　And my mockeries of the world.

"Fill the cup and fill the can;
　　Mingle madness, mingle scorn!
Dregs of life, and lees of man;
　　Yet we will not die forlorn."

v

The voice grew faint; there came a further change;
Once more uprose the mystic mountain-range.
Below were men and horses pierced with worms,
And slowly quickening into lower forms; 　　　210
By shards and scurf of salt, and scum of dross,
Old plash of rains, and refuse patch'd with moss.
Then some one spake: "Behold! it was a crime
Of sense avenged by sense that wore with time."
Another said: "The crime of sense became
The crime of malice, and is equal blame."
And one: "He had not wholly quench'd his power;
A little grain of conscience made him sour."
At last I heard a voice upon the slope
Cry to the summit, "Is there any hope?" 　　　220

To which an answer peal'd from that high land,
But in a tongue no man could understand;
And on the glimmering limit far withdrawn
God made Himself an awful rose of dawn.

1842

AMPHION

My father left a park to me,
  But it is wild and barren,
A garden too with scarce a tree,
  And waster than a warren;
Yet say the neighbors when they call
  It is not bad but good land,
And in it is the germ of all
  That grows within the woodland.

O, had I lived when song was great
  In days of old Amphion,   10
And ta'en my fiddle to the gate,
  Nor cared for seed or scion!
And had I lived when song was great,
  And legs of trees were limber,
And ta'en my fiddle to the gate,
  And fiddled in the timber!

'T is said he had a tuneful tongue,
  Such happy intonation,
Wherever he sat down and sung
  He left a small plantation;   20
Wherever in a lonely grove
  He set up his forlorn pipes,
The gouty oak began to move,
  And flounder into hornpipes.

The mountain stirr'd its bushy crown,
  And, as tradition teaches,
Young ashes pirouetted down
  Coquetting with young beeches;
And briony-vine and ivy-wreath
  Ran forward to his rhyming,   30
And from the valleys underneath
  Came little copses climbing.

The linden broke her ranks and rent
   The woodbine wreaths that bind her,
And down the middle, buzz! she went
   With all her bees behind her;
The poplars, in long order due,
   With cypress promenaded,
The shock-head willows two and two
   By rivers gallopaded.   40

Came wet-shod alder from the wave,
   Came yews, a dismal coterie;
Each pluck'd his one foot from the grave,
   Poussetting with a sloe-tree;
Old elms came breaking from the vine,
   The vine stream'd out to follow,
And, sweating rosin, plump'd the pine
   From many a cloudy hollow.

And was n't it a sight to see,
   When, ere his song was ended,   50
Like some great landslip, tree by tree,
   The country-side descended;
And shepherds from the mountain-eaves
   Look'd down, half-pleased, half-frighten'd,
As dash'd about the drunken leaves
   The random sunshine lighten'd?

O, Nature first was fresh to men,
   And wanton without measure;
So youthful and so flexile then,
   You moved her at your pleasure.   60
Twang out, my fiddle! shake the twigs!
   And make her dance attendance;
Blow, flute, and stir the stiff-set sprigs,
   And scirrhous roots and tendons!

'T is vain! in such a brassy age
   I could not move a thistle;
The very sparrows in the hedge
   Scarce answer to my whistle;
Or at the most, when three-parts-sick
   With strumming and with scraping,   70
A jackass heehaws from the rick,
   The passive oxen gaping.

But what is that I hear? a sound
   Like sleepy counsel pleading;
O Lord! — 't is in my neighbor's ground,
   The modern Muses reading.
They read Botanic Treatises,
   And Works on Gardening thro' there,
And Methods of Transplanting Trees
   To look as if they grew there.   80

The wither'd Misses! how they prose
   O'er books of travell'd seamen,
And show you slips of all that grows
   From England to Van Diemen.
They read in arbors clipt and cut,
   And alleys faded places,
By squares of tropic summer shut
   And warm'd in crystal cases.

But these, tho' fed with careful dirt,
   Are neither green nor sappy;   90
Half-conscious of the garden-squirt,
   The spindlings look unhappy.
Better to me the meanest weed
   That blows upon its mountain,
The vilest herb that runs to seed
   Beside its native fountain.

And I must work thro' months of toil,
   And years of cultivation,
Upon my proper patch of soil
   To grow my own plantation.   100
I 'll take the showers as they fall,
   I will not vex my bosom;
Enough if at the end of all
   A little garden blossom.
1842*

THE NEW TIMON AND THE POETS

WE know him, out of Shakespeare's art,
   And those fine curses which he spoke;
The old Timon, with his noble heart,
   That, strongly loathing, greatly broke.

So died the Old: here comes the New.
    Regard him: a familiar face:
I thought we knew him: What, it's you,
    The padded man — that wears the stays —

Who killed the girls and thrilled the boys
    With dandy pathos when you wrote!   10
A Lion, you, that made a noise,
    And shook a mane *en papillotes*.

And once you tried the Muses too;
    You failed, Sir: therefore now you turn,
To fall on those who are to you
    As Captain is to Subaltern.

But men of long-enduring hopes,
    And careless what this hour may bring,
Can pardon little would-be POPES
    And BRUMMELS, when they try to sting.   20

An Artist, Sir, should rest in Art,
    And waive a little of his claim;
To have the deep Poetic heart
    Is more than all poetic fame.

But you, Sir, you are hard to please;
    You never look but half content;
Nor like a gentleman at ease,
    With moral breadth of temperament.

And what with spites and what with fears,
    You cannot let a body be: 30
It's always ringing in your ears,
    "They call this man as good as *me*."

What profits now to understand
    The merits of a spotless shirt —
A dapper boot — a little hand —
    If half the little soul is dirt?

You talk of tinsel! why, we see
    The old mark of rouge upon your cheeks.
You prate of Nature! you are he
    That spilt his life about the cliques.   40

A TIMON you! Nay, nay, for shame:
   It looks too arrogant a jest —
The fierce old man — to take his name,
   You bandbox. Off, and let him rest.

1846*

TO ——

AFTER READING A LIFE AND LETTERS

"Cursed be he that moves my bones."
Shakespeare's Epitaph.

You might have won the Poet's name,
   If such be worth the winning now,
   And gain'd a laurel for your brow
Of sounder leaf than I can claim;

But you have made the wiser choice,
   A life that moves to gracious ends
   Thro' troops of unrecording friends,
A deedful life, a silent voice.

And you have miss'd the irreverent doom
   Of those that wear the Poet's crown;   10
   Hereafter, neither knave nor clown
Shall hold their orgies at your tomb.

For now the Poet cannot die,
   Nor leave his music as of old,
   But round him ere he scarce be cold
Begins the scandal and the cry:

"Proclaim the faults he would not show;
   Break lock and seal, betray the trust;
   Keep nothing sacred, 't is but just
The many-headed beast should know."   20

Ah, shameless! for he did but sing
   A song that pleased us from its worth;
   No public life was his on earth,
No blazon'd statesman he, nor king.

He gave the people of his best;
  His worst he kept, his best he gave.
  My Shakespeare's curse on clown and knave
Who will not let his ashes rest!

Who make it seem more sweet to be
  The little life of bank and brier,   30
  The bird that pipes his lone desire
And dies unheard within his tree,

Than he that warbles long and loud
  And drops at Glory's temple-gates,
  For whom the carrion vulture waits
To tear his heart before the crowd!

1849*

THE PRINCESS; A MEDLEY

Prologue

SIR WALTER VIVIAN all a summer's day
Gave his broad lawns until the set of sun
Up to the people; thither flock'd at noon
His tenants, wife and child, and thither half
The neighboring borough with their Institute,
Of which he was the patron. I was there
From college, visiting the son, — the son
A Walter too, — with others of our set,
Five others; we were seven at Vivian-place. . . .

There moved the multitude, a thousand heads;
The patient leaders of their Institute
Taught them with facts. One rear'd a font of stone
And drew, from butts of water on the slope,   60
The fountain of the moment, playing, now
A twisted snake, and now a rain of pearls,
Or steep-up spout whereon the gilded ball
Danced like a wisp; and somewhat lower down
A man with knobs and wires and vials fired
A cannon; Echo answer'd in her sleep
From hollow fields; and here were telescopes
For azure views; and there a group of girls
In circle waited, whom the electric shock
Dislink'd with shrieks and laughter; round the lake   70
A little clock-work steamer paddling plied
And shook the lilies; perch'd about the knolls
A dozen angry models jetted steam;
A petty railway ran; a fire-balloon
Rose gem-like up before the dusky groves
And dropt a fairy parachute and past;
And there thro' twenty posts of telegraph
They flash'd a saucy message to and fro
Between the mimic stations; so that sport
Went hand in hand with science; otherwhere   80
Pure sport; a herd of boys with clamor bowl'd
And stump'd the wicket; babies roll'd about
Like tumbled fruit in grass; and men and maids

Arranged a country dance, and flew thro' light
And shadow, while the twangling violin
Struck up with Soldier-laddie, and overhead
The broad ambrosial aisles of lofty lime
Made noise with bees and breeze from end to end.

Strange was the sight and smacking of the time;
And long we gazed, but satiated at length   90
Came to the ruins. High-arch'd and ivy-claspt,
Of finest Gothic lighter than a fire,
Thro' one wide chasm of time and frost they gave
The park, the crowd, the house; but all within
The sward was trim as any garden lawn.
And here we lit on Aunt Elizabeth,
And Lilia with the rest, and lady friends
From neighbor seats; and there was Ralph himself,
A broken statue propt against the wall,
As gay as any. Lilia, wild with sport,   100
Half child, half woman as she was, had wound
A scarf of orange round the stony helm,
And robed the shoulders in a rosy silk,
That made the old warrior from his ivied nook
Glow like a sunbeam. Near his tomb a feast
Shone, silver-set; about it lay the guests,
And there we join'd them; then the maiden aunt
Took this fair day for text, and from it preach'd
An universal culture for the crowd,
And all things great. But we, unworthier, told   110
Of college: he had climb'd across the spikes,
And he had squeezed himself betwixt the bars,
And he had breathed the Proctor's dogs; and one
Discuss'd his tutor, rough to common men,
But honeying at the whisper of a lord;
And one the Master, as a rogue in grain
Veneer'd with sanctimonious theory.

But while they talk'd, above their heads I saw
The feudal warrior lady-clad; which brought
My book to mind, and opening this I read   120
Of old Sir Ralph a page or two that rang
With tilt and tourney; then the tale of her
That drove her foes with slaughter from her walls,
And much I praised her nobleness, and "Where,"
Ask'd Walter, patting Lilia's head — she lay
Beside him — "lives there such a woman now?"

Quick answer'd Lilia: "There are thousands now
Such women, but convention beats them down;
It is but bringing up; no more than that.
You men have done it — how I hate you all!   130
Ah, were I something great! I wish I were
Some mighty poetess, I would shame you then,
That love to keep us children! O, I wish
That I were some great princess, I would build
Far off from men a college like a man's,
And I would teach them all that men are taught;
We are twice as quick!" And here she shook aside
The hand that play'd the patron with her curls.

And one said smiling: "Pretty were the sight
If our old halls could change their sex, and flaunt   140
With prudes for proctors, dowagers for deans,
And sweet girl-graduates in their golden hair.
I think they should not wear our rusty gowns,
But move as rich as Emperor-moths, or Ralph
Who shines so in the corner; yet I fear,
If there were many Lilias in the brood,
However deep you might embower the nest,
Some boy would spy it."
                                        At this upon the sward
She tapt her tiny silken-sandall'd foot:
"That's your light way; but I would make it death   150
For any male thing but to peep at us."

Petulant she spoke, and at herself she laugh'd;
A rosebud set with little wilful thorns,
And sweet as English air could make her, she!
But Walter hail'd a score of names upon her,
And "petty Ogress," and "ungrateful Puss,"
And swore he long'd at college, only long'd,
All else was well, for she-society.
They boated and they cricketed; they talk'd
At wine, in clubs, of art, of politics;   160
They lost their weeks; they vext the souls of deans;
They rode; they betted; made a hundred friends,
And caught the blossom of the flying terms,
But miss'd the mignonette of Vivian-place,
The little hearth-flower Lilia. Thus he spoke,
Part banter, part affection. . . .

[Walter describes to Lilia the chain-stories that the young men told
"from mouth to mouth" one Christmas vacation at college.]

                                        A half-disdain
Perch'd on the pouted blossom of her lips;
And Walter nodded at me: "*He* began,
The rest would follow, each in turn; and so
We forged a sevenfold story. Kind? what kind?
Chimeras, crotchets, Christmas solecisms;
Seven-headed monsters only made to kill   200
Time by the fire in winter."
                                        "Kill him now,
The tyrant! kill him in the summer too,"
Said Lilia; "Why not now?" the maiden aunt.
"Why not a summer's as a winter's tale?
A tale for summer as befits the time,
And something it should be to suit the place,
Heroic, for a hero lies beneath,
Grave, solemn!"
                        Walter warp'd his mouth at this
To something so mock-solemn, that I laugh'd,
And Lilia woke with sudden-shrilling mirth   210
An echo like a ghostly woodpecker
Hid in the ruins; till the maiden aunt —
A little sense of wrong had touch'd her face
With color — turn'd to me with "As you will;
Heroic if you will, or what you will,
Or be yourself your hero if you will."

    "Take Lilia, then, for heroine," clamor'd he,
"And make her some great princess, six feet high,
Grand, epic, homicidal; and be you
The prince to win her!"
                                "Then follow me, the prince," 220
I answer'd, "each be hero in his turn!
Seven and yet one, like shadows in a dream. —
Heroic seems our princess as required —
But something made to suit with time and place,
A Gothic ruin and a Grecian house,
A talk of college and of ladies' rights,
A feudal knight in silken masquerade,
And, yonder, shrieks and strange experiments
For which the good Sir Ralph had burnt them all —
This *were* a medley! we should have him back   230
Who told the 'Winter's Tale' to do it for us.
No matter; we will say whatever comes.
And let the ladies sing us, if they will,
From time to time, some ballad or a song

To give us breathing-space."
                    So I began,
And the rest follow'd; and the women sang
Between the rougher voices of the men,
Like linnets in the pauses of the wind:
And here I give the story and the songs.

I

A Prince I was, blue-eyed, and fair in face,
Of temper amorous as the first of May,
With lengths of yellow ringlet, like a girl,
For on my cradle shone the Northern star.

There lived an ancient legend in our house.
Some sorcerer, whom a far-off grandsire burnt
Because he cast no shadow, had foretold,
Dying, that none of all our blood should know
The shadow from the substance, and that one
Should come to fight with shadows and to fall;   10
For so, my mother said, the story ran.
And, truly, waking dreams were, more or less,
An old and strange affection of the house.
Myself too had weird seizures, Heaven knows what!
On a sudden in the midst of men and day,
And while I walk'd and talk'd as heretofore,
I seem'd to move among a world of ghosts,
And feel myself the shadow of a dream.
Our great court-Galen poised his gilt-head cane,
And paw'd his beard, and mutter'd "catalepsy."   20
My mother pitying made a thousand prayers.
My mother was as mild as any saint,
Half-canonized by all that look'd on her,
So gracious was her tact and tenderness;
But my good father thought a king a king.
He cared not for the affection of the house;
He held his sceptre like a pedant's wand
To lash offence, and with long arms and hands
Reach'd out and pick'd offenders from the mass
For judgment.
            Now it chanced that I had been,   30
While life was yet in bud and blade, betroth'd
To one, a neighboring Princess. She to me
Was proxy-wedded with a bootless calf
At eight years old; and still from time to time
Came murmurs of her beauty from the South,

And of her brethren, youths of puissance;
And still I wore her picture by my heart,
And one dark tress; and all around them both
Sweet thoughts would swarm as bees about their queen.

But when the days drew nigh that I should wed,   40
My father sent ambassadors with furs
And jewels, gifts, to fetch her. These brought back
A present, a great labor of the loom;
And therewithal an answer vague as wind.
Besides, they saw the king; he took the gifts;
He said there was a compact; that was true;
But then she had a will; was he to blame?
And maiden fancies; loved to live alone
Among her women; certain, would not wed.

That morning in the presence room I stood   50
With Cyril and with Florian, my two friends:
The first, a gentleman of broken means —
His father's fault — but given to starts and bursts
Of revel; and the last, my other heart,
And almost my half-self, for still we moved
Together, twinn'd as horse's ear and eye.

Now, while they spake, I saw my father's face
Grow long and troubled like a rising moon,
Inflamed with wrath. He started on his feet,
Tore the king's letter, snow'd it down, and rent   60
The wonder of the loom thro' warp and woof
From skirt to skirt; and at the last he sware
That he would send a hundred thousand men,
And bring her in a whirlwind; then he chew'd
The thrice-turn'd cud of wrath, and cook'd his spleen,
Communing with his captains of the war.

At last I spoke: "My father, let me go.
It cannot be but some gross error lies
In this report, this answer of a king
Whom all men rate as kind and hospitable;   70
Or, maybe, I myself, my bride once seen,
Whate'er my grief to find her less than fame,
May rue the bargain made." And Florian said:
"I have a sister at the foreign court,
Who moves about the Princess; she, you know,
Who wedded with a nobleman from thence.

He, dying lately, left her, as I hear,
The lady of three castles in that land;
Thro' her this matter might be sifted clean."
And Cyril whisper'd: "Take me with you too."   80
Then laughing, "What if these weird seizures come
Upon you in those lands, and no one near
To point you out the shadow from the truth!
Take me; I 'll serve you better in a strait;
I grate on rusty hinges here." But "No!"
Roar'd the rough king, "you shall not; we ourself
Will crush her pretty maiden fancies dead
In iron gauntlets; break the council up."

But when the council broke, I rose and past
Thro' the wild woods that hung about the town;   90
Found a still place, and pluck'd her likeness out;
Laid it on flowers, and watch'd it lying bathed
In the green gleam of dewy-tassell'd trees.
What were those fancies? wherefore break her troth?
Proud look'd the lips; but while I meditated
A wind arose and rush'd upon the South,
And shook the songs, the whispers, and the shrieks
Of the wild woods together, and a Voice
Went with it, " Follow, follow, thou shalt win."

Then, ere the silver sickle of that month   100
Became her golden shield, I stole from court
With Cyril and with Florian, unperceived,
Cat-footed thro' the town and half in dread
To hear my father's clamor at our backs
With "Ho!" from some bay-window shake the night;
But all was quiet. From the bastion'd walls
Like threaded spiders, one by one, we dropt,
And flying reach'd the frontier; then we crost
To a livelier land; and so by tilth and grange,
And vines, and blowing bosks of wilderness,
We gain'd the mother-city thick with towers,
And in the imperial palace found the king.

His name was Gama; crack'd and small his voice,
But bland the smile that like a wrinkling wind
On glassy water drove his cheek in lines;
A little dry old man, without a star,
Not like a king. Three days he feasted us,
And on the fourth I spake of why we came,

And my betroth'd. "You do us, Prince," he said,
Airing a snowy hand and signet gem,   120
"All honor. We remember love ourself
In our sweet youth. There did a compact pass
Long summers back, a kind of ceremony —
I think the year in which our olives fail'd.
I would you had her, Prince, with all my heart,
With my full heart; but there were widows here,
Two widows, Lady Psyche, Lady Blanche;
They fed her theories, in and out of place
Maintaining that with equal husbandry
The woman were an equal to the man.   130
They harp'd on this; with this our banquets rang;
Our dances broke and buzz'd in knots of talk;
Nothing but this; my very ears were hot
To hear them. Knowledge, so my daughter held,
Was all in all; they had but been, she thought,
As children; they must lose the child, assume
The woman. Then, sir, awful odes she wrote,
Too awful, sure, for what they treated of,
But all she is and does is awful; odes
About this losing of the child; and rhymes   140
And dismal lyrics, prophesying change
Beyond all reason. These the women sang;
And they that know such things — I sought but peace;
No critic I — would call them masterpieces.
They master'd *me*. At last she begg'd a boon,
A certain summer-palace which I have
Hard by your father's frontier. I said no,
Yet being an easy man, gave it; and there,
All wild to found an University
For maidens, on the spur she fled; and more   150
We know not, — only this: they see no men,
Not even her brother Arac, nor the twins
Her brethren, tho' they love her, look upon her
As on a kind of paragon; and I —
Pardon me saying it — were much loth to breed
Dispute betwixt myself and mine; but since —
And I confess with right — you think me bound
In some sort, I can give you letters to her;   .
And yet, to speak the truth, I rate your chance
Almost at naked nothing."   160
                     Thus the king;
And I, tho' nettled that he seem'd to slur
With garrulous ease and oily courtesies

Our formal compact, yet, not less — all frets
But chafing me on fire to find my bride —
Went forth again with both my friends. We rode
Many a long league back to the North. At last
From hills that look'd across a land of hope
We dropt with evening on a rustic town
Set in a gleaming river's crescent-curve,
Close at the boundary of the liberties;   170
There, enter'd an old hostel, call'd mine host
To council, plied him with his richest wines,
And show'd the late-writ letters of the king.

   He with a long low sibilation, stared
As blank as death in marble; then exclaim'd,
Averring it was clear against all rules
For any man to go; but as his brain
Began to mellow, "If the king," he said,
"Had given us letters, was he bound to speak?
The king would bear him out;" and at the last —   180
The summer of the vine in all his veins —
"No doubt that we might make it worth his while.
She once had past that way; he heard her speak;
She scared him; life! he never saw the like;
She look'd as grand as doomsday and as grave!
And he, he reverenced his liege-lady there:
He always made a point to post with mares;
His daughter and his housemaid were the boys;
The land, he understood, for miles about
Was till'd by women; all the swine were sows,   190
And all the dogs" —
                 But while he jested thus,
A thought flash'd thro' me which I clothed in act,
Remembering how we three presented Maid,
Or Nymph, or Goddess, at high tide of feast,
In masque or pageant at my father's court.
We sent mine host to purchase female gear;
He brought it, and himself, a sight to shake
The midriff of despair with laughter, holp
To lace us up, till each in maiden plumes
We rustled; him we gave a costly bribe   200
To guerdon silence, mounted our good steeds,
And boldly ventured on the liberties.

   We follow'd up the river as we rode,
And rode till midnight, when the college lights

Began to glitter firefly-like in copse
And linden alley; then we past an arch,
Whereon a woman-statue rose with wings
From four wing'd horses dark against the stars,
And some inscription ran along the front,
But deep in shadow. Further on we gain'd   210
A little street half garden and half house,
But scarce could hear each other speak for noise
Of clocks and chimes, like silver hammers falling
On silver anvils, and the splash and stir
Of fountains spouted up and showering down
In meshes of the jasmine and the rose;
And all about us peal'd the nightingale,
Rapt in her song and careless of the snare.

        There stood a bust of Pallas for a sign,
By two sphere lamps blazon'd like Heaven and Earth   220
With constellation and with continent,
Above an entry. Riding in, we call'd;
A plump-arm'd ostleress and a stable wench
Came running at the call, and help'd us down.
Then stept a buxom hostess forth, and sail'd,
Full-blown, before us into rooms which gave
Upon a pillar'd porch, the bases lost
In laurel. Her we ask'd of that and this,
And who were tutors. "Lady Blanche," she said,
"And Lady Psyche." "Which was prettiest,   230
Best natured?" "Lady Psyche." "Hers are we,"
One voice, we cried; and I sat down and wrote
In such a hand as when a field of corn
Bows all its ears before the roaring East:

        "Three ladies of the Northern empire pray
Your Highness would enroll them with your own,
As Lady Psyche's pupils."
                        This I seal'd;
The seal was Cupid bent above a scroll,
And o'er his head Uranian Venus hung,
And raised the blinding bandage from his eyes.   240
I gave the letter to be sent with dawn;
And then to bed, where half in doze I seem'd
To float about a glimmering night, and watch
A full sea glazed with muffled moonlight swell
On some dark shore just seen that it was rich.

As thro' the land at eve we went,
And pluck'd the ripen'd ears,
We fell out, my wife and I,
O, we fell out, I know not why,
And kiss'd again with tears.
And blessings on the falling out
That all the more endears,
When we fall out with those we love
And kiss again with tears!
For when we came where lies the child
We lost in other years,
There above the little grave,
O, there above the little grave,
We kiss'd again with tears.

II

At break of day the College Portress came;
She brought us academic silks, in hue
The lilac, with a silken hood to each,
And zoned with gold; and now when these were on,
And we as rich as moths from dusk cocoons,
She, curtseying her obeisance, let us know
The Princess Ida waited. Out we paced,
I first, and following thro' the porch that sang
All round with laurel, issued in a court
Compact of lucid marbles, boss'd with lengths   10
Of classic frieze, with ample awnings gay
Betwixt the pillars, and with great urns of flowers.
The Muses and the Graces, group'd in threes,
Enring'd a billowing fountain in the midst,
And here and there on lattice edges lay
Or book or lute; but hastily we past,
And up a flight of stairs into the hall.

There at a board by tome and paper sat,
With two tame leopards couch'd beside her throne,
All beauty compass'd in a female form,   20
The Princess; liker to the inhabitant
Of some clear planet close upon the sun,
Than our man's earth; such eyes were in her head,
And so much grace and power, breathing down
From over her arch'd brows, with every turn
Lived thro' her to the tips of her long hands,
And to her feet. She rose her height, and said:

"We give you welcome; not without redound
Of use and glory to yourselves ye come,
The first-fruits of the stranger; aftertime,   30
And that full voice which circles round the grave,
Will rank you nobly, mingled up with me.
What! are the ladies of your land so tall?"
"We of the court," said Cyril. "From the court,"
She answer'd, "then ye know the Prince?" and he:
"The climax of his age! as tho' there were
One rose in all the world, your Highness that,
He worships your ideal." She replied:
"We scarcely thought in our own hall to hear
This barren verbiage, current among men,   40
Light coin, the tinsel clink of compliment.
Your flight from out your bookless wilds would seem
As arguing love of knowledge and of power;
Your language proves you still the child. Indeed,
We dream not of him; when we set our hand
To this great work, we purposed with ourself
Never to wed. You likewise will do well,
Ladies, in entering here, to cast and fling
The tricks which make us toys of men, that so
Some future time, if so indeed you will,   50
You may with those self-styled our lords ally
Your fortunes, justlier balanced, scale with scale."

At those high words, we, conscious of ourselves,
Perused the matting; then an officer
Rose up, and read the statutes, such as these:
Not for three years to correspond with home;
Not for three years to cross the liberties;
Not for three years to speak with any men;
And many more, which hastily subscribed,
We enter'd on the boards. And "Now," she cried,   60
"Ye are green wood, see ye warp not. Look, our hall!
Our statues! — not of those that men desire,
Sleek Odalisques, or oracles of mode,
Nor stunted squaws of West or East; but she
That taught the Sabine how to rule, and she
The foundress of the Babylonian wall,
The Carian Artemisia strong in war,
The Rhodope that built the pyramid,
Clelia, Cornelia, with the Palmyrene
That fought Aurelian, and the Roman brows   70
Of Agrippina. Dwell with these, and lose

Convention, since to look on noble forms
Makes noble thro' the sensuous organism
That which is higher. O, lift your natures up;
Embrace our aims; work out your freedom. Girls,
Knowledge is now no more a fountain seal'd!
Drink deep, until the habits of the slave,
The sins of emptiness, gossip and spite
And slander, die. Better not be at all
Than not be noble. Leave us; you may go.   80
To-day the Lady Psyche will harangue
The fresh arrivals of the week before;
For they press in from all the provinces,
And fill the hive."
           She spoke, and bowing waved
Dismissal; back again we crost the court
To Lady Psyche's. As we enter'd in,
There sat along the forms, like morning doves
That sun their milky bosoms on the thatch,
A patient range of pupils; she herself
Erect behind a desk of satin-wood,   90
A quick brunette, well-moulded, falcon-eyed,
And on the hither side, or so she look'd,
Of twenty summers. At her left, a child,
In shining draperies, headed like a star,
Her maiden babe, a double April old,
Aglaïa slept. We sat; the lady glanced;
Then Florian, but no livelier than the dame
That whisper'd "Asses' ears" among the sedge,
"My sister." "Comely, too, by all that's fair,"
Said Cyril. "O, hush, hush!" and she began.   100

"This world was once a fluid haze of light,
Till toward the centre set the starry tides,
And eddied into suns, that wheeling cast
The planets; then the monster, then the man;
Tattoo'd or woaded, winter-clad in skins,
Raw from the prime, and crushing down his mate,
As yet we find in barbarous isles, and here
Among the lowest."
           Thereupon she took
A bird's-eye view of all the ungracious past;
Glanced at the legendary Amazon   110
As emblematic of a nobler age;
Appraised the Lycian custom, spoke of those
That lay at wine with Lar and Lucumo;

Ran down the Persian, Grecian, Roman lines
Of empire, and the woman's state in each,
How far from just; till warming with her theme
She fulmined out her scorn of laws Salique
And little-footed China, touch'd on Mahomet
With much contempt, and came to chivalry,
When some respect, however slight was paid   120
To woman, superstition all awry.
However, then commenced the dawn; a beam
Had slanted forward, falling in a land
Of promise; fruit would follow. Deep, indeed,
Their debt of thanks to her who first had dared
To leap the rotten pales of prejudice. . . .
                              At last
She rose upon a wind of prophecy
Dilating on the future: "everywhere
Two heads in council, two beside the hearth,
Two in the tangled business of the world,
Two in the liberal offices of life,
Two plummets dropt for one to sound the abyss
Of science and the secrets of the mind;   160
Musician, painter, sculptor, critic, more;
And everywhere the broad and bounteous Earth
Should bear a double growth of those rare souls,
Poets, whose thoughts enrich the blood of the world."

      She ended here, and beckon'd us; the rest
Parted; and, glowing full-faced welcome, she
Began to address us, and was moving on
In gratulation, till as when a boat
Tacks and the slacken'd sail flaps, all her voice
Faltering and fluttering in her throat, she cried,   170
"My brother!" "Well, my sister." "O," she said,
"What do you here? and in the dress? and these?
Why, who are these? a wolf within the fold!
A pack of wolves! the Lord be gracious to me!
A plot, a plot, a plot, to ruin all!"
"No plot, no plot," he answer'd. "Wretched boy,
How saw you not the inscription on the gate,
LET NO MAN ENTER IN ON PAIN OF DEATH?"
"And if I had," he answer'd, "who could think
The softer Adams of your Academe,   180
O sister, Sirens tho' they be, were such
As chanted on the blanching bones of men?"
"But you will find it otherwise," she said.

"You jest; ill jesting with edge-tools! my vow
Binds me to speak, and O that iron will,
That axelike edge unturnable, our Head,
The Princess!" "Well then, Psyche, take my life,
And nail me like a weasel on a grange
For warning; bury me beside the gate,
And cut this epitaph above my bones: 190
Here lies a brother by a sister slain,
All for the common good of womankind."
"Let me die too," said Cyril, "having seen
And heard the Lady Psyche." . . .

  "Are you that Lady Psyche," I rejoin'd,   220
"The fifth in line from that old Florian,
Yet hangs his portrait in my father's hall —
The gaunt old baron with his beetle brow
Sun-shaded in the heat of dusty fights —
As he bestrode my grandsire, when he fell,
And all else fled? we point to it, and we say,
The loyal warmth of Florian is not cold,
But branches current yet in kindred veins."
"Are you that Psyche," Florian added; "she
With whom I sang about the morning hills,
Flung ball, flew kite, and raced the purple fly,   230
And snared the squirrel of the glen? are you
That Psyche, wont to bind my throbbing brow,
To smooth my pillow, mix the foaming draught
Of fever, tell me pleasant tales, and read
My sickness down to happy dreams? are you
That brother-sister Psyche, both in one?
You were that Psyche, but what are you now?"
"You are that Psyche," Cyril said, "for whom
I would be that forever which I seem,
Woman, if I might sit beside your feet,   240
And glean your scatter'd sapience." . . .
                              "Out upon it!"
She answer'd, "peace! and why should I not play
The Spartan Mother with emotion, be
The Lucius Junius Brutus of my kind?
Him you call great; he for the common weal,
The fading politics of mortal Rome,
As I might slay this child, if good need were,
Slew both his sons; and I, shall I, on whom
The secular emancipation turns
Of half this world, be swerved from right to save   270

A prince, a brother? a little will I yield.
Best so, perchance, for us, and well for you.
O, hard when love and duty clash! I fear
My conscience will not count me fleckless; yet —
Hear my conditions: promise — otherwise
You perish — as you came, to slip away
To-day, to-morrow, soon. It shall be said,
These women were too barbarous, would not learn;
They fled, who might have shamed us. Promise, all."

What could we else, we promised each; and she,   280
Like some wild creature newly-caged, commenced
A to-and-fro, so pacing till she paused
By Florian; holding out her lily arms
Took both his hands, and smiling faintly said:
"I knew you at the first; tho' you have grown
You scarce have alter'd. I am sad and glad
To see you, Florian. *I* give thee to death,
My brother! it was duty spoke, not I.
My needful seeming harshness, pardon it.
Our mother, is she well?"
                                    With that she kiss'd   290
His forehead, then, a moment after, clung
About him, and betwixt them blossom'd up
From out a common vein of memory
Sweet household talk, and phrases of the hearth,
And far allusion, till the gracious dews
Began to glisten and to fall; and while
They stood, so rapt, we gazing, came a voice,
"I brought a message here from Lady Blanche."
Back started she, and turning round we saw
The Lady Blanche's daughter where she stood,   300
Melissa, with her hand upon the lock,
A rosy blonde, and in a college gown,
That clad her like an April daffodilly —
Her mother's color — with her lips apart,
And all her thoughts as fair within her eyes,
As bottom agates seen to wave and float
In crystal currents of clear morning seas.

So stood that same fair creature at the door.
Then Lady Psyche, "Ah — Melissa — you!
You heard us?" and Melissa, "O, pardon me!   310
I heard, I could not help it, did not wish;
But, dearest lady, pray you fear me not,

Nor think I bear that heart within my breast,
To give three gallant gentlemen to death." . . .

We turn'd to go, but Cyril took the child,
And held her round the knees against his waist,
And blew the swollen cheek of a trumpeter,
While Psyche watch'd them, smiling, and the child
Push'd her flat hand against his face and laugh'd;
And thus our conference closed.
          And then we strolled
For half the day thro' stately theatres
Bench'd crescent-wise. In each we sat, we heard
The grave professor. On the lecture slate
The circle rounded under female hands   350
With flawless demonstration; follow'd then
A classic lecture, rich in sentiment,
With scraps of thunderous epic lilted out
By violet-hooded Doctors, elegies
And quoted odes, and jewels five-words-long
That on the stretch'd forefinger of all Time
Sparkle forever. Then we dipt in all
That treats of whatsoever is, the state,
The total chronicles of man, the mind,
The morals, something of the frame, the rock,   360
The star, the bird, the fish, the shell, the flower,
Electric, chemic laws, and all the rest,
And whatsoever can be taught and known;
Till like three horses that have broken fence,
And glutted all night long breast-deep in corn,
We issued gorged with knowledge, and I spoke:
"Why, sirs, they do all this as well as we."
"They hunt old trails," said Cyril, "very well;
But when did woman ever yet invent?"
"Ungracious!" answer'd Florian; "have you learnt   370
No more from Psyche's lecture, you that talk'd
The trash that made me sick, and almost sad?"
"O, trash," he said, "but with a kernel in it!
Should I not call her wise who made me wise?
And learnt? I learnt more from her in a flash
Than if my brainpan were an empty hull,
And every Muse tumbled a science in.
A thousand hearts lie fallow in these halls,
And round these halls a thousand baby loves
Fly twanging headless arrows at the hearts,   380
Whence follows many a vacant pang; but O,

With me, sir, enter'd in the bigger boy,
The head of all the golden-shafted firm,
The long-limb'd lad that had a Psyche too;
He cleft me thro' the stomacher. And now
What think you of it, Florian? do I chase
The substance or the shadow? will it hold?
I have no sorcerer's malison on me,
No ghostly hauntings like his Highness. I
Flatter myself that always everywhere   390
I know the substance when I see it. Well,
Are castles shadows? Three of them? Is she
The sweet proprietress a shadow? If not,
Shall those three castles patch my tatter'd coat?
For dear are those three castles to my wants,
And dear is sister Psyche to my heart,
And two dear things are one of double worth;
And much I might have said, but that my zone
Unmann'd me. Then the Doctors! O, to hear
The Doctors! O, to watch the thirsty plants   400
Imbibing! once or twice I thought to roar,
To break my chain, to shake my mane; but thou,
Modulate me, soul of mincing mimicry!
Make liquid treble of that bassoon, my throat;
Abase those eyes that ever loved to meet
Star-sisters answering under crescent brows;
Abate the stride which speaks of man, and loose
A flying charm of blushes o'er this cheek,
Where they like swallows coming out of time
Will wonder why they came. But hark the bell   410
For dinner, let us go!" . . .
              At last a solemn grace
Concluded, and we sought the gardens. There
One walk'd reciting by herself, and one   430
In this hand held a volume as to read,
And smoothed a petted peacock down with that.
Some to a low song oar'd a shallop by,
Or under arches of the marble bridge
Hung, shadow'd from the heat; some hid and sought
In the orange thickets; others tost a ball
Above the fountain-jets, and back again
With laughter; others lay about the lawns,
Of the older sort, and murmur'd that their May
Was passing — what was learning unto them?   440
They wish'd to marry; they could rule a house;
Men hated learned women. But we three

Sat muffled like the Fates; and often came
Melissa hitting all we saw with shafts
Of gentle satire, kin to charity,
That harm'd not. Then day droopt; the chapel bells
Call'd us; we left the walks; we mixt with those
Six hundred maidens clad in purest white,
Before two streams of light from wall to wall,
While the great organ almost burst his pipes,   450
Groaning for power, and rolling thro' the court
A long melodious thunder to the sound
Of solemn psalms and silver litanies,
The work of Ida, to call down from heaven
A blessing on her labors for the world.

> Sweet and low, sweet and low,
>   Wind of the western sea,
> Low, low, breathe and blow,
>   Wind of the western sea!
> Over the rolling waters go,
> Come from the dying moon, and blow,
>   Blow him again to me;
> While my little one, while my pretty one sleeps.

> Sleep and rest, sleep and rest,
>   Father will come to thee soon;
> Rest, rest, on mother's breast,
>   Father will come to thee soon;
> Father will come to his babe in the nest,
> Silver sails all out of the west
>   Under the silver moon;
> Sleep, my little one, sleep, my pretty one, sleep.

III

Morn in the white wake of the morning star
Came furrowing all the orient into gold.
We rose, and each by other drest with care
Descended to the court that lay three parts
In shadow, but the Muses' heads were touch'd
Above the darkness from their native East.

There while we stood beside the fount, and watch'd
Or seem'd to watch the dancing bubble, approach'd
Melissa, tinged with wan from lack of sleep.
Or grief, and glowing round her dewy eyes   10
The circled Iris of a night of tears;
And "Fly," she cried, "O fly, while yet you may!

My mother knows." And when I ask'd her "how,"
"My fault," she wept, "my fault! and yet not mine;
Yet mine in part. O, hear me, pardon me!
   . . . So my mother clutch'd
The truth at once, but with no word from me;
And now thus early risen she goes to inform
The Princess. Lady Psyche will be crush'd;
But you may yet be saved, and therefore fly;
But heal me with your pardon ere you go." . . .

[Cyril goes off to plead with Lady Blanche. Melissa tells of a long
feud between Blanche and Psyche, then flees the scene.]

 Then murmur'd Florian, gazing after her:
"An open-hearted maiden, true and pure.
If I could love, why this were she. How pretty
Her blushing was, and how she blush'd again,
As if to close with Cyril's random wish!
Not like your Princess cramm'd with erring pride,
Nor like poor Psyche whom she drags in tow."

 "The crane," I said, "may chatter of the crane.
The dove may murmur of the dove, but I
An eagle clang an eagle to the sphere.   90
My princess, O my princess! true she errs,
But in her own grand way; being herself
Three times more noble than three score of men,
She sees herself in every woman else,
And so she wears her error like a crown
To blind the truth and me. For her, and her,
Hebes are they to hand ambrosia, mix
The nectar; but — ah, she — whene'er she moves
The Samian Herè rises, and she speaks
A Memnon smitten with the morning sun."   100

 So saying from the court we paced, and gain'd
The terrace ranged along the northern front,
And leaning there on those balusters, high
Above the empurpled champaign, drank the gale
That blown about the foliage underneath,
And sated with the innumerable rose,
Beat balm upon our eyelids. Hither came
Cyril, and yawning, "O hard task," he cried: . . .

[Cyril tells how he has persuaded Lady Blanche by promises of reward
to delay a little before she informs the Princess.]

He ceasing, came a message from the Head.
"That afternoon the Princess rode to take
The dip of certain strata to the north.
Would we go with her? we should find the land
Worth seeing, and the river made a fall
Out yonder;" then she pointed on to where
A double hill ran up his furrowy forks
Beyond the thick-leaved platans of the vale.

Agreed to, this, the day fled on thro' all   160
Its range of duties to the appointed hour.
Then summon'd to the porch we went. She stood
Among her maidens, higher by the head,
Her back against a pillar, her foot on one
Of those tame leopards. Kitten-like he roll'd
And paw'd about her sandal. I drew near;
I gazed. On a sudden my strange seizure came
Upon me, the weird vision of our house.
The Princess Ida seem'd a hollow show,
Her gay-furr'd cats a painted fantasy,   170
Her college and her maidens empty masks,
And I myself the shadow of a dream,
For all things were and were not. Yet I felt
My heart beat thick with passion and with awe;
Then from my breast the involuntary sigh
Brake, as she smote me with the light of eyes
That lent my knee desire to kneel, and shook
My pulses, till to horse we got, and so
Went forth in long retinue following up
The river as it narrow'd to the hills.   180

I rode beside her and to me she said:
"O friend, we trust that you esteem'd us not
Too harsh to your companion yestermorn;
Unwillingly we spake." "No — not to her,"
I answer'd, "but to one of whom we spake
Your Highness might have seem'd the thing you say."
"Again?" she cried, "are you ambassadresses
From him to me? we give you, being strange,
A license; speak, and let the topic die."

I stammer'd that I knew him — could have wish'd —   190
"Our king expects — was there no precontract?
There is no truer-hearted — ah, you seem
All he prefigured, and he could not see

The bird of passage flying south but long'd
To follow. Surely, if your Highness keep
Your purport, you will shock him even to death,
Or baser courses, children of despair."

"Poor boy," she said, "can he not read — no books?
Quoit, tennis, ball — no games? nor deals in that
Which men delight in, martial exercise?   200
To nurse a blind ideal like a girl,
Methinks he seems no better than a girl;
As girls were once, as we ourself have been.
We had our dreams; perhaps he mixt with them.
We touch on our dead self, nor shun to do it,
Being other — since we learnt our meaning here,
To lift the woman's fallen divinity
Upon an even pedestal with man."

She paused, and added with a haughtier smile,
"And as to precontracts, we move, my friend,   210
At no man's beck, but know ourself and thee,
O Vashti, noble Vashti! Summon'd out
She kept her state, and left the drunken king
To brawl at Shushan underneath the palms."

"Alas, your Highness breathes full East," I said,
"On that which leans to you! I know the Prince,
I prize his truth. And then how vast a work
To assail this gray preëminence of man!
You grant me license; might I use it? think;
Ere half be done perchance your life may fail;   220
Then comes the feebler heiress of your plan,
And takes and ruins all; and thus your pains
May only make that footprint upon sand
Which old-recurring waves of prejudice
Resmooth to nothing. Might I dread that you,
With only Fame for spouse and your great deeds
For issue, yet may live in vain, and miss
Meanwhile what every woman counts her due,
Love, children, happiness?"

                And she exclaim'd,
"Peace, you young savage of the Northern wild!   230
What! tho' your Prince's love were like a god's,
Have we not made ourself the sacrifice?
You are bold indeed; we are not talk'd to thus.
Yet will we say for children, would they grew

Like field-flowers everywhere! we like them well:
But children die; and let me tell you, girl,
Howe'er you babble, great deeds cannot die. . . ."

I answer'd nothing, doubtful in myself
If that strange poet-princess with her grand
Imaginations might at all be won.
And she broke out interpreting my thoughts:

"No doubt we seem a kind of monster to you;
We are used to that; for women, up till this   260
Cramp'd under worse than South-sea-isle taboo,
Dwarfs of the gynæceum, fail so far
In high desire, they know not, cannot guess
How much their welfare is a passion to us.
If we could give them surer, quicker proof —
O, if our end were less achievable
By slow approaches than by single act
Of immolation, any phase of death,
We were as prompt to spring against the pikes,
Or down the fiery gulf as talk of it,   270
To compass our dear sisters' liberties."

She bow'd as if to veil a noble tear;
And up we came to where the river sloped
To plunge in cataract, shattering on black blocks
A breadth of thunder. O'er it shook the woods,
And danced the color, and, below, stuck out
The bones of some vast bulk that lived and roar'd
Before man was. She gazed awhile and said,
"As these rude bones to us, are we to her
That will be." "Dare we dream of that," I ask'd,   280
"Which wrought us, as the workman and his work,
That practice betters?" "How," she cried, "you love
The metaphysics! read and earn our prize,
A golden brooch. Beneath an emerald plane
Sits Diotima, teaching him that died
Of hemlock — our device, wrought to the life —
She rapt upon her subject, he on her;
For there are schools for all." "And yet," I said,
"Methinks I have not found among them all
One anatomic." "Nay, we thought of that,"   290
She answer'd, "but it pleased us not; in truth
We shudder but to dream our maids should ape
Those monstrous males that carve the living hound,

And cram him with the fragments of the grave,
Or in the dark dissolving human heart,
And holy secrets of this microcosm,
Dabbling a shameless hand with shameful jest,
Encarnalize their spirits. Yet we know
Knowledge is knowledge, and this matter hangs.
Howbeit ourself, foreseeing casualty,   300
Nor willing men should come among us, learnt,
For many weary moons before we came,
This craft of healing. Were you sick, ourself
Would tend upon you. To your question now,
Which touches on the workman and his work.
Let there be light and there was light; 't is so,
For was, and is, and will be, are but is,
And all creation is one act at once,
The birth of light; but we that are not all,
As parts, can see but parts, now this, now that,   310
And live, perforce, from thought to thought, and make
One act a phantom of succession. Thus
Our weakness somehow shapes the shadow, Time;
But in the shadow will we work, and mould
The woman to the fuller day."
                      She spake
With kindled eyes: we rode a league beyond,
And, o'er a bridge of pinewood crossing, came
On flowery levels underneath the crag,
Full of all beauty. "O, how sweet," I said, —
For I was half-oblivious of my mask, —   320
"To linger here with one that loved us!" "Yea,"
She answer'd, "or with fair philosophies
That lift the fancy; for indeed these fields
Are lovely, lovelier not the Elysian lawns,
Where paced the demigods of old, and saw
The soft white vapor streak the crowned towers
Built to the Sun." Then, turning to her maids,
"Pitch our pavilion here upon the sward;
Lay out the viands." At the word, they raised
A tent of satin, elaborately wrought   330
With fair Corinna's triumph; here she stood,
Engirt with many a florid maiden-cheek,
The woman-conqueror; woman-conquer'd there
The bearded Victor of ten-thousand hymns,
And all the men mourn'd at his side. But we
Set forth to climb; then, climbing, Cyril kept
With Psyche, with Melissa Florian, I

With mine affianced. Many a little hand
Glanced like a touch of sunshine on the rocks,
Many a light foot shone like a jewel set   340
In the dark crag. And then we turn'd, we wound
About the cliffs, the copses, out and in,
Hammering and clinking, chattering stony names
Of shale and hornblende, rag and trap and tuff,
Amygdaloid and trachyte, till the sun
Grew broader toward his death and fell, and all
The rosy heights came out above the lawns.

    The splendor falls on castle walls
      And snowy summits old in story;
    The long light shakes across the lakes,
      And the wild cataract leaps in glory.
Blow, bugle, blow, set the wild echoes flying,
Blow, bugle; answer, echoes, dying, dying, dying.

    O, hark, O, hear! how thin and clear,
      And thinner, clearer, farther going!
    O, sweet and far from cliff and scar
      The horns of Elfland faintly blowing!
Blow, let us hear the purple glens replying,
Blow, bugle; answer, echoes, dying, dying, dying.

    O love, they die in yon rich sky,
      They faint on hill or field or river;
    Our echoes roll from soul to soul,
      And grow for ever and for ever.
Blow, bugle, blow, set the wild echoes flying,
And answer, echoes, answer, dying, dying, dying.

IV

"There sinks the nebulous star we call the sun,
If that hypothesis of theirs be sound,"
Said Ida; "let us down and rest;" and we
Down from the lean and wrinkled precipices,
By every coppice-feather'd chasm and cleft,
Dropt thro' the ambrosial gloom to where below
No bigger than a glowworm shone the tent
Lamp-lit from the inner. Once she lean'd on me,
Descending; once or twice she lent her hand,
And blissful palpitations in the blood   10
Stirring a sudden transport rose and fell.

But when we planted level feet, and dipt
Beneath the satin dome and enter'd in,
There leaning deep in broider'd down we sank
Our elbows; on a tripod in the midst
A fragrant flame rose, and before us glow'd
Fruit, blossom, viand, amber wine, and gold.

Then she, "Let some one sing to us; lightlier move
The minutes fledged with music;" and a maid,
Of those beside her, smote her harp and sang.   20

    "Tears, idle tears, I know not what they mean,
Tears from the depth of some divine despair
Rise in the heart, and gather to the eyes,
In looking on the happy autumn-fields,
And thinking of the days that are no more.

    "Fresh as the first beam glittering on a sail,
That brings our friends up from the underworld,
Sad as the last which reddens over one
That sinks with all we love below the verge;
So sad, so fresh, the days that are no more.   30

    "Ah, sad and strange as in dark summer dawns
The earliest pipe of half-awaken'd birds
To dying ears, when unto dying eyes
The casement slowly grows a glimmering square;
So sad, so strange, the days that are no more.

    "Dear as remember'd kisses after death,
And sweet as those by hopeless fancy feign'd
On lips that are for others; deep as love,
Deep as first love, and wild with all regret;
O Death in Life, the days that are no more!"   40

She ended with such passion that the tear
She sang of shook and fell, an erring pearl
Lost in her bosom; but with some disdain
Answer'd the Princess: "If indeed there haunt
About the moulder'd lodges of the past
So sweet a voice and vague, fatal to men,
Well needs it we should cram our ears with wool
And so pace by. But thine are fancies hatch'd
In silken-folded idleness; nor is it
Wiser to weep a true occasion lost,   50
But trim our sails, and let old bygones be,

While down the streams that float us each and all
To the issue, goes, like glittering bergs of ice,
Throne after throne, and molten on the waste
Becomes a cloud; for all things serve their time
Toward that great year of equal mights and rights.". . .
                                        Then to me,
"Know you no song of your own land," she said,
"Not such as moans about the retrospect,
But deals with the other distance and the hues
Of promise; not a death's-head at the wine?"
    Then I remember'd one myself had made,   70
What time I watch'd the swallow winging south

From mine own land, part made long since, and part
Now while I sang, and maiden-like as far
As I could ape their treble did I sing.

    "O Swallow, Swallow, flying, flying south,
Fly to her, and fall upon her gilded eaves,
And tell her, tell her, what I tell to thee.

    "O, tell her, Swallow, thou that knowest each,
That bright and fierce and fickle is the South,
And dark and true and tender is the North.   80

    "O Swallow, Swallow, if I could follow, and light
Upon her lattice, I would pipe and trill,
And cheep and twitter twenty million loves.

    "O, were I thou that she might take me in,
And lay me on her bosom, and her heart
Would rock the snowy cradle till I died!

    "Why lingereth she to clothe her heart with love,
Delaying as the tender ash delays
To clothe herself, when all the woods are green?

    "O, tell her, Swallow, that thy brood is flown;   90
Say to her, I do but wanton in the South,
But in the North long since my nest is made.

    "O, tell her, brief is life but love is long,
And brief the sun of summer in the North,
And brief the moon of beauty in the South.

    "O Swallow, flying from the golden woods,
Fly to her, and pipe and woo her, and make her mine,
And tell her, tell her, that I follow thee."

I ceased, and all the ladies, each at each,
Like the Ithacensian suitors in old time,   100
Stared with great eyes, and laugh'd with alien lips,
And knew not what they meant; for still my voice
Rang false. But smiling, "Not for thee," she said,
"O Bulbul, any rose of Gulistan
Shall burst her veil; marsh-divers, rather, maid,
Shall croak thee sister, or the meadow-crake
Grate her harsh kindred in the grass — and this
A mere love-poem! O, for such, my friend,
We hold them slight; they mind us of the time
When we made bricks in Egypt. Knaves are men,   110
That lute and flute fantastic tenderness,
And dress the victim to the offering up,
And paint the gates of Hell with Paradise,
And play the slave to gain the tyranny.
Poor soul! I had a maid of honor once;
She wept her true eyes blind for such a one,
A rogue of canzonets and serenades.
I loved her. Peace be with her. She is dead.
So they blaspheme the muse! But great is song
Used to great ends; ourself have often tried   120
Valkyrian hymns, or into rhythm have dash'd
The passion of the prophetess; for song
Is duer unto freedom, force and growth
Of spirit, than to junketing and love.
Love is it? Would this same mock-love, and this
Mock-Hymen were laid up like winter bats,
Till all men grew to rate us at our worth,
Not vassals to be beat, nor pretty babes
To be dandled, no, but living wills, and sphered
Whole in ourselves and owed to none. Enough!   130
But now to leaven play with profit, you,
Know you no song, the true growth of your soil,
That gives the manners of your countrywomen?"

   She spoke and turn'd her sumptuous head with eyes
Of shining expectation fixt on mine.
Then while I dragg'd my brains for such a song,
Cyril, with whom the bell-mouth'd glass had wrought,
Or master'd by the sense of sport, began
To troll a careless, careless tavern-catch
Of Moll and Meg, and strange experiences   140
Unmeet for ladies. Florian nodded at him,
I frowning; Psyche flush'd and wann'd and shook;

The lilylike Melissa droop'd her brows.
"Forbear," the Princess cried; "Forbear, sir," I;
And heated thro' and thro' with wrath and love,
I smote him on the breast. He started up;
There rose a shriek as of a city sack'd;
Melissa clamor'd, "Flee the death;" "To horse!"
Said Ida, "home! to horse!" and fled, as flies
A troop of snowy doves athwart the dusk   150
When some one batters at the dovecote doors.
Disorderly the women. Alone I stood
With Florian, cursing Cyril, vext at heart
In the pavilion. There like parting hopes
I heard them passing from me; hoof by hoof,
And every hoof a knell to my desires,
Clang'd on the bridge; and then another shriek,
"The Head, the Head, the Princess, O the Head!"
For blind with rage she miss'd the plank, and roll'd
In the river. Out I sprang from glow to gloom;   160
There whirl'd her white robe like a blossom'd branch
Rapt to the horrible fall. A glance I gave,
No more, but woman-vested as I was
Plunged, and the flood drew; yet I caught her; then
Oaring one arm, and bearing in my left
The weight of all the hopes of half the world,
Strove to buffet to land in vain. A tree
Was half-disrooted from his place and stoop'd
To drench his dark locks in the gurgling wave
Mid-channel. Right on this we drove and caught,   170
And grasping down the boughs I gain'd the shore. . . .

[Having saved Ida from drowning, the Prince escapes from her retinue. Presently he is joined by Florian, who describes Ida's efforts to track down the interlopers and to punish the women who have sheltered them. Both the Prince and Florian are soon apprehended.]

    They haled us to the Princess where she sat
High in the hall; above her droop'd a lamp,
And made the single jewel on her brow
Burn like the mystic fire on a mast-head,
Prophet of storm; a handmaid on each side
Bow'd toward her, combing out her long black hair
Damp from the river; and close behind her stood
Eight daughters of the plough, stronger than men,
Huge women blowzed with health, and wind, and rain,   260
And labor. Each was like a Druid rock;

Or like a spire of land that stands apart
Cleft from the main, and wail'd about with mews.

Then, as we came, the crowd dividing clove
An advent to the throne; and therebeside,
Half-naked as if caught at once from bed
And tumbled on the purple footcloth, lay
The lily-shining child; and on the left,
Bow'd on her palms and folded up from wrong,
Her round white shoulder shaken with her sobs,   270
Melissa knelt; but Lady Blanche erect
Stood up and spake, an affluent orator: . . .

[Lady Blanche pleads in a vain effort to excuse her delay in inform-
ing the Princess.]

She ceased; the Princess answer'd coldly, "Good;   340
Your oath is broken; we dismiss you, go.
For this lost lamb" — she pointed to the child —
"Our mind is changed; we take it to ourself." . . .

[A female courier now brings letters from the two kings announcing
that Gama has been captured and held hostage for the Prince. The
Prince declares his steadfast love for Ida, but she remains obdurate.]

A tide of fierce   450
Invective seem'd to wait behind her lips,
As waits a river level with the dam
Ready to burst and flood the world with foam;
And so she would have spoken, but there rose
A hubbub in the court of half the maids
Gather'd together; from the illumined hall
Long lanes of splendor slanted o'er a press
Of snowy shoulders, thick as herded ewes,
And rainbow robes, and gems and gemlike eyes,
And gold and golden heads. They to and fro   460
Fluctuated, as flowers in storm, some red, some pale,
All open-mouth'd, all gazing to the light,
Some crying there was an army in the land,
And some that men were in the very walls,
And some they cared not; till a clamor grew
As of a new-world Babel, woman-built,
And worse-confounded. High above them stood
The placid marble Muses, looking peace.

Not peace she look'd, the Head; but rising up
Robed in the long night of her deep hair, so   470
To the open window moved, remaining there
Fixt like a beacon-tower above the waves
Of tempest, when the crimson-rolling eye
Glares ruin, and the wild birds on the light
Dash themselves dead. She stretch'd her arms and call'd
Across the tumult, and the tumult fell.

"What fear ye, brawlers? am not I your Head?
On me, me, me, the storm first breaks; *I* dare
All these male thunderbolts; what is it ye fear?
Peace! there are those to avenge us and they come;   480
If not, — myself were like enough, O girls,
To unfurl the maiden banner of our rights,
And clad in iron burst the ranks of war,
Or, falling, protomartyr of our cause,
Die; yet I blame you not so much for fear;
Six thousand years of fear have made you that
From which I would redeem you. But for those
That stir this hubbub — you and you — I know
Your faces there in the crowd — to-morrow morn
We hold a great convention; then shall they   490
That love their voices more than duty, learn
With whom they deal, dismiss'd in shame to live
No wiser than their mothers, household stuff,
Live chattels, mincers of each other's fame,
Full of weak poison, turnspits for the clown,
The drunkard's football, laughing-stocks of Time,
Whose brains are in their hands and in their heels,
But fit to flaunt, to dress, to dance, to thrum,
To tramp, to scream, to furnish, and to scour,
For ever slaves at home and fools abroad."   500

She, ending, waved her hands; thereat the crowd
Muttering, dissolved; then with a smile, that look'd
A stroke of cruel sunshine on the cliff,
When all the glens are drown'd in azure gloom
Of thunder-shower, she floated to us and said:

"You have done well and like a gentleman,
And like a prince; you have our thanks for all.
And you look well too in your woman's dress.
Well have you done and like a gentleman.
You saved our life; we owe you bitter thanks.   510

Better have died and spilt our bones in the flood —
Then men had said — but now — what hinders me
To take such bloody vengeance on you both? —
Yet since our father — wasps in our good hive,
You would-be quenchers of the light to be,
Barbarians, grosser than your native bears —
O, would I had his sceptre for one hour!
You that have dared to break our bound, and gull'd
Our servants, wrong'd and lied and thwarted us —
I wed with thee! *I* bound by precontract   520
Your bride, your bondslave! not tho' all the gold
That veins the world were pack'd to make your crown,
And every spoken tongue should lord you. Sir,
Your falsehood and yourself are hateful to us;
I trample on your offers and on you.
Begone; we will not look upon you more.
Here, push them out at gates."

                    In wrath she spake.
Then those eight mighty daughters of the plough
Bent their broad faces toward us and address'd
Their motion. Twice I sought to plead my cause,   530
But on my shoulder hung their heavy hands,
The weight of destiny; so from her face
They push'd us, down the steps, and thro' the court,
And with grim laughter thrust us out at gates.

    We cross'd the street and gain'd a petty mound
Beyond it, whence we saw the lights and heard
The voices murmuring. While I listen'd, came
On a sudden the weird seizure and the doubt.
I seem'd to move among a world of ghosts;
The Princess with her monstrous woman-guard,   540
The jest and earnest working side by side,
The cataract and the tumult and the kings
Were shadows; and the long fantastic night
With all its doings had and had not been,
And all things were and were not.

                     This went by
As strangely as it came, and on my spirits
Settled a gentle cloud of melancholy —
Not long; I shook it off; for spite of doubts
And sudden ghostly shadowings I was one
To whom the touch of all mischance but came   550
As night to him that sitting on a hill
Sees the midsummer, midnight, Norway sun
Set into sunrise; then we moved away.

Interlude

Thy voice is heard thro' rolling drums
    That beat to battle where he stands;
Thy face across his fancy comes,
    And gives the battle to his hands.
A moment, while the trumpets blow,
    He sees his brood about thy knee;
The next, like fire he meets the foe,
    And strikes him dead for thine and thee.

So Lilia sang. We thought her half-possess'd,
She struck such warbling fury thro' the words;   10
And, after, feigning pique at what she call'd
The raillery, or grotesque, or false sublime —
Like one that wishes at a dance to change
The music — clapt her hands and cried for war,
Or some grand fight to kill and make an end.
And he that next inherited the tale,
Half turning to the broken statue, said,
"Sir Ralph has got your colors; if I prove
Your knight, and fight your battle, what for me?"
It chanced, her empty glove upon the tomb   20
Lay by her like a model of her hand.
She took it and she flung it. "Fight," she said,
"And make us all we would be, great and good."
He knightlike in his cap instead of casque,
A cap of Tyrol borrow'd from the hall,
Arranged the favor, and assumed the Prince.

V

Now, scarce three paces measured from the mound,
We stumbled on a stationary voice,
And "Stand, who goes?" "Two from the palace," I.
"The second two; they wait," he said, "pass on;
His Highness wakes;" and one, that clash'd in arms,
By glimmering lanes and walls of canvas led
Threading the soldier-city, till we heard
The drowsy folds of our great ensign shake
From blazon'd lions o'er the imperial tent
Whispers of war.
               Entering, the sudden light   10
Dazed me half-blind. I stood and seem'd to hear,

As in a poplar grove when a light wind wakes
A lisping of the innumerous leaf and dies,
Each hissing in his neighbor's ear; and then
A strangled titter, out of which there brake
On all sides, clamoring etiquette to death,
Unmeasured mirth; while now the two old kings
Began to wag their baldness up and down,
The fresh young captains flash'd their glittering teeth,
The huge bush-bearded barons heaved and blew,   20
And slain with laughter roll'd the gilded squire.

  At length my sire, his rough cheek wet with tears,
Panted from weary sides, "King, you are free!
We did but keep you surety for our son,
If this be he, — or a draggled mawkin, thou,
That tends her bristled grunters in the sludge;"
For I was drench'd with ooze, and torn with briers,
More crumpled than a poppy from the sheath,
And all one rag, disprinced from head to heel.
Then some one sent beneath his vaulted palm   30
A whisper'd jest to some one near him, "Look,
He has been among his shadows." "Satan take
The old women and their shadows!" — thus the king
Roar'd — "make yourself a man to fight with men.
Go; Cyril told us all."
                            As boys that slink
From ferule and the trespass-chiding eye,
Away we stole, and transient in a trice
From what was left of faded woman-slough
To sheathing splendors and the golden scale
Of harness, issued in the sun, that now   40
Leapt from the dewy shoulders of the earth,
And hit the Northern hills. Here Cyril met us,
A little shy at first, but by and by
We twain, with mutual pardon ask'd and given
For stroke and song, resolder'd peace, whereon
Follow'd his tale. Amazed he fled away
Thro' the dark land, and later in the night
Had come on Psyche weeping: "then we fell
Into your father's hand, and there she lies,
But will not speak nor stir."
                            He show'd a tent   50
A stone-shot off; we enter'd in, and there
Among piled arms and rough accoutrements,
Pitiful sight, wrapp'd in a soldier's cloak,

Like some sweet sculpture draped from head to foot,
And push'd by rude hands from its pedestal,
All her fair length upon the ground she lay;
And at her head a follower of the camp,
A charr'd and wrinkled piece of womanhood,
Sat watching like a watcher by the dead.

   Then Florian knelt, and "Come," he whisper'd to her,   60
"Lift up your head, sweet sister; lie not thus.
What have you done but right? you could not slay
Me, nor your prince; look up, be comforted.
Sweet is it to have done the thing one ought,
When fallen in darker ways." And likewise I:
"Be comforted; have I not lost her too,
In whose least act abides the nameless charm
That none has else for me?" She heard, she moved,
She moan'd, a folded voice; and up she sat,
And raised the cloak from brows as pale and smooth   70
As those that mourn half-shrouded over death
In deathless marble. "Her," she said, "my friend —
Parted from her — betray'd her cause and mine —
Where shall I breathe? why kept ye not your faith?
O base and bad! what comfort? none for me!"
To whom remorseful Cyril, "Yet I pray
Take comfort; live, dear lady, for your child!"
At which she lifted up her voice and cried:

   "Ah me, my babe, my blossom, ah, my child,
My one sweet child, whom I shall see no more! . . .   80
Ah! what might that man not deserve of me   101
Who gave me back my child?" "Be comforted,"
Said Cyril, "you shall have it;" but again
She veil'd her brows, and prone she sank, and so,
Like tender things that being caught feign death,
Spoke not, nor stirr'd. . . .
              Then Gama turn'd to me:
"We fear, indeed, you spent a stormy time
With our strange girl; and yet they say that still
You love her. Give us, then, your mind at large:
How say you, war or not?"
                 "Not war, if possible,
O king," I said, "lest from the abuse of war,   120
The desecrated shrine, the trampled year,
The smouldering homestead, and the household flower
Torn from the lintel — all the common wrong —

A smoke go up thro' which I loom to her
Three times a monster. Now she lightens scorn
At him that mars her plan, but then would hate —
And every voice she talk'd with ratify it,
And every face she look'd on justify it —
The general foe. More soluble is this knot
By gentleness than war. I want her love. 130
What were I nigher this altho' we dash'd
Your cities into shards with catapults? —
She would not love — or brought her chain'd, a slave,
The lifting of whose eyelash is my lord?
Not ever would she love, but brooding turn
The book of scorn, till all my flitting chance
Were caught within the record of her wrongs
And crush'd to death; and rather, Sire, than this
I would the old god of war himself were dead,
Forgotten, rusting on his iron hills, 140
Rotting on some wild shore with ribs of wreck,
Or like an old-world mammoth bulk'd in ice,
Not to be molten out."
                              And roughly spake
My father: "Tut, you know them not, the girls.
Boy, when I hear you prate I almost think
That idiot legend credible. Look you, sir!
Man is the hunter; woman is his game.
The sleek and shining creatures of the chase,
We hunt them for the beauty of their skins;
They love us for it, and we ride them down. 150
Wheedling and siding with them! Out! for shame!
Boy, there's no rose that's half so dear to them
As he that does the thing they dare not do,
Breathing and sounding beauteous battle, comes
With the air of the trumpet round him, and leaps in
Among the women, snares them by the score
Flatter'd and fluster'd, wins, tho' dash'd with death
He reddens what he kisses. Thus I won
Your mother, a good mother, a good wife,
Worth winning; but this firebrand — gentleness 160
To such as her! if Cyril spake her true,
To catch a dragon in a cherry net,
To trip a tigress with a gossamer,
Were wisdom to it."
                              "Yea, but, Sire," I cried,
"Wild natures need wise curbs. The soldier? No!
What dares not Ida do that she should prize

The soldier? I beheld her, when she rose
The yesternight, and storming in extremes
Stood for her cause, and flung defiance down
Gagelike to man, and had not shunn'd the death,   170
No, not the soldier's; yet I hold her, king,
True woman; but you clash them all in one,
That have as many differences as we.
The violet varies from the lily as far
As oak from elm. One loves the soldier, one
The silken priest of peace, one this, one that,
And some unworthily; their sinless faith,
A maiden moon that sparkles on a sty,
Glorifying clown and satyr; whence they need
More breadth of culture. Is not Ida right?   180
They worth it? truer to the law within?
Severer in the logic of a life?
Twice as magnetic to sweet influences
Of earth and heaven? and she of whom you speak,
My mother, looks as whole as some serene
Creation minted in the golden moods
Of sovereign artists; not a thought, a touch,
But pure as lines of green that streak the white
Of the first snowdrop's inner leaves; I say,
Not like the piebald miscellany, man,   190
Bursts of great heart and slips in sensual mire,
But whole and one; and take them all-in-all,
Were we ourselves but half as good, as kind,
As truthful, much that Ida claims as right
Had ne'er been mooted, but as frankly theirs
As dues of Nature. To our point; not war,
Lest I lose all."
              "Nay, nay, you spake but sense,"
Said Gama. "We remember love ourself
In our sweet youth; we did not rate him then
This red-hot iron to be shaped with blows.   200
You talk almost like Ida; *she* can talk;
And there is something in it as you say:
But you talk kindlier; we esteem you for it. —
He seems a gracious and a gallant Prince,
I would he had our daughter." . . .

[The Prince opposes "brainless war" but, taunted with cowardice, agrees to fight in a tourney. Ida, meanwhile, spurs on her irascible brother, Arac, by restating the wrongs done to womanhood in general and the college in particular. The Prince reads her letter to Arac:]

"O brother, you have known the pangs we felt,
What heats of indignation when we heard
Of those that iron-cramp'd their women's feet;
Of lands in which at the altar the poor bride
Gives her harsh groom for bridal-gift a scourge;
Of living hearts that crack within the fire
Where smoulder their dead despots; and of those, — 370
Mothers, — that, all prophetic pity, fling
Their pretty maids in the running flood, and swoops
The vulture, beak and talon, at the heart
Made for all noble motion. And I saw
That equal baseness lived in sleeker times
With smoother men; the old leaven leaven'd all;
Millions of throats would bawl for civil rights,
No woman named; therefore I set my face
Against all men, and lived but for mine own.
Far off from men I built a fold for them; 380
I stored it full of rich memorial;
I fenced it round with gallant institutes,
And biting laws to scare the beasts of prey,
And prosper'd, till a rout of saucy boys
Brake on us at our books, and marr'd our peace,
Mask'd like our maids, blustering I know not what
Of insolence and love, some pretext held
Of baby troth, invalid, since my will
Seal'd not the bond — the striplings! — for their sport! —
I tamed my leopards; shall I not tame these? 390
Or you? or I? for since you think me touch'd
In honor — what! I would not aught of false —
Is not our cause pure? and whereas I know
Your prowess, Arac, and what mother's blood
You draw from, fight! You failing, I abide
What end soever; fail you will not. Still,
Take not his life, he risk'd it for my own;
His mother lives. Yet whatsoe'er you do,
Fight and fight well; strike and strike home. O dear
Brothers, the woman's angel guards you, you 400
The sole men to be mingled with our cause,
The sole men we shall prize in the aftertime,
Your very armor hallow'd, and your statues
Rear'd, sung to, when, this gadfly brush'd aside,
We plant a solid foot into the Time,
And mould a generation strong to move
With claim on claim from right to right, till she
Whose name is yoked with children's know herself;

And Knowledge in our own land make her free,
And, ever following those two crowned twins,   **410**
Commerce and Conquest, shower the fiery grain
Of freedom broadcast over all that orbs
Between the Northern and the Southern morn."

    Then came a postscript dash'd across the rest:
"See that there be no traitors in your camp.
We seem a nest of traitors — none to trust
Since our arms fail'd — this Egypt-plague of men!
Almost our maids were better at their homes,
Than thus man-girdled here. Indeed I think
Our chiefest comfort is the little child   **420**
Of one unworthy mother, which she left.
She shall not have it back; the child shall grow
To prize the authentic mother of her mind.
I took it for an hour in mine own bed
This morning; there the tender orphan hands
Felt at my heart, and seem'd to charm from thence
The wrath I nursed against the world. Farewell." . . .

[The Prince's father crudely rejects feminism and urges him to catch
and tame the wayward Ida. But the Prince is more sensitive to the
merits of Ida's cause and is moved by her possible regard for him.]

    I pored upon her letter which I held,
And on the little clause, "take not his life;"
I mused on that wild morning in the woods,   **460**
And on the "Follow, follow, thou shalt win;"
I thought on all the wrathful king had said,
And how the strange betrothment was to end.
Then I remember'd that burnt sorcerer's curse
That one should fight with shadows and should fall;
And like a flash the weird affection came.
King, camp, and college turn'd to hollow shows;
I seem'd to move in old memorial tilts,
And doing battle with forgotten ghosts,
To dream myself the shadow of a dream;   **470**
And ere I woke it was the point of noon,
The lists were ready. Empanoplied and plumed
We enter'd in, and waited, fifty there
Opposed to fifty, till the trumpet blared
At the barrier like a wild horn in a land
Of echoes, and a moment, and once more
The trumpet, and again; at which the storm

Of galloping hoofs bare on the ridge of spears
And riders front to front, until they closed
In conflict with the crash of shivering points,   480
And thunder. Yet it seem'd a dream, I dream'd
Of fighting. On his haunches rose the steed,
And into fiery splinters leapt the lance,
And out of stricken helmets sprang the fire.
Part sat like rocks; part reel'd but kept their seats;
Part roll'd on the earth and rose again and drew;
Part stumbled mixt with floundering horses. Down
From those two bulks at Arac's side and down
From Arac's arm, as from a giant's flail,
The large blows rain'd, as here and everywhere   490
He rode the mellay, lord of the ringing lists,
And all the plain — brand, mace, and shaft, and shield —
Shock'd, like an iron-clanging anvil bang'd
With hammers; till I thought, can this be he
From Gama's dwarfish loins? if this be so,
The mother makes us most — and in my dream
I glanced aside, and saw the palace-front
Alive with fluttering scarfs and ladies' eyes,
And highest, among the statues, statue-like,
Between a cymbal'd Miriam and a Jael,   500
With Psyche's babe, was Ida watching us,
A single band of gold about her hair,
Like a saint's glory up in heaven; but she,
No saint — inexorable — no tenderness —
Too hard, too cruel. Yet she sees me fight,
Yea, let her see me fall. With that I drave
Among the thickest and bore down a prince,
And Cyril one. Yea, let me make my dream
All that I would. But that large-moulded man,
His visage all agrin as at a wake,   510
Made at me thro' the press, and, staggering back
With stroke on stroke the horse and horseman, came
As comes a pillar of electric cloud,
Flaying the roofs and sucking up the drains,
And shadowing down the champaign till it strikes
On a wood, and takes, and breaks, and cracks, and splits,
And twists the grain with such a roar that Earth
Reels, and the herdsmen cry; for everything
Gave way before him. Only Florian, he
That loved me closer than his own right eye,   520
Thrust in between; but Arac rode him down.
And Cyril seeing it, push'd against the Prince,

With Psyche's color round his helmet, tough,
Strong, supple, sinew-corded, apt at arms;
But tougher, heavier, stronger, he that smote
And threw him. Last I spurr'd; I felt my veins
Stretch with fierce heat; a moment hand to hand,
And sword to sword, and horse to horse we hung,
Till I struck out and shouted; the blade glanced,
I did but shear a feather, and dream and truth   530
Flow'd from me; darkness closed me, and I fell.

> Home they brought her warrior dead;
> > She nor swoon'd nor utter'd cry.
> All her maidens, watching, said,
> > "She must weep or she will die."

> Then they praised him, soft and low,
> > Call'd him worthy to be loved,
> Truest friend and noblest foe;
> > Yet she neither spoke nor moved.

> Stole a maiden from her place,
> > Lightly to the warrior stept,
> Took the face-cloth from the face;
> > Yet she neither moved nor wept.

> Rose a nurse of ninety years,
> > Set his child upon her knee —
> Like summer tempest came her tears —
> > "Sweet my child, I live for thee."

VI

My dream had never died or lived again;
As in some mystic middle state I lay.
Seeing I saw not, hearing not I heard;
Tho', if I saw not, yet they told me all
So often that I speak as having seen.

For so it seem'd, or so they said to me,
That all things grew more tragic and more strange;
That when our side was vanquish'd and my cause
For ever lost, there went up a great cry,
"The Prince is slain!" My father heard and ran   10
In on the lists, and there unlaced my casque
And grovell'd on my body, and after him
Came Psyche, sorrowing for Aglaïa.

But high upon the palace Ida stood
With Psyche's babe in arm; there on the roofs
Like that great dame of Lapidoth she sang.

"Our enemies have fallen, have fallen: the seed,
The little seed they laugh'd at in the dark,
Has risen and cleft the soil, and grown a bulk
Of spanless girth, that lays on every side   20
A thousand arms and rushes to the sun.

"Our enemies have fallen, have fallen: they came;
The leaves were wet with women's tears; they heard
A noise of songs they would not understand;
They mark'd it with the red cross to the fall,
And would have strewn it, and are fallen themselves.

"Our enemies have fallen, have fallen: they came,
The woodmen with their axes: lo the tree!
But we will make it faggots for the hearth,
And shape it plank and beam for roof and floor,   30
And boats and bridges for the use of men.

"Our enemies have fallen, have fallen; they struck;
With their own blows they hurt themselves, nor knew
There dwelt an iron nature in the grain;
The glittering axe was broken in their arms,
Their arms were shatter'd to the shoulder blade.

"Our enemies have fallen, but this shall grow
A night of Summer from the heat, a breadth
Of Autumn, dropping fruits of power; and roll'd
With music in the growing breeze of Time,   40
The tops shall strike from star to star, the fangs
Shall move the stony bases of the world.

"And now, O maids, behold our sanctuary
Is violate, our laws broken; fear we not
To break them more in their behoof, whose arms
Champion'd our cause and won it with a day
Blanch'd in our annals, and perpetual feast,
When dames and heroines of the golden year
Shall strip a hundred hollows bare of Spring,
To rain an April of ovation round   50
Their statues, borne aloft, the three; but come,
We will be liberal, since our rights are won.
Let them not lie in the tents with coarse mankind,
Ill nurses; but descend, and proffer these

The brethren of our blood and cause, that there
Lie bruised and maim'd, the tender ministries
Of female hands and hospitality." . . .

[Ida is disturbed to find the Prince severely wounded.]

And then once more she look'd at my pale face;
Till understanding all the foolish work   100
Of Fancy, and the bitter close of all,
Her iron will was broken in her mind;
Her noble heart was molten in her breast;
She bow'd, she set the child on the earth; she laid
A feeling finger on my brows, and presently
"O Sire," she said, "he lives; he is not dead!
O, let me have him with my brethren here
In our own palace; we will tend on him
Like one of these; if so, by any means,
To lighten this great clog of thanks, that make   110
Our progress falter to the woman's goal."

She said; but at the happy word "he lives!"
My father stoop'd, re-father'd o'er my wounds.
So those two foes above my fallen life,
With brow to brow like night and evening mixt
Their dark and gray, while Psyche ever stole
A little nearer, till the babe that by us,
Half-lapt in glowing gauze and golden brede,
Lay like a new-fallen meteor on the grass,
Uncared for, spied its mother and began   120
A blind and babbling laughter, and to dance
Its body, and reach its fatling innocent arms
And lazy lingering fingers. She the appeal
Brook'd not, but clamoring out "Mine — mine — not yours!
It is not yours, but mine; give me the child!"
Ceased all on tremble; piteous was the cry.
So stood the unhappy mother open-mouth'd,
And turn'd each face her way. Wan was her cheek
With hollow watch, her blooming mantle torn,
Red grief and mother's hunger in her eye,   130
And down dead-heavy sank her curls, and half
The sacred mother's bosom, panting, burst
The laces toward her babe; but she nor cared
Nor knew it, clamoring on, till Ida heard,
Look'd up, and rising slowly from me, stood
Erect and silent, striking with her glance

The mother, me, the child. But he that lay
Beside us, Cyril, batter'd as he was,
Trail'd himself up on one knee; then he drew
Her robe to meet his lips, and down she look'd   140
At the arm'd man sideways, pitying as it seem'd,
Or self-involved; but when she learnt his face,
Remembering his ill-omen'd song, arose
Once more thro' all her height, and o'er him grew
Tall as a figure lengthen'd on the sand
When the tide ebbs in sunshine, and he said:

    "O fair and strong and terrible! Lioness
That with your long locks play the lion's mane!
But Love and Nature, these are two more terrible
And stronger. See, your foot is on our necks,   150
We vanquish'd, you the victor of your will.
What would you more? give her the child! remain
Orb'd in your isolation; he is dead,
Or all as dead: henceforth we let you be.
Win you the hearts of women; and beware
Lest, where you seek the common love of these,
The common hate with the revolving wheel
Should drag you down, and some great Nemesis
Break from a darken'd future, crown'd with fire,
And tread you out for ever. But howsoe'er   160
Fixt in yourself, never in your own arms
To hold your own, deny not hers to her,
Give her the child!" . . .

[Ida returns the child to Psyche but refuses to forgive Psyche's defection.]

    But Ida stood nor spoke, drain'd of her force
By many a varying influence and so long.   250
Down thro' her limbs a drooping languor wept;
Her head a little bent; and on her mouth
A doubtful smile dwelt like a clouded moon
In a still water. Then brake out my sire,
Lifting his grim head from my wounds: "O you,
Woman, whom we thought woman even now,
And were half fool'd to let you tend our son,
Because he might have wish'd it — but we see
The accomplice of your madness unforgiven,
And think that you might mix his draught with death,   260
When your skies change again; the rougher hand
Is safer. On to the tents; take up the Prince."

He rose, and while each ear was prick'd to attend
A tempest, thro' the cloud that dimm'd her broke
A genial warmth and light once more, and shone
Thro' glittering drops on her sad friend.

       "Come hither,
O Psyche," she cried out, "embrace me, come,
Quick while I melt; make reconcilement sure
With one that cannot keep her mind an hour;
Come to the hollow heart they slander so!   270
Kiss and be friends, like children being chid!
I seem no more, *I* want forgiveness too;
I should have had to do with none but maids,
That have no links with men. Ah false but dear,
Dear traitor, too much loved, why? — why? — yet see
Before these kings we embrace you yet once more
With all forgiveness, all oblivion,
And trust, not love, you less.

        And now, O Sire,
Grant me your son, to nurse, to wait upon him,
Like mine own brother. For my debt to him,   280
This nightmare weight of gratitude, I know it.
Taunt me no more; yourself and yours shall have
Free adit; we will scatter all our maids
Till happier times each to her proper hearth.
What use to keep them here — now? grant my prayer.
Help, father, brother, help; speak to the king;
Thaw this male nature to some touch of that
Which kills me with myself, and drags me down
From my fixt height to mob me up with all
The soft and milky rabble of womankind,   290
Poor weakling even as they are."

         Passionate tears
Follow'd; the king replied not; Cyril said:
"Your brother, lady, — Florian, — ask for him
Of your great Head — for he is wounded too —
That you may tend upon him with the Prince."
"Ay, so," said Ida with a bitter smile,
"Our laws are broken; let him enter too."
Then Violet, she that sang the mournful song,
And had a cousin tumbled on the plain,
Petition'd too for him. "Ay, so," she said,   300
"I stagger in the stream; I cannot keep
My heart an eddy from the brawling hour.
We break our laws with ease, but let it be."
"Ay, so?" said Blanche: "Amazed am I to hear
Your Highness; but your Highness breaks with ease

The law your Highness did not make; 't was I.
I had been wedded wife, I knew mankind,
And block'd them out; but these men came to woo
Your Highness, — verily I think to win."

So she, and turn'd askance a wintry eye;   310
But Ida, with a voice that, like a bell
Toll'd by an earthquake in a trembling tower,
Rang ruin, answer'd full of grief and scorn:

"Fling our doors wide! all, all, not one, but all,
Not only he, but by my mother's soul,
Whatever man lies wounded, friend or foe,
Shall enter, if he will! Let our girls flit,
Till the storm die! but had you stood by us,
The roar that breaks the Pharos from his base
Had left us rock. She fain would sting us too,   320
But shall not. Pass, and mingle with your likes.
We brook no further insult, but are gone."

She turn'd; the very nape of her white neck
Was rosed with indignation; but the Prince
Her brother came; the king her father charm'd
Her wounded soul with words; nor did mine own
Refuse her proffer, lastly gave his hand.

Then us they lifted up, dead weights, and bare
Straight to the doors; to them the doors gave way
Groaning, and in the vestal entry shriek'd   330
The virgin marble under iron heels. . . .
                                    Then the voice
Of Ida sounded, issuing ordinance;
And me they bore up the broad stairs, and thro'
The long-laid galleries past a hundred doors
To one deep chamber shut from sound, and due
To languid limbs and sickness, left me in it;
And others otherwhere they laid; and all
That afternoon a sound arose of hoof
And chariot, many a maiden passing home
Till happier times; but some were left of those   360
Held sagest, and the great lords out and in,
From those two hosts that lay beside the walls,
Walk'd at their will, and everything was chang'd.

Ask me no more: the moon may draw the sea;
  The cloud may stoop from heaven and take the shape,
  With fold to fold, of mountain or of cape;
But O too fond, when have I answer'd thee?
    Ask me no more.

Ask me no more: what answer should I give?
  I love not hollow cheek or faded eye:
  Yet, O my friend, I will not have thee die!
Ask me no more, lest I should bid thee live;
    Ask me no more.

Ask me no more: thy fate and mine are seal'd;
  I strove against the stream and all in vain;
  Let the great river take me to the main.
No more, dear love, for at a touch I yield;
    Ask me no more.

VII

So was their sanctuary violated,
So their fair college turn'd to hospital,
At first with all confusion; by and by
Sweet order lived again with other laws,
A kindlier influence reign'd, and everywhere
Low voices with the ministering hand
Hung round the sick. The maidens came, they talk'd,
They sang, they read; till she not fair began
To gather light, and she that was became
Her former beauty treble; and to and fro   10
With books, with flowers, with angel offices,
Like creatures native unto gracious act,
And in their own clear element, they moved.

But sadness on the soul of Ida fell,
And hatred of her weakness, blent with shame.
Old studies fail'd; seldom she spoke; but oft
Clomb to the roofs, and gazed alone for hours
On that disastrous leaguer, swarms of men
Darkening her female field. Void was her use,
And she as one that climbs a peak to gaze   20
O'er land and main, and sees a great black cloud
Drag inward from the deeps, a wall of night,
Blot out the slope of sea from verge to shore,
And suck the blinding splendor from the sand,
And quenching lake by lake and tarn by tarn

Expunge the world; so fared she gazing there,
So blacken'd all her world in secret, blank
And waste it seem'd and vain; till down she came,
And found fair peace once more among the sick.

And twilight dawn'd; and morn by morn the lark   30
Shot up and shrill'd in flickering gyres, but I
Lay silent in the muffled cage of life.
And twilight gloom'd, and broader-grown the bowers
Drew the great night into themselves, and heaven,
Star after star, arose and fell; but I,
Deeper than those weird doubts could reach me, lay
Quite sunder'd from the moving Universe,
Nor knew what eye was on me, nor the hand
That nursed me, more than infants in their sleep. . . .

But I lay still, and with me oft she sat.
Then came a change; for sometimes I would catch
Her hand in wild delirium, gripe it hard,
And fling it like a viper off, and shriek,
"You are not Ida;" clasp it once again,   80
And call her Ida, tho' I knew her not,
And call her sweet, as if in irony,
And call her hard and cold, which seem'd a truth;
And still she fear'd that I should lose my mind,
And often she believed that I should die;
Till out of long frustration of her care,
And pensive tendance in the all-weary noons,
And watches in the dead, the dark, when clocks
Throbb'd thunder thro' the palace floors, or call'd
On flying Time from all their silver tongues —   90
And out of memories of her kindlier days,
And sidelong glances at my father's grief,
And at the happy lovers heart in heart —
And out of hauntings of my spoken love,
And lonely listenings to my mutter'd dream,
And often feeling of the helpless hands,
And wordless broodings on the wasted cheek —
From all a closer interest flourish'd up,
Tenderness touch by touch, and last, to these,
Love, like an Alpine harebell hung with tears   100
By some cold morning glacier; frail at first
And feeble, all unconscious of itself,
But such as gather'd color day by day.

Last I woke sane, but well-nigh close to death
For weakness. It was evening; silent light
Slept on the painted walls, wherein were wrought
Two grand designs . . . .

I saw the forms; I knew not where I was.
They did but look like hollow shows; nor more
Sweet Ida. Palm to palm she sat; the dew   120
Dwelt in her eyes, and softer all her shape
And rounder seem'd. I moved. I sigh'd; a touch
Came round my wrist, and tears upon my hand.
Then all for languor and self-pity ran
Mine down my face, and with what life I had,
And like a flower that cannot all unfold,
So drench'd it is with tempest, to the sun,
Yet, as it may, turns toward him, I on her
Fixt my faint eyes, and utter'd whisperingly:

"If you be what I think you, some sweet dream,   130
I would but ask you to fulfil yourself;
But if you be that Ida whom I knew,
I ask you nothing; only, if a dream,
Sweet dream, be perfect. I shall die tonight.
Stoop down and seem to kiss me ere I die."

I could no more, but lay like one in trance,
That hears his burial talk'd of by his friends,
And cannot speak, nor move, nor make one sign,
But lies and dreads his doom. She turn'd, she paused,
She stoop'd; and out of languor leapt a cry,   140
Leapt fiery Passion from the brinks of death,
And I believed that in the living world
My spirit closed wtih Ida's at the lips;
Till back I fell, and from mine arms she rose
Glowing all over noble shame; and all
Her falser self slipt from her like a robe,
And left her woman, lovelier in her mood
Than in her mould that other, when she came
From barren deeps to conquer all with love,
And down the streaming crystal dropt; and she   150
Far-fleeted by the purple island-sides,
Naked, a double light in air and wave,
To meet her Graces, where they deck'd her out
For worship without end — nor end of mine,
Stateliest, for thee! but mute she glided forth,

Nor glanced behind her, and I sank and slept,
Fill'd thro' and thro' with love, a happy sleep.

Deep in the night I woke: she, near me, held
A volume of the poets of her land.
There to herself, all in low tones, she read: 160

"Now sleeps the crimson petal, now the white;
Nor waves the cypress in the palace walk;
Nor winks the gold fin in the porphyry font.
The fire-fly wakens; waken thou with me.

"Now droops the milk-white peacock like a ghost,
And like a ghost she glimmers on to me.

"Now lies the Earth all Danaë to the stars,
And all thy heart lies open unto me.

"Now slides the silent meteor on, and leaves
A shining furrow, as thy thoughts in me. 170

"Now folds the lily all her sweetness up,
And slips into the bosom of the lake.
So fold thyself, my dearest, thou, and slip
Into my bosom and be lost in me."

I heard her turn the page; she found a small
Sweet idyl, and once more, as low, she read:

"Come down, O maid, from yonder mountain height.
What pleasure lives in height (the shepherd sang),
In height and cold, the splendor of the hills?
But cease to move so near the heavens, and cease 180
To glide a sunbeam by the blasted pine,
To sit a star upon the sparkling spire;
And come, for Love is of the valley, come,
For Love is of the valley, come thou down
And find him; by the happy threshold, he,
Or hand in hand with Plenty in the maize,
Or red with spirted purple of the vats,
Or foxlike in the vine; nor cares to walk
With Death and Morning on the Silver Horns,
Nor wilt thou snare him in the white ravine, 190
Nor find him dropt upon the firths of ice,
That huddling slant in furrow-cloven falls
To roll the torrent out of dusky doors.
But follow; let the torrent dance thee down

To find him in the valley; let the wild
Lean-headed eagles yelp alone, and leave
The monstrous ledges there to slope, and spill
Their thousand wreaths of dangling water-smoke,
That like a broken purpose waste in air.
So waste not thou, but come; for all the vales   200
Await thee; azure pillars of the hearth
Arise to thee; the children call, and I
Thy shepherd pipe, and sweet is every sound,
Sweeter thy voice, but every sound is sweet;
Myriads of rivulets hurrying thro' the lawn,
The moan of doves in immemorial elms,
And murmuring of innumerable bees."

So she low-toned, while with shut eyes I lay
Listening, then look'd. Pale was the perfect face;
The bosom with long sighs labor'd; and meek   210
Seem'd the full lips, and mild the luminous eyes,
And the voice trembled and the hand. She said
Brokenly, that she knew it, she had fail'd
In sweet humility, had fail'd in all;
That all her labor was but as a block
Left in the quarry; but she still were loth,
She still were loth to yield herself to one
That wholly scorn'd to help their equal rights
Against the sons of men and barbarous laws.
She pray'd me not to judge their cause from her   220
That wrong'd it, sought far less for truth than power
In knowledge. Something wild within her breast,
A greater than all knowledge, beat her down.
And she had nursed me there from week to week;
Much had she learnt in little time. In part
It was ill counsel had misled the girl
To vex true hearts; yet was she but a girl —
"Ah fool, and made myself a queen of farce!
When comes another such? never, I think,
Till the sun drop, dead, from the signs."
                              Her voice   230
Choked, and her forehead sank upon her hands,
And her great heart thro' all the faultful past
Went sorrowing in a pause I dared not break;
Till notice of a change in the dark world
Was lispt about the acacias, and a bird,
That early woke to feed her little ones,
Sent from a dewy breast a cry for light.
She moved, and at her feet the volume fell.

"Blame not thyself too much," I said, "nor blame
Too much the sons of men and barbarous laws;   240
These were the rough ways of the world till now.
Henceforth thou hast a helper, me, that know
The woman's cause is man's; they rise or sink
Together, dwarf'd or godlike, bond or free.
For she that out of Lethe scales with man
The shining steps of Nature, shares with man
His nights, his days, moves with him to one goal,
Stays all the fair young planet in her hands —
If she be small, slight-natured, miserable,
How shall men grow? but work no more alone!   250
Our place is much; as far as in us lies
We two will serve them both in aiding her —
Will clear away the parasitic forms
That seem to keep her up but drag her down —
Will leave her space to burgeon out of all
Within her — let her make herself her own
To give or keep, to live and learn and be
All that not harms distinctive womanhood.
For woman is not undevelopt man,
But diverse. Could we make her as the man,   260
Sweet Love were slain; his dearest bond is this,
Not like to like, but like in difference.
Yet in the long years liker must they grow;
The man be more of woman, she of man;
He gain in sweetness and in moral height,
Nor lose the wrestling thews that throw the world;
She mental breadth, nor fail in childward care,
Nor lose the childlike in the larger mind;
Till at the last she set herself to man,
Like perfect music unto noble words;   270
And so these twain, upon the skirts of Time,
Sit side by side, full-summ'd in all their powers,
Dispensing harvest, sowing the to-be,
Self-reverent each and reverencing each,
Distinct in individualities,
But like each other even as those who love.
Then comes the statelier Eden back to men;
Then reign the world's great bridals, chaste and calm;
Then springs the crowning race of humankind.
May these things be!"
                          Sighing she spoke: "I fear   280
They will not."
                    "Dear, but let us type them now

In our own lives, and this proud watchword rest
Of equal; seeing either sex alone
Is half itself, and in true marriage lies
Nor equal, nor unequal. Each fulfils
Defect in each, and always thought in thought,
Purpose in purpose, will in will, they grow,
The single pure and perfect animal,
The two-cell'd heart beating, with one full stroke,
Life."

  And again sighing she spoke: "A dream   290
That once was mine! what woman taught you this?"

  "Alone," I said, "from earlier than I know,
Immersed in rich foreshadowings of the world,
I loved the woman. He, that doth not, lives
A drowning life, besotted in sweet self,
Or pines in sad experience worse than death,
Or keeps his wing'd affections clipt with crime.
Yet was there one thro' whom I loved her, one
Not learned, save in gracious household ways,
Not perfect, nay, but full of tender wants,   300
No angel, but a dearer being, all dipt
In angel instincts, breathing Paradise,
Interpreter between the gods and men,
Who look'd all native to her place, and yet
On tiptoe seem'd to touch upon a sphere
Too gross to tread, and all male minds perforce
Sway'd to her from their orbits as they moved,
And girdled her with music. Happy he
With such a mother! faith in womankind
Beats with his blood, and trust in all things high   310
Comes easy to him, and tho' he trip and fall
He shall not blind his soul with clay."
             "But I,"
Said Ida, tremulously, "so all unlike —
It seems you love to cheat yourself with words;
This mother is your model. I have heard
Of your strange doubts; they well might be; I seem
A mockery to my own self. Never, Prince!
You cannot love me."
          "Nay, but thee," I said,
"From yearlong poring on thy pictured eyes,
Ere seen I loved, and loved thee seen, and saw   320
Thee woman thro' the crust of iron moods
That mask'd thee from men's reverence up, and forced

Sweet love on pranks of saucy boyhood; now,
Given back to life, to life indeed, thro' thee,
Indeed I love. The new day comes, the light
Dearer for night, as dearer thou for faults
Lived over. Lift thine eyes; my doubts are dead,
My haunting sense of hollow shows; the change,
This truthful change in thee has kill'd it. Dear,
Look up, and let thy nature strike on mine,   330
Like yonder morning on the blind half-world.
Approach and fear not; breathe upon my brows;
In that fine air I tremble, all the past
Melts mist-like into this bright hour, and this
Is morn to more, and all the rich to-come
Reels, as the golden Autumn woodland reels
Athwart the smoke of burning weeds. Forgive me,
I waste my heart in signs; let be. My bride,
My wife, my life! O, we will walk this world,
Yoked in all exercise of noble end,   340
And so thro' those dark gates across the wild
That no man knows. Indeed I love thee; come,
Yield thyself up; my hopes and thine are one.
Accomplish thou my manhood and thyself;
Lay thy sweet hands in mine and trust to me."

Conclusion

So closed our tale, of which I give you all
The random scheme as wildly as it rose.
The words are mostly mine; for when we ceased
There came a minute's pause, and Walter said,
"I wish she had not yielded!" then to me,
"What if you drest it up poetically!"
So pray'd the men, the women; I gave assent.
Yet how to bind the scatter'd scheme of seven
Together in one sheaf? What style could suit?
The men required that I should give throughout   10
The sort of mock-heroic gigantesque,
With which we banter'd little Lilia first;
The women — and perhaps they felt their power,
For something in the ballads which they sang,
Or in their silent influence as they sat,
Had ever seem'd to wrestle with burlesque,
And drove us, last, to quite a solemn close —
They hated banter, wish'd for something real,
A gallant fight, a noble princess — why

Not make her true-heroic — true-sublime?   20
Or all, they said, as earnest as the close?
Which yet with such a framework scarce could be.
Then rose a little feud betwixt the two,
Betwixt the mockers and the realists;
And I, betwixt them both, to please them both,
And yet to give the story as it rose,
I moved as in a strange diagonal,
And maybe neither pleased myself nor them. . . .

    But we went back to the Abbey, and sat on,
So much the gathering darkness charm'd; we sat
But spoke not, rapt in nameless reverie,
Perchance upon the future man. The walls
Blacken'd about us, bats wheel'd, and owls whoop'd,   110
And gradually the powers of the night,
That range above the region of the wind,
Deepening the courts of twilight broke them up
Thro' all the silent spaces of the worlds,
Beyond all thought into the heaven of heavens.

    Last little Lilia, rising quietly,
Disrobed the glimmering statue of Sir Ralph
From those rich silks, and home well-pleased we went.

1847, 1851*

IN MEMORIAM A. H. H.

OBIIT MDCCCXXXIII

Strong Son of God, immortal Love,
 Whom we, that have not seen thy face,
 By faith, and faith alone, embrace,
Believing where we cannot prove;

Thine are these orbs of light and shade;
 Thou madest Life in man and brute;
 Thou madest Death; and lo, thy foot
Is on the skull which thou hast made.

Thou wilt not leave us in the dust:
 Thou madest man, he knows not why,   10
 He thinks he was not made to die;
And thou hast made him: thou art just.

Thou seemest human and divine,
 The highest, holiest manhood, thou.
 Our wills are ours, we know not how;
Our wills are ours, to make them thine.

Our little systems have their day;
 They have their day and cease to be;
 They are but broken lights of thee,
And thou, O Lord, art more than they.   20

We have but faith: we cannot know,
 For knowledge is of things we see;
 And yet we trust it comes from thee,
A beam in darkness: let it grow.

Let knowledge grow from more to more,
 But more of reverence in us dwell;
 That mind and soul, according well,
May make one music as before,

But vaster. We are fools and slight;
 We mock thee when we do not fear: 30

178

But help thy foolish ones to bear;
Help thy vain worlds to bear thy light.

Forgive what seem'd my sin in me,
    What seem'd my worth since I began;
    For merit lives from man to man,
And not from man, O Lord, to thee.

Forgive my grief for one removed,
    Thy creature, whom I found so fair.
    I trust he lives in thee, and there
I find him worthier to be loved.   40

Forgive these wild and wandering cries,
    Confusions of a wasted youth;
    Forgive them where they fail in truth,
And in thy wisdom make me wise.

1849

I

I held it truth, with him who sings
    To one clear harp in divers tones,
    That men may rise on stepping-stones
Of their dead selves to higher things.

But who shall so forecast the years
    And find in loss a gain to match?
    Or reach a hand thro' time to catch
The far-off interest of tears?

Let Love clasp Grief lest both be drown'd,
    Let darkness keep her raven gloss.   10
    Ah, sweeter to be drunk with loss,
To dance with Death, to beat the ground,

Than that the victor Hours should scorn
    The long result of love, and boast,
    "Behold the man that loved and lost,
But all he was is overworn."

II

Old yew, which graspest at the stones
    That name the underlying dead,

Thy fibres net the dreamless head,
Thy roots are wrapt about the bones.

The seasons bring the flower again,
And bring the firstling to the flock;
And in the dusk of thee the clock
Beats out the little lives of men.

O, not for thee the glow, the bloom,
Who changest not in any gale,   10
Nor branding summer suns avail
To touch thy thousand years of gloom;

And gazing on thee, sullen tree,
Sick for thy stubborn hardihood,
I seem to fail from out my blood
And grow incorporate into thee.

III

O Sorrow, cruel fellowship,
O Priestess in the vaults of Death,
O sweet and bitter in a breath,
What whispers from thy lying lip?

"The stars," she whispers, "blindly run;
A web is woven across the sky;
From out waste places comes a cry,
And murmurs from the dying sun;

"And all the phantom, Nature, stands —
With all the music in her tone,   10
A hollow echo of my own, —
A hollow form with empty hands."

And shall I take a thing so blind,
Embrace her as my natural good;
Or crush her, like a vice of blood,
Upon the threshold of the mind?

IV

To Sleep I give my powers away;
My will is bondsman to the dark;
I sit within a helmless bark,
And with my heart I muse and say:

O heart, how fares it with thee now,
    That thou shouldst fail from thy desire,
    Who scarcely darest to inquire,
"What is it makes me beat so low?"

Something it is which thou hast lost,
    Some pleasure from thine early years.   10
    Break thou deep vase of chilling tears,
That grief hath shaken into frost!

Such clouds of nameless trouble cross
    All night below the darken'd eyes;
    With morning wakes the will, and cries,
"Thou shalt not be the fool of loss."

V

I sometimes hold it half a sin
    To put in words the grief I feel:
    For words, like Nature, half reveal
And half conceal the Soul within.

But, for the unquiet heart and brain,
    A use in measured language lies;
    The sad mechanic exercise,
Like dull narcotics, numbing pain.

In words, like weeds, I 'll wrap me o'er,
    Like coarsest clothes against the cold;   10
    But that large grief which these enfold
Is given in outline and no more.

VI

One writes, that "other friends remain,"
    That "loss is common to the race" —
    And common is the commonplace,
And vacant chaff well meant for grain.

That loss is common would not make
    My own less bitter, rather more.
    Too common! Never morning wore
To evening, but some heart did break.

O father, wheresoe'er thou be,
    Who pledgest now thy gallant son,   10
    A shot, ere half thy draught be done,
Hath still'd the life that beat from thee.

O mother, praying God will save
    Thy sailor, — while thy head is bow'd,
    His heavy-shotted hammock-shroud
Drops in his vast and wandering grave.

Ye know no more than I who wrought
    At that last hour to please him well;
    Who mused on all I had to tell,
And something written, something thought;   20

Expecting still his advent home;
    And ever met him on his way
    With wishes, thinking, "here to-day,"
Or "here to-morrow will he come."

O, somewhere, meek, unconscious dove,
    That sittest ranging golden hair;
    And glad to find thyself so fair,
Poor child, that waitest for thy love!

For now her father's chimney glows
    In expectation of a guest;   30
    And thinking "this will please him best,"
She takes a riband or a rose,

For he will see them on to-night;
    And with the thought her color burns;
    And, having left the glass, she turns
Once more to set a ringlet right;

And, even when she turn'd, the curse
    Had fallen, and her future lord
    Was drown'd in passing thro' the ford,
Or kill'd in falling from his horse.   40

O, what to her shall be the end?
    And what to me remains of good?
    To her perpetual maidenhood,
And unto me no second friend.

VII

Dark house, by which once more I stand
    Here in the long unlovely street,
    Doors, where my heart was used to beat
So quickly, waiting for a hand,

A hand that can be clasp'd no more —
  Behold me, for I cannot sleep,
  And like a guilty thing I creep
At earliest morning to the door.

He is not here; but far away
  The noise of life begins again,   10
  And ghastly thro' the drizzling rain
On the bald street breaks the blank day.

VIII

A happy lover who has come
  To look on her that loves him well,
  Who 'lights and rings the gateway bell,
And learns her gone and far from home;

He saddens, all the magic light
  Dies off at once from bower and hall,
  And all the place is dark, and all
The chambers emptied of delight:

So find I every pleasant spot
  In which we two were wont to meet,   10
  The field, the chamber, and the street,
For all is dark where thou art not.

Yet as that other, wandering there
  In those deserted walks, may find
  A flower beat with rain and wind,
Which once she foster'd up with care;

So seems it in my deep regret,
  O my forsaken heart, with thee
  And this poor flower of poesy
Which, little cared for, fades not yet.   20

But since it pleased a vanish'd eye,
  I go to plant it on his tomb,
  That if it can it there may bloom,
Or, dying, there at least may die.

IX

Fair ship, that from the Italian shore
  Sailest the placid ocean-plains
  With my lost Arthur's loved remains,
Spread thy full wings, and waft him o'er.

So draw him home to those that mourn
  In vain; a favorable speed
  Ruffle thy mirror'd mast, and lead
Thro' prosperous floods his holy urn.

All night no ruder air perplex
  Thy sliding keel, till Phosphor, bright   10
  As our pure love, thro' early light
Shall glimmer on the dewy decks.

Sphere all your lights around, above;
  Sleep, gentle heavens, before the prow;
  Sleep, gentle winds, as he sleeps now,
My friend, the brother of my love;

My Arthur, whom I shall not see
  Till all my widow'd race be run;
  Dear as the mother to the son,
More than my brothers are to me.   20

x

I hear the noise about thy keel;
  I hear the bell struck in the night;
  I see the cabin-window bright;
I see the sailor at the wheel.

Thou bring'st the sailor to his wife,
  And travell'd men from foreign lands;
  And letters unto trembling hands;
And, thy dark freight, a vanish'd life.

So bring him; we have idle dreams;
  This look of quiet flatters thus   10
  Our home-bred fancies. O, to us,
The fools of habit, sweeter seems

To rest beneath the clover sod,
  That takes the sunshine and the rains,
  Or where the kneeling hamlet drains
The chalice of the grapes of God;

Than if with thee the roaring wells
  Should gulf him fathom-deep in brine,
  And hands so often clasp'd in mine,
Should toss with tangle and with shells.   20

XI

Calm is the morn without a sound,
    Calm as to suit a calmer grief,
    And only thro' the faded leaf
The chestnut pattering to the ground;

Calm and deep peace on this high wold,
    And on these dews that drench the furze,
    And all the silvery gossamers
That twinkle into green and gold;

Calm and still light on yon great plain
    That sweeps with all its autumn bowers,   10
    And crowded farms and lessening towers,
To mingle with the bounding main;

Calm and deep peace in this wide air,
    These leaves that redden to the fall,
    And in my heart, if calm at all,
If any calm, a calm despair;

Calm on the seas, and silver sleep,
    And waves that sway themselves in rest,
    And dead calm in that noble breast
Which heaves but with the heaving deep.   20

XII

Lo, as a dove when up she springs
    To bear thro' heaven a tale of woe,
    Some dolorous message knit below
The wild pulsation of her wings;

Like her I go, I cannot stay;
    I leave this mortal ark behind,
    A weight of nerves without a mind,
And leave the cliffs, and haste away

O'er ocean-mirrors rounded large,
    And reach the glow of southern skies,   10
    And see the sails at distance rise,
And linger weeping on the marge,

And saying, "Comes he thus, my friend?
    Is this the end of all my care?"
    And circle moaning in the air,
"Is this the end? Is this the end?"

And forward dart again, and play
    About the prow, and back return
    To where the body sits, and learn
That I have been an hour away.   20

XIII

Tears of the widower, when he sees
    A late-lost form that sleep reveals,
    And moves his doubtful arms, and feels
Her place is empty, fall like these;

Which weep a loss for ever new,
    A void where heart on heart reposed;
    And, where warm hands have prest and closed,
Silence, till I be silent too;

Which weep the comrade of my choice,
    An awful thought, a life removed,   10
    The human-hearted man I loved,
A Spirit, not a breathing voice.

Come, Time, and teach me, many years,
    I do not suffer in a dream;
    For now so strange do these things seem,
Mine eyes have leisure for their tears,

My fancies time to rise on wing,
    And glance about the approaching sails,
    As tho' they brought but merchants' bales,
And not the burthen that they bring.   20

XIV

If one should bring me this report,
    That thou hadst touch'd the land to-day,
    And I went down unto the quay,
And found thee lying in the port;

And standing, muffled round with woe,
    Should see thy passengers in rank
    Come stepping lightly down the plank
And beckoning unto those they know;

And if along with these should come
    The man I held as half-divine,   10
    Should strike a sudden hand in mine,
And ask a thousand things of home;

And I should tell him all my pain,
    And how my life had droop'd of late,
    And he should sorrow o'er my state
And marvel what possess'd my brain;

And I perceived no touch of change,
    No hint of death in all his frame,
    But found him all in all the same,
I should not feel it to be strange.   20

xv

To-night the winds begin to rise
    And roar from yonder dropping day;
    The last red leaf is whirl'd away,
The rooks are blown about the skies;

The forest crack'd, the waters curl'd,
    The cattle huddled on the lea;
    And wildly dash'd on tower and tree
The sunbeam strikes along the world:

And but for fancies, which aver
    That all thy motions gently pass   10
    Athwart a plane of molten glass,
I scarce could brook the strain and stir

That makes the barren branches loud;
    And but for fear it is not so,
    The wild unrest that lives in woe
Would dote and pore on yonder cloud

That rises upward always higher,
    And onward drags a laboring breast,
    And topples round the dreary west,
A looming bastion fringed with fire.   20

xvi

What words are these have fallen from me?
    Can calm despair and wild unrest
    Be tenants of a single breast,
Or Sorrow such a changeling be?

Or doth she only seem to take
    The touch of change in calm or storm,
    But knows no more of transient form
In her deep self, than some dead lake

That holds the shadow of a lark
  Hung in the shadow of a heaven?
  Or has the shock, so harshly given,
Confused me like the unhappy bark   10

That strikes by night a craggy shelf,
  And staggers blindly ere she sink?
  And stunn'd me from my power to think
And all my knowledge of myself;

And made me that delirious man
  Whose fancy fuses old and new,
  And flashes into false and true,
And mingles all without a plan?   20

XVII

Thou comest, much wept for; such a breeze
  Compell'd thy canvas, and my prayer
  Was as the whisper of an air
To breathe thee over lonely seas.

For I in spirit saw thee move
  Thro' circles of the bounding sky,
  Week after week; the days go by;
Come quick, thou bringest all I love.

Henceforth, wherever thou mayst roam,
  My blessing, like a line of light,   10
  Is on the waters day and night,
And like a beacon guards thee home.

So may whatever tempest mars
  Mid-ocean spare thee, sacred bark,
  And balmy drops in summer dark
Slide from the bosom of the stars;

So kind an office hath been done,
  Such precious relics brought by thee,
  The dust of him I shall not see
Till all my widow'd race be run.   20

XVIII

'T is well; 't is something; we may stand
  Where he in English earth is laid,
  And from his ashes may be made
The violet of his native land.

'T is little; but it looks in truth
 As if the quiet bones were blest
 Among familiar names to rest
And in the places of his youth.

Come then, pure hands, and bear the head
 That sleeps or wears the mask of sleep, 10
 And come, whatever loves to weep,
And hear the ritual of the dead.

Ah yet, even yet, if this might be,
 I, falling on his faithful heart,
 Would breathing thro' his lips impart
The life that almost dies in me;

That dies not, but endures with pain,
 And slowly forms the firmer mind,
 Treasuring the look it cannot find,
The words that are not heard again. 20

XIX

The Danube to the Severn gave
 The darken'd heart that beat no more;
 They laid him by the pleasant shore,
And in the hearing of the wave.

There twice a day the Severn fills;
 The salt sea-water passes by,
 And hushes half the babbling Wye,
And makes a silence in the hills.

The Wye is hush'd nor moved along,
 And hush'd my deepest grief of all, 10
 When fill'd with tears that cannot fall,
I brim with sorrow drowning song.

The tide flows down, the wave again
 Is vocal in its wooded walls;
 My deeper anguish also falls,
And I can speak a little then.

XX

The lesser griefs that may be said,
 That breathe a thousand tender vows,
 Are but as servants in a house
Where lies the master newly dead;

Who speak their feeling as it is,
    And weep the fulness from the mind.
    "It will be hard," they say, "to find
Another service such as this."

My lighter moods are like to these,
    That out of words a comfort win;   10
    But there are other griefs within,
And tears that at their fountain freeze;

For by the hearth the children sit
    Cold in that atmosphere of death,
    And scarce endure to draw the breath,
Or like to noiseless phantoms flit;

But open converse is there none,
    So much the vital spirits sink
    To see the vacant chair, and think,
"How good! how kind! and he is gone."   20

XXI

I sing to him that rests below,
    And, since the grasses round me wave,
    I take the grasses of the grave,
And make them pipes whereon to blow.

The traveller hears me now and then,
    And sometimes harshly will he speak:
    "This fellow would make weakness weak,
And melt the waxen hearts of men."

Another answers: "Let him be,
    He loves to make parade of pain,   10
    That with his piping he may gain
The praise that comes to constancy."

A third is wroth: "Is this an hour
    For private sorrow's barren song,
    When more and more the people throng
The chairs and thrones of civil power?

"A time to sicken and to swoon,
    When Science reaches forth her arms
    To feel from world to world, and charms
Her secret from the latest moon?"   20

Behold, ye speak an idle thing;
    Ye never knew the sacred dust.
    I do but sing because I must,
And pipe but as the linnets sing;

And one is glad; her note is gay,
    For now her little ones have ranged;
    And one is sad; her note is changed,
Because her brood is stolen away.

XXII

The path by which we twain did go,
    Which led by tracts that pleased us well,
    Thro' four sweet years arose and fell,
From flower to flower, from snow to snow;

And we with singing cheer'd the way,
    And, crown'd with all the season lent,
    From April on to April went,
And glad at heart from May to May.

But where the path we walk'd began
    To slant the fifth autumnal slope,   **10**
    As we descended following Hope,
There sat the Shadow fear'd of man;

Who broke our fair companionship,
    And spread his mantle dark and cold,
    And wrapt thee formless in the fold,
And dull'd the murmur on thy lip,

And bore thee where I could not see
    Nor follow, tho' I walk in haste,
    And think that somewhere in the waste
The Shadow sits and waits for me.   **20**

XXIII

Now, sometimes in my sorrow shut,
    Or breaking into song by fits,
    Alone, alone, to where he sits,
The Shadow cloak'd from head to foot,

Who keeps the keys of all the creeds,
    I wander, often falling lame,
    And looking back to whence I came,
Or on to where the pathway leads;

And crying, How changed from where it ran
   Thro' lands where not a leaf was dumb,   **10**
   But all the lavish hills would hum
The murmur of a happy Pan;

When each by turns was guide to each,
   And Fancy light from Fancy caught,
   And Thought leapt out to wed with Thought
Ere Thought could wed itself with Speech;

And all we met was fair and good,
   And all was good that Time could bring,
   And all the secret of the Spring
Moved in the chambers of the blood;   **20**

And many an old philosophy
   On Argive heights divinely sang,
   And round us all the thicket rang
To many a flute of Arcady.

XXIV

And was the day of my delight
   As pure and perfect as I say?
   The very source and fount of day
Is dash'd with wandering isles of night.

If all was good and fair we met,
   This earth had been the Paradise
   It never look'd to human eyes
Since our first sun arose and set.

And is it that the haze of grief
   Makes former gladness loom so great?   **10**
   The lowness of the present state,
That sets the past in this relief?

Or that the past will always win
   A glory from its being far,
   And orb into the perfect star
We saw not when we moved therein?

XXV

I know that this was Life, — the track
   Whereon with equal feet we fared;
   And then, as now, the day prepared
The daily burden for the back.

But this it was that made me move
 As light as carrier-birds in air;
 I loved the weight I had to bear,
Because it needed help of Love;

Nor could I weary, heart or limb,
 When mighty Love would cleave in twain   10
 The lading of a single pain,
And part it, giving half to him.

XXVI

Still onward winds the dreary way;
 I with it, for I long to prove
 No lapse of moons can canker Love,
Whatever fickle tongues may say.

And if that eye which watches guilt
 And goodness, and hath power to see
 Within the green the moulder'd tree,
And towers fallen as soon as built —

O, if indeed that eye foresee
 Or see — in Him is no before —   10
 In more of life true life no more
And Love the indifference to be,

Then might I find, ere yet the morn
 Breaks hither over Indian seas,
 That Shadow waiting with the keys,
To shroud me from my proper scorn.

XXVII

I envy not in any moods
 The captive void of noble rage,
 The linnet born within the cage,
That never knew the summer woods;

I envy not the beast that takes
 His license in the field of time,
 Unfetter'd by the sense of crime,
To whom a conscience never wakes;

Nor, what may count itself as blest,
 The heart that never plighted troth   10
 But stagnates in the weeds of sloth:
Nor any want-begotten rest.

I hold it true, whate'er befall;
   I feel it, when I sorrow most;
   'T is better to have loved and lost
Than never to have loved at all.

XXVIII

The time draws near the birth of Christ.
   The moon is hid, the night is still;
   The Christmas bells from hill to hill
Answer each other in the mist.

Four voices of four hamlets round,
   From far and near, on mead and moor,
   Swell out and fail, as if a door
Were shut between me and the sound;

Each voice four changes on the wind,
   That now dilate, and now decrease,   **10**
   Peace and goodwill, goodwill and peace,
Peace and goodwill, to all mankind.

This year I slept and woke with pain,
   I almost wish'd no more to wake,
   And that my hold on life would break
Before I heard those bells again;

But they my troubled spirit rule,
   For they controll'd me when a boy;
   They bring me sorrow touch'd with joy,
The merry, merry bells of Yule.   **20**

XXIX

With such compelling cause to grieve
   As daily vexes household peace,
   And chains regret to his decease,
How dare we keep our Christmas-eve,

Which brings no more a welcome guest
   To enrich the threshold of the night
   With shower'd largess of delight
In dance and song and game and jest?

Yet go, and while the holly boughs
   Entwine the cold baptismal font,   **10**
   Make one wreath more for Use and Wont,
That guard the portals of the house;

Old sisters of a day gone by,
   Gray nurses, loving nothing new —
   Why should they miss their yearly due
Before their time? They too will die.

XXX

With trembling fingers did we weave
   The holly round the Christmas hearth;
   A rainy cloud possess'd the earth,
And sadly fell our Christmas-eve.

At our old pastimes in the hall
   We gamboll'd, making vain pretence
   Of gladness, with an awful sense
Of one mute Shadow watching all.

We paused: the winds were in the beech;
   We heard them sweep the winter land;   10
   And in a circle hand-in-hand
Sat silent, looking each at each.

Then echo-like our voices rang;
   We sung, tho' every eye was dim,
   A merry song we sang with him
Last year; impetuously we sang.

We ceased; a gentler feeling crept
   Upon us: surely rest is meet.
   "They rest," we said, "their sleep is sweet,"
And silence follow'd, and we wept.   20

Our voices took a higher range;
   Once more we sang: "They do not die
   Nor lose their mortal sympathy,
Nor change to us, although they change;

"Rapt from the fickle and the frail
   With gather'd power, yet the same,
   Pierces the keen seraphic flame
From orb to orb, from veil to veil."

Rise, happy morn, rise, holy morn,
   Draw forth the cheerful day from night: 30
   O Father, touch the east, and light
The light that shone when Hope was born.

XXXI

When Lazarus left his charnel-cave,
  And home to Mary's house return'd,
  Was this demanded — if he yearn'd
To hear her weeping by his grave?

"Where wert thou, brother, those four days?"
  There lives no record of reply,
  Which telling what it is to die
Had surely added praise to praise.

From every house the neighbors met,
  The streets were fill'd with joyful sound,   10
  A solemn gladness even crown'd
The purple brows of Olivet.

Behold a man raised up by Christ!
  The rest remaineth unreveal'd;
  He told it not, or something seal'd
The lips of that Evangelist.

XXXII

Her eyes are homes of silent prayer,
  Nor other thought, her mind admits
  But, he was dead, and there he sits,
And he that brought him back is there.

Then one deep love doth supersede
  All other, when her ardent gaze
  Roves from the living brother's face,
And rests upon the Life indeed.

All subtle thought, all curious fears,
  Borne down by gladness so complete,   10
  She bows, she bathes the Saviour's feet
With costly spikenard and with tears.

Thrice blest whose lives are faithful prayers,
  Whose loves in higher love endure;
  What souls possess themselves so pure,
Or is there blessedness like theirs?

XXXIII

O thou that after toil and storm
  Mayst seem to have reach'd a purer air,

Whose faith has centre everywhere,
Nor cares to fix itself to form,

Leave thou thy sister when she prays
   Her early heaven, her happy views;
   Nor thou with shadow'd hint confuse
A life that leads melodious days.

Her faith thro' form is pure as thine,
   Her hands are quicker unto good.   10
   O, sacred be the flesh and blood
To which she links a truth divine!

See thou, that countest reason ripe
   In holding by the law within,
   Thou fail not in a world of sin,
And even for want of such a type.

XXXIV

My own dim life should teach me this,
   That life shall live for evermore,
   Else earth is darkness at the core,
And dust and ashes all that is;

This round of green, this orb of flame,
   Fantastic beauty; such as lurks
   In some wild poet, when he works
Without a conscience or an aim.

What then were God to such as I?
   'T were hardly worth my while to choose   10
   Of things all mortal, or to use
A little patience ere I die;

'T were best at once to sink to peace,
   Like birds the charming serpent draws,
   To drop head-foremost in the jaws
Of vacant darkness and to cease.

XXXV

Yet if some voice that man could trust
   Should murmur from the narrow house,
   "The cheeks drop in, the body bows;
Man dies, nor is there hope in dust;"

Might I not say? "Yet even here,
 But for one hour, O Love, I strive
 To keep so sweet a thing alive."
But I should turn mine ears and hear

The moanings of the homeless sea,
 The sound of streams that swift or slow   10
 Draw down Æonian hills, and sow
The dust of continents to be;

And Love would answer with a sigh,
 "The sound of that forgetful shore
 Will change my sweetness more and more,
Half-dead to know that I shall die."

O me, what profits it to put
 An idle case? If Death were seen
 At first as Death, Love had not been,
Or been in narrowest working shut,   20

Mere fellowship of sluggish moods,
 Or in his coarsest Satyr-shape
 Had bruised the herb and crush'd the grape,
And bask'd and batten'd in the woods.

XXXVI

Tho' truths in manhood darkly join,
 Deep-seated in our mystic frame,
 We yield all blessing to the name
Of Him that made them current coin;

For Wisdom dealt with mortal powers,
 Where truth in closest words shall fail,
 When truth embodied in a tale
Shall enter in at lowly doors.

And so the Word had breath, and wrought
 With human hands the creed of creeds   10
 In loveliness of perfect deeds,
More strong than all poetic thought;

Which he may read that binds the sheaf,
 Or builds the house, or digs the grave,
 And those wild eyes that watch the wave
In roarings round the coral reef.

XXXVII

Urania speaks with darken'd brow:
  "Thou pratest here where thou art least;
  This faith has many a purer priest,
And many an abler voice than thou.

"Go down beside thy native rill,
  On thy Parnassus set thy feet,
  And hear thy laurel whisper sweet
About the ledges of the hill."

And my Melpomene replies,
  A touch of shame upon her cheek: 10
  "I am not worthy even to speak
Of thy prevailing mysteries;

"For I am but an earthly Muse,
  And owning but a little art
  To lull with song an aching heart,
And render human love his dues;

"But brooding on the dear one dead,
  And all he said of things divine, —
  And dear to me as sacred wine
To dying lips is all he said, —   20

"I murmur'd, as I came along,
  Of comfort clasp'd in truth reveal'd,
  And loiter'd in the master's field,
And darken'd sanctities with song."

XXXVIII

With weary steps I loiter on,
  Tho' always under alter'd skies
  The purple from the distance dies,
My prospect and horizon gone.

No joy the blowing season gives,
  The herald melodies of spring,
  But in the songs I love to sing
A doubtful gleam of solace lives.

If any care for what is here
  Survive in spirits render'd free,   10
  Then are these songs I sing of thee
Not all ungrateful to thine ear.

XXXIX

Old warder of these buried bones,
    And answering now my random stroke
    With fruitful cloud and living smoke,
Dark yew, that graspest at the stones

And dippest toward the dreamless head,
    To thee too comes the golden hour
    When flower is feeling after flower;
But Sorrow, — fixt upon the dead,

And darkening the dark graves of men, —
    What whisper'd from her lying lips?   10
    Thy gloom is kindled at the tips,
And passes into gloom again.

XL

Could we forget the widow'd hour
    And look on Spirits breathed away,
    As on a maiden in the day
When first she wears her orange-flower!

When crown'd with blessing she doth rise
    To take her latest leave of home,
    And hopes and light regrets that come
Make April of her tender eyes;

And doubtful joys the father move,
    And tears are on the mother's face,   10
    As parting with a long embrace
She enters other realms of love;

Her office there to rear, to teach,
    Becoming as is meet and fit
    A link among the days, to knit
The generations each with each;

And, doubtless, unto thee is given
    A life that bears immortal fruit
    In those great offices that suit
The full-grown energies of heaven.   20

Ay me, the difference I discern!
    How often shall her old fireside
    Be cheer'd with tidings of the bride,
How often she herself return,

And tell them all they would have told,
   And bring her babe, and make her boast,
   Till even those that miss'd her most
Shall count new things as dear as old;

But thou and I have shaken hands,
   Till growing winters lay me low;
   My paths are in the fields I know,
And thine in undiscover'd lands.   30

XLI

Thy spirit ere our fatal loss
   Did ever rise from high to higher,
   As mounts the heavenward altar-fire,
As flies the lighter thro' the gross.

But thou art turn'd to something strange,
   And I have lost the links that bound
   Thy changes; here upon the ground,
No more partaker of thy change.

Deep folly! yet that this could be —
   That I could wing my will with might   10
   To leap the grades of life and light,
And flash at once, my friend, to thee!

For tho' my nature rarely yields
   To that vague fear implied in death,
   Nor shudders at the gulfs beneath,
The howlings from forgotten fields;

Yet oft when sundown skirts the moor
   An inner trouble I behold,
   A spectral doubt which makes me cold,
That I shall be thy mate no more,   20

Tho' following with an upward mind
   The wonders that have come to thee,
   Thro' all the secular to-be,
But evermore a life behind.

XLII

I vex my heart with fancies dim.
   He still outstript me in the race;
   It was but unity of place
That made me dream I rank'd with him.

And so may Place retain us still,
    And he the much-beloved again,
    A lord of large experience, train
To riper growth the mind and will;

And what delights can equal those
    That stir the spirit's inner deeps,
    When one that loves, but knows not, reaps   10
A truth from one that loves and knows?

XLIII

If Sleep and Death be truly one,
    And every spirit's folded bloom
    Thro' all its intervital gloom
In some long trance should slumber on;

Unconscious of the sliding hour,
    Bare of the body, might it last,
    And silent traces of the past
Be all the color of the flower:

So then were nothing lost to man;
    So that still garden of the souls   10
    In many a figured leaf enrolls
The total world since life began;

And love will last as pure and whole
    As when he loved me here in Time,
    And at the spiritual prime
Rewaken with the dawning soul.

XLIV

How fares it with the happy dead?
    For here the man is more and more;
    But he forgets the days before
God shut the doorways of his head.

The days have vanish'd, tone and tint,
    And yet perhaps the hoarding sense
    Gives out at times — he knows not whence —
A little flash, a mystic hint;

And in the long harmonious years —
    If Death so taste Lethean springs —   10
    May some dim touch of earthly things
Surprise thee ranging with thy peers.

If such a dreamy touch should fall,
   O, turn thee round, resolve the doubt;
   My guardian angel will speak out
In that high place, and tell thee all.

XLV

The baby new to earth and sky,
   What time his tender palm is prest
   Against the circle of the breast,
Has never thought that "this is I;"

But as he grows he gathers much,
   And learns the use of "I" and "me,"
   And finds "I am not what I see,
And other than the things I touch."

So rounds he to a separate mind
   From whence clear memory may begin,   10
   As thro' the frame that binds him in
His isolation grows defined.

This use may lie in blood and breath,
   Which else were fruitless of their due,
   Had man to learn himself anew
Beyond the second birth of death.

XLVI

We ranging down this lower track,
   The path we came by, thorn and flower,
   Is shadow'd by the growing hour,
Lest life should fail in looking back.

So be it: there no shade can last
   In that deep dawn behind the tomb,
   But clear from marge to marge shall bloom
The eternal landscape of the past;

A lifelong tract of time reveal'd,
   The fruitful hours of still increase;   10
   Days order'd in a wealthy peace,
And those five years its richest field.

O Love, thy province were not large,
   A bounded field, nor stretching far;
   Look also, Love, a brooding star,
A rosy warmth from marge to marge.

XLVII

That each, who seems a separate whole,
   Should move his rounds, and fusing all
   The skirts of self again, should fall
Remerging in the general Soul,

Is faith as vague as all unsweet.
   Eternal form shall still divide
   The eternal soul from all beside;
And I shall know him when we meet;

And we shall sit at endless feast,
   Enjoying each the other's good.
   What vaster dream can hit the mood   10
Of Love on earth? He seeks at least

Upon the last and sharpest height,
   Before the spirits fade away,
   Some landing-place, to clasp and say,
"Farewell! We lose ourselves in light."

XLVIII

If these brief lays, of Sorrow born,
   Were taken to be such as closed
   Grave doubts and answers here proposed,
Then these were such as men might scorn.

Her care is not to part and prove;
   She takes, when harsher moods remit,
   What slender shade of doubt may flit,
And makes it vassal unto love;

And hence, indeed, she sports with words,
   But better serves a wholesome law,
   And holds it sin and shame to draw   10
The deepest measure from the chords;

Nor dare she trust a larger lay,
   But rather loosens from the lip
   Short swallow-flights of song, that dip
Their wings in tears, and skim away.

XLIX

From art, from nature, from the schools,
   Let random influences glance,

Like light in many a shiver'd lance
That breaks about the dappled pools.

The lightest wave of thought shall lisp,
    The fancy's tenderest eddy wreathe,
    The slightest air of song shall breathe
To make the sullen surface crisp.

And look thy look, and go thy way,
    But blame not thou the winds that make   10
    The seeming-wanton ripple break,
The tender-pencill'd shadow play.

Beneath all fancied hopes and fears
    Ay me, the sorrow deepens down,
    Whose muffled motions blindly drown
The bases of my life in tears.

L

Be near me when my light is low,
    When the blood creeps, and the nerves prick
    And tingle; and the heart is sick,
And all the wheels of being slow.

Be near me when the sensuous frame
    Is rack'd with pangs that conquer trust;
    And Time, a maniac scattering dust,
And Life, a Fury slinging flame.

Be near me when my faith is dry,
    And men the flies of latter spring,   10
    That lay their eggs, and sting and sing
And weave their petty cells and die.

Be near me when I fade away,
    To point the term of human strife,
    And on the low dark verge of life
The twilight of eternal day.

LI

Do we indeed desire the dead
    Should still be near us at our side?
    Is there no baseness we would hide?
No inner vileness that we dread?

Shall he for whose applause I strove,
    I had such reverence for his blame,
    See with clear eye some hidden shame
And I be lessen'd in his love?

I wrong the grave with fears untrue.
    Shall love be blamed for want of faith?   10
    There must be wisdom with great Death;
The dead shall look me thro' and thro'.

Be near us when we climb or fall;
    Ye watch, like God, the rolling hours
    With larger other eyes than ours,
To make allowance for us all.

LII

I cannot love thee as I ought,
    For love reflects the thing beloved;
    My words are only words, and moved
Upon the topmost froth of thought.

"Yet blame not thou thy plaintive song,"
    The Spirit of true love replied;
    "Thou canst not move me from thy side,
Nor human frailty do me wrong.

"What keeps a spirit wholly true
    To that ideal which he bears?   10
    What record? not the sinless years
That breathed beneath the Syrian blue;

"So fret not, like an idle girl,
    That life is dash'd with flecks of sin.
    Abide; thy wealth is gather'd in,
When Time hath sunder'd shell from pearl."

LIII

How many a father have I seen,
    A sober man, among his boys,
    Whose youth was full of foolish noise,
Who wears his manhood hale and green;

And dare we to this fancy give,
    That had the wild oat not been sown,
    The soil, left barren, scarce had grown
The grain by which a man may live?

Or, if we held the doctrine sound
   For life outliving heats of youth,   10
   Yet who would preach it as a truth
To those that eddy round and round?

Hold thou the good, define it well;
   For fear divine Philosophy
   Should push beyond her mark, and be
Procuress to the Lords of Hell.

LIV

O, yet we trust that somehow good
   Will be the final goal of ill,
   To pangs of nature, sins of will,
Defects of doubt, and taints of blood;

That nothing walks with aimless feet;
   That not one life shall be destroy'd,
   Or cast as rubbish to the void,
When God hath made the pile complete;

That not a worm is cloven in vain;
   That not a moth with vain desire   10
   Is shrivell'd in a fruitless fire,
Or but subserves another's gain.

Behold, we know not anything;
   I can but trust that good shall fall
   At last — far off — at last, to all,
And every winter change to spring.

So runs my dream; but what am I?
   An infant crying in the night;
   An infant crying for the light,
And with no language but a cry.   20

LV

The wish, that of the living whole
   No life may fail beyond the grave,
   Derives it not from what we have
The likest God within the soul?

Are God and Nature then at strife,
   That Nature lends such evil dreams?
   So careful of the type she seems,
So careless of the single life,

That I, considering everywhere
    Her secret meaning in her deeds,   10
    And finding that of fifty seeds
She often brings but one to bear,

I falter where I firmly trod,
    And falling with my weight of cares
    Upon the great world's altar-stairs
That slope thro' darkness up to God,

I stretch lame hands of faith, and grope,
    And gather dust and chaff, and call
    To what I feel is Lord of all,
And faintly trust the larger hope.   20

LVI

"So careful of the type?" but no.
    From scarped cliff and quarried stone
    She cries, "A thousand types are gone;
I care for nothing, all shall go.

"Thou makest thine appeal to me.
    I bring to life, I bring to death;
    The spirit does but mean the breath:
I know no more." And he, shall he,

Man, her last work, who seem'd so fair,
    Such splendid purpose in his eyes,   10
    Who roll'd the psalm to wintry skies,
Who built him fanes of fruitless prayer,

Who trusted God was love indeed
    And love Creation's final law —
    Tho' Nature, red in tooth and claw
With ravine, shriek'd against his creed —

Who loved, who suffer'd countless ills,
    Who battled for the True, the Just,
    Be blown about the desert dust,
Or seal'd within the iron hills?   20

No more? A monster then, a dream,
    A discord. Dragons of the prime,
    That tare each other in their slime,
Were mellow music match'd with him.

O life as futile, then, as frail!
　　O for thy voice to soothe and bless!
　　What hope of answer, or redress?
Behind the veil, behind the veil.

LVII

Peace; come away: the song of woe
　　Is after all an earthly song.
　　Peace; come away: we do him wrong
To sing so wildly: let us go.

Come; let us go: your cheeks are pale;
　　But half my life I leave behind.
　　Methinks my friend is richly shrined;
But I shall pass, my work will fail.

Yet in these ears, till hearing dies,
　　One set slow bell will seem to toll　　　　　10
　　The passing of the sweetest soul
That ever look'd with human eyes.

I hear it now, and o'er and o'er,
　　Eternal greetings to the dead;
　　And "Ave, Ave, Ave," said,
"Adieu, adieu," for evermore.

LVIII

In those sad words I took farewell.
　　Like echoes in sepulchral halls,
　　As drop by drop the water falls
In vaults and catacombs, they fell;

And, falling, idly broke the peace
　　Of hearts that beat from day to day,
　　Half-conscious of their dying clay,
And those cold crypts where they shall cease.

The high Muse answer'd: "Wherefore grieve
　　Thy brethren with a fruitless tear?　　　　　10
　　Abide a little longer here,
And thou shalt take a nobler leave."

LIX

O Sorrow, wilt thou live with me
　　No casual mistress, but a wife,

My bosom-friend and half of life;
As I confess it needs must be?

O Sorrow, wilt thou rule my blood,
   Be sometimes lovely like a bride,
   And put thy harsher moods aside,
If thou wilt have me wise and good?

My centred passion cannot move,
   Nor will it lessen from to-day;
   But I'll have leave at times to play   10
As with the creature of my love;

And set thee forth, for thou art mine,
   With so much hope for years to come,
   That, howsoe'er I know thee, some
Could hardly tell what name were thine.

LX

He past, a soul of nobler tone;
   My spirit loved and loves him yet,
   Like some poor girl whose heart is set
On one whose rank exceeds her own.

He mixing with his proper sphere,
   She finds the baseness of her lot,
   Half jealous of she knows not what,
And envying all that meet him there.

The little village looks forlorn;
   She sighs amid her narrow days,
   Moving about the household ways,   10
In that dark house where she was born.

The foolish neighbors come and go,
   And tease her till the day draws by;
   At night she weeps, "How vain am I!
How should he love a thing so low?"

LXI

If, in thy second state sublime,
   Thy ransom'd reason change replies
   With all the circle of the wise,
The perfect flower of human time;

And if thou cast thine eyes below,
   How dimly character'd and slight,
   How dwarf'd a growth of cold and night,
How blanch'd with darkness must I grow!

Yet turn thee to the doubtful shore,
   Where thy first form was made a man;   10
   I loved thee, Spirit, and love, nor can
The soul of Shakespeare love thee more.

LXII

Tho' if an eye that's downward cast
   Could make thee somewhat blench or fail,
   Then be my love an idle tale
And fading legend of the past;

And thou, as one that once declined,
   When he was little more than boy,
   On some unworthy heart with joy,
But lives to wed an equal mind,

And breathes a novel world, the while
   His other passion wholly dies,   10
   Or in the light of deeper eyes
Is matter for a flying smile.

LXIII

Yet pity for a horse o'er-driven,
   And love in which my hound has part
   Can hang no weight upon my heart
In its assumptions up to heaven;

And I am so much more than these,
   As thou, perchance, art more than I,
   And yet I spare them sympathy,
And I would set their pains at ease.

So mayst thou watch me where I weep,
   As, unto vaster motions bound,   10
   The circuits of thine orbit round
A higher height, a deeper deep.

LXIV

Dost thou look back on what hath been,
   As some divinely gifted man,

Whose life in low estate began
And on a simple village green;

Who breaks his birth's invidious bar,
    And grasps the skirts of happy chance,
    And breasts the blows of circumstance,
And grapples with his evil star;

Who makes by force his merit known
    And lives to clutch the golden keys,   10
    To mould a mighty state's decrees,
And shape the whisper of the throne;

And moving up from high to higher,
    Becomes on Fortune's crowning slope
    The pillar of a people's hope,
The centre of a world's desire;

Yet feels, as in a pensive dream,
    When all his active powers are still,
    A distant dearness in the hill,
A secret sweetness in the stream,   20

The limit of his narrower fate,
    While yet beside its vocal springs
    He play'd at counsellors and kings,
With one that was his earliest mate;

Who ploughs with pain his native lea
    And reaps the labor of his hands,
    Or in the furrow musing stands:
"Does my old friend remember me?"

LXV

Sweet soul, do with me as thou wilt;
    I lull a fancy trouble-tost
    With "Love 's too precious to be lost,
A little grain shall not be spilt."

And in that solace can I sing,
    Till out of painful phases wrought
    There flutters up a happy thought,
Self-balanced on a lightsome wing;

Since we deserved the name of friends,
    And thine effect so lives in me,   10
    A part of mine may live in thee
And move thee on to noble ends.

LXVI

You thought my heart too far diseased;
    You wonder when my fancies play
    To find me gay among the gay,
Like one with any trifle pleased.

The shade by which my life was crost,
    Which makes a desert in the mind,
    Has made me kindly with my kind,
And like to him whose sight is lost;

Whose feet are guided thro' the land,
    Whose jest among his friends is free,   10
    Who takes the children on his knee,
And winds their curls about his hand.

He plays with threads, he beats his chair
    For pastime, dreaming of the sky;
    His inner day can never die,
His night of loss is always there.

LXVII

When on my bed the moonlight falls,
    I know that in thy place of rest
    By that broad water of the west
There comes a glory on the walls:

Thy marble bright in dark appears,
    As slowly steals a silver flame
    Along the letters of thy name,
And o'er the number of thy years.

The mystic glory swims away,
    From off my bed the moonlight dies;   10
    And closing eaves of wearied eyes
I sleep till dusk is dipt in gray;

And then I know the mist is drawn
    A lucid veil from coast to coast,
    And in the dark church like a ghost
Thy tablet glimmers to the dawn.

LXVIII

When in the down I sink my head,
   Sleep, Death's twin-brother, times my breath;
   Sleep, Death's twin-brother, knows not Death,
Nor can I dream of thee as dead.

I walk as ere I walk'd forlorn,
   When all our path was fresh with dew,
   And all the bugle breezes blew
Reveillée to the breaking morn.

But what is this? I turn about,
   I find a trouble in thine eye,
   Which makes me sad I know not why,   10
Nor can my dream resolve the doubt;

But ere the lark hath left the lea
   I wake, and I discern the truth;
   It is the trouble of my youth
That foolish sleep transfers to thee.

LXIX

I dream'd there would be Spring no more,
   That Nature's ancient power was lost;
   The streets were black with smoke and frost,
They chatter'd trifles at the door;

I wander'd from the noisy town,
   I found a wood with thorny boughs;
   I took the thorns to bind my brows,
I wore them like a civic crown;

I met with scoffs, I met with scorns
   From youth and babe and hoary hairs: 10
   They call'd me in the public squares
The fool that wears a crown of thorns.

They call'd me fool, they call'd me child:
   I found an angel of the night;
   The voice was low, the look was bright;
He look'd upon my crown and smiled.

He reach'd the glory of a hand,
   That seem'd to touch it into leaf;
   The voice was not the voice of grief,
The words were hard to understand.   20

LXX

I cannot see the features right,
   When on the gloom I strive to paint
   The face I know; the hues are faint
And mix with hollow masks of night;

Cloud-towers by ghostly masons wrought,
   A gulf that ever shuts and gapes,
   A hand that points, and palled shapes
In shadowy thoroughfares of thought;

And crowds that stream from yawning doors,
   And shoals of pucker'd faces drive;   10
   Dark bulks that tumble half alive,
And lazy lengths on boundless shores;

Till all at once beyond the will
   I hear a wizard music roll,
   And thro' a lattice on the soul
Looks thy fair face and makes it still.

LXXI

Sleep, kinsman thou to death and trance
   And madness, thou hast forged at last
   A night-long present of the past
In which we went thro' summer France.

Hadst thou such credit with the soul?
   Then bring an opiate trebly strong,
   Drug down the blindfold sense of wrong,
That so my pleasure may be whole;

While now we talk as once we talk'd
   Of men and minds, the dust of change.   10
   The days that grow to something strange,
In walking as of old we walk'd

Beside the river's wooded reach,
   The fortress, and the mountain ridge,
   The cataract flashing from the bridge,
The breaker breaking on the beach.

LXXII

Risest thou thus, dim dawn, again,
   And howlest, issuing out of night,
   With blasts that blow the poplar white,
And lash with storm the streaming pane?

Day, when my crown'd estate begun
  To pine in that reverse of doom,
  Which sicken'd every living bloom,
And blurr'd the splendor of the sun;

Who usherest in the dolorous hour
  With thy quick tears that make the rose   10
  Pull sideways, and the daisy close
Her crimson fringes to the shower;

Who mightst have heaved a windless flame
  Up the deep East, or, whispering, play'd
  A chequer-work of beam and shade
Along the hills, yet look'd the same,

As wan, as chill, as wild as now;
  Day, mark'd as with some hideous crime,
  When the dark hand struck down thro' time,
And cancell'd nature's best: but thou,   20

Lift as thou mayst thy burthen'd brows
  Thro' clouds that drench the morning star,
  And whirl the ungarner'd sheaf afar,
And sow the sky with flying boughs,

And up thy vault with roaring sound
  Climb thy thick noon, disastrous day;
  Touch thy dull goal of joyless gray,
And hide thy shame beneath the ground.

LXXIII

So many worlds, so much to do,
  So little done, such things to be,
  How know I what had need of thee,
For thou wert strong as thou wert true?

The fame is quench'd that I foresaw,
  The head hath miss'd an earthly wreath:
  I curse not Nature, no, nor Death;
For nothing is that errs from law.

We pass; the path that each man trod
  Is dim, or will be dim, with weeds.   10
  What fame is left for human deeds
In endless age? It rests with God.

O hollow wraith of dying fame,
    Fade wholly, while the soul exults,
    And self-infolds the large results
Of force that would have forged a name.

LXXIV

As sometimes in a dead man's face,
    To those that watch it more and more,
    A likeness, hardly seen before,
Comes out — to some one of his race;

So, dearest, now thy brows are cold,
    I see thee what thou art, and know
    Thy likeness to the wise below,
Thy kindred with the great of old.

But there is more than I can see,
    And what I see I leave unsaid,   **10**
    Nor speak it, knowing Death has made
His darkness beautiful with thee.

LXXV

I leave thy praises unexpress'd
    In verse that brings myself relief,
    And by the measure of my grief
I leave thy greatness to be guess'd.

What practice howsoe'er expert
    In fitting aptest words to things,
    Or voice the richest-toned that sings,
Hath power to give thee as thou wert?

I care not in these fading days
    To raise a cry that lasts not long,   **10**
    And round thee with the breeze of song
To stir a little dust of praise.

Thy leaf has perish'd in the green,
    And, while we breathe beneath the sun,
    The world which credits what is done
Is cold to all that might have been.

So here shall silence guard thy fame;
    But somewhere, out of human view,
    Whate'er thy hands are set to do
Is wrought with tumult of acclaim.   **20**

LXXVI

Take wings of fancy, and ascend,
  And in a moment set thy face
  Where all the starry heavens of space
Are sharpen'd to a needle's end;

Take wings of foresight; lighten thro'
  The secular abyss to come,
  And lo, thy deepest lays are dumb
Before the mouldering of a yew;

And if the matin songs, that woke
  The darkness of our planet, last,   10
  Thine own shall wither in the vast,
Ere half the lifetime of an oak.

Ere these have clothed their branchy bowers
  With fifty Mays, thy songs are vain;
  And what are they when these remain
The ruin'd shells of hollow towers?

LXXVII

What hope is here for modern rhyme
  To him who turns a musing eye
  On songs, and deeds, and lives, that lie
Foreshorten'd in the tract of time?

These mortal lullabies of pain
  May bind a book, may line a box,
  May serve to curl a maiden's locks;
Or when a thousand moons shall wane

A man upon a stall may find,
  And, passing, turn the page that tells   10
  A grief, then changed to something else,
Sung by a long-forgotten mind.

But what of that? My darken'd ways
  Shall ring with music all the same;
  To breathe my loss is more than fame,
To utter love more sweet than praise.

LXXVIII

Again at Christmas did we weave
  The holly round the Christmas hearth;

The silent snow possess'd the earth,
And calmly fell our Christmas-eve.

The yule-clog sparkled keen with frost,
   No wing of wind the region swept,
   But over all things brooding slept
The quiet sense of something lost.

As in the winters left behind,
   Again our ancient games had place,   10
   The mimic picture's breathing grace,
And dance and song and hoodman-blind.

Who show'd a token of distress?
   No single tear, no mark of pain —
   O sorrow, then can sorrow wane?
O grief, can grief be changed to less?

O last regret, regret can die!
   No — mixt with all this mystic frame,
   Her deep relations are the same,
But with long use her tears are dry.   20

LXXIX

"More than my brothers are to me," —
   Let this not vex thee, noble heart!
   I know thee of what force thou art
To hold the costliest love in fee.

But thou and I are one in kind,
   As moulded like in Nature's mint;
   And hill and wood and field did print
The same sweet forms in either mind.

For us the same cold streamlet curl'd
   Thro' all his eddying coves, the same   10
   All winds that roam the twilight came
In whispers of the beauteous world.

At one dear knee we proffer'd vows,
   One lesson from one book we learn'd,
   Ere childhood's flaxen ringlet turn'd
To black and brown on kindred brows.

And so my wealth resembles thine,
   But he was rich where I was poor,
   And he supplied my want the more
As his unlikeness fitted mine.   20

LXXX

If any vague desire should rise,
   That holy Death ere Arthur died
   Had moved me kindly from his side,
And dropt the dust on tearless eyes;

Then fancy shapes, as fancy can,
   The grief my loss in him had wrought.
   A grief as deep as life or thought,
But stay'd in peace with God and man.

I make a picture in the brain;
   I hear the sentence that he speaks;   10
   He bears the burthen of the weeks,
But turns his burthen into gain.

His credit thus shall set me free;
   And, influence-rich to soothe and save,
   Unused example from the grave
Reach out dead hands to comfort me.

LXXXI

Could I have said while he was here,
   "My love shall now no further range;
   There cannot come a mellower change,
For now is love mature in ear"?

Love, then, had hope of richer store:
   What end is here to my complaint?
   This haunting whisper makes me faint,
"More years had made me love thee more."

But Death returns an answer sweet:
   "My sudden frost was sudden gain,   10
   And gave all ripeness to the grain
It might have drawn from after-heat."

LXXXII

I wage not any feud with Death
   For changes wrought on form and face;

No lower life that earth's embrace
May breed with him can fright my faith.

Eternal process moving on,
 From state to state the spirit walks;
 And these are but the shatter'd stalks,
Or ruin'd chrysalis of one.

Nor blame I Death, because he bare
 The use of virtue out of earth;
 I know transplanted human worth   10
Will bloom to profit, otherwhere.

For this alone on Death I wreak
 The wrath that garners in my heart:
 He put our lives so far apart
We cannot hear each other speak.

LXXXIII

Dip down upon the northern shore,
 O sweet new-year delaying long;
 Thou doest expectant Nature wrong;
Delaying long, delay no more.

What stays thee from the clouded noons,
 Thy sweetness from its proper place?
 Can trouble live with April days,
Or sadness in the summer moons?

Bring orchis, bring the foxglove spire,
 The little speedwell's darling blue,   10
 Deep tulips dash'd with fiery dew,
Laburnums, dropping-wells of fire.

O thou, new-year, delaying long,
 Delayest the sorrow in my blood,
 That longs to burst a frozen bud
And flood a fresher throat with song.

LXXXIV

When I contemplate all alone
 The life that had been thine below,
 And fix my thoughts on all the glow
To which thy crescent would have grown,

I see thee sitting crown'd with good,
    A central warmth diffusing bliss
    In glance and smile, and clasp and kiss,
On all the branches of thy blood;

Thy blood, my friend, and partly mine;
    For now the day was drawing on,   10
    When thou shouldst link thy life with one
Of mine own house, and boys of thine

Had babbled "Uncle" on my knee;
    But that remorseless iron hour
    Made cypress of her orange flower,
Despair of hope, and earth of thee.

I seem to meet their least desire,
    To clap their cheeks, to call them mine.
    I see their unborn faces shine
Beside the never-lighted fire.   20

I see myself an honor'd guest,
    Thy partner in the flowery walk
    Of letters, genial table-talk,
Or deep dispute, and graceful jest;

While now thy prosperous labor fills
    The lips of men with honest praise,
    And sun by sun the happy days
Descend below the golden hills

With promise of a morn as fair;
    And all the train of bounteous hours   30
    Conduct, by paths of growing powers,
To reverence and the silver hair;

Till slowly worn her earthly robe,
    Her lavish mission richly wrought,
    Leaving great legacies of thought,
Thy spirit should fail from off the globe;

What time mine own might also flee,
    As link'd with thine in love and fate,
    And, hovering o'er the dolorous strait
To the other shore, involved in thee,   40

Arrive at last the blessed goal,
  And He that died in Holy Land
  Would reach us out the shining hand,
And take us as a single soul.

What reed was that on which I leant?
  Ah, backward fancy, wherefore wake
  The old bitterness again, and break
The low beginnings of content?

LXXXV

This truth came borne with bier and pall,
  I felt it, when I sorrow'd most,
  'T is better to have loved and lost,
Than never to have loved at all —

O true in word, and tried in deed,
  Demanding, so to bring relief
  To this which is our common grief,
What kind of life is that I lead;

And whether trust in things above
  Be dimm'd of sorrow, or sustain'd;
  And whether love for him have drain'd
My capabilities of love;

Your words have virtue such as draws
  A faithful answer from the breast,
  Thro' light reproaches, half exprest,
And loyal unto kindly laws.

My blood an even tenor kept,
  Till on mine ear this message falls,
  That in Vienna's fatal walls
God's finger touch'd him, and he slept.

The great Intelligences fair
  That range above our mortal state,
  In circle round the blessed gate,
Received and gave him welcome there;

And led him thro' the blissful climes,
  And show'd him in the fountain fresh
  All knowledge that the sons of flesh
Shall gather in the cycled times.

10

20

But I remain'd, whose hopes were dim,
  Whose life, whose thoughts were little worth,   30
  To wander on a darken'd earth,
Where all things round me breathed of him.

O friendship, equal-poised control,
  O heart, with kindliest motion warm,
  O sacred essence, other form,
O solemn ghost, O crowned soul!

Yet none could better know than I,
  How much of act at human hands
  The sense of human will demands
By which we dare to live or die.   40

Whatever way my days decline,
  I felt and feel, tho' left alone,
  His being working in mine own,
The footsteps of his life in mine;

A life that all the Muses deck'd
  With gifts of grace, that might express
  All-comprehensive tenderness,
All-subtilizing intellect:

And so my passion hath not swerved
  To works of weakness, but I find   50
  An image comforting the mind,
And in my grief a strength reserved.

Likewise the imaginative woe,
  That loved to handle spiritual strife,
  Diffused the shock thro' all my life,
But in the present broke the blow.

My pulses therefore beat again
  For other friends that once I met;
  Nor can it suit me to forget
The mighty hopes that make us men.   60

I woo your love: I count it crime
  To mourn for any overmuch;
  I, the divided half of such
A friendship as had master'd Time;

Which masters Time indeed, and is
    Eternal, separate from fears.
    The all-assuming months and years
Can take no part away from this;

But Summer on the steaming floods,
    And Spring that swells the narrow brooks,   70
    And Autumn, with a noise of rooks,
That gather in the waning woods,

And every pulse of wind and wave
    Recalls, in change of light or gloom,
    My old affection of the tomb,
And my prime passion in the grave.

My old affection of the tomb,
    A part of stillness, yearns to speak:
    "Arise, and get thee forth and seek
A friendship for the years to come.   80

"I watch thee from the quiet shore;
    Thy spirit up to mine can reach;
    But in dear words of human speech
We two communicate no more."

And I, "Can clouds of nature stain
    The starry clearness of the free?
    How is it? Canst thou feel for me
Some painless sympathy with pain?"

And lightly does the whisper fall:
    " 'T is hard for thee to fathom this;   90
    I triumph in conclusive bliss,
And that serene result of all."

So hold I commerce with the dead;
    Or so methinks the dead would say;
    Or so shall grief with symbols play
And pining life be fancy-fed.

Now looking to some settled end,
    That these things pass, and I shall prove
    A meeting somewhere, love with love,
I crave your pardon, O my friend;   100

If not so fresh, with love as true,
 I, clasping brother-hands, aver
 I could not, if I would, transfer
The whole I felt for him to you.

For which be they that hold apart
 The promise of the golden hours?
 First love, first friendship, equal powers,
That marry with the virgin heart.

Still mine, that cannot but deplore,
 That beats within a lonely place,   110
 That yet remembers his embrace,
But at his footstep leaps no more,

My heart, tho' widow'd, may not rest
 Quite in the love of what is gone,
 But seeks to beat in time with one
That warms another living breast.

Ah, take the imperfect gift I bring,
 Knowing the primrose yet is dear,
 The primrose of the later year,
As not unlike to that of Spring.   120

LXXXVI

Sweet after showers, ambrosial air,
 That rollest from the gorgeous gloom
 Of evening over brake and bloom
And meadow, slowly breathing bare

The round of space, and rapt below
 Thro' all the dewy tassell'd wood,
 And shadowing down the horned flood
In ripples, fan my brows and blow

The fever from my cheek, and sigh
 The full new life that feeds thy breath   10
 Throughout my frame, till Doubt and Death,
Ill brethren, let the fancy fly

From belt to belt of crimson seas
 On leagues of odor streaming far,
 To where in yonder orient star
A hundred spirits whisper "Peace."

LXXXVII

I past beside the reverend walls
   In which of old I wore the gown;
   I roved at random thro' the town,
And saw the tumult of the halls;

And heard once more in college fanes
   The storm their high-built organs make,
   And thunder-music, rolling, shake
The prophet blazon'd on the panes;

And caught once more the distant shout,
   The measured pulse of racing oars   10
   Among the willows; paced the shores
And many a bridge, and all about

The same gray flats again, and felt
   The same, but not the same; and last
   Up that long walk of limes I past
To see the rooms in which he dwelt.

Another name was on the door.
   I linger'd; all within was noise
   Of songs, and clapping hands, and boys
That crash'd the glass and beat the floor;   20

Where once we held debate, a band
   Of youthful friends, on mind and art,
   And labor, and the changing mart,
And all the framework of the land;

When one would aim an arrow fair,
   But send it slackly from the string;
   And one would pierce on outer ring,
And one an inner, here and there;

And last the master-bowman, he,
   Would cleave the mark. A willing ear   30
   We lent him. Who but hung to hear
The rapt oration flowing free

From point to point, with power and grace
   And music in the bounds of law,
   To those conclusions when we saw
The God within him light his face,

And seem to lift the form, and glow
  In azure orbits heavenly-wise;
  And over those ethereal eyes
The bar of Michael Angelo?   40

LXXXVIII

Wild bird, whose warble, liquid sweet,
  Rings Eden thro' the budded quicks,
  O, tell me where the senses mix,
O, tell me where the passions meet,

Whence radiate: fierce extremes employ
  Thy spirits in the darkening leaf,
  And in the midmost heart of grief
Thy passion clasps a secret joy;

And I — my harp would prelude woe —
  I cannot all command the strings;   10
  The glory of the sum of things
Will flash along the chords and go.

LXXXIX

Witch-elms that counterchange the floor
Of this flat lawn with dusk and bright;
  And thou, with all thy breadth and height
Of foliage, towering sycamore;

How often, hither wandering down,
  My Arthur found your shadows fair,
  And shook to all the liberal air
The dust and din and steam of town!

He brought an eye for all he saw;
  He mixt in all our simple sports;   10
  They pleased him, fresh from brawling courts
And dusty purlieus of the law.

O joy to him in this retreat,
  Immantled in ambrosial dark,
  To drink the cooler air, and mark
The landscape winking thro' the heat!

O sound to rout the brood of cares,
  The sweep of scythe in morning dew,
  The gust that round the garden flew,
And tumbled half the mellowing pears!   20

O bliss, when all in circle drawn
　About him, heart and ear were fed
　To hear him, as he lay and read
The Tuscan poets on the lawn!

Or in the all-golden afternoon
　A guest, or happy sister, sung,
　Or here she brought the harp and flung
A ballad to the brightening moon.

Nor less it pleased in livelier moods,
　Beyond the bounding hill to stray,　　　　　　30
　And break the livelong summer day
With banquet in the distant woods;

Whereat we glanced from theme to theme,
　Discuss'd the books to love or hate,
　Or touch'd the changes of the state,
Or threaded some Socratic dream;

But if I praised the busy town,
　He loved to rail against it still,
　For "ground in yonder social mill
We rub each other's angles down,　　　　　　40

"And merge," he said, "in form and gloss
　The picturesque of man and man."
　We talk'd: the stream beneath us ran,
The wine-flask lying couch'd in moss,

Or cool'd within the glooming wave;
　And last, returning from afar,
　Before the crimson-circled star
Had fallen into her father's grave,

And brushing ankle-deep in flowers,
　We heard behind the woodbine veil　　　　　　50
　The milk that bubbled in the pail,
And buzzings of the honeyed hours.

XC

He tasted love with half his mind,
　Nor ever drank the inviolate spring
　Where nighest heaven, who first could fling
This bitter seed among mankind:

That could the dead, whose dying eyes
    Were closed with wail, resume their life,
    They would but find in child and wife
An iron welcome when they rise.

'T was well, indeed, when warm with wine,
    To pledge them with a kindly tear,   10
    To talk them o'er, to wish them here,
To count their memories half divine;

But if they came who past away,
    Behold their brides in other hands;
    The hard heir strides about their lands,
And will not yield them for a day.

Yea, tho' their sons were none of these,
    Not less the yet-loved sire would make
    Confusion worse than death, and shake
The pillars of domestic peace.   20

Ah, dear, but come thou back to me!
    Whatever change the years have wrought,
    I find not yet one lonely thought
That cries against my wish for thee.

XCI

When rosy plumelets tuft the larch,
    And rarely pipes the mounted thrush,
    Or underneath the barren bush
Flits by the sea-blue bird of March;

Come, wear the form by which I know
    Thy spirit in time among thy peers;
    The hope of unaccomplish'd years
Be large and lucid round thy brow.

When summer's hourly-mellowing change
    May breathe, with many roses sweet,   10
    Upon the thousand waves of wheat
That ripple round the lowly grange,

Come; not in watches of the night,
    But where the sunbeam broodeth warm,
    Come, beauteous in thine after form,
And like a finer light in light.

XCII

If any vision should reveal
   Thy likeness, I might count in vain
   As but the canker of the brain;
Yea, tho' it spake and made appeal

To chances where our lots were cast
   Together in the days behind,
   I might but say, I hear a wind
Of memory murmuring the past.

Yea, tho' it spake and bared to view
   A fact within the coming year;   10
   And tho' the months, revolving near,
Should prove the phantom-warning true,

They might not seem thy prophecies,
   But spiritual presentiments,
   And such refraction of events
As often rises ere they rise.

XCIII

I shall not see thee. Dare I say
   No spirit ever brake the band
   That stays him from the native land
Where first he walk'd when claspt in clay?

No visual shade of some one lost,
   But he, the Spirit himself, may come
   Where all the nerve of sense is numb,
Spirit to Spirit, Ghost to Ghost.

O, therefore from thy sightless range
   With gods in unconjectured bliss,   10
   O, from the distance of the abyss
Of tenfold-complicated change,

Descend, and touch, and enter; hear
   The wish too strong for words to name,
   That in this blindness of the frame
My Ghost may feel that thine is near.

XCIV

How pure at heart and sound in head,
   With what divine affections bold

Should be the man whose thought would hold
An hour's communion with the dead.

In vain shalt thou, or any, call
 The spirits from their golden day,
 Except, like them, thou too canst say,
My spirit is at peace with all.

They haunt the silence of the breast,
 Imaginations calm and fair,   10
 The memory like a cloudless air,
The conscience as a sea at rest;

But when the heart is full of din,
 And doubt beside the portal waits,
 They can but listen at the gates,
And hear the household jar within.

XCV

By night we linger'd on the lawn,
 For underfoot the herb was dry;
 And genial warmth; and o'er the sky
The silvery haze of summer drawn;

And calm that let the tapers burn
 Unwavering: not a cricket chirr'd;
 The brook alone far-off was heard,
And on the board the fluttering urn.

And bats went round in fragrant skies,
 And wheel'd or lit the filmy shapes   10
 That haunt the dusk, with ermine capes
And woolly breasts and beaded eyes;

While now we sang old songs that peal'd
 From knoll to knoll, where, couch'd at ease,
 The white kine glimmer'd, and the trees
Laid their dark arms about the field.

But when those others, one by one,
 Withdrew themselves from me and night,
 And in the house light after light
Went out, and I was all alone,   20

A hunger seized my heart; I read
 Of that glad year which once had been,

In those fallen leaves which kept their green,
The noble letters of the dead.

And strangely on the silence broke
   The silent-speaking words, and strange
   Was love's dumb cry defying change
To test his worth; and strangely spoke

The faith, the vigor, bold to dwell
   On doubts that drive the coward back,   30
   And keen thro' wordy snares to track
Suggestion to her inmost cell.

So word by word, and line by line,
   The dead man touch'd me from the past,
   And all at once it seem'd at last
The living soul was flash'd on mine,

And mine in this was wound, and whirl'd
   About empyreal heights of thought,
   And came on that which is, and caught
The deep pulsations of the world,   40

Æonian music measuring out
   The steps of Time — the shocks of Chance —
   The blows of Death. At length my trance
Was cancell'd, stricken thro' with doubt.

Vague words! but ah, how hard to frame
   In matter-moulded forms of speech,
   Or even for intellect to reach
Thro' memory that which I became;

Till now the doubtful dusk reveal'd
   The knolls once more where, couch'd at ease,   50
   The white kine glimmer'd, and the trees
Laid their dark arms about the field;

And suck'd from out the distant gloom
   A breeze began to tremble o'er
   The large leaves of the sycamore,
And fluctuate all the still perfume,

And gathering freshlier overhead,
   Rock'd the full-foliaged elms, and swung

The heavy-folded rose, and flung
The lilies to and fro, and said,   60

"The dawn, the dawn," and died away;
   And East and West, without a breath,
   Mixt their dim lights, like life and death,
To broaden into boundless day.

XCVI

You say, but with no touch of scorn,
   Sweet-hearted, you, whose light-blue eyes
   Are tender over drowning flies,
You tell me, doubt is Devil-born.

I know not: one indeed I knew
   In many a subtle question versed,
   Who touch'd a jarring lyre at first,
But ever strove to make it true;

Perplext in faith, but pure in deeds,
   At last he beat his music out.   10
   There lives more faith in honest doubt,
Believe me, than in half the creeds.

He fought his doubts and gather'd strength,
   He would not make his judgment blind,
   He faced the spectres of the mind
And laid them; thus he came at length

To find a stronger faith his own,
   And Power was with him in the night,
   Which makes the darkness and the light,
And dwells not in the light alone,   20

But in the darkness and the cloud,
   As over Sinaï 's peaks of old,
   While Israel made their gods of gold,
Altho' the trumpet blew so loud.

XCVII

My love has talk'd with rocks and trees;
   He finds on misty mountain-ground
   His own vast shadow glory-crown'd;
He sees himself in all he sees.

Two partners of a married life —
    I look'd on these and thought of thee
    In vastness and in mystery,
And of my spirit as of a wife.

These two — they dwelt with eye on eye,
    Their hearts of old have beat in tune,   10
    Their meetings made December June,
Their every parting was to die.

Their love has never past away;
    The days she never can forget
    Are earnest that he loves her yet,
Whate'er the faithless people say.

Her life is lone, he sits apart;
    He loves her yet, she will not weep,
    Tho' rapt in matters dark and deep
He seems to slight her simple heart.   20

He thrids the labyrinth of the mind,
    He reads the secret of the star,
    He seems so near and yet so far,
He looks so cold: she thinks him kind.

She keeps the gift of years before,
    A wither'd violet is her bliss;
    She knows not what his greatness is,
For that, for all, she loves him more.

For him she plays, to him she sings
    Of early faith and plighted vows;   30
    She knows but matters of the house,
And he, he knows a thousand things.

Her faith is fixt and cannot move,
    She darkly feels him great and wise,
    She dwells on him with faithful eyes,
"I cannot understand; I love."

XCVIII

You leave us: you will see the Rhine,
    And those fair hills I sail'd below,
    When I was there with him; and go
By summer belts of wheat and vine

To where he breathed his latest breath,
  That city. All her splendor seems
  No livelier than the wisp that gleams
On Lethe in the eyes of Death.

Let her great Danube rolling fair
  Enwind her isles, unmark'd of me;   10
  I have not seen, I will not see
Vienna; rather dream that there,

A treble darkness, Evil haunts
  The birth, the bridal; friend from friend
  Is oftener parted, fathers bend
Above more graves, a thousand wants

Gnarr at the heels of men, and prey
  By each cold hearth, and sadness flings
  Her shadow on the blaze of kings.
And yet myself have heard him say,   20

That not in any mother town
  With statelier progress to and fro
  The double tides of chariots flow
By park and suburb under brown

Of lustier leaves; nor more content,
  He told me, lives in any crowd,
  When all is gay with lamps, and loud
With sport and song, in booth and tent,

Imperial halls, or open plain;
  And wheels the circled dance, and breaks   30
  The rocket molten into flakes
Of crimson or in emerald rain.

XCIX

Risest thou thus, dim dawn, again,
  So loud with voices of the birds,
  So thick with lowings of the herds,
Day, when I lost the flower of men;

Who tremblest thro' thy darkling red
  On yon swollen brook that bubbles **fast**
  By meadows breathing of the past,
And woodlands holy to the dead;

Who murmurest in the foliage eaves
   A song that slights the coming care,   10
   And Autumn laying here and there
A fiery finger on the leaves;

Who wakenest with thy balmy breath
   To myriads on the genial earth,
   Memories of bridal, or of birth,
And unto myriads more, of death.

O, wheresoever those may be,
   Betwixt the slumber of the poles,
   To-day they count as kindred souls;
They know me not, but mourn with me.   20

C

I climb the hill: from end to end
   Of all the landscape underneath,
   I find no place that does not breathe
Some gracious memory of my friend;

No gray old grange, or lonely fold,
   Or low morass and whispering reed,
   Or simple stile from mead to mead,
Or sheepwalk up the windy wold;

Nor hoary knoll of ash and haw
   That hears the latest linnet trill,   10
   Nor quarry trench'd along the hill
And haunted by the wrangling daw;

Nor runlet tinkling from the rock;
   Nor pastoral rivulet that swerves
   To left and right thro' meadowy curves,
That feed the mothers of the flock;

But each has pleased a kindred eye,
   And each reflects a kindlier day;
   And, leaving these, to pass away,
I think once more he seems to die.   20

CI

Unwatch'd, the garden bough shall sway,
   The tender blossom flutter down,
   Unloved, that beech will gather brown,
This maple burn itself away;

Unloved, the sunflower, shining fair,
    Ray round with flames her disk of seed,
    And many a rose-carnation feed
With summer spice the humming air;

Unloved, by many a sandy bar,
    The brook shall babble down the plain,   **10**
    At noon or when the Lesser Wain
Is twisting round the polar star;

Uncared for, gird the windy grove,
    And flood the haunts of hern and crake,
    Or into silver arrows break
The sailing moon in creek and cove;

Till from the garden and the wild
    A fresh association blow,
    And year by year the landscape grow
Familiar to the stranger's child;   **20**

As year by year the laborer tills
    His wonted glebe, or lops the glades,
    And year by year our memory fades
From all the circle of the hills.

CII

We leave the well-beloved place
    Where first we gazed upon the sky;
    The roofs that heard our earliest cry
Will shelter one of stranger race.

We go, but ere we go from home,
    As down the garden-walks I move,
    Two spirits of a diverse love
Contend for loving masterdom.

One whispers, "Here thy boyhood sung
    Long since its matin song, and heard   **10**
    The low love-language of the bird
In native hazels tassel-hung."

The other answers, "Yea, but here
    Thy feet have stray'd in after hours
    With thy lost friend among the bowers,
And this hath made them trebly dear."

These two have striven half the day,
   And each prefers his separate claim,
   Poor rivals in a losing game,
That will not yield each other way.   20

I turn to go; my feet are set
   To leave the pleasant fields and farms;
   They mix in one another's arms
To one pure image of regret.

CIII

On that last night before we went
   From out the doors where I was bred,
   I dream'd a vision of the dead,
Which left my after-morn content.

Methought I dwelt within a hall,
   And maidens with me; distant hills
   From hidden summits fed with rills
A river sliding by the wall.

The hall with harp and carol rang.
   They sang of what is wise and good   10
   And graceful. In the centre stood
A statue veil'd, to which they sang;

And which, tho' veil'd, was known to me,
   The shape of him I loved, and love
   For ever. Then flew in a dove
And brought a summons from the sea;

And when they learnt that I must go,
   They wept and wail'd, but led the way
   To where a little shallop lay
At anchor in the flood below;   20

And on by many a level mead,
   And shadowing bluff that made the banks,
   We glided winding under ranks
Of iris and the golden reed;

And still as vaster grew the shore
   And roll'd the floods in grander space,
   The maidens gather'd strength and grace
And presence, lordlier than before;

And I myself, who sat apart
 And watch'd them, wax'd in every limb;   30
 I felt the thews of Anakim,
The pulses of a Titan's heart;

As one would sing the death of war,
 And one would chant the history
 Of that great race which is to be,
And one the shaping of a star;

Until the forward-creeping tides
 Began to foam, and we to draw
 From deep to deep, to where we saw
A great ship lift her shining sides.   40

The man we loved was there on deck,
 But thrice as large as man he bent
 To greet us. Up the side I went,
And fell in silence on his neck;

Whereat those maidens with one mind
 Bewail'd their lot; I did them wrong:
 "We served thee here," they said, "so long,
And wilt thou leave us now behind?"

So rapt I was, they could not win
 An answer from my lips, but he   50
 Replying, "Enter likewise ye
And go with us:" they enter'd in.

And while the wind began to sweep
 A music out of sheet and shroud,
 We steer'd her toward a crimson cloud
That landlike slept along the deep.

CIV

The time draws near the birth of Christ;
 The moon is hid, the night is still;
 A single church below the hill
Is pealing, folded in the mist.

A single peal of bells below,
 That wakens at this hour of rest
 A single murmur in the breast,
That these are not the bells I know.

Like strangers' voices here they sound,
   In lands where not a memory strays,
   Nor landmark breathes of other days,
But all is new unhallow'd ground.

CV

To-night ungather'd let us leave
   This laurel, let this holly stand:
   We live within the stranger's land,
And strangely falls our Christmas-eve.

Our father's dust is left alone
   And silent under other snows:
   There in due time the woodbine blows,
The violet comes, but we are gone.

No more shall wayward grief abuse
   The genial hour with mask and mime;
   For change of place, like growth of time,
Has broke the bond of dying use.

Let cares that petty shadows cast,
   By which our lives are chiefly proved,
   A little spare the night I loved,
And hold it solemn to the past.

But let no footstep beat the floor,
   Nor bowl of wassail mantle warm;
   For who would keep an ancient form
Thro' which the spirit breathes no more?

Be neither song, nor game, nor feast;
   Nor harp be touch'd, nor flute be blown;
   No dance, no motion, save alone
What lightens in the lucid East

Of rising worlds by yonder wood.
   Long sleeps the summer in the seed;
   Run out your measured arcs, and lead
The closing cycle rich in good.

CVI

Ring out, wild bells, to the wild sky,
   The flying cloud, the frosty light:
   The year is dying in the night;
Ring out, wild bells, and let him die.

Ring out the old, ring in the new,
  Ring, happy bells, across the snow:
  The year is going, let him go;
Ring out the false, ring in the true.

Ring out the grief that saps the mind,
  For those that here we see no more;
  Ring out the feud of rich and poor,
Ring in redress to all mankind.

10

Ring out a slowly dying cause,
  And ancient forms of party strife;
  Ring in the nobler modes of life,
With sweeter manners, purer laws.

Ring out the want, the care, the sin,
  The faithless coldness of the times;
  Ring out, ring out my mournful rhymes,
But ring the fuller minstrel in.

20

Ring out false pride in place and blood,
  The civic slander and the spite;
  Ring in the love of truth and right,
Ring in the common love of good.

Ring out old shapes of foul disease;
  Ring out the narrowing lust of gold;
  Ring out the thousand wars of old,
Ring in the thousand years of peace.

Ring in the valiant man and free,
  The larger heart, the kindlier hand;
  Ring out the darkness of the land,
Ring in the Christ that is to be.

30

CVII

It is the day when he was born,
  A bitter day that early sank
  Behind a purple-frosty bank
Of vapor, leaving night forlorn.

The time admits not flowers or leaves
  To deck the banquet. Fiercely flies
  The blast of North and East, and ice
Makes daggers at the sharpen'd eaves,

And bristles all the brakes and thorns
   To yon hard crescent, as she hangs   10
   Above the wood which grides and clangs
Its leafless ribs and iron horns

Together, in the drifts that pass
   To darken on the rolling brine
   That breaks the coast. But fetch the wine,
Arrange the board and brim the glass;

Bring in great logs and let them lie,
   To make a solid core of heat;
   Be cheerful-minded, talk and treat
Of all things even as he were by;   20

We keep the day. With festal cheer,
   With books and music, surely we
   Will drink to him, whate'er he be,
And sing the songs he loved to hear.

CVIII

I will not shut me from my kind,
   And, lest I stiffen into stone,
   I will not eat my heart alone,
Nor feed with sighs a passing wind:

What profit lies in barren faith,
   And vacant yearning, tho' with might
   To scale the heaven's highest height,
Or dive below the wells of death?

What find I in the highest place,
   But mine own phantom chanting hymns?   10
   And on the depths of death there swims
The reflex of a human face.

I'll rather take what fruit may be
   Of sorrow under human skies:
   'T is held that sorrow makes us wise,
Whatever wisdom sleep with thee.

CIX

Heart-affluence in discursive talk
   From household fountains never dry;
   The critic clearness of an eye
That saw thro' all the Muses' walk;

Seraphic intellect and force
    To seize and throw the doubts of man;
    Impassion'd logic, which outran
The hearer in its fiery course;

High nature amorous of the good,
    But touch'd with no ascetic gloom;   10
    And passion pure in snowy bloom
Thro' all the years of April blood;

A love of freedom rarely felt,
    Of freedom in her regal seat
    Of England; not the schoolboy heat,
The blind hysterics of the Celt;

And manhood fused with female grace
    In such a sort, the child would twine
    A trustful hand, unask'd, in thine,
And find his comfort in thy face;   20

All these have been, and thee mine eyes
    Have look'd on: if they look'd in vain,
    My shame is greater who remain,
Nor let thy wisdom make me wise.

CX

Thy converse drew us with delight,
    The men of rathe and riper years;
    The feeble soul, a haunt of fears,
Forgot his weakness in thy sight.

On thee the loyal-hearted hung,
    The proud was half disarm'd of pride,
    Nor cared the serpent at thy side
To flicker with his double tongue.

The stern were mild when thou wert by,
    The flippant put himself to school   10
    And heard thee, and the brazen fool
Was soften'd, and he knew not why;

While I, thy nearest, sat apart,
    And felt thy triumph was as mine;
    And loved them more, that they were thine,
The graceful tact, the Christian art;

Nor mine the sweetness or the skill,
    But mine the love that will not tire,
    And, born of love, the vague desire
That spurs an imitative will.   20

CXI

The churl in spirit, up or down
    Along the scale of ranks, thro' all,
    To him who grasps a golden ball,
By blood a king, at heart a clown, —

The churl in spirit, howe'er he veil
    His want in forms for fashion's sake,
    Will let his coltish nature break
At seasons thro' the gilded pale;

For who can always act? but he,
    To whom a thousand memories call,   10
    Not being less but more than all
The gentleness he seem'd to be,

Best seem'd the thing he was, and join'd
    Each office of the social hour
    To noble manners, as the flower
And native growth of noble mind;

Nor ever narrowness or spite,
    Or villain fancy fleeting by,
    Drew in the expression of an eye
Where God and Nature met in light;   20

And thus he bore without abuse
    The grand old name of gentleman,
    Defamed by every charlatan,
And soil'd with all ignoble use.

CXII

High wisdom holds my wisdom less,
    That I, who gaze with temperate eyes
    On glorious insufficiencies,
Set light by narrower perfectness.

But thou, that fillest all the room
    Of all my love, art reason why
    I seem to cast a careless eye
On souls, the lesser lords of doom.

For what wert thou? some novel power
   Sprang up for ever at a touch,
   And hope could never hope too much,   **10**
In watching thee from hour to hour,

Large elements in order brought,
   And tracts of calm from tempest made,
   And world-wide fluctuation sway'd
In vassal tides that follow'd thought.

CXIII

'T is held that sorrow makes us wise;
   Yet how much wisdom sleeps with thee
   Which not alone had guided me,
But served the seasons that may rise;

For can I doubt, who knew thee keen
   In intellect, with force and skill
   To strive, to fashion, to fulfil —
I doubt not what thou wouldst have been:

A life in civic action warm,
   A soul on highest mission sent,   **10**
   A potent voice of Parliament,
A pillar steadfast in the storm,

Should licensed boldness gather force,
   Becoming, when the time has birth,
   A lever to uplift the earth
And roll it in another course,

With thousand shocks that come and go,
   With agonies, with energies,
   With overthrowings, and with cries,
And undulations to and fro.   **20**

CXIV

Who loves not Knowledge? Who shall rail
   Against her beauty? May she mix
   With men and prosper! Who shall fix
Her pillars? Let her work prevail.

But on her forehead sits a fire;
   She sets her forward countenance
   And leaps into the future chance,
Submitting all things to desire.

Half-grown as yet, a child, and vain —
　　She cannot fight the fear of death.
　　What is she, cut from love and faith,
But some wild Pallas from the brain

Of demons? fiery-hot to burst
　　All barriers in her onward race
　　For power. Let her know her place;
She is the second, not the first.

A higher hand must make her mild,
　　If all be not in vain, and guide
　　Her footsteps, moving side by side
With Wisdom, like the younger child;

For she is earthly of the mind,
　　But Wisdom heavenly of the soul.
　　O friend, who camest to thy goal
So early, leaving me behind,

I would the great world grew like thee,
　　Who grewest not alone in power
　　And knowledge, but by year and hour
In reverence and in charity.

CXV

Now fades the last long streak of snow,
　　Now burgeons every maze of quick
　　About the flowering squares, and thick
By ashen roots the violets blow.

Now rings the woodland loud and long,
　　The distance takes a lovelier hue,
　　And drown'd in yonder living blue
The lark becomes a sightless song.

Now dance the lights on lawn and lea,
　　The flocks are whiter down the vale,
　　And milkier every milky sail
On winding stream or distant sea;

Where now the seamew pipes, or dives
　　In yonder greening gleam, and fly
　　The happy birds, that change their sky
To build and brood, that live their lives

10

20

10

From land to land; and in my breast
   Spring wakens too, and my regret
   Becomes an April violet,
And buds and blossoms like the rest.   20

CXVI

Is it, then, regret for buried time
   That keenlier in sweet April wakes,
   And meets the year, and gives and takes
The colors of the crescent prime?

Not all: the songs, the stirring air,
   The life re-orient out of dust,
   Cry thro' the sense to hearten trust
In that which made the world so fair.

Not all regret: the face will shine
   Upon me, while I muse alone,   10
   And that dear voice, I once have known,
Still speak to me of me and mine.

Yet less of sorrow lives in me
   For days of happy commune dead,
   Less yearning for the friendship fled
Than some strong bond which is to be.

CXVII

O days and hours, your work is this,
   To hold me from my proper place,
   A little while from his embrace,
For fuller gain of after bliss;

That out of distance might ensue
   Desire of nearness doubly sweet,
   And unto meeting, when we meet,
Delight a hundredfold accrue,

For every grain of sand that runs,
   And every span of shade that steals,   10
   And every kiss of toothed wheels,
And all the courses of the suns.

CXVIII

Contemplate all this work of Time,
   The giant laboring in his youth;

Nor dream of human love and truth,
As dying Nature's earth and lime;

But trust that those we call the dead
    Are breathers of an ampler day
    For ever nobler ends. They say,
The solid earth whereon we tread

In tracts of fluent heat began,
    And grew to seeming-random forms,   10
    The seeming prey of cyclic storms,
Till at the last arose the man;

Who throve and branch'd from clime to clime,
    The herald of a higher race,
    And of himself in higher place,
If so he type this work of time

Within himself, from more to more;
    Or, crown'd with attributes of woe
    Like glories, move his course, and show
That life is not as idle ore,   20

But iron dug from central gloom,
    And heated hot with burning fears,
    And dipt in baths of hissing tears,
And batter'd with the shocks of doom

To shape and use. Arise and fly
    The reeling Faun, the sensual feast;
    Move upward, working out the beast,
And let the ape and tiger die.

CXIX

Doors, where my heart was used to beat
    So quickly, not as one that weeps
    I come once more; the city sleeps;
I smell the meadow in the street;

I hear a chirp of birds; I see
    Betwixt the black fronts long-withdrawn
    A light-blue lane of early dawn,
And think of early days and thee,

And bless thee, for thy lips are bland,
 And bright the friendship of thine eye;   10
 And in my thoughts with scarce a sigh
I take the pressure of thine hand.

CXX

I trust I have not wasted breath:
 I think we are not wholly brain,
 Magnetic mockeries; not in vain,
Like Paul with beasts, I fought with Death;

Not only cunning casts in clay:
 Let Science prove we are, and then
 What matters Science unto men,
At least to me? I would not stay.

Let him, the wiser man who springs
 Hereafter, up from childhood shape   10
 His action like the greater ape,
But I was *born* to other things.

CXXI

Sad Hesper o'er the buried sun
 And ready, thou, to die with him,
 Thou watchest all things ever dim
And dimmer, and a glory done.

The team is loosen'd from the wain,
 The boat is drawn upon the shore;
 Thou listenest to the closing door,
And life is darken'd in the brain.

Bright Phosphor, fresher for the night,
 By thee the world's great work is heard   10
 Beginning, and the wakeful bird;
Behind thee comes the greater light.

The market boat is on the stream,
 And voices hail it from the brink;
 Thou hear'st the village hammer clink,
And see'st the moving of the team.

Sweet Hesper-Phosphor, double name
 For what is one, the first, the last,
 Thou, like my present and my past,
Thy place is changed; thou art the same.   20

CXXII

O, wast thou with me, dearest, then,
  While I rose up against my doom,
  And yearn'd to burst the folded gloom,
To bare the eternal heavens again,

To feel once more, in placid awe,
  The strong imagination roll
  A sphere of stars about my soul,
In all her motion one with law?

If thou wert with me, and the grave
  Divide us not, be with me now,   10
  And enter in at breast and brow,
Till all my blood, a fuller wave,

Be quicken'd with a livelier breath,
  And like an inconsiderate boy,
  As in the former flash of joy,
I slip the thoughts of life and death;

And all the breeze of Fancy blows,
  And every dewdrop paints a bow,
  The wizard lightnings deeply glow,
And every thought breaks out a rose.   20

CXXIII

There rolls the deep where grew the tree.
  O earth, what changes hast thou seen!
  There where the long street roars hath been
The stillness of the central sea.

The hills are shadows, and they flow
  From form to form, and nothing stands;
  They melt like mist, the solid lands,
Like clouds they shape themselves and go.

But in my spirit will I dwell,
  And dream my dream, and hold it true;   10
  For tho' my lips may breathe adieu,
I cannot think the thing farewell.

CXXIV

That which we dare invoke to bless;
  Our dearest faith; our ghastliest doubt;

He, They, One, All; within, without;
The Power in darkness whom we guess, —

I found Him not in world or sun,
 Or eagle's wing, or insect's eye,
 Nor thro' the questions men may try,
The petty cobwebs we have spun.

If e'er when faith had fallen asleep,
 I heard a voice, "believe no more,"   10
 And heard an ever-breaking shore
That tumbled in the Godless deep,

A warmth within the breast would melt
 The freezing reason's colder part,
 And like a man in wrath the heart
Stood up and answer'd, "I have felt."

No, like a child in doubt and fear:
 But that blind clamor made me wise;
 Then was I as a child that cries,
But, crying, knows his father near;   20

And what I am beheld again
 What is, and no man understands;
 And out of darkness came the hands
That reach thro' nature, moulding men.

CXXV

Whatever I have said or sung,
 Some bitter notes my harp would give,
 Yea, tho' there often seem'd to live
A contradiction on the tongue,

Yet Hope had never lost her youth,
 She did but look through dimmer eyes;
 Or Love but play'd with gracious lies,
Because he felt so fix'd in truth;

And if the song were full of care,
 He breathed the spirit of the song;   10
 And if the words were sweet and strong
He set his royal signet there;

Abiding with me till I sail
  To seek thee on the mystic deeps,
  And this electric force, that keeps
A thousand pulses dancing, fail.

CXXVI

Love is and was my lord and king,
  And in his presence I attend
  To hear the tidings of my friend,
Which every hour his couriers bring.

Love is and was my king and lord,
  And will be, tho' as yet I keep
  Within the court on earth, and sleep
Encompass'd by his faithful guard,

And hear at times a sentinel
  Who moves about from place to place,   10
  And whispers to the worlds of space,
In the deep night, that all is well.

CXXVII

And all is well, tho' faith and form
  Be sunder'd in the night of fear;
  Well roars the storm to those that hear
A deeper voice across the storm,

Proclaiming social truth shall spread,
  And justice, even tho' thrice again
  The red fool-fury of the Seine
Should pile her barricades with dead.

But ill for him that wears a crown,
  And him, the lazar, in his rags!   10
  They tremble, the sustaining crags;
The spires of ice are toppled down,

And molten up, and roar in flood;
  The fortress crashes from on high,
  The brute earth lightens to the sky,
And the great Æon sinks in blood,

And compass'd by the fires of hell,
  While thou, dear spirit, happy star,
  O'erlook'st the tumult from afar,
And smilest, knowing all is well.   20

CXXVIII

The love that rose on stronger wings,
  Unpalsied when he met with Death,
  Is comrade of the lesser faith
That sees the course of human things.

No doubt vast eddies in the flood
  Of onward time shall yet be made,
  And throned races may degrade;
Yet, O ye mysteries of good,

Wild Hours that fly with Hope and Fear,
  If all your office had to do   10
  With old results that look like new —
If this were all your mission here,

To draw, to sheathe a useless sword,
  To fool the crowd with glorious lies,
  To cleave a creed in sects and cries,
To change the bearing of a word,

To shift an arbitrary power,
  To cramp the student at his desk,
  To make old bareness picturesque
And tuft with grass a feudal tower,   20

Why, then my scorn might well descend
  On you and yours. I see in part
  That all, as in some piece of art,
Is toil coöperant to an end.

CXXIX

Dear friend, far off, my lost desire,
  So far, so near in woe and weal,
  O loved the most, when most I feel
There is a lower and a higher;

Known and unknown, human, divine;
  Sweet human hand and lips and eye;
  Dear heavenly friend that canst not die,
Mine, mine, for ever, ever mine;

Strange friend, past, present, and to be;
  Loved deeplier, darklier understood;   10
  Behold, I dream a dream of good,
And mingle all the world with thee.

CXXX

Thy voice is on the rolling air;
   I hear thee where the waters run;
   Thou standest in the rising sun,
And in the setting thou art fair.

What art thou then? I cannot guess;
   But tho' I seem in star and flower
   To feel thee some diffusive power,
I do not therefore love thee less.

My love involves the love before;
   My love is vaster passion now;   10
   Tho' mix'd with God and Nature thou,
I seem to love thee more and more.

Far off thou art, but ever nigh;
   I have thee still, and I rejoice;
   I prosper, circled with thy voice;
I shall not lose thee tho' I die.

CXXXI

O living will that shalt endure
   When all that seems shall suffer shock,
   Rise in the spiritual rock,
Flow thro' our deeds and make them pure,

That we may lift from out of dust
   A voice as unto him that hears,
   A cry above the conquer'd years
To one that with us works, and trust,

With faith that comes of self-control,
   The truths that never can be proved   10
   Until we close with all we loved,
And all we flow from, soul in soul.

O true and tried, so well and long,
   Demand not thou a marriage lay;
   In that it is thy marriage day
Is music more than any song.

Nor have I felt so much of bliss
  Since first he told me that he loved
  A daughter of our house, nor proved
Since that dark day a day like this;

Tho' I since then have number'd o'er
  Some thrice three years; they went and came,   10
  Remade the blood and changed the frame,
And yet is love not less, but more;

No longer caring to embalm
  In dying songs a dead regret,
  But like a statue solid-set,
And moulded in colossal calm.

Regret is dead, but love is more
  Than in the summers that are flown,
  For I myself with these have grown
To something greater than before;   20

Which makes appear the songs I made
  As echoes out of weaker times,
  As half but idle brawling rhymes,
The sport of random sun and shade.

But where is she, the bridal flower,
  That must be made a wife ere noon?
  She enters, glowing like the moon
Of Eden on its bridal bower.

On me she bends her blissful eyes
  And then on thee; they meet thy look   30
  And brighten like the star that shook
Betwixt the palms of Paradise.

O, when her life was yet in bud,
  He too foretold the perfect rose.
  For thee she grew, for thee she grows
For ever, and as fair as good.

And thou art worthy, full of power;
  As gentle; liberal-minded, great,
  Consistent; wearing all that weight
Of learning lightly like a flower.   40

But now set out: the noon is near,
   And I must give away the bride;
   She fears not, or with thee beside
And me behind her, will not fear.

For I that danced her on my knee,
   That watch'd her on her nurse's arm,
   That shielded all her life from harm,
At last must part with her to thee;

Now waiting to be made a wife,
   Her feet, my darling, on the dead;   50
   Their pensive tablets round her head,
And the most living words of life

Breathed in her ear. The ring is on,
   The "Wilt thou?" answer'd, and again
   The "Wilt thou?" ask'd, till out of twain
Her sweet "I will" has made you one.

Now sign your names, which shall be read,
   Mute symbols of a joyful morn,
   By village eyes as yet unborn.
The names are sign'd, and overhead   60

Begins the clash and clang that tells
   The joy to every wandering breeze;
   The blind wall rocks, and on the trees
The dead leaf trembles to the bells.

O happy hour, and happier hours
   Await them. Many a merry face
   Salutes them — maidens of the place,
That pelt us in the porch with flowers.

O happy hour, behold the bride
   With him to whom her hand I gave.   70
   They leave the porch, they pass the grave
That has to-day its sunny side.

To-day the grave is bright for me,
   For them the light of life increased,
   Who stay to share the morning feast,
Who rest to-night beside the sea.

Let all my genial spirits advance
   To meet and greet a whiter sun;
   My drooping memory will not shun
The foaming grape of eastern France.   80

It circles round, and fancy plays.
   And hearts are warm'd and faces bloom,
   As drinking health to bride and groom
We wish them store of happy days.

Nor count me all to blame if I
   Conjecture of a stiller guest,
   Perchance, perchance, among the rest,
And, tho' in silence, wishing joy.

But they must go, the time draws on,
   And those white-favor'd horses wait: 90
   They rise, but linger; it is late;
Farewell, we kiss, and they are gone.

A shade falls on us like the dark
   From little cloudlets on the grass,
   But sweeps away as out we pass
To range the woods, to roam the park,

Discussing how their courtship grew,
   And talk of others that are wed,
   And how she look'd, and what he said,
And back we come at fall of dew.   100

Again the feast, the speech, the glee,
   The shade of passing thought, the wealth
   Of words and wit, the double health,
The crowning cup, the three-times-three,

And last the dance;— till I retire.
   Dumb is that tower which spake so loud,
   And high in heaven the streaming cloud,
And on the downs a rising fire:

And rise, O moon, from yonder down,
   Till over down and over dale   110
   All night the shining vapor sail
And pass the silent-lighted town,

The white-faced halls, the glancing rills,
  And catch at every mountain head.
  And o'er the friths that branch and spread
Their sleeping silver thro' the hills;

And touch with shade the bridal doors,
  With tender gloom the roof, the wall;
  And breaking let the splendor fall
To spangle all the happy shores   120

By which they rest, and ocean sounds,
  And, star and system rolling past,
  A soul shall draw from out the vast
And strike his being into bounds,

And, moved thro' life of lower phase,
  Result in man, be born and think,
  And act and love, a closer link
Betwixt us and the crowning race

Of those that, eye to eye, shall look
  On knowledge; under whose command   130
  Is Earth and Earth's, and in their hand
Is Nature like an open book;

No longer half-akin to brute,
  For all we thought and loved and did,
  And hoped, and suffer'd, is but seed
Of what in them is flower and fruit;

Whereof the man that with me trod
  This planet was a noble type
  Appearing ere the times were ripe,
That friend of mine who lives in God,   140

That God, which ever lives and loves,
  One God, one law, one element,
  And one far-off divine event,
To which the whole creation moves.

1833–1849 (1850)*

THE EAGLE

FRAGMENT

He clasps the crag with crooked hands;
Close to the sun in lonely lands,
Ring'd with the azure world, he stands.

The wrinkled sea beneath him crawls;
He watches from his mountain walls,
And like a thunderbolt he falls.
1851

DE PROFUNDIS

THE TWO GREETINGS

I

Out of the deep, my child, out of the deep,
Where all that was to be, in all that was,
Whirl'd for a million æons thro' the vast
Waste dawn of multitudinous-eddying light —
Out of the deep, my child, out of the deep,
Thro' all this changing world of changeless law,
And every phase of ever-heightening life,
And nine long months of antenatal gloom,
With this last moon, this crescent — her dark orb
Touch'd with earth's light — thou comest, darling boy;   10
Our own; a babe in lineament and limb
Perfect, and prophet of the perfect man;
Whose face and form are hers and mine in one,
Indissolubly married like our love.
Live, and be happy in thyself, and serve
This mortal race thy kin so well that men
May bless thee as we bless thee, O young life
Breaking with laughter from the dark; and may
The fated channel where thy motion lives
Be prosperously shaped, and sway thy course   20
Along the years of haste and random youth

Unshatter'd; then full-current thro' full man;
And last in kindly curves, with gentlest fall,
By quiet fields, a slowly-dying power,
To that last deep where we and thou are still.

II

I

Out of the deep, my child, out of the deep,
From that great deep, before our world begins,
Whereon the Spirit of God moves as he will —
Out of the deep, my child, out of the deep,
From that true world within the world we see,   30
Whereof our world is but the bounding shore —
Out of the deep, Spirit, out of the deep,
With this ninth moon, that sends the hidden sun
Down yon dark sea, thou comest, darling boy.

II

For in the world which is not ours They said,
"Let us make man," and that which should be man,
From that one light no man can look upon,
Drew to this shore lit by the suns and moons
And all the shadows. O dear Spirit, half-lost
In thine own shadow and this fleshly sign   40
That thou art thou — who wailest being born
And banish'd into mystery, and the pain
Of this divisible-indivisible world
Among the numerable-innumerable
Sun, sun, and sun, thro' finite-infinite space
In finite-infinite Time — our mortal veil
And shatter'd phantom of that infinite One,
Who made thee unconceivably Thyself
Out of His whole World-self and all in all —
Live thou! and of the grain and husk, the grape   50
And ivy-berry, choose; and still depart
From death to death thro' life and life, and find
Nearer and ever nearer Him, who wrought
Not matter, nor the finite-infinite,
But this main-miracle, that thou art thou,
With power on thine own act and on the world.

THE HUMAN CRY

I

HALLOWED be Thy name — Halleluiah! —
  Infinite Ideality!
  Immeasurable Reality!
  Infinite Personality!   60
Hallowed be Thy name — Halleluiah!

II

We feel we are nothing — for all is Thou and in Thee;
We feel we are something — *that* also has come from Thee;
We know we are nothing — but Thou wilt help us to be.
Hallowed be Thy name — Halleluiah!

1852 + (1880) *

ODE ON THE DEATH OF THE
DUKE OF WELLINGTON

I

BURY the Great Duke
  With an empire's lamentation;
Let us bury the Great Duke
  To the noise of the mourning of a mighty nation;
Mourning when their leaders fall,
Warriors carry the warrior's pall,
And sorrow darkens hamlet and hall.

II

Where shall we lay the man whom we deplore?
Here, in streaming London's central roar.
Let the sound of those he wrought for,   10
And the feet of those he fought for,
Echo round his bones for evermore.

III

Lead out the pageant: sad and slow,
As fits an universal woe,
Let the long, long procession go,
And let the sorrowing crowd about it grow,

And let the mournful martial music blow;
The last great Englishman is low.

IV

Mourn, for to us he seems the last,
Remembering all his greatness in the past.   20
No more in soldier fashion will he greet
With lifted hand the gazer in the street.
O friends, our chief state-oracle is mute!
Mourn for the man of long-enduring blood,
The statesman-warrior, moderate, resolute,
Whole in himself, a common good.
Mourn for the man of amplest influence,
Yet clearest of ambitious crime,
Our greatest yet with least pretence,
Great in council and great in war,   30
Foremost captain of his time,
Rich in saving common-sense,
And, as the greatest only are,
In his simplicity sublime.
O good gray head which all men knew,
O voice from which their omens all men drew,
O iron nerve to true occasion true,
O fallen at length that tower of strength
Which stood four-square to all the winds that blew!
Such was he whom we deplore.   40
The long self-sacrifice of life is o'er.
The great World-victor's victor will be seen no more.

V

All is over and done.
Render thanks to the Giver,
England, for thy son.
Let the bell be toll'd.
Render thanks to the Giver,
And render him to the mould.
Under the cross of gold
That shines over city and river,   50
There he shall rest for ever
Among the wise and the bold.
Let the bell be toll'd,
And a reverent people behold
The towering car, the sable steeds.
Bright let it be with its blazon'd deeds,
Dark in its funeral fold.

Let the bell be toll'd,
And a deeper knell in the heart be knoll'd;
And the sound of the sorrowing anthem roll'd   60
Thro' the dome of the golden cross;
And the volleying cannon thunder his loss;
He knew their voices of old.
For many a time in many a clime
His captain's-ear has heard them boom
Bellowing victory, bellowing doom.
When he with those deep voices wrought,
Guarding realms and kings from shame,
With those deep voices our dead captain taught
The tyrant, and asserts his claim   70
In that dread sound to the great name
Which he has worn so pure of blame,
In praise and in dispraise the same,
A man of well-attemper'd frame.
O civic muse, to such a name,
To such a name for ages long,
To such a name,
Preserve a broad approach of fame,
And ever-echoing avenues of song!

VI

"Who is he that cometh, like an honor'd guest,   80
With banner and with music, with soldier and with priest,
With a nation weeping, and breaking on my rest?" —
Mighty Seaman, this is he
Was great by land as thou by sea.
Thine island loves thee well, thou famous man,
The greatest sailor since our world began.
Now, to the roll of muffled drums,
To thee the greatest soldier comes;
For this is he
Was great by land as thou by sea.   90
His foes were thine; he kept us free;
O, give him welcome, this is he
Worthy of our gorgeous rites,
And worthy to be laid by thee;
For this is England's greatest son,
He that gain'd a hundred fights,
Nor ever lost an English gun;
This is he that far away
Against the myriads of Assaye
Clash'd with his fiery few and won;   100

And underneath another sun,
Warring on a later day,
Round affrighted Lisbon drew
The treble works, the vast designs
Of his labor'd rampart-lines,
Where he greatly stood at bay,
Whence he issued forth anew,
And ever great and greater grew,
Beating from the wasted vines
Back to France her banded swarms,   110
Back to France with countless blows,
Till o'er the hills her eagles flew
Beyond the Pyrenean pines,
Follow'd up in valley and glen
With blare of bugle, clamor of men,
Roll of cannon and clash of arms,
And England pouring on her foes.
Such a war had such a close.
Again their ravening eagle rose
In anger, wheel'd on Europe-shadowing wings,   120
And barking for the thrones of kings;
Till one that sought but Duty's iron crown
On that loud Sabbath shook the spoiler down;
A day of onsets of despair!
Dash'd on every rocky square,
Their surging charges foam'd themselves away;
Last, the Prussian trumpet blew;
Thro' the long-tormented air
Heaven flash'd a sudden jubilant ray,
And down we swept and charged and overthrew.   130
So great a soldier taught us there
What long-enduring hearts could do
In that world-earthquake, Waterloo!
Mighty Seaman, tender and true,
And pure as he from taint of craven guile,
O saviour of the silver-coasted isle,
O shaker of the Baltic and the Nile,
If aught of things that here befall
Touch a spirit among things divine,
If love of country move thee there at all,   140
Be glad, because his bones are laid by thine
And thro' the centuries let a people's voice
In full acclaim,
A people's voice,
The proof and echo of all human fame,

A people's voice, when they rejoice
At civic revel and pomp and game,
Attest their great commander's claim
With honor, honor, honor, honor to him,
Eternal honor to his name.   150

VII

A people's voice! we are a people yet.
Tho' all men else their nobler dreams forget,
Confused by brainless mobs and lawless Powers,
Thank Him who isled us here, and roughly set
His Briton in blown seas and storming showers,
We have a voice with which to pay the debt
Of boundless love and reverence and regret
To those great men who fought, and kept it ours.
And keep it ours, O God, from brute control!
O Statesmen, guard us, guard the eye, the soul   160
Of Europe, keep our noble England whole,
And save the one true seed of freedom sown
Betwixt a people and their ancient throne,
That sober freedom out of which there springs
Our loyal passion for our temperate kings!
For, saving that, ye help to save mankind
Till public wrong be crumbled into dust,
And drill the raw world for the march of mind,
Till crowds at length be sane and crowns be just.
But wink no more in slothful overtrust.   170
Remember him who led your hosts;
He bade you guard the sacred coasts.
Your cannons moulder on the seaward wall;
His voice is silent in your council-hall
For ever; and whatever tempests lour
For ever silent; even if they broke
In thunder, silent; yet remember all
He spoke among you, and the Man who spoke;
Who never sold the truth to serve the hour,
Nor palter'd with Eternal God for power;   180
Who let the turbid streams of rumor flow
Thro' either babbling world of high and low;
Whose life was work, whose language rife
With rugged maxims hewn from life;
Who never spoke against a foe;
Whose eighty winters freeze with one rebuke
All great self-seekers trampling on the right.
Truth-teller was our England's Alfred named;

Truth-lover was our English Duke;
Whatever record leap to light   190
He never shall be shamed.

VIII

Lo! the leader in these glorious wars
Now to glorious burial slowly borne,
Follow'd by the brave of other lands,
He, on whom from both her open hands
Lavish Honor shower'd all her stars,
And affluent Fortune emptied all her horn
Yea, let all good things await
Him who cares not to be great
But as he saves or serves the state.   200
Not once or twice in our rough island-story
The path of duty was the way to glory.
He that walks it, only thirsting
For the right, and learns to deaden
Love of self, before his journey closes,
He shall find the stubborn thistle bursting
Into glossy purples, which outredden
All voluptuous garden-roses.
Not once or twice in our fair island-story
The path of duty was the way to glory.   210
He, that ever following her commands,
On with toil of heart and knees and hands,
Thro' the long gorge to the far light has won
His path upward, and prevail'd,
Shall find the toppling crags of Duty scaled
Are close upon the shining table-lands
To which our God Himself is moon and sun.
Such was he: his work is done.
But while the races of mankind endure
Let his great example stand   220
Colossal, seen of every land,
And keep the soldier firm, the statesman pure;
Till in all lands and thro' all human story
The path of duty be the way to glory.
And let the land whose hearths he saved from shame
For many and many an age proclaim
At civic revel and pomp and game,
And when the long-illumined cities flame,
Their ever-loyal iron leader's fame,
With honor, honor, honor, honor to him,   230
Eternal honor to his name.

IX

Peace, his triumph will be sung
By some yet unmoulded tongue
Far on in summers that we shall not see.
Peace, it is a day of pain
For one about whose patriarchal knee
Late the little children clung.
O peace, it is a day of pain
For one upon whose hand and heart and brain
Once the weight and fate of Europe hung.   240
Ours the pain, be his the gain!
More than is of man's degree
Must be with us, watching here
At this, our great solemnity.
Whom we see not we revere;
We revere, and we refrain
From talk of battles loud and vain,
And brawling memories all too free
For such a wise humility
As befits a solemn fane: 250
We revere, and while we hear
The tides of Music's golden sea
Setting toward eternity,
Uplifted high in heart and hope are we,
Until we doubt not that for one so true
There must be other nobler work to do
Than when he fought at Waterloo,
And Victor he must ever be.
For tho' the Giant Ages heave the hill
And break the shore, and evermore   260
Make and break, and work their will,
Tho' world on world in myriad myriads roll
Round us, each with different powers,
And other forms of life than ours,
What know we greater than the soul?
On God and Godlike men we build our trust.
Hush, the Dead March wails in the people's ears;
The dark crowd moves, and there are sobs and tears;
The black earth yawns; the mortal disappears;
Ashes to ashes, dust to dust;   270
He is gone who seem'd so great. —
Gone, but nothing can bereave him
Of the force he made his own
Being here, and we believe him
Something far advanced in State,

And that he wears a truer crown
Than any wreath that man can weave him.
Speak no more of his renown,
Lay your earthly fancies down,
And in the vast cathedral leave him,   280
God accept him, Christ receive him!

1852, 1855*

TO E. L., ON HIS TRAVELS IN GREECE

ILLYRIAN woodlands, echoing falls
    Of water, sheets of summer glass,
    The long divine Peneïan pass,
The vast Akrokeraunian walls,

Tomohrit, Athos, all things fair,
    With such a pencil, such a pen,
    You shadow forth to distant men,
I read and felt that I was there.

And trust me while I turn'd the page,
    And track'd you still on classic ground,   10
    I grew in gladness till I found
My spirits in the golden age.

For me the torrent ever pour'd
    And glisten'd — here and there alone
    The broad-limb'd Gods at random thrown
By fountain-urns; — and Naiads oar'd

A glimmering shoulder under gloom
    Of cavern pillars; on the swell
    The silver lily heaved and fell;
And many a slope was rich in bloom,   20

From him that on the mountain lea
    By dancing rivulets fed his flocks
    To him who sat upon the rocks
And fluted to the morning sea.

1853*

THE DAISY

WRITTEN AT EDINBURGH

O LOVE, what hours were thine and mine,
In lands of palm and southern pine;
   In lands of palm, or orange-blossom,
Of olive, aloe, and maize and vine!

What Roman strength Turbìa show'd
In ruin, by the mountain road;
   How like a gem, beneath, the city
Of little Monaco, basking, glow'd!

How richly down the rocky dell
The torrent vineyard streaming fell   10
   To meet the sun and sunny waters,
That only heaved with a summer swell!

What slender campanili grew
By bays, the peacock's neck in hue;
   Where, here and there, on sandy beaches
A milky-bell'd amaryllis blew!

How young Columbus seem'd to rove,
Yet present in his natal grove,
   Now watching high on mountain cornice,
And steering, now, from a purple cove,   20

Now pacing mute by ocean's rim;
Till, in a narrow street and dim,
   I stay'd the wheels at Cogoletto,
And drank, and loyally drank to him!

Nor knew we well what pleased us most;
Not the clipt palm of which they boast,
   But distant color, happy hamlet,
A moulder'd citadel on the coast,

Or tower, or high hill-convent, seen
A light amid its olives green;   30
   Or olive-hoary cape in ocean;
Or rosy blossom in hot ravine,

Where oleanders flush'd the bed
Of silent torrents, gravel-spread;
   And, crossing, oft we saw the glisten
Of ice, far up on a mountain head.

We loved that hall, tho' white and cold,
Those niched shapes of noble mould,
   A princely people's awful princes,
The grave, severe Genovese of old.   40

At Florence too what golden hours,
In those long galleries, were ours;
   What drives about the fresh Cascinè,
Or walks in Boboli's ducal bowers!

In bright vignettes, and each complete,
Of tower or duomo, sunny-sweet,
   Or palace, how the city glitter'd,
Thro' cypress avenues, at our feet!

But when we crost the Lombard plain
Remember what a plague of rain;   50
   Of rain at Reggio, rain at Parma,
At Lodi rain, Piacenza rain.

And stern and sad — so rare the smiles
Of sunlight — look'd the Lombard piles;
   Porch-pillars on the lion resting,
And sombre, old, colonnaded aisles.

O Milan, O the chanting quires,
The giant windows' blazon'd fires,
   The height, the space, the gloom, the glory!
A mount of marble, a hundred spires!   60

I climb'd the roofs at break of day;
Sun-smitten Alps before me lay.
   I stood among the silent statues,
And statued pinnacles, mute as they.

How faintly-flush'd, how phantom-fair,
Was Monte Rosa, hanging there
   A thousand shadowy-pencill'd valleys
And snowy dells in a golden air!

Remember how we came at last
To Como; shower and storm and blast　　　　70
　　Had blown the lake beyond his limit,
And all was flooded; and how we past

From Como, when the light was gray,
And in my head, for half the day,
　　The rich Virgilian rustic measure
Of "Lari Maxume," all the way,

Like ballad-burthen music, kept,
As on the Lariano crept
　　To that fair port below the castle
Of Queen Theodolind, where we slept;　　　　80

Or hardly slept, but watch'd awake
A cypress in the moonlight shake,
　　The moonlight touching o'er a terrace
One tall agavè above the lake.

What more? we took our last adieu,
And up the snowy Splügen drew;
　　But ere we reach'd the highest summit
I pluck'd a daisy, I gave it you.

It told of England then to me,
And now it tells of Italy.　　　　90
　　O love, we two shall go no longer
To lands of summer across the sea.

So dear a life your arms enfold
Whose crying is a cry for gold;
　　Yet here to-night in this dark city,
When ill and weary, alone and cold,

I found, tho' crush'd to hard and dry,
This nursling of another sky
　　Still in the little book you lent me,
And where you tenderly laid it by;　　　　100

And I forgot the clouded Forth,
The gloom that saddens heaven and earth,
　　The bitter east, the misty summer
And gray metropolis of the North.

Perchance to lull the throbs of pain,
Perchance to charm a vacant brain,
　Perchance to dream you still beside me,
My fancy fled to the South again.

1853 (1855)*

TO THE REV. F. D. MAURICE

Come, when no graver cares employ,
Godfather, come and see your boy;
　Your presence will be sun in winter,
Making the little one leap for joy.

For, being of that honest few
Who give the Fiend himself his due,
　Should eighty thousand college-councils
Thunder "Anathema," friend, at you,

Should all our churchmen foam in spite
At you, so careful of the right,   10
　Yet one lay-hearth would give you welcome —
Take it and come — to the Isle of Wight;

Where, far from noise and smoke of town,
I watch the twilight falling brown
　All round a careless-order'd garden
Close to the ridge of a noble down.

You 'll have no scandal while you dine,
But honest talk and wholesome wine,
　And only hear the magpie gossip
Garrulous under a roof of pine;   20

For groves of pine on either hand,
To break the blast of winter, stand,
　And further on, the hoary Channel
Tumbles a billow on chalk and sand;

Where, if below the milky steep
Some ship of battle slowly creep,
　And on thro' zones of light and shadow
Glimmer away to the lonely deep,

We might discuss the Northern sin
Which made a selfish war begin, 30
  Dispute the claims, arrange the chances, —
Emperor, Ottoman, which shall win;

Or whether war's avenging rod
Shall lash all Europe into blood;
  Till you should turn to dearer matters,
Dear to the man that is dear to God, —

How best to help the slender store,
How mend the dwellings, of the poor,
  How gain in life, as life advances,
Valor and charity more and more. 40

Come, Maurice, come; the lawn as yet
Is hoar with rime or spongy-wet,
  But when the wreath of March has blossom'd, —
Crocus, anemone, violet, —

Or later, pay one visit here,
For those are few we hold as dear;
  Nor pay but one, but come for many,
Many and many a happy year.

1854 (1855)*

THE CHARGE OF THE LIGHT BRIGADE

I

Half a league, half a league,
Half a league onward,
All in the valley of Death
  Rode the six hundred.
"Forward the Light Brigade!
Charge for the guns!" he said.
Into the valley of Death
  Rode the six hundred.

II

"Forward, the Light Brigade!"
Was there a man dismay'd? 10
Not tho' the soldier knew
  Some one had blunder'd.

Theirs not to make reply,
Theirs not to reason why,
Theirs but to do and die.
Into the valley of Death
  Rode the six hundred.

III

Cannon to right of them,
Cannon to left of them,
Cannon in front of them   20
  Volley'd and thunder'd;
Storm'd at with shot and shell,
Boldly they rode and well,
Into the jaws of Death,
Into the mouth of hell
  Rode the six hundred.

IV

Flash'd all their sabres bare,
Flash'd as they turn'd in air
Sabring the gunners there,
Charging an army, while   30
  All the world wonder'd.
Plunged in the battery-smoke
Right thro' the line they broke;
Cossack and Russian
Reel'd from the sabre-stroke
  Shatter'd and sunder'd.
Then they rode back, but not,
  Not the six hundred.

V

Cannon to right of them,
Cannon to left of them,   40
Cannon behind them
  Volley'd and thunder'd;
Storm'd at with shot and shell,
While horse and hero fell,
They that had fought so well
Came thro' the jaws of Death,
Back from the mouth of hell,
All that was left of them,
  Left of six hundred.

VI

When can their glory fade?
O the wild charge they made!
  All the world wonder'd.
Honor the charge they made!
Honor the Light Brigade,
  Noble six hundred!

50

1854*

MAUD; A MONODRAMA

PART I

I

i

I HATE the dreadful hollow behind the little wood;
Its lips in the field above are dabbled with blood-red heath,
The red-ribb'd ledges drip with a silent horror of blood,
And Echo there, whatever is ask'd her, answers "Death."

ii

For there in the ghastly pit long since a body was found,
His who had given me life — O father! O God! was it well? —
Mangled, and flatten'd, and crush'd, and dinted into the ground;
There yet lies the rock that fell with him when he fell.

iii

Did he fling himself down? who knows? for a vast speculation had
    fail'd,
And ever he mutter'd and madden'd, and ever wann'd with despair,
And out he walk'd when the wind like a broken worldling wail'd,   11
And the flying gold of the ruin'd woodlands drove thro' the air.

iv

I remember the time, for the roots of my hair were stirr'd
By a shuffled step, by a dead weight trail'd, by a whisper'd fright.
And my pulses closed their gates with a shock on my heart as I heard
The shrill-edged shriek of a mother divide the shuddering night.

v

Villainy somewhere! whose? One says, we are villains all.
Not he! his honest fame should at least by me be maintained;
But that old man, now lord of the broad estate and the Hall,   19
Dropt off gorged from a scheme that had left us flaccid and drain'd.

vi

Why do they prate of the blessings of peace? we have made them a
    curse,
Pickpockets, each hand lusting for all that is not its own;
And lust of gain, in the spirit of Cain, is it better or worse
Than the heart of the citizen hissing in war on his own hearthstone?

VII

But these are the days of advance, the works of the men of mind,
When who but a fool would have faith in a tradesman's ware or his
    word?
Is it peace or war? Civil war, as I think, and that of a kind
The viler, as underhand, not openly bearing the sword.

VIII

Sooner or later I too may passively take the print
Of the golden age — why not? I have neither hope nor trust;   30
May make my heart as a millstone, set my face as a flint,
Cheat and be cheated, and die — who knows? we are ashes and dust.

IX

Peace sitting under her olive, and slurring the days gone by,
When the poor are hovell'd and hustled together, each sex, like swine,
When only the ledger lives, and when only not all men lie;
Peace in her vineyard — yes! — but a company forges the wine.

X

And the vitriol madness flushes up in the ruffiian's head,
Till the filthy by-lane rings to the yell of the trampled wife,
And chalk and alum and plaster are sold to the poor for bread,
And the spirit of murder works in the very means of life,   40

XI

And Sleep must lie down arm'd, for the villainous centre-bits
Grind on the wakeful ear in the hush of the moonless nights,
While another is cheating the sick of a few last gasps, as he sits
To pestle a poison'd poison behind his crimson lights.

XII

When a Mammonite mother kills her babe for a burial fee,
And Timour-Mammon grins on a pile of children's bones,
Is it peace or war? better, war! loud war by land and by sea,
War with a thousand battles, and shaking a hundred thrones!

XIII

For I trust if an enemy's fleet came yonder round by the hill,
And the rushing battle-bolt sang from the three-decker out of the
    foam,   50
That the smooth-faced, snub-nosed rogue would leap from his counter
    and till,
And strike, if he could, were it but with his cheating yardwand, home.

XIV

What! am I raging alone as my father raged in his mood?
Must *I* too creep to the hollow and dash myself down and die
Rather than hold by the law that I made, nevermore to brood
On a horror of shatter'd limbs and a wretched swindler's lie?

XV

Would there be sorrow for *me*? there was *love* in the passionate shriek,
Love for the silent thing that had made false haste to the grave —
Wrapt in a cloak, as I saw him, and thought he would rise and speak
And rave at the lie and the liar, ah God, as he used to rave.   60

XVI

I am sick of the Hall and the hill, I am sick of the moor and the main.
Why should I stay? can a sweeter chance ever come to me here?
O, having the nerves of motion as well as the nerves of pain,
Were it not wise if I fled from the place and the pit and the fear?

XVII

Workmen up at the Hall! — they are coming back from abroad;
The dark old place will be gilt by the touch of a millionaire
I have heard, I know not whence, of the singular beauty of Maud;
I play'd with the girl when a child; she promised then to be fair.

XVIII

Maud, with her venturous climbings and tumbles and childish escapes,
Maud, the delight of the village, the ringing joy of the Hall,   70
Maud, with her sweet purse-mouth when my father dangled the grapes,
Maud, the beloved of my mother, the moon-faced darling of all, —

XIX

What is she now? My dreams are bad. She may bring me a curse.
No, there is fatter game on the moor; she will let me alone.
Thanks; for the fiend best knows whether woman or man be the worse.
I will bury myself in myself, and the Devil may pipe to his own.

II

Long have I sigh'd for a calm; God grant I may find it at last!
It will never be broken by Maud; she has neither savor nor salt,
But a cold and clear-cut face, as I found when her carriage past,
Perfectly beautiful; let it be granted her; where is the fault?   80
All that I saw — for her eyes were downcast, not to be seen —
Faultily faultless, icily regular, splendidly null,
Dead perfection, no more; nothing more, if it had not been

For a chance of travel, a paleness, an hour's defect of the rose,
Or an underlip, you may call it a little too ripe, too full,
Or the least little delicate aquiline curve in a sensitive nose,
From which I escaped heart-free, with the least little touch of spleen.

III

Cold and clear-cut face, why come you so cruelly meek,
Breaking a slumber in which all spleenful folly was drown'd?
Pale with the golden beam of an eyelash dead on the cheek,   90
Passionless, pale, cold face, star-sweet on a gloom profound;
Womanlike, taking revenge too deep for a transient wrong
Done but in thought to your beauty, and ever as pale as before
Growing and fading and growing upon me without a sound,
Luminous, gemlike, ghostlike, deathlike, half the night long
Growing and fading and growing, till I could bear it no more,
But arose, and all by myself in my own dark garden ground,
Listening now to the tide in its broad-flung shipwrecking roar,
Now to the scream of a madden'd beach dragg'd down by the wave,
Walk'd in a wintry wind by a ghastly glimmer, and found   100
The shining daffodil dead, and Orion low in his grave.

IV

I

A million emeralds break from the ruby-budded lime
In the little grove where I sit — ah, wherefore cannot I be
Like things of the season gay, like the bountiful season bland,
When the far-off sail is blown by the breeze of a softer clime,
Half-lost in the liquid azure bloom of a crescent of sea,
The silent sapphire-spangled marriage ring of the land?

II

Below me, there, is the village, and looks how quiet and small!
And yet bubbles o'er like a city, with gossip, scandal, and spite;
And Jack on his ale-house bench has as many lies as a Czar;   110
And here on the landward side, by a red rock, glimmers the Hall;
And up in the high Hall-garden I see her pass like a light;
But sorrow seize me if ever that light be my leading star!

III

When have I bow'd to her father, the wrinkled head of the race?
I met her to-day with her brother, but not to her brother I bow'd;
I bow'd to his lady-sister as she rode by on the moor,
But the fire of a foolish pride flash'd over her beautiful face.
O child, you wrong your beauty, believe it, in being so proud;
Your father has wealth well-gotten, and I am nameless and poor.

IV

I keep but a man and a maid, ever ready to slander and steal;   120
I know it, and smile a hard-set smile, like a stoic, or like
A wiser epicurean, and let the world have its way.
For nature is one with rapine, a harm no preacher can heal;
The Mayfly is torn by the swallow, the sparrow spear'd by the shrike,
And the whole little wood where I sit is a world of plunder and prey.

V

We are puppets, Man in his pride, and Beauty fair in her flower;
Do we move ourselves, or are moved by an unseen hand at a game
That pushes us off from the board, and others ever succeed?
Ah yet, we cannot be kind to each other here for an hour;
We whisper, and hint, and chuckle, and grin at a brother's shame;   130
However we brave it out, we men are a little breed.

VI

A monstrous eft was of old the lord and master of earth,
For him did his high sun flame, and his river billowing ran,
And he felt himself in his force to be Nature's crowning race.
As nine months go to the shaping an infant ripe for his birth,
So many a million of ages have gone to the making of man:
He now is first, but is he the last? is he not too base?

VII

The man of science himself is fonder of glory, and vain,
An eye well-practised in nature, a spirit bounded and poor;
The passionate heart of the poet is whirl'd into folly and vice.   140
I would not marvel at either, but keep a temperate brain;
For not to desire or admire, if a man could learn it, were more
Than to walk all day like the sultan of old in a garden of spice.

VIII

For the drift of the Maker is dark, an Isis hid by the veil.
Who knows the ways of the world, how God will bring them about?
Our planet is one, the suns are many, the world is wide.
Shall I weep if a Poland fall? shall I shriek if a Hungary fail?
Or an infant civilization be ruled with rod or with knout?
I have not made the world, and He that made it will guide.

IX

Be mine a philosopher's life in the quiet woodland ways,   150
Where if I cannot be gay let a passionless peace be my lot,
Far-off from the clamor of liars belied in the hubbub of lies;
From the long-neck'd geese of the world that are ever hissing dispraise

Because their natures are little, and, whether he heed it or not,
Where each man walks with his head in a cloud of poisonous flies.

X

And most of all would I flee from the cruel madness of love
The honey of poison-flowers and all the measureless ill.
Ah, Maud, you milk-white fawn, you are all unmeet for a wife.
Your mother is mute in her grave as her image in marble above;
Your father is ever in London, you wander about at your will;   160
You have but fed on the roses and lain in the lilies of life.

V

I

A voice by the cedar tree
In the meadow under the Hall!
She is singing an air that is known to me,
A passionate ballad gallant and gay,
A martial song like a trumpet's call!
Singing alone in the morning of life,
In the happy morning of life and of May,
Singing of men that in battle array,
Ready in heart and ready in hand,   170
March with banner and bugle and fife
To the death, for their native land.

II

Maud with her exquisite face,
And wild voice pealing up to the sunny sky,
And feet like sunny gems on an English green,
Maud in the light of her youth and her grace,
Singing of Death, and of Honor that cannot die,
Till I well could weep for a time so sordid and mean,
And myself so languid and base.

III

Silence, beautiful voice!   180
Be still, for you only trouble the mind
With a joy in which I cannot rejoice,
A glory I shall not find.
Still! I will hear you no more,
For your sweetness hardly leaves me a choice
But to move to the meadow and fall before
Her feet on the meadow grass, and adore,
Not her, who is neither courtly nor kind,
Not her, not her, but a voice.

VI

I

Morning arises stormy and pale, 190
No sun, but a wannish glare
In fold upon fold of hueless cloud;
And the budded peaks of the wood, are bow'd,
Caught, and cuff'd by the gale:
I had fancied it would be fair.

II

Whom but Maud should I meet
Last night, when the sunset burn'd
On the blossom'd gable-ends
At the head of the village street,
Whom but Maud should I meet? 200
And she touch'd my hand with a smile so sweet,
She made me divine amends
For a courtesy not return'd.

III

And thus a delicate spark
Of glowing and growing light
Thro' the livelong hours of the dark
Kept itself warm in the heart of my dreams,
Ready to burst in a color'd flame;
Till at last, when the morning came
In a cloud, it faded, and seems 210
But an ashen-gray delight.

IV

What if with her sunny hair,
And smile as sunny as cold,
She meant to weave me a snare
Of some coquettish deceit,
Cleopatra-like as of old
To entangle me when we met,
To have her lion roll in a silken net
And fawn at a victor's feet.

V

Ah, what shall I be at fifty 220
Should Nature keep me alive,
If I find the world so bitter
When I am but twenty-five?

Yet, if she were not a cheat,
If Maud were all that she seem'd,
And her smile were all that I dream'd,
Then the world were not so bitter
But a smile could make it sweet.

VI

What if, tho' her eye seem'd full
Of a kind intent to me,   230
What if that dandy-despot, he,
That jewell'd mass of millinery,
That oil'd and curl'd Assyrian bull
Smelling of musk and of insolence,
Her brother, from whom I keep aloof,
Who wants the finer politic sense
To mask, tho' but in his own behoof,
With a glassy smile his brutal scorn —
What if he had told her yestermorn
How prettily for his own sweet sake   240
A face of tenderness might be feign'd,
And a moist mirage in desert eyes,
That so, when the rotten hustings shake
In another month to his brazen lies,
A wretched vote may be gain'd?

VII

For a raven ever croaks, at my side,
Keep watch and ward, keep watch and ward,
Or thou wilt prove their tool.
Yea, too, myself from myself I guard,
For often a man's own angry pride   250
Is cap and bells for a fool.

VIII

Perhaps the smile and tender tone
Came out of her pitying womanhood,
For am I not, am I not, here alone
So many a summer since she died,
My mother, who was so gentle and good?
Living alone in an empty house,
Here half-hid in the gleaming wood,
Where I hear the dead at midday moan,
And the shrieking rush of the wainscot mouse,   260
And my own sad name in corners cried,
When the shiver of dancing leaves is thrown

About its echoing chambers wide,
Till a morbid hate and horror have grown
Of a world in which I have hardly mixt,
And a morbid eating lichen fixt
On a heart half-turn'd to stone.

IX

O heart of stone, are you flesh, and caught
By that you swore to withstand?
For what was it else within me wrought   270
But, I fear, the new strong wine of love,
That made my tongue so stammer and trip
When I saw the treasured splendor, her hand,
Come sliding out of her sacred glove,
And the sunlight broke from her lip?

X

I have play'd with her when a child;
She remembers it now we meet.
Ah, well, well, well, I *may* be beguiled
By some coquettish deceit.
Yet, if she were not a cheat,   280
If Maud were all that she seem'd,
And her smile had all that I dream'd,
Then the world were not so bitter
But a smile could make it sweet.

VII

I

Did I hear it half in a doze
    Long since, I know not where?
Did I dream it an hour ago,
    When asleep in this arm-chair?

II

Men were drinking together,
    Drinking and talking of me: 290
"Well, if it prove a girl, the boy
    Will have plenty; so let it be."

III

Is it an echo of something
    Read with a boy's delight,
Viziers nodding together
    In some Arabian night?

IV

Strange, that I hear two men,
   Somewhere, talking of me:
"Well, if it prove a girl, my boy
   Will have plenty; so let it be."   300

VIII

She came to the village church,
And sat by a pillar alone;
An angel watching an urn
Wept over her, carved in stone;
And once, but once, she lifted her eyes,
And suddenly, sweetly, strangely blush'd
To find they were met by my own;
And suddenly, sweetly, my heart beat stronger
And thicker, until I heard no longer
The snowy-banded, dilettante,   310
Delicate-handed priest intone;
And thought, is it pride? and mused and sigh'd,
"No surely, now it cannot be pride."

IX

I was walking a mile,
   More than a mile from the shore,
The sun look'd out with a smile
   Betwixt the cloud and the moor;
And riding at set of day
   Over the dark moor land,
Rapidly riding far away,   320
   She waved to me with her hand.
There were two at her side,
   Something flash'd in the sun,
Down by the hill I saw them ride,
   In a moment they were gone;
Like a sudden spark
   Struck vainly in the night,
Then returns the dark
   With no more hope of light.

X

I

Sick, am I sick of a jealous dread?   330
Was not one of the two at her side
This new-made lord, whose splendor plucks

The slavish hat from the villager's head?
Whose old grandfather has lately died,
Gone to a blacker pit, for whom
Grimy nakedness dragging his trucks
And laying his trams in a poison'd gloom
Wrought, till he crept from a gutted mine
Master of half a servile shire,
And left his coal all turn'd into gold   340
To a grandson, first of his noble line,
Rich in the grace all women desire,
Strong in the power that all men adore,
And simper and set their voices lower,
And soften as if to a girl, and hold
Awe-stricken breaths at a work divine,
Seeing his gewgaw castle shine,
New as his title, built last year,
There amid perky larches and pine,
And over the sullen-purple moor —   350
Look at it — pricking a cockney ear.

II

What, has he found my jewel out?
For one of the two that rode at her side
Bound for the Hall, I am sure was he;
Bound for the Hall, and I think for a bride.
Blithe would her brother's acceptance be
Maud could be gracious too, no doubt,
To a lord, a captain, a padded shape,
A bought commission, a waxen face,
A rabbit mouth that is ever agape —   360
Bought? what is it he cannot buy?
And therefore splenetic, personal, base,
A wounded thing with a rancorous cry,
At war with myself and a wretched race,
Sick, sick to the heart of life, am I.

III

Last week came one to the county town,
To preach our poor little army down,
And play the game of the despot kings,
Tho' the state has done it and thrice as well.
This broad-brimm'd hawker of holy things,   370
Whose ear is cramm'd with his cotton, and rings
Even in dreams to the chink of his pence,
This huckster put down war! can he tell
Whether war be a cause or a consequence?

Put down the passions that make earth hell!
Down with ambition, avarice, pride,
Jealousy, down! cut off from the mind
The bitter springs of anger and fear!
Down too, down at your own fireside,
With the evil tongue and the evil ear,   380
For each is at war with mankind!

IV

I wish I could hear again
The chivalrous battle-song
That she warbled alone in her joy!
I might persuade myself then
She would not do herself this great wrong,
To take a wanton dissolute boy
For a man and leader of men.

V

Ah God, for a man with heart, head, hand,
Like some of the simple great ones gone   390
For ever and ever by,
One still strong man in a blatant land,
Whatever they call him — what care I? —
Aristocrat, democrat, autocrat — one
Who can rule and dare not lie!

VI

And ah for a man to arise in me,
That the man I am may cease to be!

XI

I

O, let the solid ground
   Not fail beneath my feet
Before my life has found   400
   What some have found so sweet!
Then let come what come may,
What matter if I go mad,
I shall have had my day.

II

Let the sweet heavens endure,
   Not close and darken above me
Before I am quite quite sure
   That there is one to love me!

Then let come what come may
To a life that has been so sad,   410
I shall have had my day.

XII

I

Birds in the high Hall-garden
    When twilight was falling,
Maud, Maud, Maud, Maud,
    They were crying and calling.

II

Where was Maud? in our wood;
    And I — who else? — was with her,
Gathering woodland lilies,
    Myriads blow together.

III

Birds in our wood sang   420
    Ringing thro' the valleys,
Maud is here, here, here
    In among the lilies.

IV

I kiss'd her slender hand,
    She took the kiss sedately;
Maud is not seventeen,
    But she is tall and stately.

V

I to cry out on pride.
    Who have won her favor!
O, Maud were sure of heaven   430
    If lowliness could save her!

VI

I know the way she went
    Home with her maiden posy,
For her feet have touch'd the meadows
    And left the daisies rosy.

VII

Birds in the high Hall-garden
    Were crying and calling to her,
Where is Maud, Maud, Maud?
    One is come to woo her.

VIII

Look, a horse at the door,   440
    And little King Charley snarling!
Go back, my lord, across the moor,
    You are not her darling.

XIII

I

Scorn'd, to be scorn'd by one that I scorn,
Is that a matter to make me fret?
That a calamity hard to be borne?
Well, he may live to hate me yet.
Fool that I am to be vext with his pride!
I past him, I was crossing his lands;
He stood on the path a little aside;   450
His face, as I grant, in spite of spite,
Has a broad-blown comeliness, red and white,
And six feet two, as I think, he stands;
But his essences turn'd the live air sick,
And barbarous opulence jewel-thick
Sunn'd itself on his breast and his hands.

II

Who shall call me ungentle, unfair?
I long'd so heartily then and there
To give him the grasp of fellowship;
But while I past he was humming an air,   460
Stopt, and then with a riding-whip
Leisurely tapping a glossy boot,
And curving a contumelious lip,
Gorgonized me from head to foot
With a stony British stare.

III

Why sits he here in his father's chair?
That old man never comes to his place;
Shall I believe him ashamed to be seen?
For only once, in the village street,
Last year, I caught a glimpse of his face,   470
A gray old wolf and a lean.
Scarcely, now, would I call him a cheat;
For then, perhaps, as a child of deceit,
She might by a true descent be untrue;
And Maud is as true as Maud is sweet,
Tho' I fancy her sweetness only due

To the sweeter blood by the other side;
Her mother has been a thing complete,
However she came to be so allied.
And fair without, faithful within,   480
Maud to him is nothing akin.
Some peculiar mystic grace
Made her only the child of her mother,
And heap'd the whole inherited sin
On that huge scapegoat of the race,
All, all upon the brother.

IV

Peace, angry spirit, and let him be!
Has not his sister smiled on me?

XIV

I

Maud has a garden of roses   490
And lilies fair on a lawn;
There she walks in her state
And tends upon bed and bower,
And thither I climb'd at dawn
And stood by her garden-gate.
A lion ramps at the top,
He is claspt by a passion-flower.

II

Maud's own little oak-room —
Which Maud, like a precious stone
Set in the heart of the carven gloom,
Lights with herself, when alone   500
She sits by her music and books
And her brother lingers late
With a roystering company — looks
Upon Maud's own garden-gate;
And I thought as I stood, if a hand, as white
As ocean-foam in the moon, were laid
On the hasp of the window, and my Delight
Had a sudden desire, like a glorious ghost, to glide,
Like a beam of the seventh heaven, down to my side,
There were but a step to be made.   510

III

The fancy flatter'd my mind,
And again seem'd overbold;

Now I thought that she cared for me,
Now I thought she was kind
Only because she was cold.

IV

I heard no sound where I stood
But the rivulet on from the lawn
Running down to my own dark wood,
Or the voice of the long sea-wave as it swell'd
Now and then in the dim-gray dawn;   520
But I look'd, and round, all round the house I beheld
The death-white curtain drawn,
Felt a horror over me creep,
Prickle my skin and catch my breath,
Knew that the death-white curtain meant but sleep,
Yet I shudder'd and thought like a fool of the sleep of death.

XV

So dark a mind within me dwells,
    And I make myself such evil cheer,
That if *I* be dear to some one else,
    Then some one else may have much to fear;   530
But if *I* be dear to some one else,
    Then I should be to myself more dear.
Shall I not take care of all that I think,
Yea, even of wretched meat and drink,
If I be dear,
If I be dear to some one else?

XVI

I

This lump of earth has left his estate
The lighter by the loss of his weight;
And so that he find what he went to seek,
And fulsome pleasure clog him, and drown   540
His heart in the gross mud-honey of town,
He may stay for a year who has gone for a week.
But this is the day when I must speak,
And I see my Oread coming down,
O, this is the day!
O beautiful creature, what am I
That I dare to look her way?
Think I may hold dominion sweet,
Lord of the pulse that is lord of her breast,

And dream of her beauty with tender dread,   550
From the delicate Arab arch of her feet
To the grace that, bright and light as the crest
Of a peacock, sits on her shining head,
And she knows it not — O, if she knew it,
To know her beauty might half undo it!
I know it the one bright thing to save
My yet young life in the wilds of Time,
Perhaps from madness, perhaps from crime,
Perhaps from a selfish grave.

II

What, if she be fasten'd to this fool lord,   560
Dare I bid her abide by her word?
Should I love her so well if she
Had given her word to a thing so low?
Shall I love her as well if she
Can break her word were it even for me?
I trust that it is not so.

III

Catch not my breath, O clamorous heart,
Let not my tongue be a thrall to my eye,
For I must tell her before we part,
I must tell her, or die.   570

XVII

Go not, happy day,
    From the shining fields,
Go not, happy day,
    Till the maiden yields.
Rosy is the West,
    Rosy is the South,
Roses are her cheeks,
    And a rose her mouth.
When the happy Yes
    Falters from her lips,   580
Pass and blush the news
    Over glowing ships;
Over blowing seas,
    Over seas at rest,
Pass the happy news,
    Blush it thro' the West;
Till the red man dance
    By his red cedar-tree,

And the red man's babe
　　Leap, beyond the sea.　　　　　　　　590
Blush from West to East,
　　Blush from East to West,
Till the West is East,
　　Blush it thro' the West.
Rosy is the West,
　　Rosy is the South,
Roses are her cheeks,
　　And a rose her mouth.

XVIII

I

I have led her home, my love, my only friend.
There is none like her, none.　　　　　　　600
And never yet so warmly ran my blood
And sweetly, on and on
Calming itself to the long-wish'd-for end,
Full to the banks, close on the promised good.

II

None like her, none.
Just now the dry-tongued laurels' pattering talk
Seem'd her light foot along the garden walk,
And shook my heart to think she comes once more.
But even then I heard her close the door;
The gates of heaven are closed, and she is gone.　　610

III

There is none like her, none,
Nor will be when our summers have deceased.
O, art thou sighing for Lebanon
In the long breeze that streams to thy delicious East,
Sighing for Lebanon,
Dark cedar, tho' thy limbs have here increased,
Upon a pastoral slope as fair,
And looking to the South and fed
With honey'd rain and delicate air,
And haunted by the starry head　　　　　　　620
Of her whose gentle will has changed my fate,
And made my life a perfumed altar-flame;
And over whom thy darkness must have spread
With such delight as theirs of old, thy great
Forefathers of the thornless garden, there
Shadowing the snow-limb'd Eve from whom she came?

IV

Here will I lie, while these long branches sway,
And you fair stars that crown a happy day
Go in and out as if at merry play,
Who am no more so all forlorn   630
As when it seem'd far better to be born
To labor and the mattock-harden'd hand
Than nursed at ease and brought to understand
A sad astrology, the boundless plan
That makes you tyrants in your iron skies,
Innumerable, pitiless, passionless eyes,
Cold fires, yet with power to burn and brand
His nothingness into man.

V

But now shine on, and what care I,
Who in this stormy gulf have found a pearl   640
The countercharm of space and hollow sky,
And do accept my madness, and would die
To save from some slight shame one simple girl? —

VI

Would die, for sullen-seeming Death may give
More life to Love than is or ever was
In our low world, where yet 't is sweet to live.
Let no one ask me how it came to pass;
It seems that I am happy, that to me
A livelier emerald twinkles in the grass,
A purer sapphire melts into the sea.   650

VII

Not die, but live a life of truest breath,
And teach true life to fight with mortal wrongs.
O, why should Love, like men in drinking-songs,
Spice his fair banquet with the dust of death?
Make answer, Maud my bliss,
Maud made my Maud by that long loving kiss,
Life of my life, wilt thou not answer this?
"The dusky strand of Death inwoven here
With dear Love's tie, makes Love himself more dear."

VIII

Is that enchanted moan only the swell   660
Of the long waves that roll in yonder bay?
And hark the clock within, the silver knell

Of twelve sweet hours that past in bridal white,
And died to live, long as my pulses play;
But now by this my love has closed her sight
And given false death her hand, and stolen away
To dreamful wastes where footless fancies dwell
Among the fragments of the golden day.
May nothing there her maiden grace affright!
Dear heart, I feel with thee the drowsy spell.   670
My bride to be, my evermore delight,
My own heart's heart, my ownest own, farewell;
It is but for a little space I go.
And ye meanwhile far over moor and fell
Beat to the noiseless music of the night!
Has our whole earth gone nearer to the glow
Of your soft splendors that you look so bright?
I have climb'd nearer out of lonely hell.
Beat, happy stars, timing with things below,
Beat with my heart more blest than heart can tell,   680
Blest, but for some dark undercurrent woe
That seems to draw — but it shall not be so;
Let all be well, be well.

XIX

I

Her brother is coming back to-night,
Breaking up my dream of delight.

II

My dream? do I dream of bliss?
I have walk'd awake with Truth.
O, when did a morning shine
So rich in atonement as this
For my dark-dawning youth,   690
Darken'd watching a mother decline
And that dead man at her heart and mine;
For who was left to watch her but I?
Yet so did I let my freshness die.

III

I trust that I did not talk
To gentle Maud in our walk -
For often in lonely wanderings
I have cursed him even to life.ess things —
But I trust that I did not talk,
Not touch on her father's sin.   700

I am sure I did but speak
Of my mother's faded cheek
When it slowly grew so thin
That I felt she was slowly dying
Vext with lawyers and harrass'd with debt;
For how often I caught her with eyes all wet,
Shaking her head at her son and sighing
A world of trouble within!

IV

And Maud too, Maud was moved
To speak of the mother she loved   710
As one scarce less forlorn,
Dying abroad and it seems apart
From him who had ceased to share her heart,
And ever mourning over the feud,
The household Fury sprinkled with blood
By which our houses are torn.
How strange was what she said,
When only Maud and the brother
Hung over her dying bed —
That Maud's dark father and mine   720
Had bound us one to the other,
Betrothed us over their wine,
On the day when Maud was born;
Seal'd her mine from her first sweet breath!
Mine, mine by a right, from birth till death!
Mine, mine — our fathers have sworn!

V

But the true blood spilt had in it a heat
To dissolve the precious seal on a bond,
That, if left uncancell'd, had been so sweet;
And none of us thought of a something beyond,   730
A desire that awoke in the heart of the child,
As it were a duty done to the tomb,
To be friends for her sake, to be reconciled;
And I was cursing them and my doom,
And letting a dangerous thought run wild
While often abroad in the fragrant gloom
Of foreign churches — I see her there,
Bright English lily, breathing a prayer
To be friends, to be reconciled!

VI

But then what a flint is he!　　　　　　　　740
Abroad, at Florence, at Rome,
I find whenever she touch'd on me
This brother had laugh'd her down,
And at last, when each came home,
He had darken'd into a frown,
Chid her, and forbid her to speak
To me, her friend of the years before;
And this was what had redden'd her cheek
When I bow'd to her on the moor.

VII

Yet Maud, altho' not blind　　　　　　　　750
To the faults of his heart and mind,
I see she cannot but love him,
And says he is rough but kind,
And wishes me to approve him,
And tells me, when she lay
Sick once, with a fear of worse,
That he left his wine and horses and play,
Sat with her, read to her, night and day,
And tended her like a nurse.

VIII

Kind? but the death-bed desire　　　　　　　760
Spurn'd by this heir of the liar —
Rough but kind? yet I know
He has plotted against me in this,
That he plots against me still.
Kind to Maud? that were not amiss.
Well, rough but kind; why, let it be so,
For shall not Maud have her will?

IX

For, Maud, so tender and true,
As long as my life endures
I feel I shall owe you a debt　　　　　　　770
That I never can hope to pay;
And if ever I should forget
That I owe this debt to you
And for your sweet sake to yours,
O, then, what then shall I say? —
If ever I *should* forget,
May God make me more wretched
Than ever I have been yet!

X

So now I have sworn to bury
All this dead body of hate,   780
I feel so free and so clear
By the loss of that dead weight,
That I should grow light-headed, I fear,
Fantastically merry,
But that her brother comes, like a blight
On my fresh hope, to the Hall to-night.

XX

I

Strange, that I felt so gay,
Strange, that I tried to-day
To beguile her melancholy;
The Sultan, as we name him —   790
She did not wish to blame him —
But he vext her and perplext her
With his worldy talk and folly.
Was it gentle to reprove her
For stealing out of view
From a little lazy lover
Who but claims her as his due?
Or for chilling his caresses
By the coldness of her manners,
Nay, the plainness of her dresses?   800
Now I know her but in two,
Nor can pronounce upon it
If one should ask me whether
The habit, hat, and feather,
Or the frock and gipsy bonnet
Be the neater and completer;
For nothing can be sweeter
Than maiden Maud in either.

II

But to-morrow, if we live,
Our ponderous squire will give   810
A grand political dinner
To half the squirelings near;
And Maud will wear her jewels,
And the bird of prey will hover,
And the titmouse hope to win her
With his chirrup at her ear.

III

A grand political dinner
To the men of many acres,
A gathering of the Tory,
A dinner and then a dance   820
For the maids and marriage-makers,
And every eye but mine will glance
At Maud in all her glory.

IV

For I am not invited,
But, with the Sultan's pardon,
I am all as well delighted,
For I know her own rose-garden,
And mean to linger in it
Till the dancing will be over;
And then, O, then, come out to me   830
For a minute, but for a minute,
Come out to your own true lover,
That your true lover may see
Your glory also, and render
All homage to his own darling,
Queen Maud in all her splendor.

XXI

Rivulet crossing my ground,
And bringing me down from the Hall
This garden-rose that I found,
Forgetful of Maud and me,   840
And lost in trouble and moving round
Here at the head of a tinkling fall,
And trying to pass to the sea;
O rivulet, born at the Hall,
My Maud has sent it by thee —
If I read her sweet will right —
On a blushing mission to me,
Saying in odor and color, "Ah, be
Among the roses to-night."

XXII

I

Come into the garden, Maud,   850
    For the black bat, night, has flown,
Come into the garden, Maud,

I am here at the gate alone;
And the woodbine spices are wafted abroad,
 And the musk of the rose is blown.

II

For a breeze of morning moves,
 And the planet of Love is on high,
Beginning to faint in the light that she loves
 On a bed of daffodil sky,
To faint in the light of the sun she loves,   860
 To faint in his light, and to die.

III

All night have the roses heard
 The flute, violin, bassoon;
All night has the casement jessamine stirr'd
 To the dancers dancing in tune;
Till a silence fell with the waking bird,
 And a hush with the setting moon.

IV

I said to the lily, "There is but one,
 With whom she has heart to be gay.
When will the dancers leave her alone?   870
 She is weary of dance and play."
Now half to the setting moon are gone,
 And half to the rising day;
Low on the sand and loud on the stone
 The last wheel echoes away.

V

I said to the rose, "The brief night goes
 In babble and revel and wine.
O young lord-lover, what sighs are those,
 For one that will never be thine?
But mine, but mine," so I sware to the rose,   880
 "For ever and ever, mine."

VI

And the soul of the rose went into my blood,
 As the music clash'd in the hall;
And long by the garden lake I stood,
 For I heard your rivulet fall
From the lake to the meadow and on to the wood,
 Our wood, that is dearer than all;

VII

From the meadow your walks have left so sweet
    That whenever a March-wind sighs
He sets the jewel-print of your feet   890
    In violets blue as your eyes,
To the woody hollows in which we meet
    And the valleys of Paradise.

VIII

The slender acacia would not shake
    One long milk-bloom on the tree;
The white lake-blossom fell into the lake
    As the pimpernel dozed on the lea;
But the rose was awake all night for your sake,
    Knowing your promise to me;
The lilies and roses were all awake,   900
    They sigh'd for the dawn and thee.

IX

Queen rose of the rosebud garden of girls,
    Come hither, the dances are done,
In gloss of satin and glimmer of pearls,
    Queen lily and rose in one;
Shine out, little head, sunning over with curls,
    To the flowers, and be their sun.

X

There has fallen a splendid tear
    From the passion-flower at the gate.
She is coming, my dove, my dear;
    She is coming, my life, my fate.   910
The red rose cries, "She is near, she is near;"
    And the white rose weeps, "She is late;"
The larkspur listens, "I hear, I hear;"
    And the lily whispers, "I wait."

XI

She is coming, my own, my sweet;
    Were it ever so airy a tread,
My heart would hear her and beat,
    Were it earth in an earthy bed;
My dust would hear her and beat,
    Had I lain for a century dead,   920
Would start and tremble under her feet,
    And blossom in purple and red.

PART II

I

1

"The fault was mine, the fault was mine" —
Why am I sitting here so stunn'd and still,
Plucking the harmless wild-flower on the hill? —
It is this guilty hand! —
And there rises ever a passionate cry
From underneath in the darkening land —
What is it, that has been done?
O dawn of Eden bright over earth and sky,
The fires of hell brake out of thy rising sun,
The fires of hell and of hate;   10
For she, sweet soul, had hardly spoken a word,
When her brother ran in his rage to the gate,
He came with the babe-faced lord,
Heap'd on her terms of disgrace;
And while she wept, and I strove to be cool,
He fiercely gave me the lie,
Till I with as fierce an anger spoke,
And he struck me, madman, over the face,
Struck me before the languid fool,
Who was gaping and grinning by;   20
Struck for himself an evil stroke,
Wrought for his house an irredeemable woe.
For front to front in an hour we stood,
And a million horrible bellowing echoes broke
From the red-ribb'd hollow behind the wood,
And thunder'd up into heaven the Christless code
That must have life for a blow.
Ever and ever afresh they seem'd to grow.
Was it he lay there with a fading eye?
"The fault was mine," he whisper'd, "fly!"   30
Then glided out of the joyous wood
The ghastly Wraith of one that I know,
And there rang on a sudden a passionate cry,
A cry for a brother's blood;
It will ring in my heart and my ears, till I die, till I die.

II

Is it gone? my pulses beat —
What was it? a lying trick of the brain?

Yet I thought I saw her stand,
A shadow there at my feet,
High over the shadowy land.   40
It is gone; and the heavens fall in a gentle rain,
When they should burst and drown with deluging storms
The feeble vassals of wine and anger and lust,
The little hearts that know not how to forgive.
Arise, my God, and strike, for we hold Thee just,
Strike dead the whole weak race of venomous worms,
That sting each other here in the dust;
We are not worthy to live.

II

I

See what a lovely shell,
Small and pure as a pearl,   50
Lying close to my foot,
Frail, but a work divine,
Made so fairily well
With delicate spire and whorl,
How exquisitely minute,
A miracle of design!

II

What is it? a learned man
Could give it a clumsy name.
Let him name it who can,
The beauty would be the same.   60

III

The tiny cell is forlorn,
Void of the little living will
That made it stir on the shore.
Did he stand at the diamond door
Of his house in a rainbow frill?
Did he push, when he was uncurl'd,
A golden foot or a fairy horn
Thro' his dim water-world?

IV

Slight, to be crush'd with a tap
Of my finger-nail on the sand,   70
Small, but a work divine,
Frail, but of force to withstand,
Year upon year, the shock

Of cataract seas that snap
The three-decker's oaken spine
Athwart the ledges of rock,
Here on the Breton strand!

V

Breton, not Briton; here
Like a shipwreck'd man on a coast
Of ancient fable and fear —   80
Plagued with a flitting to and fro,
A disease, a hard mechanic ghost
That never came from on high
Nor ever arose from below,
But only moves with the moving eye,
Flying along the land and the main —
Why should it look like Maud?
Am I to be overawed
By what I cannot but know
Is a juggle born of the brain?   90

VI

Back from the Breton coast,
Sick of a nameless fear,
Back to the dark sea-line
Looking, thinking of all I have lost;
An old song vexes my ear,
But that of Lamech is mine.

VII

For years, a measureless ill,
For years, for ever, to part —
But she, she would love me still;
And as long, O God, as she   100
Have a grain of love for me,
So long, no doubt, no doubt,
Shall I nurse in my dark heart,
However weary, a spark of will
Not to be trampled out.

VIII

Strange, that the mind, when fraught
With a passion so intense
One would think that it well
Might drown all life in the eye, —
That it should, by being so overwrought,   110
Suddenly strike on a sharper sense

For a shell, or a flower, little things
Which else would have been past by!
And now I remember, I,
When he lay dying there,
I noticed one of his many rings —
For he had many, poor worm — and thought,
It is his mother's hair.

IX

Who knows if he be dead?
Whether I need have fled?   120
Am I guilty of blood?
However this may be,
Comfort her, comfort her, all things good,
While I am over the sea!
Let me and my passionate love go by,
But speak to her all things holy and high,
Whatever happen to me!
Me and my harmful love go by;
But come to her waking, find her asleep,
Powers of the height, Powers of the deep,   130
And comfort her tho' I die!

III

Courage, poor heart of stone!
I will not ask thee why
Thou canst not understand
That thou art left for ever alone;
Courage, poor stupid heart of stone! —
Or if I ask thee why,
Care not thou to reply:
She is but dead, and the time is at hand
When thou shalt more than die.   140

IV

I

O that 't were possible
After long grief and pain
To find the arms of my true love
Round me once again!

II

When I was wont to meet her
In the silent woody places

By the home that gave me birth,
We stood tranced in long embraces
Mixt with kisses sweeter, sweeter
Than anything on earth.   150

III

A shadow flits before me,
Not thou, but like to thee.
Ah, Christ, that it were possible
For one short hour to see
The souls we loved, that they might tell us
What and where they be!

IV

It leads me forth at evening,
It lightly winds and steals
In a cold white robe before me,
When all my spirit reels   160
At the shouts, the leagues of lights,
And the roaring of the wheels.

V

Half the night I waste in sighs,
Half in dreams I sorrow after
The delight of early skies;
In a wakeful doze I sorrow
For the hand, the lips, the eyes,
For the meeting of the morrow,
The delight of happy laughter,
The delight of low replies.   170

VI

'T is a morning pure and sweet,
And a dewy splendor falls
On the little flower that clings
To the turrets and the walls;
'T is a morning pure and sweet,
And the light and shadow fleet.
She is walking in the meadow,
And the woodland echo rings;
In a moment we shall meet.
She is singing in the meadow,   180
And the rivulet at her feet
Ripples on in light and shadow
To the ballad that she sings.

VII

Do I hear her sing as of old,
My bird with the shining head,
My own dove with the tender eye?
But there rings on a sudden a passionate cry,
There is some one dying or dead,
And a sullen thunder is roll'd;
For a tumult shakes the city,   190
And I wake, my dream is fled.
In the shuddering dawn, behold,
Without knowledge, without pity,
By the curtains of my bed
That abiding phantom cold!

VIII

Get thee hence, nor come again,
Mix not memory with doubt,
Pass, thou deathlike type of pain,
Pass and cease to move about!
'T is the blot upon the brain   200
That *will* show itself without.

IX

Then I rise, the eave-drops fall,
And the yellow vapors choke
The great city sounding wide;
The day comes, a dull red ball
Wrapt in drifts of lurid smoke
On the misty river-tide.

X

Thro' the hubbub of the market
I steal, a wasted frame;
It crosses here, it crosses there,   210
Thro' all that crowd confused and loud,
The shadow still the same;
And on my heavy eyelids
My anguish hangs like shame.

XI

Alas for her that met me,
That heard me softly call,
Came glimmering thro' the laurels
At the quiet evenfall,

In the garden by the turrets
Of the old manorial hall!   220

XII

Would the happy spirit descend
From the realms of light and song,
In the chamber or the street,
As she looks among the blest,
Should I fear to greet my friend
Or to say "Forgive the wrong,"
Or to ask her, "Take me, sweet,
To the regions of thy rest"?

XIII

But the broad light glares and beats,
And the shadow flits and fleets   230
And will not let me be;
And I loathe the squares and streets,
And the faces that one meets,
Hearts with no love for me.
Always I long to creep
Into some still cavern deep,
There to weep, and weep, and weep
My whole soul out to thee.

V

I

Dead, long dead,
Long dead!   240
And my heart is a handful of dust,
And the wheels go over my head,
And my bones are shaken with pain,
For into a shallow grave they are thrust,
Only a yard beneath the street,
And the hoofs of the horses beat, beat,
The hoofs of the horses beat,
Beat into my scalp and my brain,
With never an end to the stream of passing feet,
Driving, hurrying, marrying, burying,   250
Clamor and rumble, and ringing and clatter;
And here beneath it is all as bad,
For I thought the dead had peace, but it is not so.
To have no peace in the grave, is that not sad?
But up and down and to and fro,

Ever about me the dead men go;
And then to hear a dead man chatter
Is enough to drive one mad.

II

Wretchedest age, since Time began,
They cannot even bury a man;
And tho' we paid our tithes in the days that are gone,   260
Not a bell was rung, not a prayer was read.
It is that which makes us loud in the world of the dead;
There is none that does his work, not one.
A touch of their office might have sufficed,
But the churchmen fain would kill their church,
As the churches have kill'd their Christ.

III

See, there is one of us sobbing,
No limit to his distress;
And another, a lord of all things, praying   270
To his own great self, as I guess;
And another, a statesman there, betraying
His party-secret, fool, to the press;
And yonder a vile physician, blabbing
The case of his patient — all for what?
To tickle the maggot born in an empty head,
And wheedle a world that loves him not,
For it is but a world of the dead.

IV

Nothing but idiot gabble!
For the prophecy given of old   280
And then not understood,
Has come to pass as foretold;
Not let any man think for the public good,
But babble, merely for babble.
For I never whisper'd a private affair
Within the hearing of cat or mouse,
No, not to myself in the closet alone,
But I heard it shouted at once from the top of the house;
Everything came to be known.
Who told *him* we were there?   290

V

Not that gray old wolf, for he came not back
From the wilderness, full of wolves, where he used to lie;

He has gather'd the bones for his o'ergrown whelp to crack —
Crack them now for yourself, and howl, and die.

VI

Prophet, curse me the blabbing lip,
And curse me the British vermin, the rat;
I know not whether he came in the Hanover ship,
But I know that he lies and listens mute
In an ancient mansion's crannies and holes.
Arsenic, arsenic, sure, would do it,   300
Except that now we poison our babes, poor souls!
It is all used up for that.

VII

Tell him now: she is standing here at my head;
Not beautiful now, not even kind;
He may take her now; for she never speaks her mind,
But is ever the one thing silent here.
She is not *of* us, as I divine;
She comes from another stiller world of the dead,
Stiller, not fairer than mine.

VIII

But I know where a garden grows,   310
Fairer than aught in the world beside,
All made up of the lily and rose
That blow by night, when the season is good,
To the sound of dancing music and flutes:
It is only flowers, they had no fruits,
And I almost fear they are not roses, but blood;
For the keeper was one, so full of pride,
He linkt a dead man there to a spectral bride;
For he, if he had not been a Sultan of brutes,
Would he have that hole in his side?   320

IX

But what will the old man say?
He laid a cruel snare in a pit
To catch a friend of mine one stormy day;
Yet now I could even weep to think of it;
For what will the old man say
When he comes to the second corpse in the pit?

X

Friend, to be struck by the public foe,
Then to strike him and lay him low,

That were a public merit, far,
Whatever the Quaker holds, from sin;   330
But the red life spilt for a private blow —
I swear to you, lawful and lawless war
Are scarcely even akin.

XI

O me, why have they not buried me deep enough?
Is it kind to have made me a grave so rough,
Me, that was never a quiet sleeper?
Maybe still I am but half-dead;
Then I cannot be wholly dumb.
I will cry to the steps above my head
And somebody, surely, some kind heart will come   340
To bury me, bury me
Deeper, ever so little deeper.

PART III

I

My life has crept so long on a broken wing
Thro' cells of madness, haunts of horror and fear,
That I come to be grateful at last for a little thing.
My mood is changed, for it fell at a time of year
When the face of night is fair on the dewy downs,
And the shining daffodil dies, and the Charioteer
And starry Gemini hang like glorious crowns
Over Orion's grave low down in the west,
That like a silent lightning under the stars
She seem'd to divide in a dream from a band of the blest,   10
And spoke of a hope for the world in the coming wars —
"And in that hope, dear soul, let trouble have rest,
Knowing I tarry for thee," and pointed to Mars
As he glow'd like a ruddy shield on the Lion's breast.

II

And it was but a dream, yet it yielded a dear delight
To have look'd tho' but in a dream, upon eyes so fair,
That had been in a weary world my one thing bright;
And it was but a dream, yet it lighten'd my despair
When I thought that a war would arise in defence of the right,
That an iron tyranny now should bend or cease,   20
The glory of manhood stand on his ancient height,
Nor Britain's one sole God be the millionaire.
No more shall commerce be all in all, and Peace

Pipe on her pastoral hillock a languid note,
And watch her harvest ripen, her herd increase,
Nor the cannon-bullet rust on a slothful shore,
And the cobweb woven across the cannon's throat
Shall shake its threaded tears in the wind no more.

III

And as months ran on and rumor of battle grew,
"It is time, it is time, O passionate heart," said I, —   30
For I cleaved to a cause that I felt to be pure and true, —
"It is time, O passionate heart and morbid eye,
That old hysterical mock-disease should die."
And I stood on a giant deck and mixt my breath
With a loyal people shouting a battlecry,
Till I saw the dreary phantom arise and fly
Far into the North, and battle, and seas of death.

IV

Let it go or stay, so I wake to the higher aims
Of a land that has lost for a little her lust of gold,
And love of a peace that was full of wrongs and shames,   40
Horrible, hateful, monstrous, not to be told;
And hail once more to the banner of battle unroll'd!
Tho' many a light shall darken, and many shall weep
For those that are crush'd in the clash of jarring claims
Yet God's just wrath shall be wreak'd on a giant liar,
And many a darkness into the light shall leap,
And shine in the sudden making of splendid names,
And noble thought be freer under the sun,
And the heart of a people beat with one desire;
For the peace, that I deem'd no peace, is over and done,   50
And now by the side of the Black and the Baltic deep,
And deathful-grinning mouths of the fortress, flames
The blood-red blossom of war with a heart of fire.

V

Let it flame or fade, and the war roll down like a wind,
We have proved we have hearts in a cause, we are noble still,
And myself have awaked, as it seems, to the better mind.
It is better to fight for the good than to rail at the ill;
I have felt with my native land, I am one with my kind,
I embrace the purpose of God, and the doom assign'd.

1855, 1856°

IN THE VALLEY OF CAUTERETZ

ALL along the valley, stream that flashest white,
Deepening thy voice with the deepening of the night,
All along the valley, where thy waters flow,
I walk'd with one I loved two and thirty years ago.
All along the valley, while I walk'd to-day,
The two and thirty years were a mist that rolls away;
For all along the valley, down thy rocky bed,
Thy living voice to me was as the voice of the dead,
And all along the valley, by rock and cave and tree,
The voice of the dead was a living voice to me.　　10

1861 (1864)*

HELEN'S TOWER

[Written at the request of my friend, Lord Dufferin.]

HELEN'S TOWER, here I stand,
Dominant over sea and land.
Son's love built me, and I hold
Mother's love in letter'd gold.
Love is in and out of time,
I am mortal stone and lime.
Would my granite girth were strong
As either love, to last as long!
I should wear my crown entire
To and thro' the Doomsday fire,　　10
And be found of angel eyes
In earth's recurring Paradise.

1861 (1884)*

MILTON

(ALCAICS)

O MIGHTY-MOUTH'D inventor of harmonies,
O skill'd to sing of Time or Eternity,
　　God-gifted organ-voice of England,
　　　　Milton, a name to resound for ages;

314

Whose Titan angels, Gabriel, Abdiel,
Starr'd from Jehovah's gorgeous armories,
   Tower, as the deep-domed empyrean
     Rings to the roar of an angel onset!
Me rather all that bowery loneliness,
The brooks of Eden mazily murmuring,   10
   And bloom profuse and cedar arches
     Charm, as a wanderer out in ocean,
Where some refulgent sunset of India
Streams o'er a rich ambrosial ocean isle,
   And crimson-hued the stately palm-woods
     Whisper in odorous heights of even.

1863*

THE VOYAGE

I

WE left behind the painted buoy
   That tosses at the harbor-mouth;
And madly danced our hearts with joy,
   As fast we fleeted to the south.
How fresh was every sight and sound
   On open main or winding shore!
We knew the merry world was round,
   And we might sail for evermore.

II

Warm broke the breeze against the brow,
   Dry sang the tackle, sang the sail;   10
The Lady's-head upon the prow
   Caught the shrill salt, and sheer'd the gale.
The broad seas swell'd to meet the keel,
   And swept behind; so quick the run,
We felt the good ship shake and reel,
   We seem'd to sail into the sun!

III

How oft we saw the sun retire,
   And burn the threshold of the night,
Fall from his Ocean-lane of fire,
   And sleep beneath his pillar'd light!   20
How oft the purple-skirted robe
   Of twilight slowly downward drawn,

As thro' the slumber of the globe
    Again we dash'd into the dawn!

IV

New stars all night above the brim
    Of waters lighten'd into view;
They climb'd as quickly, for the rim
    Changed every moment as we flew.
Far ran the naked moon across
    The houseless ocean's heaving field,   30
Or flying shone, the silver boss
    Of her own halo's dusky shield.

V

The peaky islet shifted shapes,
    High towns on hills were dimly seen;
We past long lines of Northern capes
    And dewy Northern meadows green.
We came to warmer waves, and deep
    Across the boundless east we drove,
Where those long swells of breaker sweep
    The nutmeg rocks and isles of clove.   40

VI

By peaks that flamed, or, all in shade,
    Gloom'd the low coast and quivering brine
With ashy rains, that spreading made
    Fantastic plume or sable pine;
By sands and steaming flats, and floods
    Of mighty mouth, we scudded fast,
And hills and scarlet-mingled woods
    Glow'd for a moment as we past.

VII

O hundred shores of happy climes,
    How swiftly stream'd ye by the bark!   50
At times the whole sea burn'd, at times
    With wakes of fire we tore the dark;
At times a carven craft would shoot
    From havens hid in fairy bowers,
With naked limbs and flowers and fruit,
    But we nor paused for fruit nor flowers.

VIII

For one fair Vision ever fled
    Down the waste waters day and night,

And still we follow'd where she led,
    In hope to gain upon her flight.   60
Her face was evermore unseen,
    And fixt upon the far sea-line;
But each man murmur'd, "O my Queen,
    I follow till I make thee mine."

IX

And now we lost her, now she gleam'd
    Like Fancy made of golden air,
Now nearer to the prow she seem'd
    Like Virtue firm, like Knowledge fair,
Now high on waves that idly burst
    Like Heavenly Hope she crown'd the sea,   70
And now, the bloodless point reversed,
    She bore the blade of Liberty.

X

And only one among us — him
    We pleased not — he was seldom pleased;
He saw not far, his eyes were dim,
    But ours he swore were all diseased.
"A ship of fools," he shriek'd in spite,
    "A ship of fools," he sneer'd and wept.
And overboard one stormy night
    He cast his body, and on we swept.   80

XI

And never sail of ours was furl'd,
    Nor anchor dropt at eve or morn;
We loved the glories of the world,
    But laws of nature were our scorn.
For blasts would rise and rave and cease,
    But whence were those that drove the sail
Across the whirlwind's heart of peace,
    And to and thro' the counter gale?

XII

Again to colder climes we came,
    For still we follow'd where she led;   90
Now mate is blind and captain lame,
    And half the crew are sick or dead,
But, blind or lame or sick or sound,
    We follow that which flies before;
We know the merry world is round,
    And we may sail for evermore.
1864

ENOCH ARDEN

LONG lines of cliff breaking have left a chasm;
And in the chasm are foam and yellow sands;
Beyond, red roofs about a narrow wharf
In cluster; then a moulder'd church; and higher
A long street climbs to one tall-tower'd mill;
And high in heaven behind it a gray down
With Danish barrows; and a hazel-wood,
By autumn nutters haunted, flourishes
Green in a cuplike hollow of the down.
Here on this beach a hundred years ago,   10
Three children of three houses, Annie Lee,
The prettiest little damsel in the port,
And Philip Ray, the miller's only son,
And Enoch Arden, a rough sailor's lad
Made orphan by a winter shipwreck, play'd
Among the waste and lumber of the shore,
Hard coils of cordage, swarthy fishing-nets,
Anchors of rusty fluke, and boats updrawn;
And built their castles of dissolving sand
To watch them overflow'd, or following up   20
And flying the white breaker, daily left
The little footprint daily wash'd away.

A narrow cave ran in beneath the cliff;
In this the children play'd at keeping house.
Enoch was host one day, Philip the next,
While Annie still was mistress; but at times
Enoch would hold possession for a week:
"This is my house and this my little wife."
"Mine too," said Philip; "turn and turn about;"
When, if they quarrell'd, Enoch stronger-made   30
Was master. Then would Philip, his blue eyes
All flooded with the helpless wrath of tears,
Shriek out, "I hate you, Enoch," and at this
The little wife would weep for company,
And pray them not to quarrel for her sake,
And say she would be little wife to both.

But when the dawn of rosy childhood past,
And the new warmth of life's ascending sun

Was felt by either, either fixt his heart
On that one girl; and Enoch spoke his love,   40
But Philip loved in silence; and the girl
Seem'd kinder unto Philip than to him;
But she loved Enoch, tho' she knew it not,
And would if ask'd deny it. Enoch set
A purpose evermore before his eyes,
To hoard all savings to the uttermost,
To purchase his own boat, and make a home
For Annie; and so prosper'd that at last
A luckier or a bolder fisherman,
A carefuller in peril, did not breathe   50
For leagues along that breaker-beaten coast
Than Enoch. Likewise had he served a year
On board a merchantman, and made himself
Full sailor; and he thrice had pluck'd a life
From the dread sweep of the down-streaming seas,
And all men look'd upon him favorably.
And ere he touch'd his one-and-twentieth May
He purchased his own boat, and made a home
For Annie, neat and nestlike, halfway up
The narrow street that clamber'd toward the mill.   60

    Then, on a golden autumn eventide,
The younger people making holiday,
With bag and sack and basket, great and small,
Went nutting to the hazels. Philip stay'd —
His father lying sick and needing him —
An hour behind; but as he climb'd the hill,
Just where the prone edge of the wood began
To feather toward the hollow, saw the pair,
Enoch and Annie, sitting hand-in-hand,
His large gray eyes and weather-beaten face   70
All-kindled by a still and sacred fire,
That burn'd as on an altar. Philip look'd,
And in their eyes and faces read his doom;
Then, as their faces drew together, groan'd,
And slipt aside, and like a wounded life
Crept down into the hollows of the wood;
There, while the rest were loud in merrymaking,
Had his dark hour unseen, and rose and past
Bearing a lifelong hunger in his heart.

    So these were wed, and merrily rang the bells,   80
And merrily ran the years, seven happy years,

Seven happy years of health and competence,
And mutual love and honorable toil,
With children, first a daughter. In him woke,
With his first babe's first cry, the noble wish
To save all earnings to the uttermost,
And give his child a better bringing-up
Than his had been, or hers; a wish renew'd,
When two years after came a boy to be
The rosy idol of her solitudes,   90
While Enoch was abroad on wrathful seas,
Or often journeying landward; for in truth
Enoch's white horse, and Enoch's ocean-spoil
In ocean-smelling osier, and his face,
Rough-redden'd with a thousand winter gales,
Not only to the market-cross were known,
But in the leafy lanes behind the down,
Far as the portal-warding lion-whelp
And peacock yew-tree of the lonely Hall,
Whose Friday fare was Enoch's ministering.   100

Then came a change, as all things human change.
Ten miles to northward of the narrow port
Open'd a larger haven. Thither used
Enoch at times to go by land or sea;
And once when there, and clambering on a mast
In harbor, by mischance he slipt and fell.
A limb was broken when they lifted him;
And while he lay recovering there, his wife
Bore him another son, a sickly one.
Another hand crept too across his trade   110
Taking her bread and theirs; and on him fell,
Altho' a grave and staid God-fearing man,
Yet lying thus inactive, doubt and gloom.
He seem'd, as in a nightmare of the night,
To see his children leading evermore
Low miserable lives of hand-to-mouth,
And her he loved a beggar. Then he pray'd,
"Save them from this, whatever comes to me."
And while he pray'd, the master of that ship
Enoch had served in, hearing his mischance,   120
Came, for he knew the man and valued him,
Reporting of his vessel China-bound,
And wanting yet a boatswain. Would he go?
There yet were many weeks before she sail'd,
Sail'd from this port. Would Enoch have the place?

And Enoch all at once assented to it,
Rejoicing at that answer to his prayer.

So now that shadow of mischance appear'd
No graver than as when some little cloud
Cuts off the fiery highway of the sun,   130
And isles a light in the offing. Yet the wife —
When he was gone — the children — what to do?
Then Enoch lay long-pondering on his plans:
To sell the boat — and yet he loved her well —
How many a rough sea had he weather'd in her!
He knew her, as a horseman knows his horse —
And yet to sell her — then with what she brought
Buy goods and stores — set Annie forth in trade
With all that seamen needed or their wives —
So might she keep the house while he was gone.   140
Should he not trade himself out yonder? go
This voyage more than once? yea, twice or thrice —
As oft as needed — last, returning rich,
Become the master of a larger craft,
With fuller profits lead an easier life,
Have all his pretty young ones educated,
And pass his days in peace among his own.

Thus Enoch in his heart determined all;
Then moving homeward came on Annie pale,
Nursing the sickly babe, her latest-born.   150
Forward she started with a happy cry,
And laid the feeble infant in his arms;
Whom Enoch took, and handled all his limbs,
Appraised his weight and fondled fatherlike,
But had no heart to break his purposes
To Annie, till the morrow, when he spoke.

Then first since Enoch's golden ring had girt
Her finger, Annie fought against his will;
Yet not with brawling opposition she,
But manifold entreaties, many a tear,   160
Many a sad kiss by day, by night, renew'd —
Sure that all evil would come out of it —
Besought him, supplicating, if he cared
For her or his dear children, not to go.
He not for his own self caring, but her,
Her and her children, let her plead in vain;
So grieving held his will, and bore it thro'.

For Enoch parted with his old sea-friend,
Bought Annie goods and stores, and set his hand
To fit their little streetward sitting-room   170
With shelf and corner for the goods and stores.
So all day long till Enoch's last at home,
Shaking their pretty cabin, hammer and axe,
Auger and saw, while Annie seem'd to hear
Her own death-scaffold raising, shrill'd and rang,
Till this was ended, and his careful hand, —
The space was narrow, — having order'd all
Almost as neat and close as Nature packs
Her blossom or her seedling, paused; and he,
Who needs would work for Annie to the last,   180
Ascending tired, heavily slept till morn.

And Enoch faced this morning of farewell
Brightly and boldly. All his Annie's fears,
Save as his Annie's, were a laughter to him.
Yet Enoch as a brave God-fearing man
Bow'd himself down, and in that mystery
Where God-in-man is one with man-in-God,
Pray'd for a blessing on his wife and babes,
Whatever came to him; and then he said:
"Annie, this voyage by the grace of God   190
Will bring fair weather yet to all of us.
Keep a clean hearth and a clear fire for me,
For I'll be back, my girl, before you know it;"
Then lightly rocking baby's cradle, "and he,
This pretty, puny, weakly little one, —
Nay — for I love him all the better for it —
God bless him, he shall sit upon my knees
And I will tell him tales of foreign parts,
And make him merry, when I come home again.
Come, Annie, come, cheer up before I go."   200

Him running on thus hopefully she heard,
And almost hoped herself; but when he turn'd
The current of his talk to graver things
In sailor fashion roughly sermonizing
On providence and trust in heaven, she heard,
Heard and not heard him; as the village girl,
Who sets her pitcher underneath the spring,
Musing on him that used to fill it for her,
Hears and not hears, and lets it overflow.

At length she spoke: "O Enoch, you are wise;   210
And yet for all your wisdom well know I
That I shall look upon your face no more."

"Well, then," said Enoch, "I shall look on yours.
Annie, the ship I sail in passes here" —
He named the day; — "get you a seaman's glass,
Spy out my face, and laugh at all your fears."

But when the last of those last moments came:
"Annie, my girl, cheer up, be comforted,
Look to the babes, and till I come again
Keep everything shipshape, for I must go.   220
And fear no more for me; or if you fear,
Cast all your cares on God; that anchor holds.
Is He not yonder in those uttermost
Parts of the morning? if I flee to these,
Can I go from Him? and the sea is His,
The sea is His; He made it."

                       Enoch rose,
Cast his strong arms about his drooping wife,
And kiss'd his wonder-stricken little ones;
But for the third, the sickly one, who slept
After a night of feverous wakefulness,   230
When Annie would have raised him Enoch said,
"Wake him not, let him sleep; how should the child
Remember this?" and kiss'd him in his cot.
But Annie from her baby's forehead clipt
A tiny curl, and gave it; this he kept
Thro' all his future, but now hastily caught
His bundle, waved his hand, and went his way.

She, when the day that Enoch mention'd came,
Borrow'd a glass, but all in vain. Perhaps
She could not fix the glass to suit her eye;   240
Perhaps her eye was dim, hand tremulous;
She saw him not, and while he stood on deck
Waving, the moment and the vessel past.

Even to the last dip of the vanishing sail
She watch'd it, and departed weeping for him;
Then, tho' she mourn'd his absence as his grave,
Set her sad will no less to chime with his,
But throve not in her trade, not being bred

To barter, nor compensating the want
By shrewdness, neither capable of lies, 250
Nor asking overmuch and taking less,
And still foreboding "what would Enoch say?"
For more than once, in days of difficulty
And pressure, had she sold her wares for less
Than what she gave in buying what she sold.
She fail'd and sadden'd knowing it; and thus,
Expectant of that news which never came,
Gain'd for her own a scanty sustenance,
And lived a life of silent melancholy.

Now the third child was sickly-born and grew 260
Yet sicklier, tho' the mother cared for it
With all a mother's care; nevertheless,
Whether her business often call'd her from it,
Or thro' the want of what it needed most,
Or means to pay the voice who best could tell
What most it needed — howsoe'er it was,
After a lingering, — ere she was aware, —
Like the caged bird escaping suddenly,
The little innocent soul flitted away.

In that same week when Annie buried it, 270
Philip's true heart, which hunger'd for her peace, —
Since Enoch left he had not look'd upon her, —
Smote him, as having kept aloof so long.
"Surely," said Philip, "I may see her now,
May be some little comfort;" therefore went,
Past thro' the solitary room in front,
Paused for a moment at an inner door,
Then struck it thrice, and, no one opening,
Enter'd, but Annie, seated with her grief,
Fresh from the burial of her little one, 280
Cared not to look on any human face,
But turn'd her own toward the wall and wept.
Then Philip standing up said falteringly,
"Annie, I came to ask a favor of you."

He spoke; the passion in her moan'd reply,
"Favor from one so sad and so forlorn
As I am!" half abash'd him; yet unask'd,
His bashfulness and tenderness at war,
He set himself beside her, saying to her:

"I came to speak to you of what he wish'd,   290
Enoch, your husband. I have ever said
You chose the best among us — a strong man;
For where he fixt his heart he set his hand
To do the thing he will'd, and bore it thro'.
And wherefore did he go this weary way,
And leave you lonely? not to see the world —
For pleasure? — nay, but for the wherewithal
To give his babes a better bringing up
Than his had been, or yours; that was his wish.
And if he come again, vext will he be   300
To find the precious morning hours were lost.
And it would vex him even in his grave,
If he could know his babes were running wild
Like colts about the waste. So, Annie, now —
Have we not known each other all our lives?
I do beseech you by the love you bear
Him and his children not to say me nay —
For, if you will, when Enoch comes again
Why then he shall repay me — if you will,
Annie — for I am rich and well-to-do.   310
Now let me put the boy and girl to school;
This is the favor that I came to ask."

Then Annie with her brows against the wall
Answer'd, "I cannot look you in the face;
I seem so foolish and so broken down.
When you came in my sorrow broke me down;
And now I think your kindness breaks me down.
But Enoch lives; that is borne in on me;
He will repay you. Money can be repaid,
Not kindness such as yours."

                And Philip ask'd,   320
"Then you will let me, Annie?"

                    There she turn'd,
She rose, and fixt her swimming eyes upon him,
And dwelt a moment on his kindly face,
Then calling down a blessing on his head
Caught at his hand, and wrung it passionately,
And past into the little garth beyond.
So lifted up in spirit he moved away.

Then Philip put the boy and girl to school,
And bought them needful books, and every way,
Like one who does his duty by his own,   330
Made himself theirs; and tho' for Annie's sake,
Fearing the lazy gossip of the port,
He oft denied his heart his dearest wish,
And seldom crost her threshold, yet he sent
Gifts by the children, garden-herbs and fruit,
The late and early roses from his wall,
Or conies from the down, and now and then,
With some pretext of fineness in the meal
To save the offence of charitable, flour
From his tall mill that whistled on the waste.   340

But Philip did not fathom Annie's mind;
Scarce could the woman, when he came upon her,
Out of full heart and boundless gratitude
Light on a broken word to thank him with.
But Philip was her children's all-in-all;
From distant corners of the street they ran
To greet his hearty welcome heartily;
Lords of his house and of his mill were they,
Worried his passive ear with petty wrongs
Or pleasures, hung upon him, play'd with him   350
And call'd him Father Philip. Philip gain'd
As Enoch lost, for Enoch seem'd to them
Uncertain as a vision or a dream,
Faint as a figure seen in early dawn
Down at the far end of an avenue,
Going we know not where; and so ten years,
Since Enoch left his hearth and native land,
Fled forward, and no news of Enoch came.

It chanced one evening Annie's children long'd
To go with others nutting to the wood,   360
And Annie would go with them; then they begg'd
For Father Philip, as they call'd him, too.
Him, like the working bee in blossom-dust,
Blanch'd with his mill, they found; and saying to him,
"Come with us, Father Philip," he denied;
But when the children pluck'd at him to go,
He laugh'd, and yielded readily to their wish,
For was not Annie with them? and they went.

But after scaling half the weary down,
Just where the prone edge of the wood began   370
To feather toward the hollow, all her force
Fail'd her; and sighing, "Let me rest," she said.
So Philip rested with her well-content;
While all the younger ones with jubilant cries
Broke from their elders, and tumultuously
Down thro' the whitening hazels made a plunge
To the bottom, and dispersed, and bent or broke
The lithe reluctant boughs to tear away
Their tawny clusters, crying to each other
And calling, here and there, about the wood.   380

    But Philip sitting at her side forgot
Her presence, and remember'd one dark hour
Here in this wood, when like a wounded life
He crept into the shadow. At last he said,
Lifting his honest forehead, "Listen, Annie,
How merry they are down yonder in the wood.
Tired, Annie?" for she did not speak a word.
"Tired?" but her face had fallen upon her hands;
At which, as with a kind of anger in him,
"The ship was lost," he said, "the ship was lost!   390
No more of that! why should you kill yourself
And make them orphans quite?" And Annie said,
"I thought not of it; but — I know not why —
Their voices make me feel so solitary."

    Then Philip coming somewhat closer spoke:
"Annie, there is a thing upon my mind,
And it has been upon my mind so long
That, tho' I know not when it first came there,
I know that it will out at last. O Annie,
It is beyond all hope, against all chance,   400
That he who left you ten long years ago
Should still be living; well, then — let me speak.
I grieve to see you poor and wanting help;
I cannot help you as I wish to do
Unless — they say that women are so quick —
Perhaps you know what I would have you know —
I wish you for my wife. I fain would prove
A father to your chidren; I do think
They love me as a father; I am sure
That I love them as if they were mine own;   410
And I believe, if you were fast my wife,

That after all these sad uncertain years
We might be still as happy as God grants
To any of his creatures. Think upon it;
For I am well-to-do — no kin, no care,
No burthen, save my care for you and yours,
And we have known each other all our lives,
And I have loved you longer than you know."

Then answer'd Annie — tenderly she spoke:
"You have been as God's good angel in our house.　　　420
God bless you for it, God reward you for it,
Philip, with something happier than myself.
Can one love twice? can you be ever loved
As Enoch was? what is it that you ask?"
"I am content," he answer'd, "to be loved
A little after Enoch." "O," she cried,
Scared as it were, "dear Philip, wait a while.
If Enoch comes — but Enoch will not come —
Yet wait a year, a year is not so long.
Surely I shall be wiser in a year.　　　430
O, wait a little!" Philip sadly said,
"Annie, as I have waited all my life
I well may wait a little." "Nay," she cried,
"I am bound: you have my promise — in a year.
Will you not bide your year as I bide mine?"
And Philip answer'd, "I will bide my year."

Here both were mute, till Philip glancing up
Beheld the dead flame of the fallen day
Pass from the Danish barrow overhead;
Then, fearing night and chill for Annie, rose　　　440
And sent his voice beneath him thro' the wood.
Up came the children laden with their spoil;
Then all descended to the port, and there
At Annie's door he paused and gave his hand,
Saying gently, "Annie, when I spoke to you,
That was your hour of weakness. I was wrong,
I am always bound to you, but you are free."
Then Annie weeping answer'd, "I am bound."

She spoke; and in one moment as it were,
While yet she went about her household ways,　　　450
Even as she dwelt upon his latest words,
That he had loved her longer than she knew,
That autumn into autumn flash'd again,

And there he stood once more before her face,
Claiming her promise. "Is it a year?" she ask'd.
"Yes, if the nuts," he said, "be ripe again;
Come out and see." But she — she put him off —
So much to look to — such a change — a month —
Give her a month — she knew that she was bound —
A month — no more. Then Philip with his eyes   460
Full of that lifelong hunger, and his voice
Shaking a little like a drunkard's hand,
"Take your own time, Annie, take your own time."
And Annie could have wept for pity of him;
And yet she held him on delayingly
With many a scarce-believable excuse,
Trying his truth and his long-sufferance,
Till half another year had slipt away.

      By this the lazy gossips of the port,
Abhorrent of a calculation crost,   470
Began to chafe as at a personal wrong.
Some thought that Philip did but trifle with her;
Some that she but held off to draw him on;
And others laugh'd at her and Philip too,
As simple folk that knew not their own minds;
And one, in whom all evil fancies clung
Like serpent eggs together, laughingly
Would hint at worse in either. Her own son
Was silent, tho' he often look'd his wish;
But evermore the daughter prest upon her   480
To wed the man so dear to all them
And lift the household out of poverty;
And Philip's rosy face contracting grew
Careworn and wan; and all these things fell on her
Sharp as reproach.

                    At last one night it chanced
That Annie could not sleep, but earnestly
Pray'd for a sign, "My Enoch, is he gone?"
Then compass'd round by the blind wall of night
Brook'd not the expectant terror of her heart,
Started from bed, and struck herself a light,   490
Then desperately seized the holy Book,
Suddenly set it wide to find a sign,
Suddenly put her finger on the text,
"Under the palm-tree." That was nothing to her,
No meaning there; she closed the Book and slept.

When lo! her Enoch sitting on a height,
Under a palm-tree, over him the sun.
"He is gone," she thought, "he is happy, he is singing
Hosanna in the highest; yonder shines
The Sun of Righteousness, and these be palms   500
Whereof the happy people strowing cried
'Hosanna in the highest!' " Here she woke,
Resolved, sent for him and said wildly to him,
"There is no reason why we should not wed."
"Then for God's sake," he answer'd, "both our sakes,
So you will wed me, let it be at once."

So these were wed, and merrily rang the bells,
Merrily rang the bells, and they were wed.
But never merrily beat Annie's heart.
A footstep seem'd to fall beside her path,   510
She knew not whence; a whisper on her ear,
She knew not what; nor loved she to be left
Alone at home, nor ventured out alone.
What ail'd her then that, ere she enter'd, often
Her hand dwelt lingeringly on the latch,
Fearing to enter? Philip thought he knew:
Such doubts and fears were common to her state,
Being with child; but when her child was born,
Then her new child was as herself renew'd,
Then the new mother came about her heart,   520
Then her good Philip was her all-in-all,
And that mysterious instinct wholly died.

And where was Enoch? Prosperously sail'd
The ship "Good Fortune," tho' at setting forth
The Biscay, roughly ridging eastward, shook
And almost overwhelm'd her, yet unvext
She slipt across the summer of the world,
Then after a long tumble about the Cape
And frequent interchange of foul and fair,
She passing thro' the summer world again,   530
The breath of heaven came continually
And sent her sweetly by the golden isles,
Till silent in her oriental haven.

There Enoch traded for himself, and bought
Quaint monsters for the market of those times,
A gilded dragon also for the babes.

Less lucky her home-voyage: at first indeed
Thro' many a fair sea-circle, day by day,
Scarce-rocking, her full-busted figure-head
Stared o'er the ripple feathering from her bows: 540
Then follow'd calms, and then winds variable,
Then baffling, a long course of them; and last
Storm, such as drove her under moonless heavens
Till hard upon the cry of "breakers" came
The crash of ruin, and the loss of all
But Enoch and two others. Half the night,
Buoy'd upon floating tackle and broken spars,
These drifted, stranding on an isle at morn
Rich, but the loneliest in a lonely sea.

No want was there of human sustenance,   550
Soft fruitage, mighty nuts, and nourishing roots;
Nor save for pity was it hard to take
The helpless life so wild that it was tame.
There in a seaward-gazing mountain-gorge
They built, and thatch'd with leaves of palm, a hut,
Half hut, half native cavern. So the three,
Set in this Eden of all plenteousness,
Dwelt with eternal summer, ill-content.
For one, the youngest, hardly more than boy,
Hurt in that night of sudden ruin and wreck,   560
Lay lingering out a five-years' death-in-life.
They could not leave him. After he was gone,
The two remaining found a fallen stem;
And Enoch's comrade, careless of himself,
Fire-hollowing this in Indian fashion, fell
Sun-stricken, and that other lived alone.
In those two deaths he read God's warning "wait."

The mountain wooded to the peak, the lawns
And winding glades high up like ways to heaven,
The slender coco's drooping crown of plumes,   570
The lightning flash of insect and of bird,
The lustre of the long convolvuluses
That coil'd around the stately stems, and ran
Even to the limit of the land, the glows
And glories of the broad belt of the world, —
All these he saw; but what he fain had seen
He could not see, the kindly human face,
Nor ever hear a kindly voice, but heard
The myriad shriek of wheeling ocean-fowl,

The league-long roller thundering on the reef,   580
The moving whisper of huge trees that branch'd
And blossom'd in the zenith, or the sweep
Of some precipitous rivulet to the wave,
As down the shore he ranged, or all day long
Sat often in the seaward-gazing gorge,
A shipwreck'd sailor, waiting for a sail.
No sail from day to day, but every day
The sunrise broken into scarlet shafts
Among the palms and ferns and precipices;
The blaze upon the waters to the east;   590
The blaze upon his island overhead;
The blaze upon the waters to the west;
Then the great stars that globed themselves in heaven,
The hollower-bellowing ocean, and again
The scarlet shafts of sunrise — but no sail.

There often as he watch'd or seem'd to watch,
So still the golden lizard on him paused,
A phantom made of many phantoms moved
Before him haunting him, or he himself
Moved haunting people, things, and places, known   600
Far in a darker isle beyond the line;
The babes, their babble, Annie, the small house,
The climbing street, the mill, the leafy lanes,
The peacock yew-tree and the lonely Hall,
The horse he drove, the boat he sold, the chill
November dawns and dewy-glooming downs,
The gentle shower, the smell of dying leaves,
And the low moan of leaden-color'd seas.

Once likewise, in the ringing of his ears,
Tho' faintly, merrily — far and far away —   610
He heard the pealing of his parish bells;
Then, tho' he knew not wherefore, started up
Shuddering, and when the beauteous hateful isle
Return'd upon him, had not his poor heart
Spoken with That which being everywhere
Lets none who speaks with Him seem all alone,
Surely the man had died of solitude.

Thus over Enoch's early-silvering head
The sunny and rainy seasons came and went
Year after year. His hopes to see his own,   620
And pace the sacred old familiar fields,

Not yet had perish'd, when his lonely doom
Came suddenly to an end. Another ship —
She wanted water — blown by baffling winds,
Like the "Good Fortune," from her destined course,
Stay'd by this isle, not knowing where she lay;
For since the mate had seen at early dawn
Across a break on the mist-wreathen isle
The silent water slipping from the hills,
They sent a crew that landing burst away   630
In search of stream or fount, and fill'd the shores
With clamor. Downward from his mountain gorge
Stept the long-hair'd, long-bearded solitary,
Brown, looking hardly human, strangely clad,
Muttering and mumbling, idiot-like it seem'd,
With inarticulate rage, and making signs
They knew not what; and yet he led the way
To where the rivulets of sweet water ran,
And ever as he mingled with the crew,
And heard them talking, his long-bounden tongue   640
Was loosen'd, till he made them understand;
Whom, when their casks were fill'd, they took aboard.
And there the tale he utter'd brokenly,
Scarce-credited at first but more and more,
Amazed and melted all who listen'd to it;
And clothes they gave him and free passage home,
But oft he work'd among the rest and shook
His isolation from him. None of these
Came from his country, or could answer him,
If question'd, aught of what he cared to know.   650
And dull the voyage was with long delays,
The vessel scarce sea-worthy; but evermore
His fancy fled before the lazy wind
Returning, till beneath a clouded moon
He like a lover down thro' all his blood
Drew in the dewy meadowy morning-breath
Of England, blown across her ghostly wall.
And that same morning officers and men
Levied a kindly tax upon themselves,
Pitying the lonely man, and gave him it;   660
Then moving up the coast they landed him,
Even in that harbor whence he sail'd before.

    There Enoch spoke no word to any one,
But homeward — home — what home? had he a home? —
His home, he walk'd. Bright was that afternoon,

Sunny but chill; till drawn thro' either chasm,
Where either haven open'd on the deeps,
Roll'd a sea-haze and whelm'd the world in gray,
Cut off the length of highway on before,
And left but narrow breadth to left and right   670
Of wither'd holt or tilth or pasturage.
On the nigh-naked tree the robin piped
Disconsolate, and thro' the dripping haze
The dead weight of the dead leaf bore it down.
Thicker the drizzle grew, deeper the gloom;
Last, as it seem'd, a great mist-blotted light
Flared on him, and he came upon the place.

Then down the long street having slowly stolen,
His heart foreshadowing all calamity,
His eyes upon the stones, he reach'd the home   680
Where Annie lived and loved him, and his babes
In those far-off seven happy years were born;
But finding neither light nor murmur there —
    A bill of sale gleam'd thro' the drizzle — crept
Still downward thinking, "dead or dead to me!"

Down to the pool and narrow wharf he went,
Seeking a tavern which of old he knew,
A front of timber-crost antiquity,
So propt, worm-eaten, ruinously old,
He thought it must have gone; but he was gone   690
Who kept it, and his widow Miriam Lane,
With daily-dwindling profits held the house;
A haunt of brawling seamen once, but now
Stiller, with yet a bed for wandering men.
There Enoch rested silent many days.

But Miriam Lane was good and garrulous,
Nor let him be, but often breaking in,
Told him, with other annals of the port,
Not knowing — Enoch was so brown, so bow'd,
So broken — all the story of his house: 700
His baby's death, her growing poverty,
How Philip put her little ones to school,
And kept them in it, his long wooing her,
Her slow consent and marriage, and the birth
Of Philip's child; and o'er his countenance
No shadow past, nor motion. Any one,
Regarding, well had deem'd he felt the tale

Less than the teller; only when she closed,
"Enoch, poor man, was cast away and lost,"
He, shaking his gray head pathetically,   710
Repeated muttering, "cast away and lost;"
Again in deeper inward whispers, "lost!"

    But Enoch yearn'd to see her face again:
"If I might look on her sweet face again,
And know that she is happy." So the thought
Haunted and harass'd him, and drove him forth,
At evening when the dull November day
Was growing duller twilight, to the hill.
There he sat down gazing on all below;
There did a thousand memories roll upon him,   720
Unspeakable for sadness. By and by
The ruddy square of comfortable light,
Far-blazing from the rear of Philip's house,
Allured him, as the beacon-blaze allures
The bird of passage, till he madly strikes
Against it and beats out his weary life.

    For Philip's dwelling fronted on the street,
The latest house to landward; but behind,
With one small gate that open'd on the waste,
Flourish'd a little garden square and wall'd,   730
And in it throve an ancient evergreen,
A yew-tree, and all round it ran a walk
Of shingle, and a walk divided it.
But Enoch shunn'd the middle walk and stole
Up by the wall, behind the yew; and thence
That which he better might have shunn'd, if griefs
Like his have worse or better, Enoch saw.

    For cups and silver on the burnish'd board
Sparkled and shone; so genial was the hearth;
And on the right hand of the hearth he saw   740
Philip, the slighted suitor of old times,
Stout, rosy, with his babe across his knees;
And o'er her second father stoopt a girl,
A later but a loftier Annie Lee,
Fair-hair'd and tall, and from her lifted hand
Dangled a length of ribbon and a ring
To tempt the babe, who rear'd his creasy arms,
Caught at and ever miss'd it, and they laugh'd;
And on the left hand of the hearth he saw

The mother glancing often toward her babe,　　　　750
But turning now and then to speak with him,
Her son, who stood beside her tall and strong,
And saying that which pleased him, for he smiled.

Now when the dead man come to life beheld
His wife his wife no more, and saw the babe
Hers, yet not his, upon the father's knee,
And all the warmth, the peace, the happiness,
And his own children tall and beautiful,
And him, that other, reigning in his place,
Lord of his rights and of his children's love —　　　　760
Then he, tho' Miriam Lane had told him all,
Because things seen are mightier than things heard,
Stagger'd and shook, holding the branch, and fear'd
To send abroad a shrill and terrible cry,
Which in one moment, like the blast of doom,
Would shatter all the happiness of the hearth.

He therefore turning softly like a thief,
Lest the harsh shingle should grate underfoot,
And feeling all along the garden-wall,
Lest he should swoon and tumble and be found,　　　　770
Crept to the gate, and open'd it and closed,
As lightly as a sick man's chamber-door,
Behind him, and came out upon the waste.

And there he would have knelt, but that his knees
Were feeble, so that falling prone he dug
His fingers into the wet earth, and pray'd:

"Too hard to bear! why did they take me thence?
O God Almighty, blessed Saviour, Thou
That didst uphold me on my lonely isle,
Uphold me, Father, in my loneliness　　　　780
A little longer! aid me, give me strength
Not to tell her, never to let her know.
Help me not to break in upon her peace.
My children too! must I not speak to these?
They know me not. I should betray myself.
Never! no father's kiss for me — the girl
So like her mother, and the boy, my son."

There speech and thought and nature fail'd a little,
And he lay tranced; but when he rose and paced

Back toward his solitary home again,   790
All down the long and narrow street he went
Beating it in upon his weary brain,
As tho' it were the burthen of a song,
"Not to tell her, never to let her know."

   He was not all unhappy. His resolve
Upbore him, and firm faith, and evermore
Prayer from a living source within the will,
And beating up thro' all the bitter world,
Like fountains of sweet water in the sea,
Kept him a living soul. "This miller's wife,"   800
He said to Miriam, "that you spoke about,
Has she no fear that her first husband lives?"
"Ay, ay, poor soul," said Miriam, "fear enow!
If you could tell her you had seen him dead,
Why, that would be her comfort;" and he thought,
"After the Lord has call'd me she shall know,
I wait His time;" and Enoch set himself,
Scorning an alms, to work whereby to live.
Almost to all things could he turn his hand.
Cooper he was and carpenter, and wrought   810
To make the boatmen fishing-nets, or help'd
At lading and unlading the tall barks
That brought the stinted commerce of those days,
Thus earn'd a scanty living for himself.
Yet since he did but labor for himself,
Work without hope, there was not life in it
Whereby the man could live; and as the year
Roll'd itself round again to meet the day
When Enoch had return'd, a languor came
Upon him, gentle sickness, gradually   820
Weakening the man, till he could do no more,
But kept the house, his chair, and last his bed.
And Enoch bore his weakness cheerfully.
For sure no gladlier does the stranded wreck
See thro' the gray skirts of a lifting squall
The boat that bears the hope of life approach
To save the life despair'd of, than he saw
Death dawning on him, and the close of all.

   For thro' that dawning gleam'd a kindlier hope
On Enoch thinking, "after I am gone,   830
Then may she learn I loved her to the last."
He call'd aloud for Miriam Lane and said:

"Woman, I have a secret — only swear,
Before I tell you — swear upon the book
Not to reveal it, till you see me dead."
"Dead," clamor'd the good woman, "hear him talk!
I warrant, man, that we shall bring you round."
"Swear," added Enoch sternly, "on the book;"
And on the book, half-frighted, Miriam swore.
Then Enoch rolling his gray eyes upon her,   840
"Did you know Enoch Arden of this town?"
"Know him?" she said, "I knew him far away.
Ay, ay, I mind him coming down the street;
Held his head high, and cared for no man, he."
Slowly and sadly Enoch answer'd her:
"His head is low, and no man cares for him.
I think I have not three days more to live;
I am the man." At which the woman gave
A half-incredulous, half-hysterical cry:
"You Arden, you! nay, — sure he was a foot   850
Higher than you be." Enoch said again:
"My God has bow'd me down to what I am;
My grief and solitude have broken me;
Nevertheless, know you that I am he
Who married — but that name has twice been changed —
I married her who married Philip Ray.
Sit, listen." Then he told her of his voyage,
His wreck, his lonely life, his coming back,
His gazing in on Annie, his resolve,
And how he kept it. As the woman heard,   860
Fast flow'd the current of her easy tears,
While in her heart she yearn'd incessantly
To rush abroad all round the little haven,
Proclaiming Enoch Arden and his woes;
But awed and promise-bounden she forbore,
Saying only, "See your bairns before you go!
Eh, let me fetch 'em, Arden," and arose
Eager to bring them down, for Enoch hung
A moment on her words, but then replied:

"Woman, disturb me not now at the last,   870
But let me hold my purpose till I die.
Sit down again; mark me and understand,
While I have power to speak. I charge you **now**,
When you shall see her, tell her that I died
Blessing her, praying for her, loving her;
Save for the bar between us, loving her

As when she laid her head beside my own.
And tell my daughter Annie, whom I saw
So like her mother, that my latest breath
Was spent in blessing her and praying for her.   880
And tell my son that I died blessing him.
And say to Philip that I blest him too;
He never meant us anything but good.
But if my children care to see me dead,
Who hardly knew me living, let them come,
I am their father; but she must not come,
For my dead face would vex her after-life.
And now there is but one of all my blood
Who will embrace me in the world-to-be.
This hair is his, she cut it off and gave it,   890
And I have borne it with me all these years,
And thought to bear it with me to my grave;
But now my mind is changed, for I shall see him,
My babe in bliss. Wherefore when I am gone,
Take, give her this, for it may comfort her;
It will moreover be a token to her
That I am he."

        He ceased; and Miriam Lane
Made such a voluble answer promising all,
That once again he roll'd his eyes upon her
Repeating all he wish'd, and once again   900
She promised.

        Then the third night after this,
While Enoch slumber'd motionless and pale,
And Miriam watch'd and dozed at intervals,
There came so loud a calling of the sea
That all the houses in the haven rang.
He woke, he rose, he spread his arms abroad,
Crying with a loud voice, "A sail! a sail!
I am saved;" and so fell back and spoke no more.

  So past the strong heroic soul away.
And when they buried him the little port   910
Had seldom seen a costlier funeral.

1864*

NORTHERN FARMER

OLD STYLE

I

Wheer 'asta beän saw long and meä liggin' 'ere aloän?
Noorse? thoort nowt o' a noorse; whoy, Doctor's abeän an' agoän;
Says that I moänt 'a naw moor aäle, but I beänt a fool;
Git ma my aäle, fur I beänt a-gawin' to breäk my rule.

II

Doctors, they knaws nowt, fur a says what 's nawways true;
Naw soort o' koind o' use to saäy the things that a do.
I 've 'ed my point o' aäle ivry noight sin' I beän 'ere.
An' I 've 'ed my quart ivry market-noight for foorty year.

III

Parson's a beän loikewoise, an' a sittin' ere o' my bed.
"The Amoighty 's a taäkin o' you [1] to 'issén, my friend," a said,   10
An' a towd ma my sins, an' 's toithe were due, an' I gied it in hond;
I done moy duty boy 'um, as I 'a done boy the lond.

IV

Larn'd a ma' beä. I reckons I 'annot sa moch to larn.
But a cast oop, thot a did, 'bout Bessy Marris's barne.
Thaw a knaws I hallus voäted wi' Squoire an' choorch an' staäte,
An' i' the woost o' toimes I wur niver agin the raäte.

V

An' I hallus coom'd to 's choorch afoor moy Sally wur deäd,
An' 'eärd 'um a bummin' awaäy loike a buzzard-clock [2] ower my 'eäd,
An' I niver knaw'd whot a meän'd but I thowt a 'ad summut to saäy,
An' I thowt a said whot a owt to 'a said, an' I coom'd awaäy.   20

VI

Bessy Marris's barne! tha knaws she laäid it to meä.
Mowt a beän, mayhap, for she wur a bad un, sheä.
'Siver, I kep 'um, I kep 'um, my lass, tha mun understond;
I done moy duty boy 'um, as I 'a done boy the lond.

[1] *ou* as in *hour*.
[2] Cockchafer.

VII

But Parson a cooms an' a goäs, an' a says it easy an' freeë.
"The Amoighty 's taäkin o' to you to 'issén, my friend," say 'eä.
I weänt saäy men be loiars, thaw summun said it in 'aäste;
But 'e reäds wonn sarmin a weeäk, an' I' a stubb'd Thurnaby waäste.

VIII

D' ya moind the waäste, my lass? naw, naw, tha was not born then;
Theer wur a boggle in it, I often 'eärd 'um mysén;   30
Moäst loike a butter-bump,[3] fur I 'eärd 'um about an' about,
But I stubb'd 'um oop wi' the lot, an' raäved an' rembled 'um out.

IX

Keäper's it wur; fo' they fun 'um theer a-laäid of 'is faäce
Down i' the woild 'enemies[4] afor I com'd to the plaäce.
Noäks or Thimbleby — toäner[5] 'ed shot 'um as deäd as a naäil.
Noäks wur 'ang'd for it oop at 'soize — but git ma my aäle.

X

Dubbut looök at the waäste; theer warn't not feeäd for a cow;
Nowt at all but bracken an' fuzz, an' looök at it now —
Warn't worth nowt a haäcre, an' now theer 's lots o' feeäd,
Fourscoor[6] yows upon it, an' some on it down i' seeäd.[7]   40

XI

Nobbut a bit on it 's left, an' I meän'd to 'a stubb'd it at fall,
Done it ta-year I meän'd, an' runn'd plow thruff it an' all,
If Godamoighty an' parson 'ud nobbut let ma aloän, —
Meä, wi' haäte hoonderd haäcre o' Squoire's, an' lond o' my oän.

XII

Do Godamoighty knaw what a 's doing a-taäkin' o' meä?
I beänt wonn as saws 'ere a beän an' yonder a peä;
An' Squoire 'ull be sa mad an' all — a' dear, a' dear!
And I 'a managed for Squoire coom Michaelmas thutty year.

XIII

A mowt 'a taäen owd Joänes, as 'ant not a 'aäpoth o' sense,
Or a mowt 'a taäen young Robins — a niver mended a fence;   50
But Godamoighty a moost taäke meä an' taäke ma now,
Wi' aäf the cows to cauve an' Thurnaby hoälms to plow!

---

[3] Bittern.   [4] Anemones.   [5] One or other.
[6] *ou* as in *hour*.   [7] Clover.

XIV

Looök 'ow quoloty smoiles when they seeäs ma a passin' boy,
Says to thessén, naw doubt, "What a man a beä sewer-loy!"
Fur they knaws what I beän to Squoire sin' fust a coom'd to the 'All;
I done moy duty by Squoire an' I done moy duty boy hall.

XV

Squoire 's i' Lunnon, an' summun I reckons 'ull 'a to wroite,
For whoä 's to howd the lond ater meä, thot muddles ma quoit;
Sartin-sewer I beä thot a weänt niver give it to Joänes,
Naw, nor a moänt to Robins — a niver rembles the stoäns.   60

XVI

But summun 'ull come ater meä mayhap wi' 'is kittle o' steäm
Huzzin' an' maäzin' the blessed feälds wi' the divil's oän teäm.
Sin' I mun doy I mun doy, thaw loife they says is sweet,
But sin' I mun doy I mun doy, for I couldn abeär to see it.

XVII

What atta stannin' theer fur, an' doesn bring ma the aäle?
Doctor 's a 'toättler, lass, an a 's hallus i' the owd taäle;
I weänt breäk rules fur Doctor, a knaws naw moor nor a floy;
Git ma my aäle, I tell tha, an' if I mun doy I mun doy.

1864*

NORTHERN FARMER

NEW STYLE

I

Dosn't thou 'ear my 'erse's legs, as they canters awaäy?
Proputty, proputty, proputty — that 's what I 'ears 'em saäy.
Proputty, proputty, proputty — Sam, thou 's an ass for thy païns;
Theer 's moor sense i' one o' 'is legs, nor in all thy braïns.

II

Woä — theer 's a craw to pluck wi' tha, Sam: yon 's parson's 'ouse —
Dosn't thou knaw that man mun be eäther a man or a mouse?
Time to think on it then; for thou 'll be twenty to weeäk.[1]
Proputty, proputty — woä then, woä — let ma 'ear mysén speäk.

[1] This week.

III

Me an' thy muther, Sammy, 'as beän a-talkin' o' thee;
Thou 's beän talkin' to muther, an' she beä a-tellin' it me.   10
Thou 'll not marry for munny — thou's sweet upo' parson's lass —
Noä — thou 'll marry for luvv — an' we boäth on us thinks tha an ass.

IV

Seeä'd her to-daäy goä by — Saäint's-daäy — they was ringing the
    bells.
She 's a beauty, thou thinks — an' soä is scoors o' gells,
Them as 'as munny an' all — wot 's a beauty? — the flower as blaws.
But proputty, proputty sticks, an' proputty, proputty graws.

V

Do'ant be stunt;[2] taäke time. I knaws what maäkes tha sa mad.
Warn't I craäzed fur the lasses mysén when I wur a lad?
But I knaw'd a Quaäker feller as often 'as towd ma this:
"Doänt thou marry for munny, but goä wheer munny is!"   20

VI

An' I went wheer munny war; an' thy muther coom to 'and,
Wi' lots o' munny laaïd by, an' a nicetish bit o' land.
Maäybe she warn't a beauty — I niver giv it a thowt —
But warn't she as good to cuddle an' kiss as a lass as 'ant nowt?

VII

Parson's las 'ant nowt, an' she weänt 'a nowt when 'e 's deäd,
Mun be a guvness, lad, or summut, and addle [3] her breäd.
Why? fur 'e 's nobbut a curate, an' weänt niver get hissén clear,
An' 'e maäde the bed as 'e ligs on afoor 'e coom'd to the shere.

VIII

An' thin 'e coom'd to the parish wi' lots o' Varsity debt,
Stook to his taaïl they did, an' 'e 'ant got shut on 'em yet.   30
An' 'e ligs on 'is back i' the grip, wi' noän to lend 'im a shove,
Woorse nor a far-welter'd [4] yowe; fur, Sammy, 'e married fur luvv.

IX

Luvv? what 's luvv? thou can luvv thy lass an' 'er munny too,
Maäkin' 'em goä togither, as they 've good right to do.
Couldn I luvv thy muther b' y cause o' 'er munny laaïd by?
Naäy — fur I luvv'd 'er a vast sight moor fur it; reäson why.

---

[2] Obstinate.   [3] Earn.
[4] Or, fow-welter'd, — said of a sheep lying on its back in the furrow.

X

Ay, an' thy muther says thou wants to marry the lass,
Cooms of a gentleman burn; an' we boäth on us thinks tha an ass.
Woä then, proputty, wiltha? — an ass as near as mays nowt [5]
Woä then, wiltha? dangtha! — the bees is as fell as owt.[6]   40

XI

Breäk me a bit o' the esh for his 'eäd, lad, out o' the fence!
Gentleman burn! what 's gentleman burn? is it shillins an' pence?
Proputty, proputty 's ivrything 'ere, an', Sammy, I 'm blest
If it is n't the saäme oop yonder, fur them as 'as it 's the best.

XII

Tis 'n them as 'as munny as breäks into 'ouses an' steäls,
Them as 'as coäts to their backs an' taäkes their regular meäls.
Noä, but it 's them as niver knaws wheer a meäl 's to be 'ad.
Taäke my word for it, Sammy, the poor in a loomp is bad.

XIII

Them or thir feythers, tha sees, mun 'a beän a laäzy lot,
Fur work mun 'a gone to the gittin' whiniver munny was got.   50
Feyther 'ad ammost nowt; leästways 's munny was 'id.
But 'e tued an' moil'd issén deäd, an' 'e died a good un, 'e did.

XIV

Looök thou theer wheer Wrigglesby beck cooms out by the 'll!
Feyther run oop to the farm, an' I runs oop to the mill;
An' I 'll run oop to the brig, an' that thou 'll live to see;
And if thou marries a good un I 'll leäve the land to thee.

XV

Thim 's my noätions, Sammy, wheerby I meäns to stick;
But if thou marries a bad un, I 'll leäve the land to Dick. —
Com oop, proputty, proputty — that 's what I 'ears 'im saäy —
Proputty, proputty, proputty — canter an' canter awaäy.   60
1866 (1869) *

LUCRETIUS

LUCILIA, wedded to Lucretius, found
Her master cold; for when the morning flush

---

[5] Makes nothing.
[6] The flies are as fierce as anything.

Of passion and the first embrace had died
Between them, tho' he loved her none the less,
Yet often when the woman heard his foot
Return from pacings in the field, and ran
To greet him with a kiss, the master took
Small notice, or austerely, for — his mind
Half buried in some weightier argument,
Or fancy-borne perhaps upon the rise   10
And long roll of the hexameter — he past
To turn and ponder those three hundred scrolls
Left by the Teacher, whom he held divine.
She brook'd it not, but wrathful, petulant,
Dreaming some rival, sought and found a witch
Who brew'd the philtre which had power, they said,
To lead an errant passion home again.
And this, at times, she mingled with his drink,
And this destroy'd him; for the wicked broth
Confused the chemic labor of the blood,   20
And tickling the brute brain within the man's
Made havoc among those tender cells, and check'd
His power to shape. He loathed himself, and once
After a tempest woke upon a morn
That mock'd him with returning calm, and cried:

"Storm in the night! for thrice I heard the rain
Rushing; and once the flash of a thunderbolt —
Methought I never saw so fierce a fork —
Struck out the streaming mountain-side, and show'd
A riotous confluence of watercourses   30
Blanching and billowing in a hollow of it,
Where all but yester-eve was dusty-dry.

"Storm, and what dreams, ye holy Gods, what dreams!
For thrice I waken'd after dreams. Perchance
We do but recollect the dreams that come
Just ere the waking. Terrible: for it seem'd
A void was made in Nature; all her bonds
Crack'd; and I saw the flaring atom-streams
And torrents of her myriad universe,
Ruining along the illimitable inane,   40
Fly on to clash together again, and make
Another and another frame of things
For ever. That was mine, my dream, I knew it —
Of and belonging to me, as the dog
With inward yelp and restless forefoot plies

His function of the woodland; but the next!
I thought that all the blood by Sylla shed
Came driving rainlike down again on earth,
And where it dash'd the reddening meadow, sprang
No dragon warriors from Cadmean teeth,   50
For these I thought my dream would show to me,
But girls, Hetairai, curious in their art,
Hired animalisms, vile as those that made
The mulberry-faced Dictator's orgies worse
Than aught they fable of the quiet Gods.
And hands they mixt, and yell'd and round me drove
In narrowing circles till I yell'd again
Half-suffocated, and sprang up, and saw —
Was it the first beam of my latest day?

    "Then, then, from utter gloom stood out the breasts,   60
The breasts of Helen, and hoveringly a sword
Now over and now under, now direct,
Pointed itself to pierce, but sank down shamed
At all that beauty; and as I stared, a fire,
The fire that left a roofless Ilion,
Shot out of them, and scorch'd me that I woke.

    "Is this thy vengeance, holy Venus, thine,
Because I would not one of thine own doves,
Not even a rose, were offer'd to thee? thine,
Forgetful how my rich procœmion makes   70
Thy glory fly along the Italian field,
In lays that will outlast thy deity?

    "Deity? nay, thy worshippers. My tongue
Trips, or I speak profanely. Which of these
Angers thee most, or angers thee at all?
Not if thou be'st of those who, far aloof
From envy, hate and pity, and spite and scorn,
Live the great life which all our greatest fain
Would follow, centred in eternal calm.

    "Nay, if thou canst, O Goddess, like ourselves   80
Touch, and be touch'd, then would I cry to thee
To kiss thy Mavors, roll thy tender arms
Round him, and keep him from the lust of blood
That makes a steaming slaughter-house of Rome.

"Ay, but I meant not thee; I meant not her
Whom all the pines of Ida shook to see
Slide from that quiet heaven of hers, and tempt
The Trojan, while his neatherds were abroad;
Nor her that o'er her wounded hunter wept
Her deity false in human-amorous tears; 90
Nor whom her beardless apple-arbiter
Decided fairest. Rather, O ye Gods,
Poet-like, as the great Sicilian called
Calliope to grace his golden verse —
Ay, and this Kypris also — did I take
That popular name of thine to shadow forth
The all-generating powers and genial heat
Of Nature, when she strikes thro' the thick blood
Of cattle, and light is large, and lambs are glad
Nosing the mother's udder, and the bird 100
Makes his heart voice amid the blaze of flowers;
Which things appear the work of mighty Gods.

"The Gods! and if I go *my* work is left
Unfinish'd — *if* I go. The Gods, who haunt
The lucid interspace of world and world,
Where never creeps a cloud, or moves a wind,
Nor ever falls the least white star of snow,
Nor ever lowest roll of thunder moans,
Nor sound of human sorrow mounts to mar
Their sacred everlasting calm! and such, 110
Not all so fine, nor so divine a calm,
Not such, nor all unlike it, man may gain
Letting his own life go. The Gods, the Gods!
If all be atoms, how then should the Gods
Being atomic not be dissoluble,
Not follow the great law? My master held
That Gods there are, for all men so believe.
I prest my footsteps into his, and meant
Surely to lead my Memmius in a train
Of flowery clauses onward to the proof 120
That Gods there are, and deathless. Meant? I meant?
I have forgotten what I meant; my mind
Stumbles, and all my faculties are lamed.

"Look where another of our Gods, the Sun,
Apollo, Delius, or of older use
All-seeing Hyperion — what you will —
Has mounted yonder; since he never sware,

Except his wrath were wreak'd on wretched man,
That he would only shine among the dead
Hereafter — tales! for never yet on earth 130
Could dead flesh creep, or bits of roasting ox
Moan round the spit — nor knows he what he sees;
King of the East altho' he seem, and girt
With song and flame and fragrance, slowly lifts
His golden feet on those empurpled stairs
That climb into the windy halls of heaven
And here he glances on an eye new-born,
And gets for greeting but a wail of pain;
And here he stays upon a freezing orb
That fain would gaze upon him to the last; 140
And here upon a yellow eyelid fallen
And closed by those who mourn a friend in vain,
Not thankful that his troubles are no more.
And me, altho' his fire is on my face
Blinding, he sees not, nor at all can tell
Whether I mean this day to end myself.
Or lend an ear to Plato where he says,
That men like soldiers may not quit the post
Allotted by the Gods. But he that holds
The Gods are careless, wherefore need he care 150
Greatly for them, nor rather plunge at once,
Being troubled, wholly out of sight, and sink
Past earthquake — ay, and gout and stone, that break
Body toward death, and palsy, death-in-life,
And wretched age — and worst disease of all,
These prodigies of myriad nakednesses,
And twisted shapes of lust, unspeakable,
Abominable, strangers at my hearth
Not welcome, harpies miring every dish,
The phantom husks of something foully done, 160
And fleeting thro' the boundless universe,
And blasting the long quiet of my breast
With animal heat and dire insanity?

"How should the mind, except it loved them, clasp
These idols to herself? or do they fly
Now thinner, and now thicker, like the flakes
In a fall of snow, and so press in, perforce
Of multitude, as crowds that in an hour
Of civic tumult jam the doors, and bear
The keepers down, and throng, their rags and they 170
The basest, far into that council-hall
Where sit the best and stateliest of the land?

"Can I not fling this horror off me again,
Seeing with how great ease Nature can smile,
Balmier and nobler from her bath of storm,
At random ravage? and how easily
The mountain there has cast his cloudy slough,
Now towering o'er him in serenest air,
A mountain o'er a mountain, — ay, and within
All hollow as the hopes and fears of men?   180

"But who was he that in the garden snared
Picus and Faunus, rustic Gods? a tale
To laugh at — more to laugh at in myself —
For look! what is it? there? yon arbutus
Totters; a noiseless riot underneath
Strikes through the wood, sets all the tops quivering —
The mountain quickens into Nymph and Faun,
And here an Oread — how the sun delights
To glance and shift about her slippery sides,
And rosy knees and supple roundedness,   190
And budded bosom-peaks — who this way runs
Before the rest! — a satyr, a satyr, see,
Follows; but him I proved impossible;
Twy-natured is no nature. Yet he draws
Nearer and nearer, and I scan him now
Beastlier than any phantom of his kind
That ever butted his rough brother-brute
For lust or lusty blood or provender.
I hate, abhor, spit, sicken at him; and she
Loathes him as well; such a precipitate heel,   200
Fledged as it were with Mercury's ankle-wing,
Whirls her to me — but will she fling herself
Shameless upon me? Catch her, goatfoot! nay,
Hide, hide them, million-myrtled wilderness,
And cavern-shadowing laurels, hide! do I wish —
What? — that the bush were leafless? or to whelm
All of them in one massacre? O ye Gods,
I know you careless, yet, behold, to you
From childly wont and ancient use I call —
I thought I lived securely as yourselves —   210
No lewdness, narrowing envy, monkey-spite,
No madness of ambition, avarice, none;
No larger feast than under plane or pine
With neighbors laid along the grass, to take
Only such cups as left us friendly-warm,
Affirming each his own philosophy —
Nothing to mar the sober majesties

Of settled, sweet, Epicurean life.
But now it seems some unseen monster lays
His vast and filthy hands upon my will,   220
Wrenching it backward into his, and spoils
My bliss in being; and it was not great,
For save when shutting reasons up in rhythm,
Or Heliconian honey in living words,
To make a truth less harsh, I often grew
Tired of so much within our little life,
Or of so little in our little life —
Poor little life that toddles half an hour
Crown'd with a flower or two, and there an end —
And since the nobler pleasure seems to fade,   230
Why should I, beastlike as I find myself,
Not manlike end myself? — our privilege —
What beast has heart to do it? And what man,
What Roman would be dragg'd in triumph thus?
Not I; not he, who bears one name with her
Whose death-blow struck the dateless doom of kings,
When, brooking not the Tarquin in her veins,
She made her blood in sight of Collatine
And all his peers, flushing the guiltless air,
Spout from the maiden fountain in her heart.   240
And from it sprang the Commonwealth, which breaks
As I am breaking now!

              "And therefore now
Let her, that is the womb and tomb of all,
Great Nature, take, and forcing far apart
Those blind beginnings that have made me man,
Dash them anew together at her will
Thro' all her cycles — into man once more,
Or beast or bird or fish, or opulent flower.
But till this cosmic order everywhere
Shatter'd into one earthquake in one day   250
Cracks all to pieces, — and that hour perhaps
Is not so far when momentary man
Shall seem no more a something to himself,
But he, his hopes and hates, his homes and fanes,
And even his bones long laid within the grave,
The very sides of the grave itself shall pass,
Vanishing, atom and void, atom and void,
Into the unseen for ever, — till that hour,
My golden work in which I told a truth
That stays the rolling Ixionian wheel,   260

And numbs the Fury's ringlet-snake, and plucks
The mortal soul from out immortal hell,
Shall stand. Ay, surely; then it fails at last
And perishes as I must; for O Thou,
Passionless bride, divine Tranquillity,
Yearn'd after by the wisest of the wise,
Who fail to find thee, being as thou art
Without one pleasure and without one pain,
Howbeit I know thou surely must be mine
Or soon or late, yet out of season, thus   270
I woo thee roughly, for thou carest not
How roughly men may woo thee so they win —
Thus — thus — the soul flies out and dies in the air."

    With that he drove the knife into his side.
She heard him raging, heard him fall, ran in,
Beat breast, tore hair, cried out upon herself
As having fail'd in duty to him, shriek'd
That she but meant to win him back, fell on him,
Clasp'd, kiss'd him, wail'd. He answer'd, "Care not thou!
Thy duty? What is duty? Fare thee well!"   280
1868°

"FLOWER IN THE CRANNIED WALL"

        FLOWER in the crannied wall,
        I pluck you out of the crannies,
        I hold you here, root and all, in my hand,
        Little flower — but *if* I could understand
        What you are, root and all, and all in all,
        I should know what God and man is.
        1869

THE HIGHER PANTHEISM

THE sun, the moon, the stars, the seas, the hills and the plains, —
Are not these, O Soul, the Vision of Him who reigns?

Is not the Vision He, tho' He be not that which He seems?
Dreams are true while they last, and do we not live in dreams?

Earth, these solid stars, this weight of body and limb,
Are they not sign and symbol of thy division from Him?

Dark is the world to thee; thyself art the reason why,
For is He not all but thou, that hast power to feel "I am I"?

Glory about thee, without thee; and thou fulfillest thy doom,
Making Him broken gleams and a stifled splendor and gloom.   10

Speak to Him, thou, for He hears, and Spirit with Spirit can meet —
Closer is He than breathing, and nearer than hands and feet.

God is law, say the wise; O Soul, and let us rejoice,
For if He thunder by law the thunder is yet His voice.

Law is God, say some; no God at all, says the fool,
For all we have power to see is a straight staff bent in a pool;

And the ear of man cannot hear, and the eye of man cannot see;
But if we could see and hear, this Vision — were it not He?
1869

IN THE GARDEN AT SWAINSTON

NIGHTINGALES warbled without,
    Within was weeping for thee;
Shadows of three dead men
    Walk'd in the walks with me,
        Shadows of three dead men, and thou wast one of the three.

Nightingales sang in his woods,
    The Master was far away;
Nightingales warbled and sang
    Of a passion that lasts but a day;
        Still in the house in his coffin the Prince of courtesy lay.   10

Two dead men have I known
    In courtesy like to thee;
Two dead men have I loved
    With a love that ever will be;
        Three dead men have I loved, and thou art last of the three.

1870 (1874) *

IDYLLS OF THE KING

"Flos Regum Arthurus." — JOSEPH OF EXETER

THE COMING OF ARTHUR

LEODOGRAN, the king of Cameliard,
Had one fair daughter, and none other child;
And she was fairest of all flesh on earth,
Guinevere, and in her his one delight.

    For many a petty king ere Arthur came
Ruled in this isle and, ever waging war
Each upon other, wasted all the land;
And still from time to time the heathen host
Swarm'd over-seas, and harried what was left.
And so there grew great tracts of wilderness,   **10**
Wherein the beast was ever more and more,
But man was less and less, till Arthur came.
For first Aurelius lived and fought and died,
And after him King Uther fought and died,
But either fail'd to make the kingdom one.
And after these King Arthur for a space,
And thro' the puissance of his Table Round,
Drew all their petty princedoms under him,
Their king and head, and made a realm and reign'd.

    And thus the land of Cameliard was waste,   **20**
Thick with wet woods, and many a beast therein,
And none or few to scare or chase the beast;
So that wild dog and wolf and boar and bear
Came night and day, and rooted in the fields,
And wallow'd in the gardens of the King.
And ever and anon the wolf would steal
The children and devour, but now and then,
Her own brood lost or dead, lent her fierce teat
To human sucklings; and the children, housed
In her foul den, there at their meat would growl,   **30**
And mock their foster-mother on four feet,
Till, straighten'd, they grew up to wolf-like men,
Worse than the wolves. And King Leodogran
Groan'd for the Roman legions here again

And Cæsar's eagle. Then his brother king,
Urien, assail'd him; last a heathen horde,
Reddening the sun with smoke and earth with blood,
And on the spike that split the mother's heart
Spitting the child, brake on him, till, amazed,
He knew not whither he should turn for aid.   40

But — for he heard of Arthur newly crown'd,
Tho' not without an uproar made by those
Who cried, "He is not Uther's son" — the King
Sent to him, saying, "Arise, and help us thou!
For here between the man and beast we die."

And Arthur yet had done no deed of arms,
But heard the call and came; and Guinevere
Stood by the castle walls to watch him pass;
But since he neither wore on helm or shield
The golden symbol of his kinglihood,   50
But rode a simple knight among his knights,
And many of these in richer arms than he,
She saw him not, or mark'd not, if she saw,
One among many, tho' his face was bare.
But Arthur, looking downward as he past,
Felt the light of her eyes into his life
Smite on the sudden, yet rode on, and pitch'd
His tents beside the forest. Then he drave
The heathen; after, slew the beast, and fell'd
The forest, letting in the sun, and made   60
Broad pathways for the hunter and the knight,
And so return'd.

                    For while he linger'd there,
A doubt that ever smoulder'd in the hearts
Of those great lords and barons of his realm
Flash'd forth and into war; for most of these,
Colleaguing with a score of petty kings,
Made head against him, crying: "Who is he
That he should rule us? who hath proven him
King Uther's son? for lo! we look at him,
And find nor face nor bearing, limbs nor voice,   70
Are like to those of Uther whom we knew.
This is the son of Gorloïs, not the King;
This is the son of Anton, not the King."

And Arthur, passing thence to battle, felt
Travail, and throes and agonies of the life,

Desiring to be join'd with Guinevere,
And thinking as he rode: "Her father said
That there between the man and beast they die.
Shall I not lift her from this land of beasts
Up to my throne and side by side with me?   80
What happiness to reign a lonely king,
Vext — O ye stars that shudder over me,
O earth that soundest hollow under me,
Vext with waste dreams? for saving I be join'd
To her that is the fairest under heaven,
I seem as nothing in the mighty world,
And cannot will my will nor work my work
Wholly, nor make myself in mine own realm
Victor and lord. But were I join'd with her,
Then might we live together as one life,   90
And reigning with one will in everything
Have power on this dark land to lighten it,
And power on this dead world to make it live."

      Thereafter — as he speaks who tells the tale —
When Arthur reach'd a field of battle bright
With pitch'd pavilions of his foe, the world
Was all so clear about him that he saw
The smallest rock far on the faintest hill,
And even in high day the morning star.
So when the King had set his banner broad,   100
At once from either side, with trumpet-blast,
And shouts, and clarions shrilling unto blood,
The long-lanced battle let their horses run.
And now the barons and the kings prevail'd,
And now the King, as here and there that war
Went swaying; but the Powers who walk the world
Made lightnings and great thunders over him,
And dazed all eyes, till Arthur by main might,
And mightier of his hands with every blow,
And leading all his knighthood threw the kings,   110
Carádos, Urien, Cradlemont of Wales,
Claudius, and Clariance of Northumberland,
The King Brandagoras of Latangor,
With Anguisant of Erin, Morganore,
And Lot of Orkney. Then, before a voice
As dreadful as the shout of one who sees
To one who sins, and deems himself alone
And all the world asleep, they swerved and brake
Flying, and Arthur call'd to stay the brands

That hack'd among the flyers, "Ho! they yield!"   120
So like a painted battle the war stood
Silenced, the living quiet as the dead,
And in the heart of Arthur joy was lord.
He laugh'd upon his warrior whom he loved
And honor'd most. "Thou dost not doubt me King,
So well thine arm hath wrought for me today."
"Sir and my liege," he cried, "the fire of God
Descends upon thee in the battle-field.
I know thee for my King!" Whereat the two,
For each had warded either in the fight,   130
Sware on the field of death a deathless love.
And Arthur said, "Man's word is God in man;
Let chance what will, I trust thee to the death."

Then quickly from the foughten field he sent
Ulfius, and Brastias, and Bedivere,
His new-made knights, to King Leodogran,
Saying, "If I in aught have served thee well,
Give me thy daughter Guinevere to wife."

Whom when he heard, Leodogran in heart
Debating — "How should I that am a king,   140
However much he holp me at my need,
Give my one daughter saving to a king,
And a king's son?" — lifted his voice, and call'd
A hoary man, his chamberlain, to whom
He trusted all things, and of him required
His counsel: "Knowest thou aught of Arthur's birth?"

Then spake the hoary chamberlain and said:
"Sir King, there be but two old men that know;
And each is twice as old as I; and one
Is Merlin, the wise man that ever served   150
King Uther thro' his magic art, and one
Is Merlin's master — so they call him — Bleys,
Who taught him magic; but the scholar ran
Before the master, and so far that Bleys
Laid magic by, and sat him down, and wrote
All things and whatsoever Merlin did
In one great annal-book, where after-years
Will learn the secret of our Arthur's birth."

To whom the King Leodogran replied:
"O friend, had I been holpen half as well   160

By this King Arthur as by thee to-day,
Then beast and man had had their share of me;
But summon here before us yet once more
Ulfius, and Brastias, and Bedivere."

Then, when they came before him, the king said:
"I have seen the cuckoo chased by lesser fowl,
And reason in the chase; but wherefore now
Do these your lords stir up the heat of war,
Some calling Arthur born of Gorloïs,
Others of Anton? Tell me, ye yourselves,   170
Hold ye this Arthur for King Uther's son?"

And Ulfius and Brastias answer'd, "Ay."
Then Bedivere, the first of all his knights
Knighted by Arthur at his crowning, spake —
For bold in heart and act and word was he,
Whenever slander breathed against the King —

"Sir, there be many rumors on this head;
For there be those who hate him in their hearts,
Call him baseborn, and since his ways are sweet,
And theirs are bestial, hold him less than man;   180
And there be those who deem him more than man,
And dream he dropt from heaven. But my belief
In all this matter — so ye care to learn —
Sir, for ye know that in King Uther's time
The prince and warrior Gorloïs, he that held
Tintagil castle by the Cornish sea,
Was wedded with a winsome wife, Ygerne.
And daughters had she borne him, — one whereof,
Lot's wife, the Queen of Orkney, Bellicent,
Hath ever like a loyal sister cleaved
To Arthur, — but a son she had not borne.
And Uther cast upon her eyes of love;
But she, a stainless wife to Gorloïs,
So loathed the bright dishonor of his love
That Gorloïs and King Uther went to war,
And overthrown was Gorloïs and slain.
Then Uther in his wrath and heat besieged
Ygerne within Tintagil, where her men,
Seeing the mighty swarm about their walls,
Left her and fled, and Uther enter'd in,   200
And there was none to call to but himself.
So, compass'd by the power of the king,

Enforced she was to wed him in her tears,
And with a shameful swiftness; afterward
Not many moons, King Uther died himself,
Moaning and wailing for an heir to rule
After him, lest the realm should go to wrack.
And that same night, the night of the new year,
By reason of the bitterness and grief
That vext his mother, all before his time   210
Was Arthur born, and all as soon as born
Deliver'd at a secret postern-gate
To Merlin, to be holden far apart
Until his hour should come, because the lords
Of that fierce day were as the lords of this,
Wild beasts, and surely would have torn the child
Piecemeal among them, had they known; for each
But sought to rule for his own self and hand,
And many hated Uther for the sake
Of Gorloïs. Wherefore Merlin took the child,   220
And gave him to Sir Anton, an old knight
And ancient friend of Uther; and his wife
Nursed the young prince, and rear'd him with her own;
And no man knew. And ever since the lords
Have foughten like wild beasts among themselves,
So that the realm has gone to wrack; but now,
This year, when Merlin — for his hour had come —
Brought Arthur forth, and set him in the hall,
Proclaiming, 'Here is Uther's heir, your king,'
A hundred voices cried: 'Away with him!   230
No king of ours! a son of Gorloïs he,
Or else the child of Anton, and no king,
Or else baseborn.' Yet Merlin thro' his craft,
And while the people clamor'd for a king,
Had Arthur crown'd; but after, the great lords
Banded, and so brake out in open war."

Then while the king debated with himself
If Arthur were the child of shamefulness,
Or born the son of Gorloïs after death,
Or Uther's son and born before his time.   240
Or whether there were truth in anything
Said by these three, there came to Cameliard,
With Gawain and young Modred, her two sons,
Lot's wife, the Queen of Orkney, Bellicent;
Whom as he could, not as he would, the king
Made feast for, saying, as they sat at meat:

"A doubtful throne is ice on summer seas.
Ye come from Arthur's court. Victor his men
Report him! Yea, but ye — think ye this king —
So many those that hate him, and so strong,   250
So few his knights, however brave they be —
Hath body enow to hold his foemen down?"

    "O King," she cried, "and I will tell thee: few,
Few, but all brave, all of one mind with him;
For I was near him when the savage yells
Of Uther's peerage died, and Arthur sat
Crowned on the daïs, and his warriors cried,
'Be thou the king, and we will work thy will
Who love thee.' Then the King in low deep tones,
And simple words of great authority,   260
Bound them by so strait vows to his own self
That when they rose, knighted from kneeling, some
Were pale as at the passing of a ghost,
Some flush'd, and others dazed, as one who wakes
Half-blinded at the coming of a light.

    "But when he spake, and cheer'd his Table Round
With large, divine, and comfortable words,
Beyond my tongue to tell thee — I beheld
From eye to eye thro' all their Order flash
A momentary likeness of the King;   270
And ere it left their faces, thro' the cross
And those around it and the Crucified,
Down from the casement over Arthur smote
Flame-color, vert, and azure, in three rays,
One falling upon each of three fair queens
Who stood in silence near his throne, the friends
Of Arthur, gazing on him, tall, with bright
Sweet faces, who will help him at his need.

    "And there I saw mage Merlin, whose vast wit
And hundred winters are but as the hands   280
Of loyal vassals toiling for their liege.

    "And near him stood the Lady of the Lake,
Who knows a subtler magic than his own —
Clothed in white samite, mystic, wonderful.
She gave the King his huge cross-hilted sword,
Whereby to drive the heathen out. A mist
Of incense curl'd about her, and her face

Wellnigh was hidden in the minster gloom;
But there was heard among the holy hymns
A voice as of the waters, for she dwells   290
Down in a deep — calm, whatsoever storms
May shake the world — and when the surface rolls,
Hath power to walk the waters like our Lord.

"There likewise I beheld Excalibur
Before him at his crowning borne, the sword
That rose from out the bosom of the lake,
And Arthur row'd across and took it — rich
With jewels, elfin Urim, on the hilt,
Bewildering heart and eye — the blade so bright
That men are blinded by it — on one side,   300
Graven in the oldest tongue of all this world,
'Take me,' but turn the blade and ye shall see,
And written in the speech ye speak yourself,
'Cast me away!' And sad was Arthur's face
Taking it, but old Merlin counsell'd him,
'Take thou and strike! the time to cast away
Is yet far-off.' So this great brand the king
Took, and by this will beat his foemen down."

Thereat Leodogran rejoiced, but thought
To sift his doubtings to the last, and ask'd,   310
Fixing full eyes of question on her face,
"The swallow and the swift are near akin,
But thou art closer to this noble prince,
Being his own dear sister;" and she said,
"Daughter of Gorloïs and Ygerne am I;"
"And therefore Arthur's sister?" ask'd the king.
She answer'd, "These be secret things," and sign'd
To those two sons to pass, and let them be.
And Gawain went, and breaking into song
Sprang out, and follow'd by his flying hair   320
Ran like a colt, and leapt at all he saw;
But Modred laid his ear beside the doors,
And there half-heard — the same that afterward
Struck for the throne, and striking found his doom.

And then the Queen made answer: "What know I?
For dark my mother was in eyes and hair,
And dark in hair and eyes am I; and dark
Was Gorloïs; yea, and dark was Uther too,
Wellnigh to blackness; but this king is fair

Beyond the race of Britons and of men.   330
Moreover, always in my mind I hear
A cry from out the dawning of my life,
A mother weeping, and I hear her say,
'O that ye had some brother, pretty one,
To guard thee on the rough ways of the world.' "

    "Ay," said the king, "and hear ye such a cry?
But when did Arthur chance upon thee first?"

    "O King!" she cried, "and I will tell thee true.
He found me first when yet a little maid.
Beaten I had been for a little fault   340
Whereof I was not guilty; and out I ran
And flung myself down on a bank of heath,
And hated this fair world and all therein,
And wept, and wish'd that I were dead; and he —
I know not whether of himself he came,
Or brought by Merlin, who, they say, can walk
Unseen at pleasure — he was at my side,
And spake sweet words, and comforted my heart,
And dried my tears, being a child with me.
And many a time he came, and evermore   350
As I grew greater grew with me; and sad
At times he seem'd, and sad with him was I,
Stern too at times, and then I loved him not,
But sweet again, and then I loved him well.
And now of late I see him less and less,
But those first days had golden hours for me,
For then I surely thought he would be king.

    "But let me tell thee now another tale:
For Bleys, our Merlin's master, as they say,
Died but of late, and sent his cry to me,   360
To hear him speak before he left his life.
Shrunk like a fairy changeling lay the mage;
And when I enter'd told me that himself
And Merlin ever served about the king,
Uther, before he died; and on the night
When Uther in Tintagil past away
Moaning and wailing for an heir, the two
Left the still king, and passing forth to breathe,
Then from the castle gateway by the chasm
Descending thro' the dismal night — a night   370
In which the bounds of heaven and earth were lost —

Beheld, so high upon the dreary deeps
It seem'd in heaven, a ship, the shape thereof
A dragon wing'd, and all from stem to stern
Bright with a shining people on the decks,
And gone as soon as seen. And then the two
Dropt to the cove, and watch'd the great sea fall,
Wave after wave, each mightier than the last,
Till last, a ninth one, gathering half the deep
And full of voices, slowly rose and plunged   380
Roaring, and all the wave was in a flame;
And down the wave and in the flame was borne
A naked babe, and rode to Merlin's feet,
Who stoopt and caught the babe, and cried, 'The King!
Here is an heir for Uther!' And the fringe
Of that great breaker, sweeping up the strand,
Lash'd at the wizard as he spake the word,
And all at once all round him rose in fire,
So that the child and he were clothed in fire.
And presently thereafter follow'd calm,   390
Free sky and stars. 'And this same child,' he said,
'Is he who reigns; nor could I part in peace
Till this were told.' And saying this the seer
Went thro' the strait and dreadful pass of death,
Not ever to be question'd any more
Save on the further side; but when I met
Merlin, and ask'd him if these things were truth —
The shining dragon and the naked child
Descending in the glory of the seas —
He laugh'd as is his wont, and answer'd me   400
In riddling triplets of old time, and said: —

   " 'Rain, rain, and sun! a rainbow in the sky!
A young man will be wiser by and by;
An old man's wit may wander ere he die.

   " 'Rain, rain, and sun! a rainbow on the lea!
And truth is this to me, and that to thee;
And truth or clothed or naked let it be.

   " 'Rain, sun, and rain! and the free blossom blows;
Sun, rain, and sun! and where is he who knows?
From the great deep to the great deep he goes.'   410

   "So Merlin riddling anger'd me; but thou
Fear not to give this King thine only child,
Guinevere; so great bards of him will sing

Hereafter, and dark sayings from of old
Ranging and ringing thro' the minds of men,
And echo'd by old folk beside their fires
For comfort after their wage-work is done,
Speak of the King; and Merlin in our time
Hath spoken also, not in jest, and sworn
Tho' men may wound him that he will not die,   420
But pass, again to come, and then or now
Utterly smite the heathen underfoot,
Till these and all men hail him for their king."

   She spake and King Leodogran rejoiced,
But musing "Shall I answer yea or nay?"
Doubted, and drowsed, nodded and slept, and saw,
Dreaming, a slope of land that ever grew,
Field after field, up to a height, the peak
Haze-hidden, and thereon a phantom king,
Now looming, and now lost; and on the slope   430
The sword rose, the hind fell, the herd was driven,
Fire glimpsed; and all the land from roof and rick,
In drifts of smoke before a rolling wind,
Stream'd to the peak, and mingled with the haze
And made it thicker; while the phantom king
Sent out at times a voice; and here or there
Stood one who pointed toward the voice, the rest
Slew on and burnt, crying, "No king of ours,
No son of Uther, and no king of ours;"
Till with a wink his dream was changed, the haze   440
Descended, and the solid earth became
As nothing, but the King stood out in heaven,
Crown'd. And Leodogran awoke, and sent
Ulfius, and Brastias, and Bedivere,
Back to the court of Arthur answering yea.

   Then Arthur charged his warrior whom he loved
And honor'd most, Sir Lancelot, to ride forth
And bring the Queen, and watch'd him from the gates;
And Lancelot past away among the flowers —
For then was latter April — and return'd   450
Among the flowers, in May, with Guinevere.
To whom arrived, by Dubric the high saint,
Chief of the church in Britain, and before
The stateliest of her altar-shrines, the King
That morn was married, while in stainless white,
The fair beginners of a nobler time,

And glorying in their vows and him, his knights
Stood round him, and rejoicing in his joy.
Far shone the fields of May thro' open door,
The sacred altar blossom'd white with May,   460
The sun of May descended on their King,
They gazed on all earth's beauty in their Queen,
Roll'd incense, and there past along the hymns
A voice as of the waters, while the two
Sware at the shrine of Christ a deathless love.
And Arthur said, "Behold, thy doom is mine.
Let chance what will, I love thee to the death!"
To whom the Queen replied with drooping eyes,
"King and my lord, I love thee to the death!"
And holy Dubric spread his hands and spake: 470
"Reign ye, and live and love, and make the world
Other, and may thy Queen be one with thee,
And all this Order of thy Table Round
Fulfil the boundless purpose of their King!"

So Dubric said; but when they left the shrine
Great lords from Rome before the portal stood,
In scornful stillness gazing as they past;
Then while they paced a city all on fire
With sun and cloth of gold, the trumpets blew,
And Arthur's knighthood sang before the King: —   480

"Blow trumpet, for the world is white with May!
Blow trumpet, the long night hath roll'd away!
Blow thro' the living world — 'Let the King reign!'

"Shall Rome or Heathen rule in Arthur's realm?
Flash brand and lance, fall battle-axe upon helm,
Fall battle-axe, and flash brand! Let the King reign!

"Strike for the King and live! his knights have heard
That God hath told the King a secret word.
Fall battle-axe, and flash brand! Let the King reign!

"Blow trumpet! he will lift us from the dust.   490
Blow trumpet! live the strength, and die the lust!
Clang battle-axe, and clash brand! Let the King reign!

"Strike for the King and die! and if thou diest,
The King is king, and ever wills the highest.
Clang battle-axe, and clash brand! Let the King reign!

"Blow, for our Sun is mighty in his May!
Blow, for our Sun is mightier day by day!
Clang battle-axe, and clash brand! Let the King reign!

"The King will follow Christ, and we the King,
In whom high God hath breathed a secret thing.   500
Fall battle-axe, and clash brand! Let the King reign!"

So sang the knighthood, moving to their hall.
There at the banquet those great lords from Rome,
The slowly-fading mistress of the world,
Strode in and claim'd their tribute as of yore.
But Arthur spake: "Behold, for these have sworn
To wage my wars, and worship me their King;
The old order changeth, yielding place to new,
And we that fight for our fair father Christ,
Seeing that ye be grown too weak and old   510
To drive the heathen from your Roman wall,
No tribute will we pay." So those great lords
Drew back in wrath, and Arthur strove with Rome.

And Arthur and his knighthood for a space
Were all one will, and thro' that strength the King
Drew in the petty princedoms under him,
Fought, and in twelve great battles overcame
The heathen hordes, and made a realm and reign'd.
1869*

MERLIN AND VIVIEN

A STORM was coming, but the winds were still,
And in the wild woods of Broceliande,
Before an oak, so hollow, huge, and old
It look'd a tower of ivied masonwork,
At Merlin's feet the wily Vivien lay.

For he that always bare in bitter grudge
The slights of Arthur and his Table, Mark
The Cornish King, had heard a wandering voice,
A minstrel of Caerleon by strong storm
Blown into shelter at Tintagil, say   10
That out of naked knight-like purity
Sir Lancelot worshipt no unmarried girl,

But the great Queen herself, fought in her name,
Sware by her — vows like theirs that high in heaven
Love most, but neither marry nor are given
In marriage, angels of our Lord's report.

He ceased, and then — for Vivien sweetly said —
She sat beside the banquet nearest Mark, —
"And is the fair example follow'd, sir,
In Arthur's household?" — answer'd innocently: 20

"Ay, by some few — ay, truly — youths that hold
It more beseems the perfect virgin knight
To worship woman as true wife beyond
All hopes of gaining, than as maiden girl.
They place their pride in Lancelot and the Queen.
So passionate for an utter purity
Beyond the limit of their bond are these,
For Arthur bound them not to singleness.
Brave hearts and clean! and yet — God guide them! — young."

Then Mark was half in heart to hurl his cup   30
Straight at the speaker, but forbore. He rose
To leave the hall, and, Vivien following him,
Turn'd to her: "Here are snakes within the grass;
And you methinks, O Vivien, save ye fear
The monkish manhood, and the mask of pure
Worn by this court, can stir them till they sting."

And Vivien answer'd, smiling scornfully:
"Why fear? because that foster'd at *thy* court
I savor of thy — virtues? fear them? no,
As love, if love be perfect, casts out fear,   40
So hate, if hate be perfect, casts out fear.
My father died in battle against the King,
My mother on his corpse in open field;
She bore me there, for born from death was I
Among the dead and sown upon the wind —
And then on thee! and shown the truth betimes,
That old true filth, and bottom of the well,
Where Truth is hidden. Gracious lessons thine,
And maxims of the mud! 'This Arthur pure!
Great Nature thro' the flesh herself hath made   50
Gives him the lie! There is no being pure,
My Cherub; saith not Holy Writ the same?' —
If I were Arthur, I would have thy blood.

Thy blessing, stainless King! I bring thee back,
When I have ferreted out their burrowings,
The hearts of all this Order in mine hand —
Ay — so that fate and craft and folly close,
Perchance, one curl of Arthur's golden beard.
To me this narrow grizzled fork of thine
Is cleaner-fashion'd — Well, I loved thee first;   60
That warps the wit."

           Loud laugh'd the graceless Mark.
But Vivien, into Camelot stealing, lodged
Low in the city, and on a festal day
When Guinevere was crossing the great hall
Cast herself down, knelt to the Queen, and wail'd.

  "Why kneel ye there? What evil have ye wrought?
Rise!" and the damsel bidden rise arose
And stood with folded hands and downward eyes
Of glancing corner and all meekly said:
"None wrought, but suffer'd much, an orphan maid!   70
My father died in battle for thy King,
My mother on his corpse — in open field,
The sad sea-sounding wastes of Lyonnesse —
Poor wretch — no friend! — and now by Mark the king,
For that small charm of feature mine, pursued —
If any such be mine — I fly to thee.
Save, save me thou! Woman of women — thine
The wreath of beauty, thine the crown of power,
Be thine the balm of pity, O heaven's own white
Earth-angel, stainless bride of stainless King —   80
Help, for he follows! take me to thyself!
O yield me shelter for mine innocency
Among thy maidens!"

           Here her slow sweet eyes
Fear-tremulous, but humbly hopeful, rose
Fixt on her hearer's, while the Queen who stood
All glittering like May sunshine on May leaves
In green and gold, and plumed with green replied:
"Peace, child! of over-praise and over-blame
We choose the last. Our noble Arthur, him
Ye scarce can overpraise, will hear and know.   90
Nay — we believe all evil of thy Mark —
Well, we shall test thee farther; but this hour
We ride a-hawking with Sir Lancelot.

He hath given us a fair falcon which he train'd;
We go to prove it. Bide ye here the while."

    She past; and Vivien murmur'd after, "Go!
I bide the while." Then thro' the portal-arch
Peering askance, and muttering brokenwise,
As one that labors with an evil dream,
Beheld the Queen and Lancelot get to horse.   100

    "Is that the Lancelot? goodly — ay, but gaunt;
Courteous — amends for gauntness — takes her hand —
That glance of theirs, but for the street, had been
A clinging kiss — how hand lingers in hand!
Let go at last! — they ride away — to hawk
For waterfowl. Royaller game is mine.
For such a supersensual sensual bond
As that gray cricket chirpt of at our hearth —
Touch flax with flame — a glance will serve — the liars!
Ah little rat that borest in the dyke   110
Thy hole by night to let the boundless deep
Down upon far-off cities while they dance —
Or dream — of thee they dream'd not — nor of me
These — ay, but each of either; ride, and dream
The mortal dream that never yet was mine —
Ride, ride and dream until ye wake — to me!
Then, narrow court and lubber King, farewell!
For Lancelot will be gracious to the rat,
And our wise Queen, if knowing that I know,
Will hate, loathe, fear — but honor me the more."   120

    Yet while they rode together down the plain,
Their talk was all of training, terms of art,
Diet and seeling, jesses, leash and lure.
"She is too noble," he said, "to check at pies,
Nor will she rake: there is no baseness in her."
Here when the Queen demanded as by chance,
"Know ye the stranger woman?" "Let her be,"
Said Lancelot, and unhooded casting off
The goodly falcon free; she tower'd; her bells,
Tone under tone, shrill'd; and they lifted up   130
Their eager faces, wondering at the strength,
Boldness, and royal knighthood of the bird,
Who pounced her quarry and slew it. Many a time
As once — of old — among the flowers — they rode.

But Vivien half-forgotten of the Queen
Among her damsels broidering sat, heard, watch'd,
And whisper'd. Thro' the peaceful court she crept
And whisper'd; then, as Arthur in the highest
Leaven'd the world, so Vivien in the lowest,
Arriving at a time of golden rest,   140
And sowing one ill hint from ear to ear,
While all the heathen lay at Arthur's feet,
And no quest came, but all was joust and play,
Leaven'd his hall. They heard and let her be.

Thereafter, as an enemy that has left
Death in the living waters and withdrawn,
The wily Vivien stole from Arthur's court.

She hated all the knights, and heard in thought
Their lavish comment when her name was named.
For once, when Arthur walking all alone,   150
Vext at a rumor issued from herself
Of some corruption crept among his knights,
Had met her, Vivien, being greeted fair,
Would fain have wrought upon his cloudy mood
With reverent eyes mock-loyal, shaken voice,
And flutter'd adoration, and at last
With dark sweet hints of some who prized him more
Than who should prize him most; at which the King
Had gazed upon her blankly and gone by.
But one had watch'd, and had not held his peace;   160
It made the laughter of an afternoon
That Vivien should attempt the blameless King.
And after that, she set herself to gain
Him, the most famous man of all those times,
Merlin, who knew the range of all their arts,
Had built the King his havens, ships, and halls,
Was also bard, and knew the starry heavens;
The people call'd him wizard; whom at first
She play'd about with slight and sprightly talk,
And vivid smiles, and faintly-venom'd points   170
Of slander, glancing here and grazing there;
And yielding to his kindlier moods, the seer
Would watch her at her petulance and play,
Even when they seem'd unlovable, and laugh
As those that watch a kitten. Thus he grew
Tolerant of what he half disdain'd, and she,
Perceiving that she was but half disdain'd,

Began to break her sports with graver fits,
Turn red or pale, would often when they met
Sigh fully, or all-silent gaze upon him   180
With such a fixt devotion that the old man,
Tho' doubtful, felt the flattery, and at times
Would flatter his own wish in age for love,
And half believe her true; for thus at times
He waver'd, but that other clung to him,
Fixt in her will, and so the seasons went.

Then fell on Merlin a great melancholy;
He walk'd with dreams and darkness, and he found
A doom that ever poised itself to fall,
An ever-moaning battle in the mist,   190
World-war of dying flesh against the life,
Death in all life and lying in all love,
The meanest having power upon the highest,
And the high purpose broken by the worm.

So leaving Arthur's court he gain'd the beach,
There found a little boat and stept into it;
And Vivien follow'd, but he mark'd her not.
She took the helm and he the sail; the boat
Drave with a sudden wind across the deeps,
And, touching Breton sands, they disembark'd.   200
And then she follow'd Merlin all the way,
Even to the wild woods of Broceliande.
For Merlin once had told her of a charm,
The which if any wrought on any one
With woven paces and with waving arms,
The man so wrought on ever seem'd to lie
Closed in the four walls of a hollow tower,
From which was no escape for evermore;
And none could find that man for evermore,
Nor could he see but him who wrought the charm   210
Coming and going, and he lay as dead
And lost to life and use and name and fame.
And Vivien ever sought to work the charm
Upon the great enchanter of the time,
As fancying that her glory would be great
According to his greatness whom she quench'd.

There lay she all her length and kiss'd his feet,
As if in deepest reverence and in love.

A twist of gold was round her hair; a robe
Of samite without price, that more exprest   220
Than hid her, clung about her lissome limbs,
In color like the satin-shining palm
On sallows in the windy gleams of March.
And while she kiss'd them, crying, "Trample me,
Dear feet, that I have follow'd thro' the world,
And I will pay you worship; tread me down
And I will kiss you for it;" he was mute.
So dark a forethought roll'd about his brain,
As on a dull day in an ocean cave
The blind wave feeling round his long sea-hall   230
In silence; wherefore, when she lifted up
A face of sad appeal, and spake and said,
"O Merlin, do ye love me?" and again,
"O Merlin, do ye love me?" and once more,
"Great Master, do ye love me?" he was mute.
And lissome Vivien, holding by his heel,
Writhed toward him, slided up his knee and sat,
Behind his ankle twined her hollow feet
Together, curved an arm about his neck,
Clung like a snake; and letting her left hand   240
Droop from his mighty shoulder, as a leaf,
Made with her right a comb of pearl to part
The lists of such a beard as youth gone out
Had left in ashes. Then he spoke and said,
Not looking at her, "Who are wise in love
Love most, say least, " and Vivien answer'd quick:
"I saw the little elf-god eyeless once
In Arthur's arras hall at Camelot;
But neither eyes nor tongue — O stupid child!
Yet you are wise who say it; let me think   250
Silence is wisdom. I am silent then,
And ask no kiss;" then adding all at once,
"And lo, I clothe myself with wisdom," drew
The vast and shaggy mantle of his beard
Across her neck and bosom to her knee,
And call'd herself a gilded summer fly
Caught in a great old tyrant spider's web,
Who meant to eat her up in that wild wood
Without one word. So Vivien call'd herself,
But rather seem'd a lovely baleful star   260
Veil'd in gray vapor; till he sadly smiled:
"To what request for what strange boon," he said,
"Are these your pretty tricks and fooleries,

O Vivien, the preamble? yet my thanks,
For these have broken up my melancholy."

And Vivien answer'd smiling saucily:
"What, O my Master, have ye found your voice?
I bid the stranger welcome. Thanks at last!
But yesterday you never open'd lip,
Except indeed to drink. No cup had we;   270
In mine own lady palms I cull'd the spring
That gather'd trickling dropwise from the cleft,
And made a pretty cup of both my hands
And offer'd you it kneeling. Then you drank
And knew no more, nor gave me one poor word;
O, no more thanks than might a goat have given
With no more sign of reverence than a beard.
And when we halted at that other well,
And I was faint to swooning, and you lay
Foot-gilt with all the blossom-dust of those   280
Deep meadows we had traversed, did you know
That Vivien bathed your feet before her own?
And yet no thanks; and all thro' this wild wood
And all this morning when I fondled you.
Boon, ay, there was a boon, one not so strange —
How had I wrong'd you? surely ye are wise,
But such a silence is more wise than kind."

And Merlin lock'd his hand in hers and said:
"O, did ye never lie upon the shore,
And watch the curl'd white of the coming wave   290
Glass'd in the slippery sand before it breaks?
Even such a wave, but not so pleasurable,
Dark in the glass of some presageful mood,
Had I for three days seen, ready to fall.
And then I rose and fled from Arthur's court
To break the mood. You follow'd me unask'd;
And when I look'd, and saw you following still,
My mind involved yourself the nearest thing
In that mind-mist — for shall I tell you truth?
You seem'd that wave about to break upon me   300
And sweep me from my hold upon the world,
My use and name and fame. Your pardon, child.
Your pretty sports have brighten'd all again.
And ask your boon, for boon I owe you thrice,
Once for wrong done you by confusion, next
For thanks it seems till now neglected, last

For these your dainty gambols; wherefore ask,
And take this boon so strange and not so strange."

And Vivien answer'd smiling mournfully:
"O, not so strange as my long asking it,   310
Not yet so strange as you yourself are strange,
Nor half so strange as that dark mood of yours.
I ever fear'd ye were not wholly mine;
And see, yourself have own'd ye did me wrong.
The people call you prophet; let it be;
But not of those that can expound themselves.
Take Vivien for expounder; she will call
That three-days-long presageful gloom of yours
No presage, but the same mistrustful mood
That makes you seem less noble than yourself,   320
Whenever I have ask'd this very boon,
Now ask'd again; for see you not, dear love,
That such a mood as that which lately gloom'd
Your fancy when ye saw me following you
Must make me fear still more you are not mine,
Must make me yearn still more to prove you mine,
And make me wish still more to learn this charm
Of woven paces and of waving hands,
As proof of trust. O Merlin, teach it me!
The charm so taught will charm us both to rest.   330
For, grant me some slight power upon your fate,
I, feeling that you felt me worthy trust,
Should rest and let you rest, knowing you mine.
And therefore be as great as ye are named,
Not muffled round with selfish reticence.
How hard you look and how denyingly!
O, if you think this wickedness in me,
That I should prove it on you unawares,
That makes me passing wrathful; then our bond
Had best be loosed for ever; but think or not,   340
By Heaven that hears, I tell you the clean truth,
As clean as blood of babes, as white as milk!
O Merlin, may this earth, if ever I,
If these unwitty wandering wits of mine,
Even in the jumbled rubbish of a dream,
Have tript on such conjectural treachery —
May this hard earth cleave to the nadir hell
Down, down, and close again and nip me flat,
If I be such a traitress! Yield my boon,
Till which I scarce can yield you all I am;   350

And grant my re-reiterated wish,
The great proof of your love; because I think,
However wise, ye hardly know me yet."

    And Merlin loosed his hand from hers and said:
"I never was less wise, however wise,
Too curious Vivien, tho' you talk of trust,
Than when I told you first of such a charm.
Yea, if ye talk of trust I tell you this,
Too much I trusted when I told you that,
And stirr'd this vice in you which ruin'd man   360
Thro' woman the first hour; for howsoe'er
In children a great curiousness be well,
Who have to learn themselves and all the world,
In you, that are no child, for still I find
Your face is practised when I spell the lines,
I call it, — well, I will not call it vice;
But since you name yourself the summer fly,
I well could wish a cobweb for the gnat
That settles beaten back, and beaten back
Settles, till one could yield for weariness.   370
But since I will not yield to give you power
Upon my life and use and name and fame,
Why will ye never ask some other boon?
Yea, by God's rood, I trusted you too much!"

    And Vivien, like the tenderest-hearted maid
That ever bided tryst at village stile,
Made answer, either eyelid wet with tears:
"Nay, Master, be not wrathful with your maid;
Caress her, let her feel herself forgiven
Who feels no heart to ask another boon.   380
I think ye hardly know the tender rhyme
Of 'trust me not at all or all in all.'
I heard the great Sir Lancelot sing it once,
And it shall answer for me. Listen to it.

            " 'In love, if love be love, if love be ours,
            Faith and unfaith can ne'er be equal powers:
            Unfaith in aught is want of faith in all.

            " 'It is the little rift within the lute,
            That by and by will make the music mute,
            And ever widening slowly silence all.   390

" 'The little rift within the lover's lute,
Or little pitted speck in garner'd fruit,
That rotting inward slowly moulders all.

" 'It is not worth the keeping; let it go:
But shall it? answer, darling, answer, no.
And trust me not at all or all in all.'

"O master, do ye love my tender rhyme?"

And Merlin look'd and half believed her true,
So tender was her voice, so fair her face,
So sweetly gleam'd her eyes behind her tears   400
Like sunlight on the plain behind a shower;
And yet he answer'd half indignantly:

"Far other was the song that once I heard
By this huge oak, sung nearly where we sit;
For here we met, some ten or twelve of us,
To chase a creature that was current then
In these wild woods, the hart with golden horns.
It was the time when first the question rose
About the founding of a Table Round,
That was to be, for love of God and men   410
And noble deeds, the flower of all the world;
And each incited each to noble deeds.
And while we waited, one, the youngest of us,
We could not keep him silent, out he flash'd,
And into such a song, such fire for fame,
Such trumpet-blowings in it, coming down
To such a stern and iron-clashing close,
That when he stopt we long'd to hurl together,
And should have done it, but the beauteous beast
Scared by the noise upstarted at our feet,   420
And like a silver shadow slipt away
Thro' the dim land. And all day long we rode
Thro' the dim land against a rushing wind,
That glorious roundel echoing in our ears,
And chased the flashes of his golden horns
Until they vanish'd by the fairy well
That laughs at iron — as our warriors did —
Where children cast their pins and nails, and cry,
'Laugh, little well!' but touch it with a sword,
It buzzes fiercely round the point; and there   430
We lost him — such a noble song was that.
But, Vivien, when you sang me that sweet rhyme,

I felt as tho' you knew this cursed charm,
Were proving it on me, and that I lay
And felt them slowly ebbing, name and fame."

And Vivien answer'd smiling mournfully:
"O, mine have ebb'd away for evermore,
And all thro' following you to this wild wood,
Because I saw you sad, to comfort you.
Lo now, what hearts have men! they never mount   440
As high as woman in her selfless mood.
And touching fame, howe'er ye scorn my song,
Take one verse more — the lady speaks it — this:

    " 'My name, once mine, now thine, is closelier mine,
    For fame, could fame be mine, that fame were thine,
    And shame, could shame be thine, that shame were mine.
    So trust me not at all or all in all.'

"Says she not well? and there is more — this rhyme
Is like the fair pearl-necklace of the Queen,
That burst in dancing and the pearls were spilt;   450
Some lost, some stolen, some as relics kept;
But nevermore the same two sister pearls
Ran down the silken thread to kiss each other
On her white neck — so is it with this rhyme.
It lives dispersedly in many hands,
And every minstrel sings it differently;
Yet is there one true line, the pearl of pearls:
'Man dreams of fame while woman wakes to love.'
Yea! love, tho' love were of the grossest, carves
A portion from the solid present, eats   460
And uses, careless of the rest; but fame,
The fame that follows death is nothing to us;
And what is fame in life but half-disfame
And counterchanged with darkness? ye yourself
Know well that envy calls you devil's son,
And since ye seem the master of all art,
They fain would make you master of all vice."

And Merlin lock'd his hand in hers and said:
"I once was looking for a magic weed,
And found a fair young squire who sat alone,   470
Had carved himself a knightly shield of wood,
And then was painting on it fancied arms,
Azure, an eagle rising or, the sun
In dexter chief; the scroll, 'I follow fame.'

And speaking not, but leaning over him,
I took his brush and blotted out the bird,
And made a gardener putting in a graff,
With this for motto, 'Rather use than fame.'
You should have seen him blush; but afterwards
He made a stalwart knight. O Vivien,   480
For you, methinks you think you love me well;
For me, I love you somewhat. Rest; and Love
Should have some rest and pleasure in himself,
Not ever be too curious for a boon,
Too prurient for a proof against the grain
Of him ye say ye love. But Fame with men,
Being but ampler means to serve mankind,
Should have small rest or pleasure in herself,
But work as vassal to the larger love
That dwarfs the petty love of one to one.   490
Use gave me fame at first, and fame again
Increasing gave me use. Lo, there my boon!
What other? for men sought to prove me vile,
Because I fain had given them greater wits;
And then did envy call me devil's son.
The sick weak beast, seeking to help herself
By striking at her better, miss'd, and brought
Her own claw back, and wounded her own heart.
Sweet were the days when I was all unknown,
But when my name was lifted up the storm   500
Brake on the mountain and I cared not for it.
Right well know I that fame is half-disfame,
Yet needs must work my work. That other fame,
To one at least who hath not children vague,
The cackle of the unborn about the grave,
I cared not for it. A single misty star,
Which is the second in a line of stars
That seem a sword beneath a belt of three,
I never gazed upon it but I dreamt
Of some vast charm concluded in that star   510
To make fame nothing. Wherefore, if I fear,
Giving you power upon me thro' this charm,
That you might play me falsely, having power,
However well ye think ye love me now —
As sons of kings loving in pupilage
Have turn'd to tyrants when they came to power —
I rather dread the loss of use than fame;
If you — and not so much from wickedness,
As some wild turn of anger, or a mood

Of overstrain'd affection, it may be,   520
To keep me all to your own self, — or else
A sudden spurt of woman's jealousy, —
Should try this charm on whom ye say ye love."

    And Vivien answer'd smiling as in wrath:
"Have I not sworn? I am not trusted. Good!
Well, hide it, hide it; I shall find it out,
And being found take heed of Vivien.
A woman and not trusted, doubtless I
Might feel some sudden turn of anger born
Of your misfaith; and your fine epithet   530
Is accurate too, for this full love of mine
Without the full heart back may merit well
Your term of overstrain'd. So used as I,
My daily wonder is, I love at all.
And as to woman's jealousy, O, why not?
O, to what end, except a jealous one,
And one to make me jealous if I love,
Was this fair charm invented by yourself?
I well believe that all about this world
Ye cage a buxom captive here and there,
Closed in the four walls of a hollow tower
From which is no escape for evermore."

    Then the great master merrily answer'd her:
"Full many a love in loving youth was mine;
I needed then no charm to keep them mine
But youth and love; and that full heart of yours
Whereof ye prattle, may now assure you mine;
So live uncharm'd. For those who wrought it first,
The wrist is parted from the hand that waved,
The feet unmortised from their anklebones   550
Who paced it, ages back — but will ye hear
The legend as in guerdon for your rhyme?

    "There lived a king in the most eastern East,
Less old than I, yet older, for my blood
Hath earnest in it of far springs to be.
A tawny pirate anchor'd in his port,
Whose bark had plunder'd twenty nameless isles;
And passing one, at the high peep of dawn,
He saw two cities in a thousand boats
All fighting for a woman on the sea.   560
And pushing his black craft among them all,

He lightly scatter'd theirs and brought her off,
With loss of half his people arrow-slain;
A maid so smooth, so white, so wonderful,
They said a light came from her when she moved.
And since the pirate would not yield her up,
The king impaled him for his piracy,
Then made her queen. But those isle-nurtured eyes
Waged such unwilling tho' successful war
On all the youth, they sicken'd; councils thinn'd,　570
And armies waned, for magnet-like she drew
The rustiest iron of old fighters' hearts;
And beasts themselves would worship, camels knelt
Unbidden, and the brutes of mountain back
That carry kings in castles bow'd black knees
Of homage, ringing with their serpent hands,
To make her smile, her golden ankle-bells.
What wonder, being jealous, that he sent
His horns of proclamation out thro' all
The hundred under-kingdoms that he sway'd　580
To find a wizard who might teach the king
Some charm which, being wought upon the queen,
Might keep her all his own. To such a one
He promised more than ever king has given,
A league of mountain full of golden mines,
A province with a hundred miles of coast,
A palace and a princess, all for him;
But on all those who tried and fail'd the king
Pronounced a dismal sentence, meaning by it
To keep the list low and pretenders back,　590
Or, like a king, not to be trifled with —
Their heads should moulder on the city gates.
And many tried and fail'd, because the charm
Of nature in her overbore their own;
And many a wizard brow bleach'd on the walls,
And many weeks a troop of carrion crows
Hung like a cloud above the gateway towers."

And Vivien breaking in upon him, said:
"I sit and gather honey; yet, methinks,
Thy tongue has tript a little; ask thyself.　600
The lady never made *unwilling* war
With those fine eyes; she had her pleasure in it,
And made her good man jealous with good cause.
And lived there neither dame nor damsel then
Wroth at a lover's loss? were all as tame,

I mean, as noble, as their queen was fair?
Not one to flirt a venom at her eyes,
Or pinch a murderous dust into her drink,
Or make her paler with a poison'd rose?
Well, those were not our days — but did they find   610
A wizard? Tell me, was he like to thee?"

    She ceased, and made her lithe arm round his neck
Tighten, and then drew back, and let her eyes
Speak for her, glowing on him, like a bride's
On her new lord, her own, the first of men.

    He answer'd laughing: "Nay, not like to me.
At last they found — his foragers for charms —
A little glassy-headed hairless man,
Who lived alone in a great wild on grass,
Read but one book, and ever reading grew   620
So grated down and filed away with thought,
So lean his eyes were monstrous; while the skin
Clung but to crate and basket, ribs and spine.
And since he kept his mind on one sole aim,
Nor ever touch'd fierce wine, nor tasted flesh,
Nor own'd a sensual wish, to him the wall
That sunders ghosts and shadow-casting men
Became a crystal, and he saw them thro' it,
And heard their voices talk behind the wall,
And learnt their elemental secrets, powers   630
And forces; often o'er the sun's bright eye
Drew the vast eyelid of an inky cloud,
And lash'd it at the base with slanting storm;
Or in the noon of mist and driving rain,
When the lake whiten'd and the pinewood roar'd,
And the cairn'd mountain was a shadow, sunn'd
The world to peace again. Here was the man;
And so by force they dragg'd him to the king.
And then he taught the king to charm the queen
In such-wise that no man could see her more,   640
Nor saw she save the king, who wrought the charm,
Coming and going, and she lay as dead,
And lost all use of life. But when the king
Made proffer of the league of golden mines,
The province with a hundred miles of coast,
The palace and the princess, that old man
Went back to his old wild, and lived on grass,
And vanish'd and his book came down to me."

And Vivien answer'd smiling saucily:
"Ye have the book; the charm is written in it.   650
Good! take my counsel, let me know it at once;
For keep it like a puzzle chest in chest,
With each chest lock'd and padlock'd thirty-fold,
And whelm all this beneath as vast a mound
As after furious battle turfs the slain
On some wild down above the windy deep,
I yet should strike upon a sudden means
To dig, pick, open, find and read the charm;
Then, if I tried it, who should blame me then?"

And smiling as a master smiles at one   660
That is not of his school, nor any school
But that where blind and naked Ignorance
Delivers brawling judgments, unashamed,
On all things all day long, he answer'd her:

"Thou read the book, my pretty Vivien!
O, ay, it is but twenty pages long,
But every page having an ample marge,
And every marge enclosing in the midst
A square of text that looks a little blot,
The text no larger than the limbs of fleas;   670
And every square of text an awful charm,
Writ in a language that has long gone by,
So long that mountains have arisen since
With cities on their flanks — thou read the book!
And every margin scribbled, crost, and cramm'd
With comment, densest condensation, hard
To mind and eye; but the long sleepless nights
Of my long life have made it easy to me.
And none can read the text, not even I;
And none can read the comment but myself;   680
And in the comment did I find the charm.
O, the results are simple; a mere child
Might use it to the harm of any one,
And never could undo it. Ask no more;
For tho' you should not prove it upon me,
But keep that oath ye sware, ye might, perchance,
Assay it on some one of the Table Round,
And all because ye dream they babble of you."

And Vivien, frowning in true anger, said:
"What dare the full-fed liars say of me?   690

They ride abroad redressing human wrongs!
They sit with knife in meat and wine in horn.
They bound to holy vows of chastity!
Were I not woman, I could tell a tale.
But you are man, you well can understand
The shame that cannot be explain'd for shame.
Not one of all the drove should touch me — swine!"

Then answer'd Merlin careless of her words:
"You breathe but accusation vast and vague,
Spleen-born, I think, and proofless. If ye know,   700
Set up the charge ye know, to stand or fall!"

And Vivien answer'd frowning wrathfully:
"O, ay, what say ye to Sir Valence, him
Whose kinsmen left him watcher o'er his wife
And two fair babes, and went to distant lands,
Was one year gone, and on returning found
Not two but three? there lay the reckling, one
But one hour old! What said the happy sire?
A seven-months' babe had been a truer gift.
Those twelve sweet moons confused his fatherhood."   710

Then answer'd Merlin: "Nay, I know the tale.
Sir Valence wedded with an outland dame;
Some cause had kept him sunder'd from his wife.
One child they had; it lived with her; she died.
His kinsman travelling on his own affair
Was charged by Valence to bring home the child.
He brought, not found it therefore; take the truth."

"O, ay," said Vivien, "over-true a tale!
What say ye then to sweet Sir Sagramore,
That ardent man? 'To pluck the flower in season,'   720
So says the song, 'I trow it is no treason.'
O Master, shall we call him over-quick
To crop his own sweet rose before the hour?"

And Merlin answer'd: "Over-quick art thou
To catch a loathly plume fallen from the wing
Of that foul bird of rapine whose whole prey
Is man's good name. He never wrong'd his bride.
I know the tale. An angry gust of wind
Puff'd out his torch among the myriad-room'd
And many-corridor'd complexities   730

Of Arthur's palace. Then he found a door,
And darkling felt the sculptured ornament
That wreathen round it made it seem his own,
And wearied out made for the couch and slept,
A stainless man beside a stainless maid;
And either slept, nor knew of other there,
Till the high dawn piercing the royal rose
In Arthur's casement glimmer'd chastely down,
Blushing upon them blushing, and at once
He rose without a word and parted from her.   740
But when the thing was blazed about the court,
The brute world howling forced them into bonds,
And as it chanced they are happy, being pure."

"O, ay," said Vivien, "that were likely too!
What say ye then to fair Sir Percivale
And of the horrid foulness that he wrought,
The saintly youth, the spotless lamb of Christ,
Or some black wether of Saint Satan's fold?
What, in the precincts of the chapel-yard,
Among the knightly brasses of the graves,   750
And by the cold Hic Jacets of the dead!"

And Merlin answer'd careless of her charge:
"A sober man is Percivale and pure,
But once in life was fluster'd with new wine,
Then paced for coolness in the chapel-yard,
Where one of Satan's shepherdesses caught
And meant to stamp him with her master's mark.
And that he sinn'd is not believable;
For, look upon his face! — but if he sinn'd,
The sin that practice burns into the blood,   760
And not the one dark hour which brings remorse,
Will brand us, after, of whose fold we be;
Or else were he, the holy king whose hymns
Are chanted in the minster, worse than all.
But is your spleen froth'd out, or have ye more?"

And Vivien answer'd frowning yet in wrath:
"O, ay; what say ye to Sir Lancelot, friend,
Traitor or true? that commerce with the Queen,
I ask you, is it clamor'd by the child,
Or whisper'd in the corner? do ye know it?"   770

To which he answer'd sadly: "Yea, I know it.
Sir Lancelot went ambassador, at first,
To fetch her, and she watch'd him from her walls.
A rumor runs, she took him for the king,
So fixt her fancy on him; let them be.
But have ye no one word of loyal praise
For Arthur, blameless king and stainless man?"

She answer'd with a low and chuckling laugh:
"Man! is he man at all, who knows and winks?
Sees what his fair bride is and does, and winks? 780
By which the good King means to blind himself,
And blinds himself and all the Table Round
To all the foulness that they work. Myself
Could call him — were it not for womanhood —
The pretty, popular name such manhood earns,
Could call him the main cause of all their crime,
Yea, were he not crown'd king, coward and fool."

Then Merlin to his own heart, loathing, said:
"O true and tender! O my liege and King!
O selfless man and stainless gentleman, 790
Who wouldst against thine own eye-witness fain
Have all men true and leal, all women pure!
How, in the mouths of base interpreters,
From over-fineness not intelligible
To things with every sense as false and foul
As the poach'd filth that floods the middle street,
Is thy white blamelessness accounted blame!"

But Vivien, deeming Merlin overborne
By instance, recommenced, and let her tongue
Rage like a fire among the noblest names, 800
Polluting, and imputing her whole self,
Defaming and defacing, till she left
Not even Lancelot brave nor Galahad clean.

Her words had issue other than she will'd.
He dragg'd his eyebrow bushes down, and made
A snowy pent-house for his hollow eyes,
And mutter'd in himself: "Tell *her* the charm!
So, if she had it, would she rail on me
To snare the next, and if she have it not
So will she rail. What did the wanton say? 810
'Not mount as high!' we scarce can sink as low;

For men at most differ as heaven and earth,
But women, worst and best, as heaven and hell.
I know the Table Round, my friends of old;
All brave, and many generous, and some chaste.
She cloaks the scar of some repulse with lies.
I well believe she tempted them and fail'd,
Being so bitter; for fine plots may fail,
Tho' harlots paint their talk as well as face
With colors of the heart that are not theirs.   820
I will not let her know; nine tithes of times
Face-flatterer and backbiter are the same.
And they, sweet soul, that most impute a crime
Are pronest to it, and impute themselves,
Wanting the mental range, or low desire
Not to feel lowest makes them level all;
Yea, they would pare the mountain to the plain,
To leave an equal baseness; and in this
Are harlots like the crowd that if they find
Some stain or blemish in a name of note,   830
Not grieving that their greatest are so small,
Inflate themselves with some insane delight,
And judge all nature from her feet of clay,
Without the will to lift their eyes, and see
Her godlike head crown'd with spiritual fire,
And touching other worlds. I am weary of her."

   He spoke in words part heard, in whispers part,
Half-suffocated in the hoary fell
And many-winter'd fleece of throat and chin.
But Vivien, gathering somewhat of his mood,   840
And hearing "harlot" mutter'd twice or thrice,
Leapt from her session on his lap, and stood
Stiff as a viper frozen; loathsome sight,
How from the rosy lips of life and love
Flash'd the bare-grinning skeleton of death!
White was her cheek; sharp breaths of anger puff'd
Her fairy nostril out; her hand half-clench'd
Went faltering sideways downward to her belt,
And feeling. Had she found a dagger there —
For in a wink the false love turns to hate —   850
She would have stabb'd him; but she found it not.
His eye was calm, and suddenly she took
To bitter weeping, like a beaten child,
A long, long weeping, not consolable.
Then her false voice made way, broken with sobs:

"O crueller than was ever told in tale
Or sung in song! O vainly lavish'd love!
O cruel, there was nothing wild or strange,
Or seeming shameful — for what shame in love,
So love be true, and not as yours is? — nothing   860
Poor Vivien had not done to win his trust
Who call'd her what he call'd her — all her crime,
All — all — the wish to prove him wholly hers."

She mused a little, and then clapt her hands
Together with a wailing shriek, and said:
"Stabb'd through the heart's affections to the heart!
Seethed like the kid in its own mother's milk!
Kill'd with a word worse than a life of blows!
I thought that he was gentle, being great;
O God, that I had loved a smaller man!   870
I should have found in him a greater heart.
O, I, that flattering my true passion, saw
The knights, the court, the King, dark in your light,
Who loved to make men darker than they are,
Because of that high pleasure which I had
To seat you sole upon my pedestal
Of worship — I am answer'd, and henceforth
The course of life that seem'd so flowery to me
With you for guide and master, only you,
Becomes the sea-cliff pathway broken short,   880
And ending in a ruin — nothing left
But into some low cave to crawl, and there,
If the wolf spare me, weep my life away,
Kill'd with unutterable unkindliness."

She paused, she turn'd away, she hung her head,
The snake of gold slid from her hair, the braid
Slipt and uncoil'd itself, she wept afresh,
And the dark wood grew darker toward the storm
In silence, while his anger slowly died
Within him, till he let his wisdom go   890
For ease of heart, and half believed her true;
Call'd her to shelter in the hollow oak,
"Come from the storm," and having no reply,
Gazed at the heaving shoulder and the face
Hand-hidden, as for utmost grief or shame;
Then thrice essay'd, by tenderest-touching terms,
To sleek her ruffled peace of mind, in vain.
At last she let herself be conquer'd by him,

And as the cageling newly flown returns,
The seeming-injured simple-hearted thing   900
Came to her old perch back, and settled there.
There while she sat, half-falling from his knees,
Half-nestled at his heart, and since he saw
The slow tear creep from her closed eyelid yet,
About her, more in kindness than in love,
The gentle wizard cast a shielding arm.
But she dislink'd herself at once and rose,
Her arms upon her breast across, and stood,
A virtuous gentlewoman deeply wrong'd,
Upright and flush'd before him; then she said: 910

"There must be now no passages of love
Betwixt us twain henceforward evermore;
Since, if I be what I am grossly call'd,
What should be granted which your own gross heart
Would reckon worth the taking? I will go.
In truth, but one thing now — better have died
Thrice than have ask'd it once — could make me stay —
That proof of trust — so often ask'd in vain!
How justly, after that vile term of yours,
I find with grief! I might believe you then,   920
Who knows? once more. Lo! what was once to me
Mere matter of the fancy, now hath grown
The vast necessity of heart and life.
Farewell; think gently of me, for I fear
My fate or folly, passing gayer youth
For one so old, must be to love thee still.
But ere I leave thee let me swear once more
That if I schemed against thy peace in this,
May yon just heaven, that darkens o'er me, send
One flash that, missing all things else, may make   930
My scheming brain a cinder, if I lie."

Scarce had she ceased, when out of heaven a bolt —
For now the storm was close above them — struck,
Furrowing a giant oak, and javelining
With darted spikes and splinters of the wood
The dark earth round. He raised his eyes and saw
The tree that shone white-listed thro' the gloom.
But Vivien, fearing heaven had heard her oath,
And dazzled by the livid-flickering fork,
And deafen'd with the stammering cracks and claps   940
That follow'd, flying back and crying out,

"O Merlin, tho' you do not love me, save,
Yet save me!" clung to him and hugg'd him close;
And call'd him dear protector in her fright,
Nor yet forgot her practice in her fright,
But wrought upon his mood and hugg'd him close.
The pale blood of the wizard at her touch
Took gayer colors, like an opal warm'd.
She blamed herself for telling hearsay tales;
She shook from fear, and for her fault she wept   950
Of petulancy; she call'd him lord and liege,
Her seer, her bard, her silver star of eve,
Her God, her Merlin, the one passionate love
Of her whole life; and ever overhead
Bellow'd the tempest, and the rotten branch
Snapt in the rushing of the river-rain
Above them; and in change of glare and gloom
Her eyes and neck glittering went and came;
Till now the storm, its burst of passion spent,
Moaning and calling out of other lands,   960
Had left the ravaged woodland yet once more
To peace; and what should not have been had been,
For Merlin, overtalk'd and overworn,
Had yielded, told her all the charm, and slept.

Then, in one moment, she put forth the charm
Of woven paces and of waving hands,
And in the hollow oak he lay as dead,
And lost to life and use and name and fame.

Then crying, "I have made his glory mine,"
And shrieking out, "O fool!" the harlot leapt   970
Adown the forest, and the thicket closed
Behind her, and the forest echo'd "fool."
1859°

THE HOLY GRAIL

FROM noiseful arms, and acts of prowess done
In tournament or tilt, Sir Percivale
Whom Arthur and his knighthood call'd the Pure,
Had past into the silent life of prayer,
Praise, fast, and alms; and leaving for the cowl
The helmet in an abbey far away
From Camelot, there, and not long after, died.

And one, a fellow-monk among the rest,
Ambrosius, loved him much beyond the rest,
And honor'd him, and wrought into his heart   10
A way by love that waken'd love within,
To answer that which came; and as they sat
Beneath a world-old yew-tree, darkening half
The cloisters, on a gustful April morn
That puff'd the swaying branches into smoke
Above them, ere the summer when he died,
The monk Ambrosius question'd Percivale:

"O brother, I have seen this yew-tree smoke,
Spring after spring, for half a hundred years;
For never have I known the world without,   20
Nor ever stray'd beyond the pale. But thee,
When first thou camest — such a courtesy
Spake thro' the limbs and in the voice — I knew
For one of those who eat in Arthur's hall;
For good ye are and bad, and like to coins,
Some true, some light, but every one of you
Stamp'd with the image of the King; and now
Tell me, what drove thee from the Table Round,
My brother? was it earthly passion crost?"

"Nay," said the knight; "for no such passion mine.   30
But the sweet vision of the Holy Grail
Drove me from all vainglories, rivalries,
And earthly heats that spring and sparkle out
Among us in the jousts, while women watch
Who wins, who falls, and waste the spiritual strength
Within us, better offer'd up to heaven."

To whom the monk: "The Holy Grail! — I trust
We are green in Heaven's eyes; but here too much
We moulder — as to things without I mean —
Yet one of your own knights, a guest of ours,   40
Told us of this in our refectory,
But spake with such a sadness and so low
We heard not half of what he said. What is it?
The phantom of a cup that comes and goes?"

"Nay, monk! what phantom?" answer'd Percivale.
"The cup, the cup itself, from which our Lord
Drank at the last sad supper with his own —
This, from the blessed land of Aromat —
After the day of darkness, when the dead

Went wandering o'er Moriah — the good saint   **50**
Arimathæan Joseph, journeying brought
To Glastonbury, where the winter thorn
Blossoms at Christmas, mindful of our Lord.
And there awhile it bode; and if a man
Could touch or see it, he was heal'd at once,
By faith, of all his ills. But then the times
Grew to such evil that the holy cup
Was caught away to heaven, and disappear'd."

    To whom the monk: "From our old books I know
That Joseph came of old to Glastonbury,   **60**
And there the heathen Prince, Arviragus,
Gave him an isle of marsh whereon to build;
And there he built with wattles from the marsh
A little lonely church in days of yore,
For so they say, these books of ours, but seem
Mute of this miracle, far as I have read.
But who first saw the holy thing to-day?"

    "A woman," answer'd Percivale, "a nun,
And one no further off in blood from me
Than sister; and if ever holy maid   **70**
With knees of adoration wore the stone,
A holy maid; tho' never maiden glow'd,
But that was in her earlier maidenhood,
With such a fervent flame of human love,
Which, being rudely blunted, glanced and shot
Only to holy things; to prayer and praise
She gave herself, to fast and alms. And yet,
Nun as she was, the scandal of the Court,
Sin against Arthur and the Table Round,
And the strange sound of an adulterous race,   **80**
Across the iron grating of her cell
Beat, and she pray'd and fasted all the more.

    "And he to whom she told her sins, or what
Her all but utter whiteness held for sin,
A man wellnigh a hundred winters old,
Spake often with her of the Holy Grail,
A legend handed down thro' five or six,
And each of these a hundred winters old,
From our Lord's time. And when King Arthur made
His Table Round, and all men's hearts became   **90**
Clean for a season, surely he had thought

That now the Holy Grail would come again;
But sin broke out. Ah, Christ, that it would come,
And heal the world of all their wickedness!
'O Father!' ask'd the maiden, 'might it come
To me by prayer and fasting?' 'Nay,' said he,
'I know not, for thy heart is pure as snow.'
And so she pray'd and fasted, till the sun
Shone, and the wind blew, thro' her, and I thought
She might have risen and floated when I saw her.   100

    "For on a day she sent to speak with me.
And when she came to speak, behold her eyes
Beyond my knowing of them, beautiful,
Beyond all knowing of them, wonderful,
Beautiful in the light of holiness!
And 'O my brother Percivale,' she said,
'Sweet brother, I have seen the Holy Grail;
For, waked at dead of night, I heard a sound
As of a silver horn from o'er the hills
Blown, and I thought, "It is not Arthur's use   110
To hunt by moonlight." And the slender sound
As from a distance beyond distance grew
Coming upon me — O never harp nor horn,
Nor aught we blow with breath, or touch with hand,
Was like that music as it came; and then
Stream'd thro' my cell a cold and silver beam,
And down the long beam stole the Holy Grail,
Rose-red with beatings in it, as if alive,
Till all the white walls of my cell were dyed
With rosy colors leaping on the wall;   120
And then the music faded, and the Grail
Past, and the beam decay'd, and from the walls
The rosy quiverings died into the night.
So now the Holy Thing is here again
Among us, brother, fast thou too and pray,
And tell they brother knights to fast and pray,
That so perchance the vision may be seen
By thee and those, and all the world be heal'd.'

    "Then leaving the pale nun, I spake of this
To all men; and myself fasted and pray'd   130
Always, and many among us many a week
Fasted and pray'd even to the uttermost,
Expectant of the wonder that would be.

"And one there was among us, ever moved
Among us in white armor, Galahad.
'God make thee good as thou art beautiful!'
Said Arthur, when he dubb'd him knight, and none
In so young youth was ever made a knight
Till Galahad; and this Galahad, when he heard
My sister's vision, fill'd me with amaze;   140
His eyes became so like her own, they seem'd
Hers, and himself her brother more than I.

"Sister or brother none had he; but some
Call'd him a son of Lancelot, and some said
Begotten by enchantment — chatterers they,
Like birds of passage piping up and down,
That gape for flies — we know not whence they come;
For when was Lancelot wanderingly lewd?

"But she, the wan sweet maiden, shore away
Clean from her forehead all that wealth of hair   150
Which made a silken mat-work for her feet;
And out of this she plaited broad and long
A strong sword-belt, and wove with silver thread
And crimson in the belt a strange device,
A crimson grail within a silver beam;
And saw the bright boy-knight, and bound it on him,
Saying: 'My knight, my love, my knight of heaven,
O thou, my love, whose love is one with mine,
I, maiden, round thee, maiden, bind my belt.
Go forth, for thou shalt see what I have seen,   160
And break thro' all, till one will crown thee king
Far in the spiritual city;' and as she spake
She sent the deathless passion in her eyes
Thro' him, and made him hers, and laid her mind
On him, and he believed in her belief.

"Then came a year of miracle. O brother,
In our great hall there stood a vacant chair,
Fashion'd by Merlin ere he past away,
And carven with strange figures; and in and out
The figures, like a serpent, ran a scroll   170
Of letters in a tongue no man could read.
And Merlin call'd it 'the Siege Perilous,'
Perilous for good and ill; 'for there,' he said,
'No man could sit but he should lose himself.'
And once by misadvertence Merlin sat

In his own chair, and so was lost; but he,
Galahad, when he heard of Merlin's doom,
Cried, 'If I lose myself, I save myself!'

 "Then on a summer night it came to pass,
While the great banquet lay along the hall,   180
That Galahad would sit down in Merlin's chair.

 "And all at once, as there we sat, we heard
A cracking and a riving of the roofs,
And rending, and a blast, and overhead
Thunder and in the thunder was a cry.
And in the blast there smote along the hall
A beam of light seven times more clear than day;
And down the long beam stole the Holy Grail
All over cover'd with a luminous cloud,
And none might see who bare it, and it past.   190
But every knight beheld his fellow's face
As in a glory, and all the knights arose,
And staring each at other like dumb men
Stood, till I found a voice and sware a vow.

 "I sware a vow before them all, that I,
Because I had not seen the Grail, would ride
A twelvemonth and a day in quest of it,
Until I found and saw it, as the nun
My sister saw it; and Galahad sware the vow,
And good Sir Bors, our Lancelot's cousin, sware,   200
And Lancelot sware, and many among the knights,
And Gawain sware, and louder than the rest.'

 Then spake the monk Ambrosius, asking him,
"What said the King? Did Arthur take the vow?"

 "Nay, for my lord," said Percivale, "the King,
Was not in hall; for early that same day,
Scaped thro' a cavern from a bandit bold,
An outraged maiden sprang into the hall
Crying on help; for all her shining hair
Was smear'd with earth, and either milky arm   210
Red-rent with hooks of bramble, and all she wore
Torn as a sail that leaves the rope is torn
In tempest. So the King arose and went
To smoke the scandalous hive of those wild bees
That made such honey in his realm. Howbeit

Some little of this marvel he too saw,
Returning o'er the plain that then began
To darken under Camelot; whence the King
Look'd up, calling aloud, 'Lo, there! the roofs
Of our great hall are roll'd in thunder-smoke!   220
Pray heaven, they be not smitten by the bolt!'
For dear to Arthur was that hall of ours,
As having there so oft with all his knights
Feasted, and as the stateliest under heaven.

　　"O brother, had you known our mighty hall,
Which Merlin built for Arthur long ago!
For all the sacred mount of Camelot,
And all the dim rich city, roof by roof,
Tower after tower, spire beyond spire,
By grove, and garden-lawn, and rushing brook,   230
Climbs to the mighty hall that Merlin built.
And four great zones of sculpture, set betwixt
With many a mystic symbol, gird the hall;
And in the lowest beasts are slaying men,
And in the second men are slaying beasts,
And on the third are warriors, perfect men,
And on the fourth are men with growing wings,
And over all one statue in the mould
Of Arthur, made by Merlin, with a crown,
And peak'd wings pointed to the Northern Star.   240
And eastward fronts the statue, and the crown
And both the wings are made of gold, and flame
At sunrise till the people in far fields,
Wasted so often by the heathen hordes,
Behold it, crying 'We have still a king.'

　　"And, brother had you known our hall within,
Broader and higher than any in all the lands!
Where twelve great windows blazon Arthur's wars,
And all the light that falls upon the board
Streams thro' the twelve great battles of our King.   250
Nay, one there is, and at the eastern end,
Wealthy with wandering lines of mount and mere,
Where Arthur finds the brand Excalibur.
And also one to the west, and counter to it,
And blank; and who shall blazon it? when and how? —
O, there, perchance, when all our wars are done,
The brand Excalibur will be cast away!

　　"So to this hall full quickly rode the King,

In horror lest the work by Merlin wrought,
Dreamlike, should on the sudden vanish, wrapt   260
In unremorseful folds of rolling fire.
And in he rode, and up I glanced, and saw
The golden dragon sparkling over all;
And many of those who burnt the hold, their arms
Hack'd, and their foreheads grimed with smoke and sear'd,
Follow'd, and in among bright faces, ours,
Full of the vision, prest; and then the King
Spake to me, being nearest, 'Percivale,' —
Because the hall was all in tumult — some
Vowing, and some protesting, — 'what is this?'   270

    "O brother, when I told him what had chanced,
My sister's vision and the rest, his face
Darken'd, as I have seen it more than once,
When some brave deed seem'd to be done in vain,
Darken; and 'Woe is me, my knights,' he cried,
'Had I been here, ye had not sworn the vow.'
Bold was mine answer, 'Had thyself been here,
My King, thou wouldst have sworn.' 'Yea, yea,' said he,
'Art thou so bold and hast not seen the Grail?'

    " 'Nay, lord, I heard the sound, I saw the light,   280
But since I did not see the holy thing,
I sware a vow to follow it till I saw.'

    "Then when he ask'd us, knight by knight, if any
Had seen it, all their answers were as one:
'Nay, lord, and therefore have we sworn our vows.'

    " 'Lo, now,' said Arthur, 'have ye seen a cloud?
What go ye into the wilderness to see?'

    "Then Galahad on the sudden, and in a voice
Shrilling along the hall to Arthur, call'd,
'But I, Sir Arthur, saw the Holy Grail,   290
I saw the Holy Grail and heard a cry —
"O Galahad, and O Galahad, follow me!" ' "

    " 'Ah, Galahad, Galahad,' said the King, 'for such
As thou art is the vision, not for these.
Thy holy nun and thou have seen a sign —
Holier is none, my Percivale, than she —
A sign to maim this Order which I made.

But ye that follow but the leader's bell,' —
Brother, the King was hard upon his knights, —
'Taliessin is our fullest throat of song,   300
And one hath sung and all the dumb will sing.
Lancelot is Lancelot, and hath overborne
Five knights at once, and every younger knight,
Unproven, holds himself as Lancelot,
Till overborne by one, he learns — and ye,
What are ye? Galahads? — no, nor Percivales' —
For thus it pleased the King to range me close
After Sir Galahad; — 'nay,' said he, 'but men
With strength and will to right the wrong'd, of power
To lay the sudden heads of violence flat,   310
Knights that in twelve great battles splash'd and dyed
The strong White Horse in his own heathen blood —
But one hath seen, and all the blind will see.
Go, since your vows are sacred, being made.
Yet — for ye know the cries of all my realm
Pass thro' this hall — how often, O my knights,
Your places being vacant at my side,
This chance of noble deeds will come and go
Unchallenged, while ye follow wandering fires
Lost in the quagmire! Many of you, yea most,   320
Return no more. Ye think I show myself
Too dark a prophet. Come now, let us meet
The morrow morn once more in one full field
Of gracious pastime, that once more the King,
Before ye leave him for this quest, may count
The yet-unbroken strength of all his knights,
Rejoicing in that Order which he made.'

"So when the sun broke next from underground,
All the great Table of our Arthur closed
And clash'd in such a tourney and so full,   330
So many lances broken — never yet
Had Camelot seen the like since Arthur came;
And I myself and Galahad, for a strength
Was in us from the vision, overthrew
So many knights that all the people cried,
And almost burst the barriers in their heat,
Shouting, 'Sir Galahad and Sir Percivale!'

"But when the next day brake from underground —
O brother, had you known our Camelot,
Built by old kings, age after age, so old   340

The King himself had fears that it would fall,
So strange, and rich, and dim; for where the roofs
Totter'd toward each other in the sky,
Met foreheads all along the street of those
Who watch'd us pass; and lower, and where the long
Rich galleries, lady-laden, weigh'd the necks
Of dragons clinging to the crazy walls,
Thicker than drops from thunder, showers of flowers
Fell as we past; and men and boys astride
On wyvern, lion, dragon, griffin, swan,   350
At all the corners, named us each by name,
Calling 'God speed!' but in the ways below
The knights and ladies wept, and rich and poor
Wept, and the King himself could hardly speak
For grief, and all in middle street the Queen,
Who rode by Lancelot, wail'd and shriek'd aloud,
'This madness has come on us for our sins.'
So to the Gate of the Three Queens we came,
Where Arthur's wars are render'd mystically,
And thence departed every one his way.   360

    "And I was lifted up in heart, and thought
Of all my late-shown prowess in the lists,
How my strong lance had beaten down the knights,
So many and famous names; and never yet
Had heaven appear'd so blue, nor earth so green,
For all my blood danced in me, and I knew
That I should light upon the Holy Grail.

    "Thereafter, the dark warning of our King,
That most of us would follow wandering fires,
Came like a driving gloom across my mind.   370
Then every evil word I had spoken once,
And every evil thought I had thought of old,
And every evil deed I ever did,
Awoke and cried, 'This quest is not for thee.'
And lifting up mine eyes, I found myself
Alone, and in a land of sand and thorns,
And I was thirsty even unto death;
And I, too, cried, 'This quest is not for thee.'

    "And on I rode, and when I thought my thirst
Would slay me, saw deep lawns, and then a brook,   380
With one sharp rapid, where the crisping white
Play'd ever back upon the sloping wave

And took both ear and eye; and o'er the brook
Were apple-trees, and apples by the brook
Fallen, and on the lawns. 'I will rest here,'
I said, 'I am not worthy of the quest;'
But even while I drank the brook, and ate
The goodly apples, all these things at once
Fell into dust, and I was left alone
And thirsting in a land of sand and thorns.   390

    "And then behold a woman at a door
Spinning; and fair the house whereby she sat.
And kind the woman's eyes and innocent,
And all her bearing gracious; and she rose
Opening her arms to meet me, as who should say,
'Rest here;' but when I touch'd her, lo! she, too,
Fell into dust and nothing, and the house
Became no better than a broken shed,
And in it a dead babe; and also this
Fell into dust, and I was left alone.   400

    "And on I rode, and greater was my thirst.
Then flash'd a yellow gleam across the world,
And where it smote the plowshare in the field
The plowman left his plowing and fell down
Before it; where it glitter'd on her pail
The milkmaid left her milking and fell down
Before it, and I knew not why, but thought
'The sun is rising,' tho' the sun had risen.
Then was I ware of one that on me moved
In golden armor with a crown of gold   410
About a casque all jewels, and his horse
In golden armor jewelled everywhere;
And on the splendor came, flashing me blind,
And seem'd to me the lord of all the world,
Being so huge. But when I thought he meant
To crush me, moving on me, lo! he, too,
Open'd his arms to embrace me as he came,
And up I went and touch'd him, and he, too,
Fell into dust, and I was left alone
And wearying in a land of sand and thorns.   420

    "And I rode on and found a mighty hill,
And on the top a city wall'd; the spires
Prick'd with incredible pinnacles into heaven.
And by the gateway stirr'd a crowd; and these

Cried to me climbing, 'Welcome, Percivale!
Thou mightiest and thou purest among men!'
And glad was I and clomb, but found at top
No man, nor any voice. And thence I past
Far thro' a ruinous city, and I saw
That man had once dwelt there; but there I found   430
Only one man of an exceeding age.
'Where is that goodly company,' and I,
'That so cried out upon me?' and he had
Scarce any voice to answer, and yet gasp'd,
'Whence and what art thou?' and even as he spoke
Fell into dust and disappear'd, and I
Was left alone once more and cried in grief,
'Lo, if I find the Holy Grail itself
And touch it, it will crumble into dust!'

"And thence I dropt into a lowly vale,   440
Low as the hill was high, and where the vale
Was lowest found a chapel, and thereby
A holy hermit in a hermitage,
To whom I told my phantoms, and he said:

" 'O son, thou hast not true humility,
The highest virtue, mother of them all;
For when the Lord of all things made Himself
Naked of glory for His mortal change,
"Take thou my robe," she said, "for all is thine,"
And all her form shone forth with sudden light   450
So that the angels were amazed, and she
Follow'd Him down, and like a flying star
Led on the gray-hair'd wisdom of the east.
But her thou hast not known; for what is this
Thou thoughtest of thy prowess and thy sins?
Thou hast not lost thyself to save thyself
As Galahad.' When the hermit made an end,
In silver armor suddenly Galahad shone
Before us, and against the chapel door
Laid lance and enter'd, and we knelt in prayer.   460
And there the hermit slaked my burning thirst,
And at the sacring of the mass I saw
The holy elements alone; but he,
'Saw ye no more? I, Galahad, saw the Grail,
The Holy Grail, descend upon the shrine.
I saw the fiery face as of a child
That smote itself into the bread and went;

And hither am I come; and never yet
Hath what thy sister taught me first to see,
This holy thing, fail'd from my side, nor come   470
Cover'd, but moving with me night and day,
Fainter by day, but always in the night
Blood-red, and sliding down the blacken'd marsh
Blood-red, and on the naked mountain top
Blood-red, and in the sleeping mere below
Blood-red. And in the strength of this I rode,
Shattering all evil customs everywhere,
And past thro' Pagan realms, and made them mine,
And clash'd with Pagan hordes, and bore them down,
And broke thro' all, and in the strength of this   480
Come victor. But my time is hard at hand,
And hence I go, and one will crown me king
Far in the spiritual city; and come thou, too,
For thou shalt see the vision when I go.'

"While thus he spake, his eye, dwelling on mine,
Drew me, with power upon me, till I grew
One with him, to believe as he believed.
Then, when the day began to wane, we went.

"There rose a hill that none but man could climb,
Scarr'd with a hundred wintry watercourses —   490
Storm at the top, and when we gain'd it, storm
Round us and death; for every moment glanced
His silver arms and gloom'd, so quick and thick
The lightnings here and there to left and right
Struck, till the dry old trunks about us, dead,
Yea, rotten with a hundred years of death,
Sprang into fire. And at the base we found
On either hand, as far as eye could see,
A great black swamp and of an evil smell,
Part black, part whiten'd with the bones of men,   500
Not to be crost, save that some ancient king
Had built a way, where, link'd with many a bridge,
A thousand piers ran into the great Sea.
And Galahad fled along them bridge by bridge,
And every bridge as quickly as he crost
Sprang into fire and vanish'd, tho' I yearn'd
To follow; and thrice above him all the heavens
Open'd and blazed with thunder such as seem'd
Shoutings of all the sons of God. And first
At once I saw him far on the great Sea,   510

In silver-shining armor starry-clear;
And o'er his head the Holy Vessel hung
Clothed in white samite or a luminous cloud.
And with exceeding swiftness ran the boat,
If boat it were — I saw not whence it came.
And when the heavens open'd and blazed again
Roaring, I saw him like a silver star —
And had he set the sail, or had the boat
Become a living creature clad with wings?
And o'er his head the Holy Vessel hung   520
Redder than any rose, a joy to me,
For now I knew the veil had been withdrawn.
Then in a moment when they blazed again
Opening, I saw the least of little stars
Down on the waste, and straight beyond the star
I saw the spiritual city and all her spires
And gateways in a glory like one pearl —
No larger, tho' the goal of all the saints —
Strike from the sea; and from the star there shot
A rose-red sparkle to the city, and there   530
Dwelt, and I knew it was the Holy Grail,
Which never eyes on earth again shall see.
Then fell the floods of heaven drowning the deep,
And how my feet recrost the deathful ridge
No memory in me lives; but that I touch'd
The chapel-doors at dawn I know, and thence
Taking my war-horse from the holy man,
Glad that no phantom vext me more, return'd
To whence I came, the gate of Arthur's wars."

    "O brother," ask'd Ambrosius, — "for in sooth   540
These ancient books — and they would win thee — teem,
Only I find not there this Holy Grail,
With miracles and marvels like to these,
Not all unlike; which oftentime I read,
Who read but on my breviary with ease,
Till my head swims, and then go forth and pass
Down to the little thorpe that lies so close,
And almost plaster'd like a martin's nest
To these old walls — and mingle with our folk;
And knowing every honest face of theirs   550
As well as ever shepherd knew his sheep,
And every homely secret in their hearts,
Delight myself with gossip and old wives,
And ills and aches, and teethings, lyings-in,

And mirthful sayings, children of the place,
That have no meaning half a league away;
Or lulling random squabbles when they rise,
Chafferings and chatterings at the market-cross,
Rejoice, small man, in this small world of mine,
Yea, even in their hens and in their eggs —   560
O brother, saving this Sir Galahad,
Came ye on none but phantoms in your quest,
No man, no woman?"

        Then Sir Percivale:
"All men, to one so bound by such a vow,
And women were as phantoms. O, my brother,
Why wilt thou shame me to confess to thee
How far I falter'd from my quest and vow?
For after I had lain so many nights,
A bed-mate of the snail and eft and snake,
In grass and burdock, I was changed to wan   570
And meagre, and the vision had not come;
And then I chanced upon a goodly town
With one great dwelling in the middle of it.
Thither I made, and there was I disarm'd
By maidens each as fair as any flower;
But when they led me into hall, behold,
The princess of that castle was the one,
Brother, and that one only, who had ever
Made my heart leap; for when I moved of old
A slender page about her father's hall,   580
And she a slender maiden, all my heart
Went after her with longing, yet we twain
Had never kiss'd a kiss or vow'd a vow.
And now I came upon her once again,
And one had wedded her, and he was dead,
And all his land and wealth and state were hers.
And while I tarried, every day she set
A banquet richer than the day before
By me, for all her longing and her will
Was toward me as of old; till one fair morn,   590
I walking to and fro beside a stream
That flash'd across her orchard underneath
Her castle-walls, she stole upon my walk,
And calling me the greatest of all knights,
Embraced me, and so kiss'd me the first time,
And gave herself and all her wealth to me.
Then I remember'd Arthur's warning word,

That most of us would follow wandering fires,
And the quest faded in my heart. Anon,
The heads of all her people drew to me,   600
With supplication both of knees and tongue:
'We have heard of thee; thou art our greatest knight,
Our Lady says it, and we well believe.
Wed thou our Lady, and rule over us,
And thou shalt be as Arthur in our land.'
O me, my brother! but one night my vow
Burnt me within, so that I rose and fled,
But wail'd and wept, and hated mine own self,
And even the holy quest, and all but her;
Then after I was join'd with Galahad   610
Cared not for her nor anything upon earth."

    Then said the monk: "Poor men, when yule is cold,
Must be content to sit by little fires.
And this am I, so that ye care for me
Ever so little; yea, and blest be heaven
That brought thee here to this poor house of ours
Where all the brethren are so hard, to warm
My cold heart with a friend; but O the pity
To find thine own first love once more — to hold,
Hold her a wealthy bride within thine arms,   620
Or all but hold, and then — cast her aside,
Foregoing all her sweetness, like a weed!
For we that want the warmth of double life,
We that are plagued with dreams of something sweet
Beyond all sweetness in a life so rich, —
Ah, blessed Lord, I speak too earthly-wise,
Seeing I never stray'd beyond the cell,
But live like an old badger in his earth,
With earth about him everywhere, despite
All fast and penance. Saw ye none beside,   630
None of your knights?"

                    "Yea, so," said Percivale:
"One night my pathway swerving east, I saw
The pelican on the casque of our Sir Bors
All in the middle of the rising moon,
And toward him spurr'd, and hail'd him, and he me,
And each made joy of either. Then he ask'd:
Where is he? hast thou seen him — Lancelot? — Once,'
Said good Sir Bors, 'he dash'd across me — mad,
And maddening what he rode; and when I cried,

"Ridest thou then so hotly on a quest   640
So holy?" Lancelot shouted, "Stay me not!
I have been the sluggard, and I ride apace,
For now there is a lion in the way!"
So vanish'd.'

      "Then Sir Bors had ridden on
Softly, and sorrowing for our Lancelot,
Because his former madness, once the talk
And scandal of our table, had return'd;
For Lancelot's kith and kin so worship him
That ill to him is ill to them, to Bors
Beyond the rest. He well had been content   650
Not to have seen, so Lancelot might have seen,
The Holy Cup of healing; and, indeed,
Being so clouded with his grief and love,
Small heart was his after the holy quest.
If God would send the vision, well; if not,
The quest and he were in the hands of Heaven.

    "And then, with small adventure met, Sir Bors
Rode to the lonest tract of all the realm,
And found a people there among their crags,
Our race and blood, a remnant that were left   660
Paynim amid their circles, and the stones
They pitch up straight to heaven; and their wise men
Were strong in that old magic which can trace
The wandering of the stars, and scoff'd at him
And this high quest as at a simple thing,
Told him he follow'd — almost Arthur's words —
A mocking fire: 'what other fire than he
Whereby the blood beats, and the blossom blows,
And the sea rolls, and all the world is warm'd?'
And when his answer chafed them, the rough crowd,   670
Hearing he had a difference with their priests,
Seized him, and bound and plunged him into a cell
Of great piled stones; and lying bounden there
In darkness thro' innumerable hours
He heard the hollow-ringing heavens sweep
Over him till by miracle — what else? —
Heavy as it was, a great stone slipt and fell,
Such as no wind could move; and thro' the gap
Glimmer'd the streaming scud. Then came a night
Still as the day was loud, and thro' the gap   680
The seven clear stars of Arthur's Table Round —

For, brother, so one night, because they roll
Thro' such a round in heaven, we named the stars,
Rejoicing in ourselves and in our King —
And these, like bright eyes of familiar friends,
In on him shone: 'And then to me, to me,'
Said good Sir Bors, 'beyond all hopes of mine,
Who scarce had pray'd or ask'd it for myself —
Across the seven clear stars — O grace to me! —
In color like the fingers of a hand   690
Before a burning taper, the sweet Grail
Glided and past, and close upon it peal'd
A sharp quick thunder.' Afterwards, a maid,
Who kept our holy faith among her kin
In secret, entering, loosed and let him go."

To whom the monk: "And I remember now
That pelican on the casque. Sir Bors it was
Who spake so low and sadly at our board,
And mighty reverent at our grace was he;
A square-set man and honest, and his eyes,   700
An outdoor sign of all the warmth within,
Smiled with his lips — a smile beneath a cloud,
But heaven had meant it for a sunny one.
Ay, ay, Sir Bors, who else? But when ye reach'd
The city, found ye all your knights return'd,
Or was there sooth in Arthur's prophecy,
Tell me, and what said each, and what the King?"

Then answer'd Percivale: "And that can I,
Brother, and truly; since the living words
Of so great men as Lancelot and our King   710
Pass not from door to door and out again,
But sit within the house. O, when we reach'd
The city, our horses stumbling as they trode
On heaps of ruin, hornless unicorns,
Crack'd basilisks, and splinter'd cockatrices,
And shatter'd talbots, which had left the stones
Raw that they fell from, brought us to the hall.

"And there sat Arthur on the dais-throne,
And those that had gone out upon the quest,
Wasted and worn, and but a tithe of them,   720
And those that had not, stood before the King,
Who, when he saw me, rose and bade me hail,
Saying: 'A welfare in thine eyes reproves

Our fear of some disastrous chance for thee
On hill or plain, at sea or flooding ford.
So fierce a gale made havoc here of late
Among the strange devices of our kings,
Yea, shook this newer, stronger hall of ours,
And from the statue Merlin moulded for us
Half-wrench'd a golden wing; but now — the quest,   730
This vision — hast thou seen the Holy Cup
That Joseph brought of old to Glastonbury?'

    "So when I told him all thyself hast heard,
Ambrosius, and my fresh but fixt resolve
To pass away into the quiet life,
He answer'd not, but, sharply turning, ask'd
Of Gawain, 'Gawain, was this quest for thee?'

    " 'Nay, lord,' said Gawain, 'not for such as I.
Therefore I communed with a saintly man,
Who made me sure the quest was not for me;   740
For I was much a-wearied of the quest,
But found a silk pavilion in a field,
And merry maidens in it; and then this gale
Tore my pavilion from the tenting-pin,
And blew my merry maidens all about
With all discomfort; yea, and but for this,
My twelvemonth and a day were pleasant to me.'

    "He ceased; and Arthur turn'd to whom at first
He saw not, for Sir Bors, on entering, push'd
Athwart the throng to Lancelot, caught his hand,   750
Held it, and there, half-hidden by him, stood,
Until the King espied him, saying to him,
'Hail, Bors! if ever loyal man and true
Could see it, thou hast seen the Grail;' and Bors,
'Ask me not, for I may not speak of it;
I saw it;' and the tears were in his eyes.

    "Then there remain'd but Lancelot, for the rest
Spake but of sundry perils in the storm.
Perhaps, like him of Cana in Holy Writ,
Our Arthur kept his best until the last;   760
'Thou, too, my Lancelot,' ask'd the King, 'my friend,
Our mightiest, hath this quest avail'd for thee?'

" 'Our mightiest!' answer'd Lancelot, with a groan;
'O King!' — and when he paused methought I spied
A dying fire of madness in his eyes —
'O King, my friend, if friend of thine I be,
Happier are those that welter in their sin,
Swine in the mud, that cannot see for slime,
Slime of the ditch; but in me lived a sin
So strange, of such a kind, that all of pure,   770
Noble, and knightly in me twined and clung
Round that one sin, until the wholesome flower
And poisonous grew together, each as each,
Not to be pluck'd asunder; and when thy knights
Sware, I sware with them only in the hope
That could I touch or see the Holy Grail
They might be pluck'd asunder. Then I spake
To one most holy saint, who wept and said
That, save they could be pluck'd asunder, all
My quest were but in vain; to whom I vow'd   780
That I would work according as he will'd.
And forth I went, and while I yearn'd and strove
To tear the twain asunder in my heart,
My madness came upon me as of old,
And whipt me into waste fields far away.
There was I beaten down by little men,
Mean knights, to whom the moving of my sword
And shadow of my spear had been enow
To scare them from me once; and then I came
All in my folly to the naked shore,   790
Wide flats, where nothing but coarse grasses grew;
But such a blast, my King, began to blow,
So loud a blast along the shore and sea,
Ye could not hear the waters for the blast,
Tho' heapt in mounds and ridges all the sea
Drove like a cataract, and all the sand
Swept like a river, and the clouded heavens
Were shaken with the motion and the sound.
And blackening in the sea-foam sway'd a boat,
Half-swallow'd in it, anchor'd with a chain;   800
And in my madness to myself I said,
"I will embark and I will lose myself,
And in the great sea wash away my sin."
I burst the chain, I sprang into the boat.
Seven days I drove along the dreary deep,
And with me drove the moon and all the stars;
And the wind fell, and on the seventh night

I heard the shingle grinding in the surge,
And felt the boat shock earth, and looking up,
Behold, the enchanted towers of Carbonek,   810
A castle like a rock upon a rock,
With chasm-like portals open to the sea,
And steps that met the breaker! There was none
Stood near it but a lion on each side
That kept the entry, and the moon was full.
Then from the boat I leapt, and up the stairs,
There drew my sword. With sudden-flaring manes
Those two great beasts rose upright like a man,
Each gript a shoulder, and I stood between,
And, when I would have smitten them, heard a voice,   820
"Doubt not, go forward; if thou doubt, the beasts
Will tear thee piecemeal." Then with violence
The sword was dash'd from out my hand, and fell.
And up into the sounding hall I past;
But nothing in the sounding hall I saw,
No bench nor table, painting on the wall
Or shield of knight, only the rounded moon
Thro' the tall oriel on the rolling sea.
But always in the quiet house I heard,
Clear as a lark, high o'er me as a lark,   830
A sweet voice singing in the topmost tower
To the eastward. Up I climb'd a thousand steps
With pain; as in a dream I seem'd to climb
For ever; at the last I reach'd a door,
A light was in the crannies, and I heard,
"Glory and joy and honor to our Lord
And to the Holy Vessel of the Grail!"
Then in my madness I essay'd the door;
It gave, an thro' a stormy glare, a heat
As from a seven-times-heated furnace, I,   840
Blasted and burnt, and blinded as I was,
With such a fierceness that I swoon'd away —
O, yet methought I saw the Holy Grail,
All pall'd in crimson samite, and around
Great angels, awful shapes, and wings and eyes!
And but for all my madness and my sin,
And then my swooning, I had sworn I saw
That which I saw; but what I saw was veil'd
And cover'd, and this quest was not for me.'

   "So speaking, and here ceasing, Lancelot left   850
The hall long silent, till Sir Gawain — nay,

Brother, I need not tell thee foolish words, —
A reckless and irreverent knight was he,
Now bolden'd by the silence of his King, —
Well, I will tell thee: 'O King, my liege,' he said,
'Hath Gawain fail'd in any quest of thine?
When have I stinted stroke in foughten field?
But as for thine, my good friend Percivale,
Thy holy nun and thou have driven men mad,
Yea, made our mightiest madder than our least.   860
But by mine eyes and by mine ears I swear,
I will be deafer than the blue-eyed cat,
And thrice as blind as any noonday owl,
To holy virgins in their ecstasies,
Henceforward.'

   " 'Deafer,' said the blameless King,
'Gawain, and blinder unto holy things,
Hope not to make thyself by idle vows,
Being too blind to have desire to see.
But if indeed there came a sign from heaven,
Blessed are Bors, Lancelot, and Percivale,   870
For these have seen according to their sight.
For every fiery prophet in old times,
And all the sacred madness of the bard,
When God made music thro' them, could but speak
His music by the framework and the chord;
And as ye saw it ye have spoken truth.

   " 'Nay — but thou errest, Lancelot; never yet
Could all of true and noble in knight and man
Twine round one sin, whatever it might be,
With such a closeness but apart there grew,   880
Save that he were the swine thou spakest of,
Some root of knighthood and pure nobleness;
Whereto see thou, that it may bear its flower.

   " 'And spake I not too truly, O my knights?
Was I too dark a prophet when I said
To those who went upon the Holy Quest,
That most of them would follow wandering fires,
Lost in the quagmire? — lost to me and gone,
And left me gazing at a barren board,
And a lean Order — scarce return'd a tithe —   890
And out of those to whom the vision came
My greatest hardly will believe he saw.

Another hath beheld it afar off,
And, leaving human wrongs to right themselves,
Cares but to pass into the silent life.
And one hath had the vision face to face,
And now his chair desires him here in vain,
However they may crown him otherwhere.

"'And some among you held that if the King
Had seen the sight he would have sworn the vow.   900
Not easily, seeing that the King must guard
That which he rules, and is but as the hind
To whom a space of land is given to plow,
Who may not wander from the allotted field
Before his work be done, but, being done,
Let visions of the night or of the day
Come as they will; and many a time they come,
Until this earth he walks on seems not earth,
This light that strikes his eyeball is not light,
This air that smites his forehead is not air   910
But vision — yea, his very hand and foot —
In moments when he feels he cannot die,
And knows himself no vision to himself,
Nor the high God a vision, nor that One
Who rose again. Ye have seen what ye have seen.'

"So spake the King; I knew not all he meant."
1869*

PELLEAS AND ETTARRE

KING ARTHUR made new knights to fill the gap
Left by the Holy Quest; and as he sat
In hall at old Caerleon, the high doors
Were softly sunder'd, and thro' these a youth,
Pelleas, and the sweet smell of the fields
Past, and the sunshine came along with him.

"Make me thy knight, because I know, Sir King,
All that belongs to knighthood, and I love."
Such was his cry; for having heard the King
Had let proclaim a tournament — the prize   10
A golden circlet and a knightly sword,
Full fain had Pelleas for his lady won

The golden circlet, for himself the sword.
And there were those who knew him near the King,
And promised for him; and Arthur made him knight.

   And this new knight, Sir Pelleas of the Isles —
But lately come to his inheritance,
And lord of many a barren isle was he —
Riding at noon, a day or twain before,
Across the forest call'd of Dean, to find   20
Caerleon and the King, had felt the sun
Beat like a strong knight on his helm and reel'd
Almost to falling from his horse, but saw
Near him a mound of even-sloping side
Whereon a hundred stately beeches grew,
And here and there great hollies under them;
But for a mile all round was open space
And fern and heath. And slowly Pelleas drew
To that dim day, then, binding his good horse
To a tree, cast himself down; and as he lay   30
At random looking over the brown earth
Thro' that green-glooming twilight of the grove,
It seem'd to Pelleas that the fern without
Burnt as a living fire of emeralds,
So that his eyes were dazzled looking at it.
Then o'er it crost the dimness of a cloud
Floating, and once the shadow of a bird
Flying, and then a fawn; and his eyes closed.
And since he loved all maidens, but no maid
In special, half-awake he whisper'd: "Where?   40
O, where? I love thee, tho' I know thee not.
For fair thou art and pure as Guinevere,
And I will make thee with my spear and sword
As famous — O my Queen, my Guinevere,
For I will be thine Arthur when we meet."

   Suddenly waken'd with a sound of talk
And laughter at the limit of the wood,
And glancing thro' the hoary boles, he saw,
Strange as to some old prophet might have seem'd
A vision hovering on a sea of fire,   50
Damsels in divers colors like the cloud
Of sunset and sunrise, and all of them
On horses, and the horses richly trapt
Breast-high in that bright line of bracken stood;
And all the damsels talk'd confusedly,

And one was pointing this way and one that,
Because the way was lost.

                    And Pelleas rose,
And loosed his horse, and led him to the light.
There she that seem'd the chief among them said:
"In happy time behold our pilot-star!   60
Youth, we are damsels-errant, and we ride,
Arm'd as ye see, to tilt against the knights
There at Caerleon, but have lost our way.
To right? to left? straight forward? back again?
Which? tell us quickly."

                  Pelleas gazing thought,
"Is Guinevere herself so beautiful?"
For large her violet eyes look'd, and her bloom
A rosy dawn kindled in stainless heavens,
And round her limbs, mature in womanhood;
And slender was her hand and small her shape;   70
And but for those large eyes, the haunts of scorn,
She might have seem'd a toy to trifle with,
And pass and care no more. But while he gazed
The beauty of her flesh abash'd the boy,
As tho' it were the beauty of her soul;
For as the base man, judging of the good,
Puts his own baseness in him by default
Of will and nature, so did Pelleas lend
All the young beauty of his own soul to hers,
Believing her, and when she spake to him   80
Stammer'd, and could not make her a reply.
For out of the waste islands had he come,
Where saving his own sisters he had known
Scarce any but the women of his isles,
Rough wives, that laugh'd and scream'd against the gulls,
Makers of nets, and living from the sea.

    Then with a slow smile turn'd the lady round
And look'd upon her people; and, as when
A stone is flung into some sleeping tarn
The circle widens till it lip the marge,   90
Spread the slow smile thro' all her company.
Three knights were thereamong, and they too smiled,
Scorning him; for the lady was Ettarre,
And she was a great lady in her land.

Again she said: "O wild and of the woods,
Knowest thou not the fashion of our speech?
Or have the Heavens but given thee a fair face,
Lacking a tongue?"

    "O damsel," answer'd he,
"I woke from dreams, and coming out of gloom
Was dazzled by the sudden light, and crave   100
Pardon; but will ye to Caerleon? I
Go likewise; shall I lead you to the King?"

  "Lead then," she said; and thro' the woods they went.
And while they rode, the meaning in his eyes,
His tenderness of manner, and chaste awe,
His broken utterances and bashfulness,
Were all a burthen to her, and in her heart
She mutter'd, "I have lighted on a fool,
Raw, yet so stale!" But since her mind was bent
On hearing, after trumpet blown, her name   110
And title, "Queen of Beauty," in the lists
Cried — and beholding him so strong she thought
That peradventure he will fight for me,
And win the circlet — therefore flatter'd him,
Being so gracious that he wellnigh deem'd
His wish by hers was echo'd; and her knights
And all her damsels too were gracious to him,
For she was a great lady.

      And when they reach'd
Caerleon, ere they past to lodging, she,
Taking his hand, "O the strong hand," she said,   120
"See! look at mine! but wilt thou fight for me,
And win me this fine circlet, Pelleas,
That I may love thee?"

      Then his helpless heart
Leapt, and he cried, "Ay! wilt thou if I win?"
"Ay, that will I," she answer'd, and she laugh'd,
And straitly nipt the hand, and flung it from her;
Then glanced askew at those three knights of hers,
Till all her ladies laugh'd along with her.

  "O happy world," thought Pelleas, "all, meseems,
Are happy; I the happiest of them all!"   130
Nor slept that night for pleasure in his blood,

And green wood-ways, and eyes among the leaves;
Then being on the morrow knighted, sware
To love one only. And as he came away,
The men who met him rounded on their heels
And wonder'd after him, because his face
Shone like the countenance of a priest of old
Against the flame about a sacrifice
Kindled by fire from heaven; so glad was he.

Then Arthur made vast banquets, and strange knights   140
From the four winds came in; and each one sat,
Tho' served with choice from air, land, stream, and sea,
Oft in mid-banquet measuring with his eyes
His neighbor's make and might; and Pelleas look'd
Noble among the noble, for he dream'd
His lady loved him, and he knew himself
Loved of the King; and him his new-made knight
Worshipt, whose lightest whisper moved him more
Than all the ranged reasons of the world.

Then blush'd and brake the morning of the jousts,   150
And this was call'd "The Tournament of Youth;"
For Arthur, loving his young knight, withheld
His older and his mightier from the lists,
That Pelleas might obtain his lady's love,
According to her promise, and remain
Lord of the tourney. And Arthur had the jousts
Down in the flat field by the shore of Usk
Holden; the gilded parapets were crown'd
With faces, and the great tower fill'd with eyes
Up to the summit, and the trumpets blew.   160
There all day long Sir Pelleas kept the field
With honor; so by that strong hand of his
The sword and golden circlet were achieved.

Then rang the shout his lady loved; the heat
Of pride and glory fired her face, her eye
Sparkled; she caught the circlet from his lance,
And there before the people crown'd herself.
So for the last time she was gracious to him.

Then at Caerleon for a space — her look
Bright for all others, cloudier on her knight —   170
Linger'd Ettarre; and, seeing Pelleas droop,
Said Guinevere, "We marvel at thee much,

O damsel, wearing this unsunny face
To him who won thee glory!" And she said,
"Had ye not held your Lancelot in your bower,
My Queen, he had not won." Whereat the Queen,
As one whose foot is bitten by an ant,
Glanced down upon her, turn'd and went her way.

But after, when her damsels, and herself,
And those three knights all set their faces home,   180
Sir Pelleas follow'd. She that saw him cried:
"Damsels — and yet I should be shamed to say it —
I cannot bide Sir Baby. Keep him back
Among yourselves. Would rather that we had
Some rough old knight who knew the worldly way,
Albeit grizzlier than a bear, to ride
And jest with! Take him to you, keep him off,
And pamper him with papmeat, if ye will,
Old milky fables of the wolf and sheep,
Such as the wholesome mothers tell their boys.   190
Nay, should ye try him with a merry one
To find his mettle, good; and if he fly us,
Small matter! let him." This her damsels heard,
And, mindful of her small and cruel hand,
They, closing round him thro' the journey home,
Acted her hest, and always from her side
Restrain'd him with all manner of device,
So that he could not come to speech with her.
And when she gain'd her castle, upsprang the bridge,
Down rang the grate of iron thro' the groove,   200
And he was left alone in open field.

"These be the ways of ladies," Pelleas thought,
"To those who love them, trials of our faith.
Yea, let her prove me to the uttermost,
For loyal to the uttermost am I."
So made his moan, and, darkness falling, sought
A priory not far off, there lodged, but rose
With morning every day, and, moist or dry,
Full-arm'd upon his charger all day long
Sat by the walls, and no one open'd to him.   210

And this persistence turn'd her scorn to wrath.
Then, calling her three knights, she charged them, "Out!
And drive him from the walls." And out they came,
But Pelleas overthrew them as they dash'd

Against him one by one; and these return'd,
But still he kept his watch beneath the wall.

Thereon her wrath became a hate; and once,
A week beyond, while walking on the walls
With her three knights, she pointed downward, "Look,
He haunts me — I cannot breathe — besieges me!   220
Down! strike him! put my hate into your strokes,
And drive him from my walls." And down they went,
And Pelleas overthrew them one by one;
And from the tower above him cried Ettarre,
"Bind him, and bring him in."

                      He heard her voice;
Then let the strong hand, which had overthrown
Her minion-knights, by those he overthrew
Be bounden straight, and so they brought him in.

Then when he came before Ettarre, the sight   230
Of her rich beauty made him at one glance
More bondsman in his heart than in his bonds.
Yet with good cheer he spake: "Behold me, lady,
A prisoner, and the vassal of thy will;
And if thou keep me in thy donjon here,
Content am I so that I see thy face
But once a day; for I have sworn my vows,
And thou hast given thy promise, and I know
That all these pains are trials of my faith,
And that thyself, when thou hast seen me strain'd
And sifted to the utmost, wilt at length   240
Yield me thy love and know me for thy knight."

Then she began to rail so bitterly,
With all her damsels, he was stricken mute,
But, when she mock'd his vows and the great King,
Lighted on words: "For pity of thine own self,
Peace, lady, peace; is he not thine and mine?"
"Thou fool," she said, "I never heard his voice
But long'd to break away. Unbind him now,
And thrust him out of doors; for save he be
Fool to the midmost marrow of his bones,   250
He will return no more." And those, her three,
Laugh'd, and unbound, and thrust him from the gate.

And after this, a week beyond, again
She call'd them, saying: "There he watches yet,

There like a dog before his master's door!
Kick'd, he returns; do ye not hate him, ye?
Ye know yourselves; how can ye bide at peace,
Affronted with his fulsome innocence?
Are ye but creatures of the board and bed.
No men to strike? Fall on him all at once,   260
And if ye slay him I reck not; if ye fail,
Give ye the slave mine order to be bound,
Bind him as heretofore, and bring him in.
It may be ye shall slay him in his bonds."

    She spake, and at her will they couch'd their spears,
Three against one; and Gawain passing by,
Bound upon solitary adventure, saw
Low down beneath the shadow of those towers
A villainy, three to one; and thro' his heart
The fire of honor and all noble deeds   270
Flash'd, and he call'd, "I strike upon thy side —
The caitiffs!" "Nay," said Pelleas, "but forbear;
He needs no aid who doth his lady's will."

    So Gawain, looking at the villainy done,
Forbore, but in his heat and eagerness
Trembled and quiver'd, as the dog, withheld
A moment from the vermin that he sees
Before him, shivers ere he springs and kills.

    And Pelleas overthrew them, one to three;
And they rose up, and bound, and brought him in.   280
Then first her anger, leaving Pelleas, burn'd
Full on her knights in many an evil name
Of craven, weakling, and thrice-beaten hound:
"Yet, take him, ye that scarce are fit to touch,
Far less to bind, your victor, and thrust him out,
And let who will release him from his bonds.
And if he comes again" — there she brake short;
And Pelleas answer'd: "Lady, for indeed
I loved you and I deem'd you beautiful,
I cannot brook to see your beauty marr'd   290
Thro' evil spite; and if ye love me not,
I cannot bear to dream you so forsworn.
I had liefer ye were worthy of my love
Than to be loved again of you — farewell.
And tho' ye kill my hope, not yet my love,
Vex not yourself; ye will not see me more."

While thus he spake, she gazed upon the man
Of princely bearing, tho' in bonds, and thought:
"Why have I push'd him from me? this man loves,
If love there be; yet him I loved not. Why?   300
I deem'd him fool? yea, so? or that in him
A something — was it nobler than myself? —
Seem'd my reproach? He is not of my kind.
He could not love me, did he know me well.
Nay, let him go — and quickly." And her knights
Laugh'd not, but thrust him bounden out of door.

Forth sprang Gawain, and loosed him from his bonds,
And flung them o'er the walls; and afterward,
Shaking his hands, as from a lazar's rag,
"Faith of my body," he said, "and art thou not —   310
Yea thou art he, whom late our Arthur made
Knight of his table; yea, and he that won
The circlet? wherefore hast thou so defamed
Thy brotherhood in me and all the rest
As let these caitiffs on thee work their will?"

And Pelleas answer'd: "O, their wills are hers
For whom I won the circlet; and mine, hers,
Thus to be bounden, so to see her face,
Marr'd tho' it be with spite and mockery now,
Other than when I found her in the woods;   320
And tho' she hath me bounden but in spite,
And all to flout me, when they bring me in,
Let me be bounden, I shall see her face;
Else must I die thro' mine unhappiness."

And Gawain answer'd kindly tho' in scorn:
"Why, let my lady bind me if she will,
And let my lady beat me if she will;
But an she send her delegate to thrall
These fighting hands of mine — Christ kill me then
But I will slice him handless by the wrist,   330
And let my lady sear the stump for him,
Howl as he may! But hold me for your friend.
Come, ye know nothing; here I pledge my troth,
Yea, by the honor of the Table Round,
I will be leal to thee and work thy work,
And tame thy jailing princess to thine hand.
Lend me thine horse and arms, and I will say
That I have slain thee. She will let me in

To hear the manner of thy fight and fall;
Then, when I come within her counsels, then   340
From prime to vespers will I chant thy praise
As prowest knight and truest lover, more
Than any have sung thee living, till she long
To have thee back in lusty life again,
Not to be bound, save by white bonds and warm,
Dearer than freedom. Wherefore now thy horse
And armor; let me go; be comforted.
Give me three days to melt her fancy, and hope
The third night hence will bring thee news of gold."

     Then Pelleas lent his horse and all his arms,   350
Saving the goodly sword, his prize, and took
Gawain's, and said, "Betray me not, but help —
Art thou not he whom men call light-of-love?"

     "Ay," said Gawain, "for women be so light;"
Then bounded forward to the castle walls,
And raised a bugle hanging from his neck,
And winded it, and that so musically
That all the old echoes hidden in the wall
Rang out like hollow woods at huntingtide.

     Up ran a score of damsels to the tower;   360
"Avaunt," they cried, "our lady loves thee not!"
But Gawain lifting up his vizor said:
"Gawain am I, Gawain of Arthur's court,
And I have slain this Pelleas whom ye hate.
Behold his horse and armor. Open gates,
And I will make you merry."

                  And down they ran,
Her damsels, crying to their lady, "Lo!
Pelleas is dead — he told us — he that hath
His horse and armor; will ye let him in?
He slew him! Gawain, Gawain of the court,   370
Sir Gawain — there he waits below the wall,
Blowing his bugle as who should say him nay."

     And so, leave given, straight on thro' open door
Rode Gawain, whom she greeted courteously.
"Dead, is it so?" she ask'd. "Ay, ay," said he,
"And oft in dying cried upon your name."
"Pity on him," she answer'd, "a good knight,

But never let me bide one hour at peace."
"Ay," thought Gawain, "and you be fair enow;
But I to your dead man have given my troth,   380
That whom ye loathe, him will I make you love."

So those three days, aimless about the land,
Lost in a doubt, Pelleas wandering
Waited, until the third night brought a moon
With promise of large light on woods and ways.

Hot was the night and silent; but a sound
Of Gawain ever coming, and this lay —
Which Pelleas had heard sung before the Queen,
And seen her sadden listening — vext his heart,
And marr'd his rest — "A worm within the rose."   390

   "A rose, but one, none other rose had I,
   A rose, one rose, and this was wondrous fair,
   One rose, a rose that gladden'd earth and sky,
   One rose, my rose, that sweeten'd all mine air —
   I cared not for the thorns; the thorns were there.

   "One rose, a rose to gather by and by,
   One rose, a rose, to gather and to wear,
   No rose but one — what other rose had I?
   One rose, my rose; a rose that will not die, —
   He dies who loves it, — if the worm be there."   400

This tender rhyme, and evermore the doubt,
"Why lingers Gawain with his golden news?"
So shook him that he could not rest, but rode
Ere midnight to her walls, and bound his horse
Hard by the gates. Wide open were the gates,
And no watch kept; and in thro' these he past,
And heard but his own steps, and his own heart
Beating, for nothing moved but his own self
And his own shadow. Then he crost the court,
And spied not any light in hall or bower,   410
But saw the postern portal also wide
Yawning; and up a slope of garden, all
Of roses white and red, and brambles mixt
And overgrowing them, went on, and found,
Here too, all hush'd below the mellow moon,
Save that one rivulet from a tiny cave
Came lightening downward, and so spilt itself
Among the roses and was lost again.

Then was he ware of three pavilions rear'd
Above the bushes, gilden-peakt. In one,   420
Red after revel, droned her lurdane knights
Slumbering, and their three squires across their feet;
In one, their malice on the placid lip
Frozen by sweet sleep, four of her damsels lay;
And in the third, the circlet of the jousts
Bound on her brow, were Gawain and Ettarre.

    Back, as a hand that pushes thro' the leaf
To find a nest and feels a snake, he drew;
Back, as a coward slinks from what he fears
To cope with, or a traitor proven, or hound   430
Beaten, did Pelleas in an utter shame
Creep with his shadow thro' the court again,
Fingering at his sword-handle until he stood
There on the castle-bridge once more, and thought,
"I will go back, and slay them where they lie."

    And so went back, and seeing them yet in sleep
Said, "Ye, that so dishallow the holy sleep,
Your sleep is death," and drew the sword, and thought,
"What! slay a sleeping knight? the King hath bound
And sworn me to this brotherhood;" again,   440
"Alas that ever a knight should be so false!"
Then turn'd, and so return'd, and groaning laid
The naked sword athwart their naked throats,
There left it, and them sleeping; and she lay,
The circlet of the tourney round her brows,
And the sword of the tourney across her throat.

    And forth he past, and mounting on his horse
Stared at her towers that, larger than themselves
In their own darkness, throng'd into the moon;
Then crush'd the saddle with his thighs, and clench'd   450
His hands, and madden'd with himself and moan'd:

    "Would they had risen against me in their blood
At the last day? I might have answer'd them
Even before high God. O towers so strong,
Huge, solid, would that even while I gaze
The crack of earthquake shivering to your base
Split you, and hell burst up your harlot roofs
Bellowing, and charr'd you thro' and thro' within,
Black as the harlot's heart — hollow as a skull!

Let the fierce east scream thro' your eyelet-holes,   460
And whirl the dust of harlots round and round
In dung and nettles! hiss, snake — I saw him there —
Let the fox bark, let the wolf yell! Who yells
Here in the still sweet summer night but I —
I, the poor Pelleas whom she call'd her fool?
Fool, beast — he, she, or I? myself most fool;
Beast too, as lacking human wit — disgraced,
Dishonor'd all for trial of true love —
Love? — we be all alike; only the King
Hath made us fools and liars. O noble vows!   470
O great and sane and simple race of brutes
That own no lust because they have no law!
For why should I have loved her to my shame?
I loathe her, as I loved her to my shame.
I never loved her, I but lusted for her —
Away!" —

       He dash'd the rowel into his horse,
And bounded forth and vanish'd thro' the night.

    Then she, that felt the cold touch on her throat,
Awaking knew the sword, and turn'd herself
To Gawain: "Liar, for thou hast not slain   480
This Pelleas! here he stood, and might have slain
Me and thyself." And he that tells the tale
Says that her ever-veering fancy turn'd
To Pelleas, as the one true knight on earth
And only lover; and thro' her love her life
Wasted and pined, desiring him in vain.

    But he by wild and way, for half the night,
And over hard and soft, striking the sod
From out the soft, the spark from off the hard,
Rode till the star above the wakening sun,   490
Beside that tower where Percivale was cowl'd,
Glanced from the rosy forehead of the dawn.
For so the words were flash'd into his heart
He knew not whence or wherefore: "O sweet star,
Pure on the virgin forehead of the dawn!"
And there he would have wept, but felt his eyes
Harder and drier than a fountain bed
In summer. Thither came the village girls
And linger'd talking, and they come no more
Till the sweet heavens have fill'd it from the heights   500

Again with living waters in the change
Of seasons. Hard his eyes, harder his heart
Seem'd; but so weary were his limbs that he,
Gasping, "Of Arthur's hall am I, but here,
Here let me rest and die," cast himself down,
And gulf'd his griefs in inmost sleep; so lay,
Till shaken by a dream, that Gawain fired
The hall of Merlin, and the morning star
Reel'd in the smoke, brake into flame, and fell.

He woke, and being ware of some one nigh,   510
Sent hands upon him, as to tear him, crying,
"False! and I held thee pure as Guinevere."

But Percivale stood near him and replied,
"Am I but false as Guinevere is pure?
Or art thou mazed with dreams? or being one
Of our free-spoken Table hast not heard
That Lancelot" — there he check'd himself and paused.

Then fared it with Sir Pelleas as with one
Who gets a wound in battle, and the sword
That made it plunges thro' the wound again,   520
And pricks it deeper; and he shrank and wail'd,
"Is the Queen false?" and Percivale was mute.
"Have any of our Round Table held their vows?"
And Percivale made answer not a word.
"Is the King true?" "The King!" said Percivale.
"Why, then let men couple at once with wolves.
What! art thou mad?"

                But Pelleas, leaping up,
Ran thro' the doors and vaulted on his horse
And fled. Small pity upon his horse had he,
Or on himself, or any, and when he met   530
A cripple, one that held a hand for alms —
Hunch'd as he was, and like an old dwarf elm
That turns its back on the salt blast, the boy
Paused not, but overrode him, shouting, "False,
And false with Gawain!" and so left him bruised
And batter'd, and fled on, and hill and wood
Went ever streaming by him till the gloom
That follows on the turning of the world
Darken'd the common path. He twitch'd the reins,
And made his beast, that better knew it, swerve   540

Now off it and now on; but when he saw
High up in heaven the hall that Merlin built,
Blackening against the dead-green stripes of even,
"Black nest of rats," he groan'd, "ye build too high."

    Not long thereafter from the city gates
Issued Sir Lancelot riding airily,
Warm with a gracious parting from the Queen,
Peace at his heart, and gazing at a star
And marvelling what it was; on whom the boy,
Across the silent seeded meadow-grass   550
Borne, clash'd; and Lancelot, saying, "What name hast thou
That ridest here so blindly and so hard?"
"No name, no name," he shouted, "a scourge am I
To lash the treasons of the Table Round."
"Yea, but thy name?" "I have many names," he cried:
"I am wrath and shame and hate and evil fame,
And like a poisonous wind I pass to blast
And blaze the crime of Lancelot and the Queen."
"First over me," said Lancelot, "shalt thou pass."
"Fight therefore," yell'd the youth, and either Knight   560
Drew back a space, and when they closed, at once
The weary steed of Pelleas floundering flung
His rider, who call'd out from the dark field,
"Thou art false as hell; slay me, I have no sword."
Then Lancelot, "Yea, between thy lips — and sharp;
But here will I disedge it by thy death."
"Slay then," he shriek'd, "my will is to be slain,"
And Lancelot, with his heel upon the fallen,
Rolling his eyes, a moment stood, then spake:
"Rise, weakling; I am Lancelot; say thy say."   570

    And Lancelot slowly rode his war-horse back
To Camelot, and Sir Pelleas in brief while
Caught his unbroken limbs from the dark field,
And follow'd to the city. It chanced that both
Brake into hall together, worn and pale.
There with her knights and dames was Guinevere.
Full wonderingly she gazed on Lancelot
So soon return'd, and then on Pelleas, him
Who had not greeted her, but cast himself
Down on a bench, hard-breathing. "Have ye fought?"   580
She ask'd of Lancelot. "Ay, my Queen," he said.
"And thou hast overthrown him?" "Ay, my Queen."
Then she, turning to Pelleas, "O young knight,

Hath the great heart of knighthood in thee fail'd
So far thou canst not bide, unfrowardly,
A fall from *him?*" Then, for he answer'd not,
"Or hast thou other griefs? If I, the Queen,
May help them, loose thy tongue, and let me know."
But Pelleas lifted up an eye so fierce
She quail'd; and he, hissing "I have no sword,"   590
Sprang from the door into the dark. The Queen
Look'd hard upon her lover, he on her,
And each foresaw the dolorous day to be;
And all talk died, as in a grove all song
Beneath the shadow of some bird of prey.
Then a long silence came upon the hall,
And Modred thought, "The time is hard at hand."
1869*

THE LAST TOURNAMENT

DAGONET, the fool, whom Gawain in his mood
Had made mock-knight of Arthur's Table Round,
At Camelot, high above the yellowing woods,
Danced like a wither'd leaf before the hall.
And toward him from the hall, with harp in hand,
And from the crown thereof a carcanet
Of ruby swaying to and fro, the prize
Of Tristram in the jousts of yesterday,
Came Tristram, saying, "Why skip ye so, Sir Fool?"

   For Arthur and Sir Lancelot riding once   10
Far down beneath a winding wall of rock
Heard a child wail. A stump of oak half-dead,
From roots like some black coil of carven snakes,
Clutch'd at the crag, and started thro' mid air
Bearing an eagle's nest; and thro' the tree
Rush'd ever a rainy wind, and thro' the wind
Pierced ever a child's cry; and crag and tree
Scaling, Sir Lancelot from the perilous nest,
This ruby necklace thrice around her neck,
And all unscarr'd from beak or talon, brought   20
A maiden babe, which Arthur pitying took,
Then gave it to his Queen to rear. The Queen,
But coldly acquiescing, in her white arms
Received, and after loved it tenderly,

And named it Nestling; so forgot herself
A moment, and her cares; till that young life
Being smitten in mid heaven with mortal cold
Past from her, and in time the carcanet
Vext her with plaintive memories of the child.
So she, delivering it to Arthur, said,   30
"Take thou the jewels of this dead innocence,
And make them, an thou wilt, a tourney-prize."

To whom the King: "Peace to thine eagle-borne
Dead nestling, and this honor after death,
Following thy will! but, O my Queen, I muse
Why ye not wear on arm, or neck, or zone
Those diamonds that I rescued from the tarn,
And Lancelot won, methought, for thee to wear."

"Would rather you had let them fall," she cried,
"Plunge and be lost — ill-fated as they were,   40
A bitterness to me! — ye look amazed,
Not knowing they were lost as soon as given —
Slid from my hands when I was learning out
Above the river — that unhappy child
Past in her barge; but rosier luck will go
With these rich jewels, seeing that they came
Not from the skeleton of a brother-slayer,
But the sweet body of a maiden babe.
Perchance — who knows? — the purest of thy knights
May win them for the purest of my maids."   50

She ended, and the cry of a great jousts
With trumpet-blowings ran on all the ways
From Camelot in among the faded fields
To furthest towers; and everywhere the knights
Arm'd for a day of glory before the King.

But on the hither side of that loud morn
Into the hall stagger'd, his visage ribb'd
From ear to ear with dogwhip-weals, his nose
Bridge-broken, one eye out, and one hand off,
And one with shatter'd fingers dangling lame,   60
A churl, to whom indignantly the King:

"My churl, for whom Christ died, what evil beast
Hath drawn his claws athwart thy face? or fiend?
Man was it who marr'd heaven's image in thee thus?"

Then, sputtering thro' the hedge of splinter'd teeth,
Yet strangers to the tongue, and with blunt stump
Pitch-blacken'd sawing the air, said the maim'd churl:

"He took them and he drave them to his tower —
Some hold he was a table-knight of thine —
A hundred goodly ones — the Red Knight, he —   70
Lord, I was tending swine, and the Red Knight
Brake in upon me and drave them to his tower;
And when I call'd upon thy name as one
That doest right by gentle and by churl,
Maim'd me and maul'd, and would outright have slain,
Save that he sware me to a message, saying:
'Tell thou the King and all his liars that I
Have founded my Round Table in the North,
And whatsoever his own knights have sworn
My knights have sworn the counter to it — and say   80
My tower is full of harlots, like his court,
But mine are worthier, seeing they profess
To be none other than themselves — and say
My knights are all adulterers like his own,
But mine are truer, seeing they profess
To be none other; and say his hour is come,
The heathen are upon him, his long lance
Broken, and his Excalibur a straw.' "

Then Arthur turn'd to Kay the seneschal:
"Take thou my churl, and tend him curiously   90
Like a king's heir, till all his hurts be whole.
The heathen — but that ever-climbing wave,
Hurl'd back again so often in empty foam,
Hath lain for years at rest — and renegades,
Thieves, bandits, leavings of confusion, whom
The wholesome realm is purged of otherwhere,
Friends, thro' your manhood and your fealty, — now
Make their last head like Satan in the North.
My younger knights, new-made, in whom your flower
Waits to be solid fruit of golden deeds,   100
Move with me toward their quelling, which achieved,
The loneliest ways are safe from shore to shore.
But thou, Sir Lancelot, sitting in my place
Enchair'd to-morrow, arbitrate the field;
For wherefore shouldst thou care to mingle with it,
Only to yield my Queen her own again?
Speak, Lancelot, thou art silent; is it well?"

Thereto Sir Lancelot answer'd: "It is well;
Yet better if the King abide, and leave
The leading of his younger knights to me. 110
Else, for the King has will'd it, it is well."

Then Arthur rose and Lancelot follow'd him,
And while they stood without the doors, the King
Turn'd to him saying: "Is it then so well?
Or mine the blame that oft I seem as he
Of whom was written, 'A sound is in his ears'?
The foot that loiters, bidden go, — the glance
That only seems half-loyal to command, —
A manner somewhat fallen from reverence —
Or have I dream'd the bearing of our knights 120
Tells of a manhood ever less and lower?
Or whence the fear lest this my realm, uprear'd,
By noble deeds at one with noble vows,
From flat confusion and brute violences,
Reel back into the beast, and be no more?"

He spoke, and taking all his younger knights,
Down the slope city rode, and sharply turn'd
North by the gate. In her high bower the Queen,
Working a tapestry, lifted up her head,
Watch'd her lord pass, and knew not that she sigh'd. 130
Then ran across her memory the strange rhyme
Of bygone Merlin, "Where is he who knows?
From the great deep to the great deep he goes."

But when the morning of a tournament,
By these in earnest those in mockery call'd
The Tournament of the Dead Innocence,
Brake with a wet wind blowing, Lancelot,
Round whose sick head all night, like birds of prey,
The words of Arthur flying shriek'd, arose,
And down a streetway hung with folds of pure 140
White samite, and by fountains running wine,
Where children sat in white with cups of gold,
Moved to the lists, and there, with slow sad steps
Ascending, fill'd his double-dragon'd chair.

He glanced and saw the stately galleries,
Dame, damsel, each thro' worship of their Queen
White-robed in honor of the stainless child,
And some with scatter'd jewels, like a bank

Of maiden snow mingled with sparks of fire.
He look'd but once, and vail'd his eyes again.   150

    The sudden trumpet sounded as in a dream
To ears but half-awaked, then one low roll
Of Autumn thunder, and the jousts began;
And ever the wind blew, and yellowing leaf,
And gloom and gleam, and shower and shorn plume
Went down it. Sighing weariedly, as one
Who sits and gazes on a faded fire,
When all the goodlier guests are past away,
Sat their great umpire looking o'er the lists.
He saw the laws that ruled the tournament   160
Broken, but spake not; once, a knight cast down
Before his throne of arbitration cursed
The dead babe and the follies of the King;
And once the laces of a helmet crack'd,
And show'd him, like a vermin in its hole,
Modred, a narrow face. Anon he heard
The voice that billow'd round the barriers roar
An ocean-sounding welcome to one knight,
But newly-enter'd, taller than the rest,
And armor'd all in forest green, whereon   170
There tript a hundred tiny silver deer,
And wearing but a holly-spray for crest,
With ever-scattering berries, and on shield
A spear, a harp, a bugle — Tristram — late
From over-seas in Brittany return'd,
And marriage with a princess of that realm,
Isolt the White — Sir Tristram of the Woods —
Whom Lancelot knew, had held sometime with pain
His own against him, and now yearn'd to shake
The burthen off his heart in one full shock   180
With Tristram even to death. His strong hands gript
And dinted the gilt dragons right and left,
Until he groan'd for wrath — so many of those
That ware their ladies' colors on the casque
Drew from before Sir Tristram to the bounds,
And there with gibes and flickering mockeries
Stood, while he mutter'd, "Craven crests! O shame!
What faith have these in whom they sware to love?
The glory of our Round Table is no more."

    So Tristram won, and Lancelot gave, the gems,   190
Not speaking other word than, "Hast thou won?

Art thou the purest, brother? See, the hand
Wherewith thou takest this is red!" to whom
Tristram, half plagued by Lancelot's languorous mood,
Made answer: "Ay, but wherefore toss me this
Like a dry bone cast to some hungry hound?
Let be thy fair Queen's fantasy. Strength of heart
And might of limb, but mainly use and skill,
Are winners in this pastime of our King.
My hand — belike the lance hath dript upon it —   200
No blood of mine, I trow; but O chief knight,
Right arm of Arthur in the battle-field,
Great brother, thou nor I have made the world;
Be happy in thy fair Queen as I in mine."

    And Tristram round the gallery made his horse
Caracole; then bow'd his homage, bluntly saying,
"Fair damsels, each to him who worships each
Sole Queen of Beauty and of love, behold
This day my Queen of Beauty is not here."
And most of these were mute, some anger'd, one   210
Murmuring, "All courtesy is dead," and one,
"The glory of our Round Table is no more."

    Then fell thick rain, plume droopt and mantle clung,
And pettish cries awoke, and the wan day
Went glooming down in wet and weariness;
But under her black brows a swarthy one
Laugh'd shrilly, crying: "Praise the patient saints,
Our one white day of Innocence hath past,
Tho' somewhat draggled at the skirt. So be it.
The snowdrop only, flowering thro' the year,   220
Would make the world as blank as winter-tide.
Come — let us gladden their sad eyes, our Queen's
And Lancelot's, at this night's solemnity
With all the kindlier colors of the field."

    So dame and damsel glitter'd at the feast
Variously gay; for he that tells the tale
Liken'd them, saying, as when an hour of cold
Falls on the mountain in midsummer snows,
And all the purple slopes of mountain flowers
Pass under white, till the warm hour returns   230
With veer of wind and all are flowers again,
So dame and damsel cast the simple white,
And glowing in all colors, the live grass,

Rose-campion, bluebell, kingcup, poppy, glanced
About the revels, and with mirth so loud
Beyond all use, that, half-amazed, the Queen,
And wroth at Tristam and the lawless jousts,
Brake up their sports, then slowly to her bower
Parted, and in her bosom pain was lord.

    And little Dagonet on the morrow morn,   240
High over all the yellowing autumn-tide,
Danced like a wither'd leaf before the hall.
Then Tristram saying, "Why skip ye so, Sir Fool?"
Wheel'd round on either heel, Dagonet replied,
"Belike for lack of wiser company;
Or being fool, and seeing too much wit
Makes the world rotten, why, belike I skip
To know myself the wisest knight of all."
"Ay, fool," said Tristram, "but 't is eating dry
To dance without a catch, a roundelay   250
To dance to." Then he twangled on his harp,
And while he twangled little Dagonet stood
Quiet as any water-sodden log
Stay'd in the wandering warble of a brook,
But when the twangling ended, skipt again;
And being ask'd, "Why skipt ye not, Sir Fool?"
Made answer, "I had liefer twenty years
Skip to the broken music of my brains
Than any broken music thou canst make."
Then Tristram, waiting for the quip to come,   260
"Good now, what music have I broken, fool?"
And little Dagonet, skipping, "Arthur, the King's;
For when thou playest that air with Queen Isolt,
Thou makest broken music with thy bride,
Her daintier namesake down in Brittany —
And so thou breakest Arthur's music too."
"Save for that broken music in thy brains,
Sir Fool," said Tristram, "I would break thy head.
Fool, I came late, the heathen wars were o'er,
The life had flown, we sware but by the shell —   270
I am but a fool to reason with a fool —
Come, thou art crabb'd and sour; but lean me down,
Sir Dagonet, one of thy long asses' ears,
And harken if my music be not true.

    " 'Free love — free field — we love but while we may.
The woods are hush'd, their music is no more;

The leaf is dead, the yearning past away.
New leaf, new life — the days of frost are o'er;
New life, new love, to suit the newer day;
New loves are sweet as those that went before.   280
Free love — free field — we love but while we may.'

    "Ye might have moved slow-measure to my tune,
Not stood stock-still. I made it in the woods,
And heard it ring as true as tested gold."

    But Dagonet with one foot poised in his hand:
"Friend, did ye mark that fountain yesterday,
Made to run wine? — but this had run itself
All out like a long life to a sour end —
And them that round it sat with golden cups
To hand the wine to whosoever came —   290
The twelve small damosels white as Innocence,
In honor of poor Innocence the babe,
Who left the gems which Innocence the Queen
Lent to the King, and Innocence the King
Gave for a prize — and one of those white slips
Handed her cup and piped, the pretty one,
'Drink, drink, Sir Fool,' and thereupon I drank,
Spat — pish — the cup was gold, the draught was mud."

    And Tristram: "Was it muddier than thy gibes?
Is all the laughter gone dead out of thee? —   300
Not marking how the knighthood mock thee, fool —
'Fear God: honor the King — his one true knight —
Sole follower of the vows' — for here be they
Who knew thee swine enow before I came,
Smuttier than blasted grain. But when the King
Had made thee fool, thy vanity so shot up
It frighted all free fool from out thy heart;
Which left thee less than fool, and less than swine,
A naked aught — yet swine I hold thee still,
For I have flung thee pearls and find thee swine."   310

    And little Dagonet mincing with his feet:
"Knight, an ye fling those rubies round my neck
In lieu of hers, I 'll hold thou hast some touch
Of music, since I care not for thy pearls.
Swine? I have wallow'd, I have wash'd — the world
Is flesh and shadow — I have had my day.
The dirty nurse, Experience, in her kind

Hath foul'd me — an I wallow'd, then I wash'd —
I have had my day and my philosophies —
And thank the Lord I am King Arthur's fool.   320
Swine, say ye? swine, goats, asses, rams, and geese
Troop'd round a Paynim harper once, who thrumm'd
On such a wire as musically as thou
Some such fine song — but never a king's fool."

    And Tristram, "Then were swine, goats, asses, geese
The wiser fools, seeing thy Paynim bard
Had such a mastery of his mystery
That he could harp his wife up out of hell."

    Then Dagonet, turning on the ball of his foot,
"And whither harp'st thou thine? down! and thyself   330
Down! and two more; a helpful harper thou,
That harpest downward! Dost thou know the star
We call the Harp of Arthur up in heaven?"

    And Tristram, "Ay, Sir Fool, for when our King
Was victor wellnigh day by day, the knights,
Glorying in each new glory, set his name
High on all hills and in the signs of heaven."

    And Dagonet answer'd: "Ay, and when the land
Was freed, and the Queen false, ye set yourself
To babble about him, all to show your wit —   340
And whether he were king by courtesy,
Or king by right — and so went harping down
The black king's highway, got so far and grew
So witty that ye play'd at ducks and drakes
With Arthur's vows on the great lake of fire.
Tuwhoo! do ye see it? do ye see the star?"

    "Nay, fool," said Tristram, "not in open day."
And Dagonet: "Nay, nor will; I see it and hear.
It makes a silent music up in heaven,
And I and Arthur and the angels hear,   350
And then we skip." "Lo, fool," he said, "ye talk
Fool's treason; is the King thy brother fool?"
Then little Dagonet clapt his hands and shrill'd:
"Ay, ay, my brother fool, the king of fools!
Conceits himself as God that he can make
Figs out of thistles, silk from bristles, milk
From burning spurge, honey from hornet-combs,
And men from beasts — Long live the king of fools!"

And down the city Dagonet danced away;
But thro' the slowly-mellowing avenues   360
And solitary passes of the wood
Rode Tristram toward Lyonnesse and the west.
Before him fled the face of Queen Isolt
With ruby-circled neck, but evermore
Past, as a rustle or twitter in the wood
Made dull his inner, keen his outer eye
For all that walk'd, or crept, or perch'd, or flew.
Anon the face, as, when a gust hath blown,
Unruffling waters re-collect the shape
Of one that in them sees himself, return'd;   370
But at the slot or fewmets of a deer,
Or even a fallen feather, vanish'd again.

So on for all that day from lawn to lawn
Thro' many a league-long bower he rode. At length
A lodge of intertwisted beechen-boughs,
Furze-cramm'd and bracken-rooft, the which himself
Built for a summer day with Queen Isolt
Against a shower, dark in the golden grove
Appearing, sent his fancy back to where
She lived a moon in that low lodge with him;   380
Till Mark her lord had past, the Cornish King,
With six or seven, when Tristram was away,
And snatch'd her thence, yet, dreading worse than shame
Her warrior Tristram, spake not any word,
But bode his hour, devising wretchedness.

And now that desert lodge to Tristram lookt
So sweet that, halting, in he past and sank
Down on a drift of foliage random-blown;
But could not rest for musing how to smooth
And sleek his marriage over to the queen.   390
Perchance in lone Tintagil far from all
The tonguesters of the court she had not heard.
But then what folly had sent him over-seas
After she left him lonely here? a name?
Was it the name of one in Brittany,
Isolt, the daughter of the king? "Isolt
Of the White Hands" they call'd her: the sweet name
Allured him first, and then the maid herself,
Who served him well with those white hands of hers,
And loved him well, until himself had thought   400
He loved her also, wedded easily,

But left her all as easily, and return'd.
The black-blue Irish hair and Irish eyes
Had drawn him home — what marvel? then he laid
His brows upon the drifted leaf and dream'd.

He seem'd to pace the strand of Brittany
Between Isolt of Britain and his bride,
And show'd them both the ruby-chain, and both
Began to struggle for it, till his queen
Graspt it so hard that all her hand was red.   410
Then cried the Breton, "Look, her hand is red!
These be no rubies, this is frozen blood,
And melts within her hand — her hand is hot
With ill desires, but this I gave thee, look,
Is all as cool and white as any flower."
Follow'd a rush of eagle's wings, and then
A whimpering of the spirit of the child,
Because the twain had spoil'd her carcanet.

He dream'd; but Arthur with a hundred spears
Rode far, till o'er the illimitable reed,   420
And many a glancing plash and sallowy isle,
The wide-wing'd sunset of the misty marsh
Glared on a huge machicolated tower
That stood with open doors, whereout was roll'd
A roar of riot, as from men secure
Amid their marshes, ruffians at their ease
Among their harlot-brides, an evil song.
"Lo there," said one of Arthur's youth, for there,
High on a grim dead tree before the tower,
A goodly brother of the Table Round   430
Swung by the neck; and on the boughs a shield
Showing a shower of blood in a field noir,
And therebeside a horn, inflamed the knights
At that dishonor done the gilded spur,
Till each would clash the shield and blow the horn.
But Arthur waved them back. Alone he rode.
Then at the dry harsh roar of the great horn,
That sent the face of all the marsh aloft
An ever upward-rushing storm and cloud
Of shriek and plume, the Red Knight heard, and all,   440
Even to tipmost lance and topmost helm,
In blood-red armor sallying, howl'd to the King:

"The teeth of Hell flay bare and gnash thee flat! —
Lo! art thou not that eunuch-hearted king

Who fain had clipt free manhood from the world —
The woman-worshipper? Yea, God's curse, and I,
Slain was the brother of my paramour
By a knight of thine, and I that heard her whine
And snivel, being eunuch-hearted too,
Sware by the scorpion-worm that twists in hell   450
And stings itself to everlasting death,
To hang whatever knight of thine I fought
And tumbled. Art thou king? — Look to thy life!"

He ended. Arthur knew the voice; the face
Wellnigh was helmet-hidden, and the name
Went wandering somewhere darkling in his mind.
And Arthur deign'd not use of word or sword,
But let the drunkard, as he stretch'd from horse
To strike him, overbalancing his bulk,
Down from the causeway heavily to the swamp   460
Fall, as the crest of some slow-arching wave,
Heard in dead night along that table-shore,
Drops flat, and after the great waters break
Whitening for half a league, and thin themselves,
Far over sands marbled with moon and cloud,
From less and less to nothing; thus he fell
Head-heavy. Then the knights, who watch'd him, roar'd
And shouted and leapt down upon the fallen,
There trampled out his face from being known,
And sank his head in mire, and slimed themselves;   470
Nor heard the King for their own cries, but sprang
Thro' open doors, and swording right and left
Men, women, on their sodden faces, hurl'd
The tables over and the wines, and slew
Till all the rafters rang with woman-yells,
And all the pavement stream'd with massacre.
Then, echoing yell with yell, they fired the tower,
Which half that autumn night, like the live North,
Red-pulsing up thro' Alioth and Alcor,
Made all above it, and a hundred meres   480
About it, as the water Moab saw
Come round by the east, and out beyond them flush'd
The long low dune and lazy-plunging sea.

So all the ways were safe from shore to shore,
But in the heart of Arthur pain was lord.

Then, out of Tristram waking, the red dream
Fled with a shout, and that low lodge return'd,
Mid-forest, and the wind among the boughs.
He whistled his good war-horse left to graze
Among the forest greens, vaulted upon him,   490
And rode beneath an ever-showering leaf,
Till one lone woman, weeping near a cross,
Stay'd him. "Why weep ye?" "Lord," she said, "my man
Hath left me or is dead;" whereon he thought —
"What, if she hate me now? I would not this.
What, if she love me still? I would not that.
I know not what I would" — but said to her,
"Yet weep not thou, lest, if thy mate return,
He find thy favor changed and love thee not" —
Then pressing day by day thro' Lyonnesse   500
Last in a roky hollow, belling, heard
The hounds of Mark, and felt the goodly hounds
Yelp at his heart, but, turning, past and gain'd
Tintagil, half in sea and high on land,
A crown of towers.

                      Down in a casement sat,
A low sea-sunset glorying round her hair
And glossy-throated grace, Isolt the queen.
And when she heard the feet of Tristram grind
The spiring stone that scaled about her tower,
Flush'd, started, met him at the doors, and there   510
Belted his body with her white embrace,
Crying aloud: "Not Mark — not Mark, my soul!
The footstep flutter'd me at first — not he!
Catlike thro' his own castle steals my Mark,
But warrior-wise thou stridest thro' his halls
Who hates thee, as I him — even to the death.
My soul, I felt my hatred for my Mark
Quicken within me, and knew that thou wert nigh."
To whom Sir Tristram smiling, "I am here;
Let be thy Mark, seeing he is not thine."   520

    And drawing somewhat backward she replied:
"Can he be wrong'd who is not even his own,
But save for dread of thee had beaten me,
Scratch'd, bitten, blinded, marr'd me somehow — Mark?
What rights are his that dare not strike for them?
Not lift a hand — not, tho' he found me thus!
But harken! have ye met him? hence he went

To-day for three days' hunting — as he said —
And so returns belike within an hour.
Mark's way, my soul! — but eat not thou with Mark,   530
Because he hates thee even more than fears,
Nor drink; and when thou passest any wood
Close vizor, lest an arrow from the bush
Should leave me all alone with Mark and hell..
My God, the measure of my hate for Mark
Is as the measure of my love for thee!"

So, pluck'd one way by hate and one by love,
Drain'd of her force, again she sat, and spake
To Tristram, as he knelt before her, saying:
"O hunter, and O blower of the horn,   540
Harper, and thou hast been a rover too,
For, ere I mated with my shambling king,
Ye twain had fallen out about the bride
Of one — his name is out of me — the prize,
If prize she were — what marvel? — she could see —
Thine, friend; and ever since my craven seeks
To wreck thee villainously — but, O Sir Knight,
What dame or damsel have ye kneel'd to last?"

And Tristram, "Last to my Queen Paramount,
Here now to my queen paramount of love   550
And loveliness — ay, lovelier than when first
Her light feet fell on our rough Lyonnesse,
Sailing from Ireland."

        Softly laugh'd Isolt:
"Flatter me not, for hath not our great Queen
My dole of beauty trebled?" and he said:
"Her beauty is her beauty, and thine thine,
And thine is more to me — soft, gracious, kind —
Save when thy Mark is kindled on thy lips
Most gracious; but she, haughty, even to him,
Lancelot; for I have seen him wan enow   560
To make one doubt if ever the great Queen
Have yielded him her love."

        To whom Isolt:
"Ah, then, false hunter and false harper, thou
Who brakest thro' the scruple of my bond,
Calling me thy white hind, and saying to me
That Guinevere had sinn'd against the highest,

And I — misyoked with such a want of man —
That I could hardly sin against the lowest."

He answer'd: "O my soul, be comforted!
If this be sweet, to sin in leading-strings,   570
If here be comfort, and if ours be sin,
Crown'd warrant had we for the crowning sin
That made us happy; but how ye greet me — fear
And fault and doubt — no word of that fond tale —
Thy deep heart-yearnings, thy sweet memories
Of Tristram in that year he was away."

And, saddening on the sudden, spake Isolt:
"I had forgotten all in my strong joy
To see thee — yearnings? — ay! for, hour by hour,
Here in the never-ended afternoon,   580
O, sweeter than all memories of thee,
Deeper than any yearnings after thee
Seem'd those far-rolling, westward-smiling seas,
Watch'd from this tower. Isolt of Britain dash'd
Before Isolt of Brittany on the strand,
Would that have chill'd her bride-kiss? Wedded her?
Fought in her father's battles? wounded there?
The King was all fulfill'd with gratefulness,
And she, my namesake of the hands, that heal'd
Thy hurt and heart with unguent and caress —   590
Well — can I wish her any huger wrong
Than having known thee? her too hast thou left
To pine and waste in those sweet memories.
O, were I not my Mark's, by whom all men
Are noble, I should hate thee more than love."

And Tristram, fondling her light hands, replied:
"Grace, queen, for being loved; she loved me well.
Did I love her? the name at least I loved.
Isolt? — I fought his battles, for Isolt!
The night was dark; the true star set. Isolt!   600
The name was ruler of the dark — Isolt?
Care not for her! patient, and prayerful, meek,
Pale-blooded, she will yield herself to God."

And Isolt answer'd: "Yea, and why not I?
Mine is the larger need, who am not meek,
Pale-blooded, prayerful. Let me tell thee now.
Here one black, mute midsummer night I sat,

Lonely, but musing on thee, wondering where,
Murmuring a light song I had heard thee sing,
And once or twice I spake thy name aloud.   610
Then flash'd a levin-brand; and near me stood,
In fuming sulphur blue and green, a fiend —
Mark's way to steal behind one in the dark —
For there was Mark: 'He has wedded her,' he said,
Not said, but hiss'd it; then this crown of towers
So shook to such a roar of all the sky,
That here in utter dark I swoon'd away,
And woke again in utter dark, and cried,
'I will flee hence and give myself to God' —
And thou wert lying in thy new leman's arms."   620

    Then Tristram, ever dallying with her hand,
"May God be with thee, sweet, when old and gray,
And past desire!" a saying that anger'd her.
" 'May God be with thee, sweet, when thou art old,
And sweet no more to me!' I need Him now.
For when had Lancelot utter'd aught so gross
Even to the swineherd's malkin in the mast?
The greater man the greater courtesy.
Far other was the Tristram, Arthur's knight!
But thou, thro' ever harrying thy wild beasts —   630
Save that to touch a harp, tilt with a lance
Becomes thee well — art grown wild beast thyself.
How darest thou, if lover, push me even
In fancy from thy side, and set me far
In the gray distance, half a life away.
Her to be loved no more? Unsay it, unswear!
Flatter me rather, seeing me so weak,
Broken with Mark and hate and solitude,
Thy marriage and mine own, that I should suck
Lies like sweet wines. Lie to me; I believe.   640
Will ye not lie? not swear, as there ye kneel,
And solemnly as when ye sware to him,
The man of men, our King — My God, the power
Was once in vows when men believed the King!
They lied not then who sware, and thro' their vows
The King prevailing made his realm — I say,
Swear to me thou wilt love me even when old,
Gray-hair'd, and past desire, and in despair."

    Then Tristram, pacing moodily up and down:
"Vows! did you keep the vow you made to Mark   650

More than I mine? Lied, say ye? Nay, but learnt,
The vow that binds too strictly snaps itself —
My knighthood taught me this — ay, being snapt —
We run more counter to the soul thereof
Than had we never sworn. I swear no more.
I swore to the great King, and am forsworn.
For once — even to the height — I honor'd him.
'Man, is he man at all?' methought, when first
I rode from our rough Lyonnesse, and beheld
That victor of the Pagan throned in hall —   660
His hair, a sun that ray'd from off a brow
Like hill-snow high in heaven, the steel-blue eyes,
The golden beard that clothed his lips with light —
Moreover, that weird legend of his birth,
With Merlin's mystic babble about his end
Amazed me; then, his foot was on a stool
Shaped as a dragon; he seem'd to me no man,
But Michael trampling Satan; so I sware,
Being amazed. But this went by — The vows!
O, ay — the wholesome madness of an hour —   670
They served their use, their time; for every knight
Believed himself a greater than himself,
And every follower eyed him as a God;
Till he, being lifted up beyond himself,
Did mightier deeds than elsewise he had done,
And so the realm was made. But then their vows —
First mainly thro' that sullying of our Queen —
Began to gall the knighthood, asking whence
Had Arthur right to bind them to himself?
Dropt down from heaven? wash'd up from out the deep?   680
They fail'd to trace him thro' the flesh and blood
Of our old kings. Whence then? a doubtful lord
To bind them by inviolable vows,
Which flesh and blood perforce would violate;
For feel this arm of mine — the tide within
Red with free chase and heather-scented air,
Pulsing full man. Can Arthur make me pure
As any maiden child? lock up my tongue
From uttering freely what I freely hear?
Bind me to one? The wide world laughs at it.   690
And worldling of the world am I, and know
The ptarmigan that whitens ere his hour
Woos his own end; we are not angels here
Nor shall be. Vows — I am woodman of the woods,
And hear the garnet-headed yaffingale

Mock them — my soul, we love but while we may;
And therefore is my love so large for thee,
Seeing it is not bounded save by love."

Here ending, he moved toward her, and she said:
"Good; an I turn'd away my love for thee   700
To some one thrice as courteous as thyself —
For courtesy wins woman all as well
As valor may, but he that closes both
Is perfect, he is Lancelot — taller indeed,
Rosier and comelier, thou — but say I loved
This knightliest of all knights, and cast thee back
Thine own small saw, 'We love but while we may,'
Well then, what answer?"

                              He that while she spake,
Mindful of what he brought to adorn her with,
The jewels, had let one finger lightly touch   710
The warm white apple of her throat, replied,
"Press this a little closer, sweet, until —
Come, I am hunger'd and half-anger'd — meat,
Wine, wine — and I will love thee to the death,
And out beyond into the dream to come."

So then, when both were brought to full accord,
She rose, and set before him all he will'd;
And after these had comforted the blood
With meats and wines, and satiated their hearts —
Now talking of their woodland paradise,   720
The deer, the dews, the fern, the founts, the lawns;
Now mocking at the much ungainliness,
And craven shifts, and long crane legs of Mark —
Then Tristram laughing caught the harp and sang:

    "Ay, ay, O, ay — the winds that bend the brier!
  A star in heaven, a star within the mere!
  Ay, ay, O, ay — a star was my desire,
  And one was far apart and one was near.
  Ay, ay, O, ay — the winds that bow the grass!
  And one was water and one star was fire,   730
  And one will ever shine and one will pass.
  Ay, ay, O, ay — the winds that move the mere!"

Then in the light's last glimmer Tristram show'd
And swung the ruby carcanet. She cried,

"The collar of some Order, which our King
Hath newly founded, all for thee, my soul,
For thee, to yield thee grace beyond thy peers."

"Not so, my queen," he said, "but the red fruit
Grown on a magic oak-tree in mid-heaven,
And won by Tristram as a tourney-prize,   740
And hither brought by Tristram for his last
Love-offering and peace-offering unto thee."

He spoke, he turn'd, then, flinging round her neck,
Claspt it, and cried, "Thine Order, O my queen!"
But, while he bow'd to kiss the jewell'd throat,
Out of the dark, just as the lips had touch'd,
Behind him rose a shadow and a shriek —
"Mark's way," said Mark, and clove him thro' the brain.

That night came Arthur home, and while he climb'd,
All in a death-dumb autumn-dripping gloom,   750
The stairway to the hall, and look'd and saw
The great Queen's bower was dark, — about his feet
A voice clung sobbing till he question'd it,
"What art thou?" and the voice about his feet
Sent up an answer, sobbing, "I am thy fool,
And I shall never make thee smile again."

1871*

GUINEVERE

QUEEN GUINEVERE had fled the court, and sat
There in the holy house at Almesbury
Weeping, none with her save a little maid,
A novice. One low light betwixt them burn'd
Blurr'd by the creeping mist, for all abroad,
Beneath a moon unseen albeit at full,
The white mist, like a face-cloth to the face,
Clung to the dead earth, and the land was still.

For hither had she fled, her cause of flight
Sir Modred; he that like a subtle beast   10
Lay couchant with his eyes upon the throne,
Ready to spring, waiting a chance. For this
He chill'd the popular praises of the King

With silent smiles of slow disparagement;
And tamper'd with the Lords of the White Horse,
Heathen, the brood by Hengist left; and sought
To make disruption in the Table Round
Of Arthur, and to splinter it into feuds
Serving his traitorous end; and all his aims
Were sharpen'd by strong hate for Lancelot.   20

     For thus it chanced one morn when all the court,
Green-suited, but with plumes that mock'd the may,
Had been — their wont — a-maying and return'd,
That Modred still in green, all ear and eye,
Climb'd to the high top of the garden-wall
To spy some secret scandal if he might,
And saw the Queen who sat betwixt her best
Enid and lissome Vivien, of her court
The wiliest and the worst; and more than this
He saw not, for Sir Lancelot passing by   30
Spied where he couch'd, and as the gardener's hand
Picks from the colewort a green caterpillar,
So from the high wall and the flowering grove
Of grasses Lancelot pluck'd him by the heel,
And cast him as a worm upon the way;
But when he knew the prince tho' marr'd with dust,
He, reverencing king's blood in a bad man,
Made such excuses as he might, and these
Full knightly without scorn. For in those days
No knight of Arthur's noblest dealt in scorn;   40
But, if a man were halt, or hunch'd, in him
By those whom God had made full-limb'd and tall,
Scorn was allow'd as part of his defect,
And he was answer'd softly by the King
And all his Table. So Sir Lancelot holp
To raise the prince, who rising twice or thrice
Full sharply smote his knees, and smiled, and went;
But, ever after, the small violence done
Rankled in him and ruffled all his heart,
As the sharp wind that ruffles all day long   50
A little bitter pool about a stone
On the bare coast.

                    But when Sir Lancelot told
This matter to the Queen, at first she laugh'd
Lightly, to think of Modred's dusty fall,
Then shudder'd, as the village wife who cries,

"I shudder, some one steps across my grave;"
Then laugh'd again, but faintlier, for indeed
She half-foresaw that he, the subtle beast,
Would track her guilt until he found, and hers
Would be for evermore a name of scorn.   60
Henceforward rarely could she front in hall,
Or elsewhere, Modred's narrow foxy face,
Heart-hiding smile, and gray persistent eye.
Henceforward too, the Powers that tend the soul,
To help it from the death that cannot die,
And save it even in extremes, began
To vex and plague her. Many a time for hours,
Beside the placid breathings of the King,
In the dead night, grim faces came and went
Before her, or a vague spiritual fear —   70
Like to some doubtful noise of creaking doors,
Heard by the watcher in a haunted house,
That keeps the rust of murder on the walls —
Held her awake; or if she slept she dream'd
An awful dream, for then she seem'd to stand
On some vast plain before a setting sun,
And from the sun there swiftly made at her
A ghastly something, and its shadow flew
Before it till it touch'd her, and she turn'd —
When lo! her own, that broadening from her feet,   80
And blackening, swallow'd all the land, and in it
Far cities burnt, and with a cry she woke.
And all this trouble did not pass but grew,
Till even the clear face of the guileless King,
And trustful courtesies of household life,
Became her bane; and at the last she said:
"O Lancelot, get thee hence to thine own land,
For if thou tarry we shall meet again,
And if we meet again some evil chance
Will make the smouldering scandal break and blaze   90
Before the people and our lord the King."
And Lancelot ever promised, but remain'd,
And still they met and met. Again she said,
"O Lancelot, if thou love me get thee hence."
And then they were agreed upon a night —
When the good King should not be there — to meet
And part for ever. Vivien, lurking, heard.
She told Sir Modred. Passion-pale they met
And greeted. Hands in hands, and eye to eye,
Low on the border of her couch they sat   100

Stammering and staring. It was their last hour,
A madness of farewells. And Modred brought
His creatures to the basement of the tower
For testimony; and crying with full voice,
"Traitor, come out, ye are trapt at last," aroused
Lancelot, who rushing outward lionlike
Leapt on him, and hurl'd him headlong, and he fell
Stunn'd, and his creatures took and bare him off,
And all was still. Then she, "The end is come,
And I am shamed for ever;" and he said: 110
"Mine be the shame, mine was the sin; but rise,
And fly to my strong castle over-seas.
There will I hide thee till my life shall end,
There hold thee with my life against the world."
She answer'd: "Lancelot, wilt thou hold me so?
Nay, friend, for we have taken our farewells.
Would God that thou couldst hide me from myself!
Mine is the shame, for I was wife, and thou
Unwedded; yet rise now, and let us fly,
For I will draw me into sanctuary,   120
And bide my doom." So Lancelot got her horse,
Set her thereon, and mounted on his own,
And then they rode to the divided way,
There kiss'd and parted weeping; for he past,
Love-loyal to the least wish of the Queen,
Back to his land; but she to Almesbury
Fled all night long by glimmering waste and weald,
And heard the spirits of the waste and weald
Moan as she fled, or thought she heard them moan.
And in herself she moan'd, "Too late, too late!"   130
Till in the cold wind that foreruns the morn,
A blot in heaven, the raven, flying high,
Croak'd, and she thought, "He spies a field of death;
For now the heathen of the Northern Sea,
Lured by the crimes and frailties of the court,
Begin to slay the folk and spoil the land."

      And when she came to Almesbury she spake
There to the nuns, and said, "Mine enemies
Pursue me, but, O peaceful Sisterhood,
Receive and yield me sanctuary, nor ask   140
Her name to whom ye yield it till her time
To tell you;" and her beauty, grace, and power
Wrought as a charm upon them, and they spared
To ask it.

So the stately Queen abode
For many a week, unknown, among the nuns,
Nor with them mix'd, nor told her name, nor sought,
Wrapt in her grief, for housel or for shrift
But communed only with the little maid,
Who pleased her with a babbling heedlessness
Which often lured her from herself; but now,   150
This night, a rumor wildly blown about
Came that Sir Modred had usurp'd the realm
And leagued him with the heathen, while the King
Was waging war on Lancelot. Then she thought,
"With what a hate the people and the King
Must hate me," and bow'd down upon her hands
Silent, until the little maid, who brook'd
No silence, brake it, uttering "Late! so late!
What hour, I wonder now?" and when she drew
No answer, by and by began to hum   160
An air the nuns had taught her: "Late, so late!"
Which when she heard, the Queen look'd up, and said,
"O maiden, if indeed ye list to sing,
Sing, and unbind my heart that I may weep."
Whereat full willingly sang the little maid.

"Late, late, so late! and dark the night and chill!
Late, late, so late! but we can enter still.
Too late, too late! ye cannot enter now.

"No light had we; for that we do repent,
And learning this, the bridegroom will relent.   170
Too late, too late! ye cannot enter now.

"No light! so late! and dark and chill the night!
O, let us in, that we may find the light!
Too late, too late! ye cannot enter now.

"Have we not heard the bridegroom is so sweet?
O, let us in, tho' late, to kiss his feet!
No, no, too late! ye cannot enter now."

So sang the novice, while full passionately,
Her head upon her hands, remembering
Her thought when first she came, wept the sad Queen.   180
Then said the little novice prattling to her:

"O pray you, noble lady, weep no more:
But let my words — the words of one so small,

Who knowing nothing knows but to obey,
And if I do not there is penance given —
Comfort your sorrows, for they do not flow
From evil done; right sure am I of that,
Who see your tender grace and stateliness.
But weigh your sorrows with our lord the King's,
And weighing find them less; for gone is he   190
To wage grim war against Sir Lancelot there,
Round that strong castle where he holds the Queen;
And Modred whom he left in charge of all,
The traitor — Ah, sweet lady, the King's grief
For his own self, and his own Queen, and realm,
Must needs be thrice as great as any of ours!
For me, I thank the saints, I am not great;
For if there ever come a grief to me
I cry my cry in silence, and have done;
None knows it, and my tears have brought me good.   200
But even were the griefs of little ones
As great as those of great ones, yet this grief
Is added to the griefs the great must bear,
That, howsoever much they desire
Silence, they cannot weep behind a cloud;
As even here they talk at Almesbury
About the good King and his wicked Queen,
And were I such a King with such a Queen,
Well might I wish to veil her wickedness,
But were I such a King it could not be."   210

Then to her own sad heart mutter'd the Queen,
"Will the child kill me with her innocent talk?"
But openly she answer'd, "Must not I,
If this false traitor have displaced his lord,
Grieve with the common grief of all the realm?"

"Yea," said the maid, "this all is woman's grief,
That *she* is woman, whose disloyal life
Hath wrought confusion in the Table Round
Which good King Arthur founded, years ago,
With signs and miracles and wonders, there   220
At Camelot, ere the coming of the Queen."

Then thought the Queen within herself again,
"Will the child kill me with her foolish prate?"
But openly she spake and said to her,

"O little maid, shut in by nunnery walls,
What canst thou know of Kings and Tables Round,
Or what of signs and wonders, but the signs
And simple miracles of thy nunnery?"

To whom the little novice garrulously:
"Yea, but I know; the land was full of signs   230
And wonders ere the coming of the Queen.
So said my father, and himself was knight
Of the great Table — at the founding of it,
And rode thereto from Lyonesse; and he said
That as he rode, an hour or maybe twain
After the sunset, down the coast, he heard
Strange music, and he paused, and turning — there,
All down the lonely coast of Lyonnesse,
Each with a beacon-star upon his head,
And with a wild sea-light about his feet,   240
He saw them — headland after headland flame
Far on into the rich heart of the west.
And in the light the white mermaiden swam,
And strong man-breasted things stood from the the sea,
And sent a deep sea-voice thro' all the land,
To which the little elves of chasm and cleft
Made answer, sounding like a distant horn.
So said my father — yea, and furthermore,
Next morning, while he past the dim-lit woods
Himself beheld three spirits mad with joy   250
Come dashing down on a tall wayside flower,
That shook beneath them as the thistle shakes
When three gray linnets wrangle for the seed.
And still at evenings on before his horse
The flickering fairy-circle wheel'd and broke
Flying, and link'd again, and wheel'd and broke
Flying, for all the land was full of life.
And when at last he came to Camelot,
A wreath of airy dancers hand-in-hand
Swung round the lighted lantern of the hall;   260
And in the hall itself was such a feast
As never man had dream'd; for every knight
Had whatsoever meat he long'd for served
By hands unseen; and even as he said
Down in the cellars merry bloated things
Shoulder'd the spigot, straddling on the butts
While the wine ran; so glad were spirits and men
Before the coming of the sinful Queen."

Then spake the Queen and somewhat bitterly,
"Were they so glad? ill prophets were they all,   270
Spirits and men. Could none of them foresee,
Not even thy wise father with his signs
And wonders, what has fallen upon the realm?"

To whom the novice garrulously again:
"Yea, one, a bard, of whom my father said,
Full many a noble war-song had he sung,
Even in the presence of an enemy's fleet,
Between the steep cliff and the coming wave;
And many a mystic lay of life and death
Had chanted on the smoky mountain-tops,   280
When round him bent the spirits of the hills
With all their dewy hair blown back like flame.
So said my father — and that night the bard
Sang Arthur's glorious wars, and sang the King
As wellnigh more than man, and rail'd at those
Who call'd him the false son of Gorloïs.
For there was no man knew from whence he came;
But after tempest, when the long wave broke
All down the thundering shores of Bude and Bos,
There came a day as still as heaven, and then   290
They found a naked child upon the sands
Of dark Tintagil by the Cornish sea,
And that was Arthur, and they foster'd him
Till he by miracle was approven King;
And that his grave should be a mystery
From all men, like his birth; and could he find
A woman in her womanhood as great
As he was in his manhood, then, he sang,
The twain together well might change the world.
But even in the middle of his song   300
He falterer'd, and his hand fell from the harp,
And pale he turn'd, and reel'd, and would have fallen,
But that they stay'd him up; nor would he tell
His vision; but what doubt that he foresaw
This evil work of Lancelot and the Queen?"

Then thought the Queen, "Lo! they have set her on,
Our simple-seeming abbess and her nuns,
To play upon me," and bow'd her head nor spake.
Whereat the novice crying, with clasp'd hands,
Shame on her own garrulity garrulously,   310
Said the good nuns would check her gadding tongue

Full often, "and, sweet lady, if I seem
To vex an ear too sad to listen to me,
Unmannerly, with prattling and the tales
Which my good father told me, check me too
Nor let me shame my father's memory, one
Of noblest manners, tho' himself would say
Sir Lancelot had the noblest; and he died,
Kill'd in a tilt, come next, five summers back,
And left me; but of others who remain,   320
And of the two first-famed for courtesy —
And pray you check me if I ask amiss —
But pray you, which had noblest, while you moved
Among them, Lancelot or our lord the King?"

     Then the pale Queen look'd up and answer'd her:
"Sir Lancelot, as became a noble knight,
Was gracious to all ladies, and the same
In open battle or the tilting-field
Forbore his own advantage, and the King
In open battle or the tilting-field   330
Forbore his own advantage, and these two
Were the most nobly-manner'd men of all;
For manners are not idle, but the fruit
Of loyal nature and of noble mind."

     "Yea," said the maid, "be manners such fair fruit?
Then Lancelot's needs must be a thousand fold
Less noble, being, as all rumor runs,
The most disloyal friend in all the world."

     To which a mournful answer made the Queen:
"O, closed about by narrowing nunnery-walls,   340
What knowest thou of the world and all its lights
And shadows, all the wealth and all the woe?
If ever Lancelot, that most noble knight,
Were for one hour less noble than himself,
Pray for him that he scape the doom of fire,
And weep for her who drew him to his doom."

     "Yea," said the little novice, "I pray for both;
But I should all as soon believe that his,
Sir Lancelot's, were as noble as the King's,
As I could think, sweet lady, yours would be   350
Such as they are, were you the sinful Queen."

So she, like many another babbler, hurt
Whom she would soothe, and harm'd where she would heal;
For here a sudden flush of wrathful heat
Fired all the pale face of the Queen, who cried:
"Such as thou art be never maiden more
For ever! thou their tool, set on to plague
And play upon and harry me, petty spy
And traitress!" When that storm of anger brake
From Guinevere, aghast the maiden rose,   360
White as her veil, and stood before the Queen
As tremulously as foam upon the beach
Stands in a wind, ready to break and fly,
And when the Queen had added, "Get thee hence!"
Fled frighted. Then that other left alone
Sigh'd, and began to gather heart again,
Saying in herself: "The simple, fearful child
Meant nothing, but my own too-fearful guilt,
Simpler than any child, betrays itself.
But help me, Heaven, for surely I repent!   370
For what is true repentance but in thought —
Not even in inmost thought to think again
The sins that made the past so pleasant to us?
And I have sworn never to see him more,
To see him more."

        And even in saying this,
Her memory from old habit of the mind
Went slipping back upon the golden days
In which she saw him first, when Lancelot came,
Reputed the best knight and goodliest man,
Ambassador, to yield her to his lord   380
Arthur, and led her forth, and far ahead
Of his and her retinue moving, they,
Rapt in sweet talk or lively, all on love
And sport and tilts and pleasure, — for the time
Was may-time, and as yet no sin was dream'd, —
Rode under groves that look'd a paradise
Of blossom, over sheets of hyacinth
That seem'd the heavens upbreaking thro' the earth,
And on from hill to hill, and every day
Beheld at noon in some delicious dale   390
The silk pavilions of King Arthur raised
For brief repast or afternoon repose
By couriers gone before; and on again,
Till yet once more ere set of sun they saw

The Dragon of the great Pendragonship,
That crown'd the state pavilion of the King,
Blaze by the rushing brook or silent well.

But when the Queen immersed in such a trance,
And moving thro' the past unconsciously,
Came to that point where first she saw the King   400
Ride toward her from the city, sigh'd to find
Her journey done, glanced at him, thought him cold,
High, self-contain'd, and passionless, not like him,
"Not like my Lancelot" — while she brooded thus
And grew half-guilty in her thoughts again,
There rode an armed warrior to the doors.
A murmuring whisper thro' the nunnery ran,
Then on a sudden a cry, "The King!" She sat
Stiff-stricken, listening; but when armed feet
Thro' the long gallery from the outer doors   410
Rang coming, prone from off her seat she fell,
And grovell'd with her face against the floor.
There with her milk-white arms and shadowy hair
She made her face a darkness from the King,
And in the darkness heard his armed feet
Pause by her; then came silence, then a voice,
Monotonous and hollow like a ghost's
Denouncing judgment, but, tho' changed, the King's:

"Liest thou here so low, the child of one
I honor'd, happy, dead before thy shame?   420
Well is it that no child is born of thee.
The children born of thee are sword and fire,
Red ruin, and the breaking up of laws,
The craft of kindred and the godless hosts
Of heathen swarming o'er the Northern Sea;
Whom I, while yet Sir Lancelot, my right arm,
The mightiest of my knights, abode with me,
Have everywhere about this land of Christ
In twelve great battles ruining overthrown.
And knowest thou now from whence I come — from him,   430
From waging bitter war with him; and he,
That did not shun to smite me in worse way,
Had yet that grace of courtesy in him left,
He spared to lift his hand against the King
Who made him knight. But many a knight was slain;
And many more and all his kith and kin
Clave to him, and abode in his own land.

And many more when Modred raised revolt,
Forgetful of their troth and fealty, clave
To Modred, and a remnant stays with me.   440
And of this remnant will I leave a part,
True men who love me still, for whom I live,
To guard thee in the wild hour coming on,
Lest but a hair of this low head be harm'd.
Fear not; thou shalt be guarded till my death.
Howbeit I know, if ancient prophecies
Have err'd not, that I march to meet my doom.
Thou hast not made my life so sweet to me,
That I the King should greatly care to live;
For thou hast spoilt the purpose of my life.   450
Bear with me for the last time while I show,
Even for thy sake, the sin which thou hast sinn'd.
For when the Roman left us, and their law
Relax'd its hold upon us, and the ways
Were fill'd with rapine, here and there a deed
Of prowess done redress'd a random wrong.
But I was first of all the kings who drew
The knighthood-errant of this realm and all
The realms together under me, their Head,
In that fair Order of my Table Round,   460
A glorious company, the flower of men,
To serve as model for the mighty world,
And be the fair beginning of a time.
I made them lay their hands in mine and swear
To reverence the King, as if he were
Their conscience, and their conscience as their King,
To break the heathen and uphold the Christ,
To ride abroad redressing human wrongs,
To speak no slander, no, nor listen to it,
To honor his own word as if his God's,   470
To lead sweet lives in purest chastity,
To love one maiden only, cleave to her,
And worship her by years of noble deeds,
Until they won her; for indeed I knew
Of no more subtle master under heaven
Than is the maiden passion for a maid,
Not only to keep down the base in man,
But teach high thought, and amiable words
And courtliness, and the desire of fame,
And love of truth, and all that makes a man.   480
And all this throve before I wedded thee,
Believing, 'Lo, mine helpmate, one to feel

My purpose and rejoicing in my joy!'
Then came thy shameful sin with Lancelot;
Then came the sin of Tristram and Isolt;
Then others, following these my mightiest knights,
And drawing foul ensample from fair names,
Sinn'd also, till the loathsome opposite
Of all my heart had destined did obtain,
And all thro' thee! so that this life of mine   490
I guard as God's high gift from scathe and wrong,
Not greatly care to lose; but rather think
How sad it were for Arthur, should he live,
To sit once more within his lonely hall,
And miss the wonted number of my knights,
And miss to hear high talk of noble deeds
As in the golden days before thy sin.
For which of us who might be left could speak
Of the pure heart, nor seem to glance at thee?
And in thy bowers of Camelot or of Usk   500
Thy shadow still would glide from room to room,
And I should evermore be vext with thee
In hanging robe or vacant ornament,
Or ghostly footfall echoing on the stair.
For think not, tho' thou wouldst not love thy lord,
Thy lord has wholly lost his love for thee.
I am not made of so slight elements.
Yet must I leave thee, woman, to thy shame.
I hold that man the worst of public foes
Who either for his own or children's sake,   510
To save his blood from scandal, lets the wife
Whom he knows false abide and rule the house:
For being thro' his cowardice allow'd
Her station, taken everywhere for pure,
She like a new disease, unknown to men,
Creeps, no precaution used, among the crowd,
Makes wicked lightnings of her eyes, and saps
The fealty of our friends, and stirs the pulse
With devil's leaps, and poisons half the young.
Worst of the worst were that man he that reigns!   520
Better the King's waste hearth and aching heart
Than thou reseated in thy place of light,
The mockery of my people and their bane!"

He paused, and in the pause she crept an inch
Nearer, and laid her hands about his feet.
Far off a solitary trumpet blew.

Then waiting by the doors the war-horse neigh'd
As at a friend's voice, and he spake again:

"Yet think not that I come to urge thy crimes;
I did not come to curse thee, Guinevere,   530
I, whose vast pity almost makes me die
To see thee, laying there thy golden head,
My pride in happier summers, at my feet.
The wrath of which forced my thoughts on that fierce law,
The doom of treason and the flaming death, —
When first I learnt thee hidden here, — is past.
The pang — which, while I weigh'd thy heart with one
Too wholly true to dream untruth in thee,
Made my tears burn — is also past — in part.
And all is past, the sin is sinn'd, and I,   540
Lo, I forgive thee, as Eternal God
Forgives! do thou for thine own soul the rest.
But how to take last leave of all I loved?
O golden hair, with which I used to play
Not knowing! O imperial-moulded form,
And beauty such as never woman wore,
Until it came a kingdom's curse with thee —
I cannot touch thy lips, they are not mine,
But Lancelot's; nay, they never were the King's.
I cannot take thy hand; that too is flesh,   550
And in the flesh thou hast sinn'd; and mine own flesh,
Here looking down on thine polluted, cries,
'I loathe thee;' yet not less, O Guinevere,
For I was ever virgin save for thee,
My love thro' flesh hath wrought into my life
So far that my doom is, I love thee still.
Let no man dream but that I love thee still.
Perchance, and so thou purify thy soul,
And so thou lean on our fair father Christ,
Hereafter in that world where all are pure   560
We two may meet before high God, and thou
Wilt spring to me, and claim me thine, and know
I am thine husband — not a smaller soul,
Nor Lancelot, nor another. Leave me that,
I charge thee, my last hope. Now must I hence.
Thro' the thick night I hear the trumpet blow.
They summon me their King to lead mine hosts
Far down to that great battle in the west,
Where I must strike against the man they call
My sister's son — no kin of mine, who leagues   570

With Lords of the White Horse, heathen, and knights,
Traitors — and strike him dead, and meet myself
Death, or I know not what mysterious doom.
And thou remaining here wilt learn the event;
But hither shall I never come again,
Never lie by thy side, see thee no more —
Farewell!"

      And while she grovell'd at his feet,
She felt the King's breath wander o'er her neck,
And in the darkness o'er her fallen head
Perceived the waving of his hands that blest.   580

    Then, listening till those armed steps were gone,
Rose the pale Queen, and in her anguish found
The casement: "peradventure," so she thought,
"If I might see his face, and not be seen."
And lo, he sat on horseback at the door!
And near him the sad nuns with each a light
Stood, and he gave them charge about the Queen,
To guard and foster her for evermore.
And while he spake to these his helm was lower'd,
To which for crest the golden dragon clung   590
Of Britain; so she did not see the face,
Which then was as an angel's, but she saw,
Wet with the mists and smitten by the lights,
The Dragon of the great Pendragonship
Blaze, making all the night a steam of fire.
And even then he turn'd; and more and more
The moony vapor rolling round the King,
Who seem'd the phantom of a giant in it,
Enwound him fold by fold, and made him gray
And grayer, till himself became as mist   600
Before her, moving ghostlike to his doom.

    Then she stretch'd out her arms and cried aloud,
"O Arthur!" there her voice brake suddenly,
Then — as a stream that spouting from a cliff
Fails in mid air, but gathering at the base
Re-makes itself, and flashes down the vale —
Went on in passionate utterance:

                    "Gone — my lord!
Gone thro' my sin to slay and to be slain!
And he forgave me, and I could not speak.

Farewell? I should have answer'd his farewell.   610
His mercy choked me. Gone, my lord the King,
My own true lord! how dare I call him mine?
The shadow of another cleaves to me,
And makes me one pollution. He, the King,
Call'd me polluted. Shall I kill myself?
What help in that? I cannot kill my sin,
If soul be soul, nor can I kill my shame;
No, nor by living can I live it down.
The days will grow to weeks, the weeks to months,
The months will add themselves and make the years,   620
The years will roll into the centuries,
And mine will ever be a name of scorn.
I must not dwell on that defeat of fame.
Let the world be; that is but of the world —
What else? what hope? I think there was a hope,
Except he mock'd me when he spake of hope;
His hope he call'd it; but he never mocks,
For mockery is the fume of little hearts.
And blessed be the King, who hath forgiven
My wickedness to him, and left me hope   630
That in mine own heart I can live down sin
And be his mate hereafter in the heavens
Before high God! Ah great and gentle lord,
Who wast, as is the conscience of a saint
Among his warring senses, to thy knights —
To whom my false voluptuous pride, that took
Full easily all impressions from below,
Would not look up, or half-despised the height
To which I would not or I could not climb —
I thought I could not breathe in that fine air,   640
That pure severity of perfect light —
I yearn'd for warmth and color which I found
In Lancelot — now I see thee what thou art,
Thou art the highest and most human too,
Not Lancelot, nor another. Is there none
Will tell the King I love him tho' so late?
Now — ere he goes to the great battle? none!
Myself must tell him in that purer life,
But now it were too daring. Ah my God,
What might I not have made of thy fair world,   650
Had I but loved thy highest creature here?
It was my duty to have loved the highest;
It surely was my profit had I known;
It would have been my pleasure had I seen.

We needs must love the highest when we see it,
Not Lancelot, nor another."

Here her hand
Grasp'd made her vail her eyes. She look'd and saw
The novice, weeping, suppliant, and said to her,
"Yea, little maid, for am *I* not forgiven?"
Then glancing up beheld the holy nuns   660
All round her, weeping; and her heart was loosed
Within her, and she wept with these and said:

"Ye know me then, that wicked one, who broke
The vast design and purpose of the King.
O, shut me round with narrowing nunnery-walls,
Meek maidens, from the voices crying, 'Shame!'
I must not scorn myself; he loves me still.
Let no one dream but that he loves me still.
So let me, if you do not shudder at me,
Nor shun to call me sister, dwell with you;   670
Wear black and white, and be a nun like you,
Fast with your fasts, not feasting with your feasts;
Grieve with your griefs, not grieving at your joys,
But not rejoicing; mingle with your rites;
Pray and be pray'd for; lie before your shrines;
Do each low office of your holy house;
Walk your dim cloister, and distribute dole
To poor sick people, richer in His eyes
Who ransom'd us, and haler too than I;
And treat their loathsome hurts and heal mine own;   680
And so wear out in alms-deed and in prayer
The sombre close of that voluptuous day
Which wrought the ruin of my lord the King."

She said. They took her to themselves; and she
Still hoping, fearing "Is it yet too late?"
Dwelt with them, till in time their abbess died.
Then she, for her good deeds and her pure life,
And for the power of ministration in her,
And likewise for the high rank she had borne,
Was chosen abbess, there, an abbess, lived   690
For three brief years, and there, an abbess, past
To where beyond these voices there is peace.

1859*

THE PASSING OF ARTHUR

THAT story which the bold Sir Bedivere,
First made and latest left of all the knights,
Told, when the man was no more than a voice
In the white winter of his age, to those
With whom he dwelt, new faces, other minds.

    For on their march to westward, Bedivere,
Who slowly paced among the slumbering host,
Heard in his tent the moanings of the King:

    "I found Him in the shining of the stars,
I mark'd Him in the flowering of His fields,   10
But in His ways with men I find Him not.
I waged His wars, and now I pass and die.
O me! for why is all around us here
As if some lesser god had made the world,
But had not force to shape it as he would,
Till the High God behold it from beyond,
And enter it, and make it beautiful?
Or else as if the world were wholly fair,
But that these eyes of men are dense and dim,
And have not power to see it as it is —   20
Perchance, because we see not to the close; —
For I, being simple, thought to work His will,
And have but stricken with the sword in vain,
And all whereon I lean'd in wife and friend
Is traitor to my peace, and all my realm
Reels back into the beast, and is no more.
My God, thou hast forgotten me in my death!
Nay — God my Christ — I pass but shall not die."

    Then, ere that last weird battle in the west,
There came on Arthur sleeping, Gawain kill'd   30
In Lancelot's war, the ghost of Gawain blown
Along a wandering wind, and past his ear
Went shrilling: "Hollow, hollow all delight!
Hail, King! to-morrow thou shalt pass away.
Farewell! there is an isle of rest for thee.
And I am blown along a wandering wind,
And hollow, hollow, hollow all delight!"
And fainter onward, like wild birds that change

Their season in the night and wail their way
From cloud to cloud, down the long wind the dream   40
Shrill'd; but in going mingled with dim cries
Far in the moonlit haze among the hills,
As of some lonely city sack'd by night,
When all is lost, and wife and child with wail
Pass to new lords; and Arthur woke and call'd:
"Who spake? A dream. O, light upon the wind,
Thine, Gawain, was the voice — are these dim cries
Thine? or doth all that haunts the waste and wild
Mourn, knowing it will go along with me?"

    This heard the bold Sir Bedivere and spake: 50
"O me, my King, let pass whatever will,
Elves, and the harmless glamour of the field;
But in their stead thy name and glory cling
To all high places like a golden cloud
For ever; but as yet thou shall not pass.
Light was Gawain in life, and light in death
Is Gawain, for the ghost is as the man;
And care not thou for dreams from him, but rise —
I hear the steps of Modred in the west,
And with him many of thy people, and knights   60
Once thine, whom thou hast loved, but grosser grown
Than heathen, spitting at their vows and thee.
Right well in heart they know thee for the King.
Arise, go forth and conquer as of old."

    Then spake King Arthur to Sir Bedivere:
"Far other is this battle in the west
Whereto we move than when we strove in youth,
And brake the petty kings, and fought with Rome,
Or thrust the heathen from the Roman wall,
And shook him thro' the north. Ill doom is mine   70
To war against my people and my knights.
The king who fights his people fights himself.
And they my knights, who loved me once, the stroke
That strikes them dead is as my death to me.
Yet let us hence, and find or feel a way
Thro' this blind haze which, ever since I saw
One lying in the dust at Almesbury,
Hath folded in the passes of the world."

    Then rose the King and moved his host by night,
And ever push'd Sir Modred, league by league,   80

Back to the sunset bound of Lyonnesse —
A land of old upheaven from the abyss
By fire, to sink into the abyss again;
Where fragments of forgotten peoples dwelt,
And the long mountains ended in a coast
Of ever-shifting sand, and far away
The phantom circle of a moaning sea.
There the pursuer could pursue no more,
And he that fled no further fly the King;
And there, that day when the great light of heaven   90
Burn'd at his lowest in the rolling year,
On the waste sand by the waste sea they closed.
Nor ever yet had Arthur fought a fight
Like this last, dim, weird battle of the west.
A death-white mist slept over sand and sea,
Whereof the chill, to him who breathed it, drew
Down with his blood, till all his heart was cold
With formless fear; and even on Arthur fell
Confusion, since he saw not whom he fought.
For friend and foe were shadows in the mist,   100
And friend slew friend not knowing whom he slew;
And some had visions out of golden youth,
And some beheld the faces of old ghosts
Look in upon the battle; and in the mist
Was many a noble deed, many a base,
And chance and craft and strength in single fights,
And ever and anon with host to host
Shocks, and the splintering spear, the hard mail hewn,
Shield-breakings, and the clash of brands, the crash
Of battle-axes on shatter'd helms, and shrieks   110
After the Christ, of those who falling down
Look'd up for heaven, and only saw the mist;
And shouts of heathen and the traitor knights,
Oaths, insult, filth, and monstrous blasphemies,
Sweat, writhings, anguish, laboring of the lungs
In that close mist, and cryings for the light,
Moans of the dying, and voices of the dead.

Last, as by some one death-bed after wail
Of suffering, silence follows, or thro' death
Or death-like swoon, thus over all that shore,   120
Save for some whisper of the seething seas,
A dead hush fell; but when the dolorous day
Grew drearier toward twilight falling, came
A bitter wind, clear from the north, and blew

The mist aside, and with that wind the tide
Rose, and the pale King glanced across the field
Of battle. But no man was moving there;
Nor any cry of Christian heard thereon,
Nor yet of heathen; only the wan wave
Brake in among dead faces, to and fro   130
Swaying the helpless hands, and up and down
Tumbling the hollow helmets of the fallen,
And shiver'd brands that once had fought with Rome,
And rolling far along the gloomy shores
The voice of days of old and days to be.

    Then spake King Arthur to Sir Bedivere,
And whiter than the mist that all day long
Had held the field of battle was the King:

    "Hearest thou this great voice that shakes the world,
And wastes the narrow realm whereon we move,   140
And beats upon the faces of the dead,
My dead, as tho' they had not died for me? —
O Bedivere, for on my heart hath fallen
Confusion, till I know not what I am,
Nor whence I am, nor whether I be king;
Behold, I seem but king among the dead."

    Then spoke the bold Sir Bedivere: "My King!
King everywhere! and so the dead have kings,
There also will I worship thee as king.
Yet still thy life is whole, and still I live   150
Who love thee; but who hates thee, he that brought
The heathen back among us, yonder stands,
Modred, unharm'd, the traitor of thine house."

    Then spake the King: "My house hath been my doom.
But call not thou this traitor of my house
Who hath but dwelt beneath one roof with me.
My house are rather they who sware my vows,
Yea, even while they brake them, own'd me king.
And well for thee, saying in my dark hour,
When all the purport of my throne hath fail'd,   160
That quick or dead thou holdest me for king.
King am I, whatsoever be their cry;
And one last act of kinghood shalt thou see
Yet, ere I pass." And uttering this the King

Made at the man. Then Modred smote his liege
Hard on that helm which many a heathen sword
Had beaten thin; while Arthur at one blow,
Striking the last stroke with Excalibur,
Slew him, and, all but slain himself, he fell.

So all day long the noise of battle roll'd   170
Among the mountains by the winter sea,
Until King Arthur's Table, man by man,
Had fallen in Lyonnesse about their lord,
King Arthur; then, because his wound was deep,
The bold Sir Bedivere uplifted him,
And bore him to a chapel nigh the field,
A broken chancel with a broken cross,
That stood on a dark strait of barren land.
On one side lay the Ocean, and on one
Lay a great water, and the moon was full.   180

Then spake King Arthur to Sir Bedivere:
"The sequel of to-day unsolders all
The goodliest fellowship of famous knights
Whereof this world holds record. Such a sleep
They sleep — the men I loved. I think that we
Shall never more, at any future time,
Delight our souls with talk of knightly deeds,
Walking about the gardens and the halls
Of Camelot, as in the days that were.
I perish by this people which I made, —   190
Tho' Merlin sware that I should come again
To rule once more — but let what will be be,
I am so deeply smitten thro' the helm
That without help I cannot last till morn.
Thou therefore take my brand Excalibur,
Which was my pride; for thou rememberest how
In those old days, one summer noon, an arm
Rose up from out the bosom of the lake,
Clothed in white samite, mystic, wonderful,
Holding the sword — and how I row'd across   200
And took it, and have worn it, like a king;
And, wheresoever I am sung or told
In aftertime, this also shall be known.
But now delay not; take Excalibur,
And fling him far into the middle mere;
Watch what thou seest, and lightly bring me word."

To him replied the bold Sir Bedivere:
"It is not meet, Sir King, to leave thee thus,
Aidless, alone, and smitten thro' the helm —
A little thing may harm a wounded man;   210
Yet I thy hest will all perform at full,
Watch what I see, and lightly bring thee word."

So saying, from the ruin'd shrine he stept,
And in the moon athwart the place of tombs,
Where lay the mighty bones of ancient men,
Old knights, and over them the sea-wind sang
Shrill, chill, with flakes of foam. He, stepping down
By zigzag paths and juts of pointed rock,
Came on the shining levels of the lake.

There drew he forth the brand Excalibur,   220
And o'er him, drawing it, the winter moon,
Brightening the skirts of a long cloud, ran forth
And sparkled keen with frost against the hilt;
For all the haft twinkled with diamond sparks,
Myriads of topaz-lights, and jacinth-work
Of subtlest jewellery. He gazed so long
That both his eyes were dazzled as he stood,
This way and that dividing the swift mind,
In act to throw; but at the last it seem'd
Better to leave Excalibur conceal'd   230
There in the many-knotted water-flags,
That whistled stiff and dry about the marge.
So strode he back slow to the wounded King.

Then spake King Arthur to Sir Bedivere:
"Hast thou perform'd my mission which I gave?
What is it thou hast seen? or what hast heard?"

And answer made the bold Sir Bedivere:
"I heard the ripple washing in the reeds,
And the wild water lapping on the crag."

To whom replied King Arthur, faint and pale: 240
"Thou hast betray'd thy nature and thy name,
Not rendering true answer, as beseem'd
Thy fealty, nor like a noble knight;
For surer sign had follow'd, either hand,
Or voice, or else a motion of the mere.
This is a shameful thing for men to lie.

Yet now, I charge thee, quickly go again,
As thou art lief and dear, and do the thing
I bade thee, watch, and lightly bring me word."

Then went Sir Bedivere the second time   250
Across the ridge, and paced beside the mere,
Counting the dewy pebbles, fixt in thought;
But when he saw the wonder of the hilt,
How curiously and strangely chased, he smote
His palms together, and he cried aloud:

"And if indeed I cast the brand away,
Surely a precious thing, one worthy note,
Should thus be lost for ever from the earth,
Which might have pleased the eyes of many men.
What good should follow this, if this were done?   260
What harm, undone? Deep harm to disobey,
Seeing obedience is the bond of rule.
Were it well to obey then, if a king demand
An act unprofitable, against himself?
The King is sick, and knows not what he does.
What record or what relic of my lord
Should be to aftertime, but empty breath
And rumors of a doubt? But were this kept,
Stored in some treasure-house of mighty kings,
Some one might show it at a joust of arms,   270
Saying: 'King Arthur's sword, Excalibur,
Wrought by the lonely Maiden of the Lake.
Nine years she wrought it, sitting in the deeps
Upon the hidden bases of the hills.'
So might some old man speak in the aftertime
To all the people, winning reverence.
But now much honor and much fame were lost."

So spake he, clouded with his own conceit,
And hid Excalibur the second time,
And so strode back slow to the wounded King.   280

Then spoke King Arthur, breathing heavily:
"What is it thou hast seen? or what hast heard?"

And answer made the bold Sir Bedivere:
"I heard the water lapping on the crag,
And the long ripple washing in the reeds."

To whom replied King Arthur, much in wrath:
"Ah miserable, and unkind, untrue,
Unknightly, traitor-hearted! Woe is me!
Authority forgets a dying king,
Laid widow'd of the power in his eye   290
That bow'd the will. I see thee what thou art,
For thou, the latest-left of all my knights,
In whom should meet the offices of all,
Thou wouldst betray me for the precious hilt;
Either from lust of gold, or like a girl
Valuing the giddy pleasure of the eyes.
Yet, for a man may fail in duty twice,
And the third time may prosper, get thee hence;
But, if thou spare to fling Excalibur,
I will arise and slay thee with my hands."   300

Then quickly rose Sir Bedivere, and ran,
And, leaping down the ridges lightly, plunged
Among the bulrush beds, and clutch'd the sword,
And strongly wheel'd and threw it. The great brand
Made lightnings in the splendor of the moon,
And flashing round and round, and whirl'd in an arch,
Shot like a streamer of the northern morn,
Seen where the moving isles of winter shock
By night, with noises of the Northern sea.
So flash'd and fell the brand Excalibur;   310
But ere he dipt the surface, rose an arm
Clothed in white samite, mystic, wonderful,
And caught him by the hilt, and brandish'd him
Three times, and drew him under in the mere.
And lightly went the other to the King.

Then spoke King Arthur, drawing thicker breath:
"Now see I by thine eyes that this is done.
Speak out; what is it thou hast heard, or seen?"

And answer made the bold Sir Bedivere:
"Sir King, I closed mine eyelids, lest the gems   320
Should blind my purpose, for I never saw,
Nor shall see, here or elsewhere, till I die,
Not tho' I live three lives of mortal men,
So great a miracle as yonder hilt.
Then with both hands I flung him, wheeling him;
But when I look'd again, behold an arm,
Clothed in white samite, mystic, wonderful,

That caught him by the hilt, and brandish'd him
Three times, and drew him under in the mere."

And answer made King Arthur, breathing hard: 330
"My end draws nigh; 't is time that I were gone.
Make broad thy shoulders to receive my weight,
And bear me to the margin; yet I fear
My wound hath taken cold, and I shall die."

So saying, from the pavement he half rose,
Slowly, with pain, reclining on his arm,
And looking wistfully with wide blue eyes
As in a picture. Him Sir Bedivere
Remorsefully regarded thro' his tears,
And would have spoken, but he found not words;   340
Then took with care, and kneeling on one knee,
O'er both his shoulders drew the languid hands,
And rising bore him thro' the place of tombs.

But, as he walk'd, King Arthur panted hard,
Like one that feels a nightmare on his bed
When all the house is mute. So sigh'd the King,
Muttering and murmuring at his ear, "Quick, quick!
I fear it is too late, and I shall die."
But the other swiftly strode from ridge to ridge,
Clothed with his breath, and looking, as he walk'd,   350
Larger than human on the frozen hills.
He heard the deep behind him, and a cry
Before. His own thought drove him like a goad.
Dry clash'd his harness in the icy caves
And barren chasms, and all to left and right
The bare black cliff clang'd round him, as he based
His feet on juts of slippery crag that rang
Sharp-smitten with the dint of armed heels —
And on a sudden, lo, the level lake,
And the long glories of the winter moon!   360

Then saw they how there hove a dusky barge,
Dark as a funeral scarf from stem to stern,
Beneath them; and descending they were ware
That all the decks were dense with stately forms,
Black-stoled, black-hooded, like a dream — by these
Three queens with crowns of gold — and from them rose
A cry that shiver'd to the tingling stars,
And, as it were one voice, an agony

Of lamentation, like a wind that shrills
All night in a waste land, where no one comes,   370
Or hath come, since the making of the world.

Then murmur'd Arthur, "Place me in the barge."
So to the barge they came. There those three queens
Put forth their hands, and took the King, and wept.
But she that rose the tallest of them all
And fairest laid his head upon her lap,
And loosed the shatter'd casque, and chafed his hands,
And call'd him by his name, complaining loud,
And dropping bitter tears against a brow
Striped with dark blood; for all his face was white   380
And colorless, and like the wither'd moon
Smote by the fresh beam of the springing east;
And all his greaves and cuisses dash'd with drops
Of onset; and the light and lustrous curls —
That made his forehead like a rising sun
High from the dais-throne — were parch'd with dust,
Or, clotted into points and hanging loose,
Mixt with the knightly growth that fringed his lips.
So like a shatter'd column lay the King;
Not like that Arthur who, with lance in rest,   390
From spur to plume a star of tournament,
Shot thro' the lists at Camelot, and charged
Before the eyes of ladies and of kings.

Then loudly cried the bold Sir Bedivere:
"Ah! my Lord Arthur, whither shall I go?
Where shall I hide my forehead and my eyes?
For now I see the true old times are dead,
When every morning brought a noble chance,
And every chance brought out a noble knight.
Such times have been not since the light that led   400
The holy Elders with the gift of myrrh.
But now the whole Round Table is dissolved
Which was an image of the mighty world;
And I, the last, go forth companionless,
And the days darken round me, and the years,
Among new men, strange faces, other minds."

And slowly answer'd Arthur from the barge:
"The old order changeth yielding place to new,
And God fulfils himself in many ways,
Lest one good custom should corrupt the world.   410

Comfort thyself; what comfort is in me?
I have lived my life, and that which I have done
May He within himself make pure! but thou,
If thou shouldst never see my face again,
Pray for my soul. More things are wrought by prayer
Than this world dreams of. Wherefore, let thy voice
Rise like a fountain for me night and day.
For what are men better than sheep or goats
That nourish a blind life within the brain,
If, knowing God, they lift not hands of prayer   420
Both for themselves and those who call them friend?
For so the whole round earth is every way
Bound by gold chains about the feet of God.
But now farewell. I am going a long way
With these thou seest — if indeed I go —
For all my mind is clouded with a doubt —
To the island-valley of Avilion;
Where falls not hail, or rain, or any snow,
Nor ever wind blows loudly; but it lies
Deep-meadow'd, happy, fair with orchard lawns   430
And bowery hollows crown'd with summer sea,
Where I will heal me of my grievous wound."

    So said he, and the barge with oar and sail
Moved from the brink, like some full-breasted swan
That, fluting a wild carol ere her death,
Ruffles her pure cold plume, and takes the flood
With swarthy webs. Long stood Sir Bedivere
Revolving many memories, till the hull
Look'd one black dot against the verge of dawn,
And on the mere the wailing died away.   440

    But when that moan had past for evermore,
The stillness of the dead world's winter dawn
Amazed him, and he groan'd, "The King is gone."
And therewithal came on him the weird rhyme,
"From the great deep to the great deep he goes."

    Whereat he slowly turn'd and slowly clomb
The last hard footstep of that iron crag,
Thence mark'd the black hull moving yet, and cried:
"He passes to be king among the dead,
And after healing of his grievous wound   450
He comes again; but — if he come no more —
O me, be yon dark queens in yon black boat,
Who shriek'd and wail'd, the three whereat we gazed

On that high day, when, clothed with living light,
They stood before his throne in silence, friends
Of Arthur, who should help him at his need?"

Then from the dawn it seem'd there came, but faint
As from beyond the limit of the world,
Like the last echo born of a great cry,
Sounds, as if some fair city were one voice   460
Around a king returning from his wars.

Thereat once more he moved about, and clomb
Even to the highest he could climb, and saw,
Straining his eyes beneath an arch of hand,
Or thought he saw, the speck that bare the King,
Down that long water opening on the deep
Somewhere far off, pass on and on, and go
From less to less and vanish into light.
And the new sun rose bringing the new year.

1833 f. (1842, 1869) °

TO THE QUEEN

O LOYAL to the royal in thyself,
And loyal to thy land, as this to thee —
Bear witness, that rememberable day,
When, pale as yet and fever-worn, the Prince
Who scarce had pluck'd his flickering life again
From halfway down the shadow of the grave
Past with thee thro' thy people and their love,
And London roll'd one tide of joy thro' all
Her trebled millions, and loud leagues of man
And welcome! witness, too, the silent cry,   10
The prayer of many a race and creed, and clime —
Thunderless lightnings striking under sea
From sunset and sunrise of all thy realm,
And that true North, whereof we lately heard
A strain to shame us, "Keep you to yourselves;
So loyal is too costly! friends — your love
Is but a burthen; loose the bond, and go."
Is this the tone of empire? here the faith
That made us rulers? this, indeed, her voice
And meaning whom the roar of Hougoumont   20
Left mightiest of all peoples under heaven?
What shock has fool'd her since, that she should speak

So feebly? wealthier — wealthier — hour by hour!
The voice of Britain, or a sinking land,
Some third-rate isle half-lost among her seas?
There rang her voice, when the full city peal'd
Thee and thy Prince! The loyal to their crown
Are loyal to their own far sons, who love
Our ocean-empire with her boundless homes
For ever-broadening England, and her throne   30
In our vast Orient, and one isle, one isle,
That knows not her own greatness; if she knows
And dreads it we are fallen. — But thou, my Queen,
Not for itself, but thro' thy living love
For one to whom I made it o'er his grave
Sacred, accept this old imperfect tale,
New-old, and shadowing Sense at war with Soul,
Ideal manhood closed in real man,
Rather than that gray king whose name, a ghost,
Streams like a cloud, man-shaped, from mountain peak,   40
And cleaves to cairn and cromlech still; or him
Of Geoffrey's book, or him of Malleor's, one
Touch'd by the adulterous finger of a time
That hover'd between war and wantonness,
And crownings and dethronements. Take withal
Thy poet's blessing, and his trust that Heaven
Will blow the tempest in the distance back
From thine and ours; for some are scared, who mark,
Or wisely or unwisely, signs of storm,
Waverings of every vane with every wind,   50
And wordy trucklings to the transient hour,
And fierce or careless looseners of the faith,
And Softness breeding scorn of simple life,
Or Cowardice, the child of lust for gold,
Or Labor, with a groan and not a voice,
Or Art with poisonous honey stolen from France,
And that which knows, but careful for itself,
And that which knows not, ruling that which knows
To its own harm. The goal of this great world
Lies beyond sight; yet — if our slowly-grown   60
And crown'd Republic's crowning common-sense,
That sav'd her many times, not fail — their fears
Are morning shadows huger than the shapes
That cast them, not those gloomier which forego
The darkness of that battle in the west
Where all of high and holy dies away.

1872*

THE VOICE AND THE PEAK

I

THE voice and the Peak
Far over summit and lawn,
The lone glow and long roar
Green-rushing from the rosy thrones of dawn!

II

All night have I heard the voice
Rave over the rocky bar,
But thou wert silent in heaven,
Above thee glided the star.

III

Hast thou no voice, O Peak,
That standest high above all?   10
"I am the voice of the Peak,
I roar and rave, for I fall.

IV

"A thousand voices go
To North, South, East, and West;
They leave the heights and are troubled,
And moan and sink to their rest.

V

"The fields are fair beside them,
The chestnut towers in his bloom;
But they — they feel the desire of the deep —
Fall, and follow their doom.   20

VI

"The deep has power on the height,
And the height has power on the deep;
They are raised for ever and ever,
And sink again into sleep."

VII

Not raised for ever and ever,
But when their cycle is o'er,
The valley, the voice, the peak, the star
Pass, and are found no more.

VIII

The Peak is high and flush'd
　　At his highest with sunrise fire;
The Peak is high, and the stars are high,
　　And the thought of a man is higher.

30

IX

A deep below the deep,
　　And a height beyond the height!
Our hearing is not hearing,
　　And our seeing is not sight.

X

The voice and the Peak
　　Far into heaven withdrawn,
The lone glow and long roar
　　Green-rushing from the rosy thrones of dawn!

40

1874

SIR JOHN FRANKLIN

ON THE CENOTAPH IN WESTMINSTER ABBEY

Not here! the white North has thy bones; and thou,
　　Heroic sailor-soul,
Art passing on thine happier voyage now
　　Toward no earthly pole.

1877 (1880) *

THE REVENGE

A BALLAD OF THE FLEET

I

At Flores in the Azores Sir Richard Grenville lay,
And a pinnace, like a flutter'd bird, came flying from far away:
"Spanish ships of war at sea! we have sighted fifty-three!"
Then sware Lord Thomas Howard: " 'Fore God I am no coward;
But I cannot meet them here, for my ships are out of gear,
And the half my men are sick. I must fly, but follow quick.
We are six ships of the line; can we fight with fifty-three?"

II

Then spake Sir Richard Grenville: "I know you are no coward;
You fly them for a moment to fight with them again.
But I 've ninety men and more that are lying sick ashore.   10
I should count myself the coward if I left them, my Lord Howard,
To these Inquisition dogs and the devildoms of Spain."

III

So Lord Howard past away with five ships of war that day,
Till he melted like a cloud in the silent summer heaven;
But Sir Richard bore in hand all his sick men from the land
Very carefully and slow,
Men of Bideford in Devon,
And we laid them on the ballast down below;
For we brought them all aboard,
And they blest him in their pain, that they were not left to Spain,   20
To the thumb-screw and the stake, for the glory of the Lord.

IV

He had only a hundred seamen to work the ship and to fight,
And he sailed away from Flores till the Spaniard came in sight,
With his huge sea-castles heaving upon the weather bow.
"Shall we fight or shall we fly?
Good Sir Richard, tell us now,
For to fight is but to die!
There 'll be little of us left by the time this sun be set."
And Sir Richard said again: "We be all good English men.
Let us bang these dogs of Seville, the children of the devil,   30
For I never turn'd my back upon Don or devil yet."

V

Sir Richard spoke and he laugh'd and we roar'd a hurrah, and so
The little Revenge ran on sheer into the heart of the foe,
With her hundred fighters on deck, and her ninety sick below;
For half of their fleet to the right and half to the left were seen,
And the little Revenge ran on thro' the long sea-lane between.

VI

Thousands of their soldiers look'd down from their decks and laugh'd,
Thousands of their seamen made mock at the mad little craft
Running on and on, till delay'd
By their mountain-like San Philip that, of fifteen hundred tons,   40
And up-shadowing high above us with her yawning tiers of guns,
Took the breath from our sails, and we stay'd.

VII

And while now the great San Philip hung above us like a cloud
Whence the thunderbolt will fall
Long and loud,
Four galleons drew away
From the Spanish fleet that day,
And two upon the larboard and two upon the starboard lay,
And the battle-thunder broke from them all.

VIII

But anon the great San Philip, she bethought herself and went,   50
Having that within her womb that had left her ill content;
And the rest they came aboard us, and they fought us hand to hand,
For a dozen times they came with their pikes and musqueteers,
And a dozen times we shook 'em off as a dog that shakes his ears
When he leaps from the water to the land.

IX

And the sun went down, and the stars came out far over the summer
    sea,
But never a moment ceased the fight of the one and the fifty-three.
Ship after ship, the whole night long, their high-built galleons came,
Ship after ship, the whole night long, with her battle-thunder and flame;
Ship after ship, the whole night long, drew back with her dead and her
    shame.   60
For some were sunk and many were shatter'd, and so could fight us no
    more —
God of battles, was ever a battle like this in the world before?

X

For he said, "Fight on! fight on!"
Tho' his vessel was all but a wreck;
And it chanced that, when half of the short summer night was gone,
With a grisly wound to be drest he had left the deck,
But a bullet struck him that was dressing it suddenly dead,
And himself he was wounded again in the side and the head,
And he said, "Fight on! fight on!"

XI

And the night went down, and the sun smiled out far over the summer
    sea,   70
And the Spanish fleet with broken sides lay round us all in a ring;
But they dared not touch us again, for they fear'd that we still could
    sting,
So they watch'd what the end would be.

And we had not fought them in vain,
But in perilous plight were we.
Seeing forty of our poor hundred were slain,
And half of the rest of us maim'd for life
In the crash of the cannonades and the desperate strife;
And the sick men down in the hold were most of them stark and cold,
And the pikes were all broken or bent, and the powder was all of it
    spent;   **80**
And the masts and the rigging were lying over the side;
But Sir Richard cried in his English pride:
"We have fought such a fight for a day and a night
As may never be fought again!
We have won great glory, my men!
And a day less or more
At sea or ashore,
We die — does it matter when?
Sink me the ship, Master Gunner — sink her, split her in twain.
Fall into the hands of God, not into the hands of Spain!"   **90**

XII

And the gunner said, "Ay, ay," but the seamen made reply:
"We have children, we have wives,
And the Lord hath spared our lives.
We will make the Spaniard promise, if we yield, to let us go;
We shall live to fight again and to strike another blow."
And the lion there lay dying, and they yielded to the foe.

XIII

And the stately Spanish men to their flagship bore him then,
Where they laid him by the mast, old Sir Richard caught at last,
And they praised him to his face with their courtly foreign grace;
But he rose upon their decks, and he cried: **100**
"I have fought for Queen and Faith like a valiant man and true;
I have only done my duty as a man is bound to do.
With a joyful spirit I Sir Richard Grenville die!"
And he fell upon their decks, and he died.

XIV

And they stared at the dead that had been so valiant and true,
And had holden the power and glory of Spain so cheap
That he dared her with one little ship and his English few;
Was he devil or man? He was devil for aught they knew,
But they sank his body with honor down into the deep,
And they mann'd the Revenge with a swarthier alien crew,   **110**
And away she sail'd with her loss and long'd for her own;

When a wind from the lands they had ruin'd awoke from sleep,
And the water began to heave and the weather to moan,
And or ever that evening ended a great gale blew,
And a wave like the wave that is raised by an earthquake grew,
Till it smote on their hulls and their sails and their masts and their flags,
And the whole sea plunged and fell on the shot-shatter'd navy of Spain,
And the little Revenge herself went down by the island crags
To be lost evermore in the main.

1878*

PREFATORY POEM TO MY BROTHER'S SONNETS

MIDNIGHT, JUNE 30, 1879

I

MIDNIGHT — in no midsummer tune
The breakers lash the shores;
The cuckoo of a joyless June
Is calling out of doors.

And thou hast vanish'd from thine own
To that which looks like rest,
True brother, only to be known
By those who love thee best.

II

Midnight — and joyless June gone by,
And from the deluged park   10
The cuckoo of a worse July
Is calling thro' the dark;

But thou art silent underground,
And o'er thee streams the rain,
True poet, surely to be found
When Truth is found again.

III

And, now to these unsummer'd skies
The summer bird is still,
Far off a phantom cuckoo cries
From out a phantom hill;   20

And thro' this midnight breaks the sun
Of sixty years away,
The light of days when life begun,
The days that seem to-day,

When all my griefs were shared with thee,
As all my hopes were thine—
As all thou wert was one with me,
May all thou art be mine!
1880*

THE VOYAGE OF MAELDUNE

FOUNDED ON AN IRISH LEGEND
A. D. 700

I

I was the chief of the race — he had stricken my father dead —
But I gather'd my fellows together, I swore I would strike off his head.
Each of them look'd like a king, and was noble in birth as in worth,
And each of them boasted he sprang from the oldest race upon earth.
Each was as brave in the fight as the bravest hero of song,
And each of them liefer had died than have done one another a wrong.
He lived on an isle in the ocean — we sail'd on a Friday morn —
He that had slain my father the day before I was born.

II

And we came to the isle in the ocean, and there on the shore was he.
But a sudden blast blew us out and away thro' a boundless sea.   10

III

And we came to the Silent Isle that we never had touch'd at before,
Where a silent ocean always broke on a silent shore,
And the brooks glitter'd on in the light without sound, and the long waterfalls
Pour'd in a thunderless plunge to the base of the mountain walls,
And the poplar and cypress unshaken by storm flourish'd up beyond sight,
And the pine shot aloft from the crag to an unbelievable height,
And high in the heaven above it there flicker'd a songless lark,
And the cock could n't crow, and the bull could n't low, and the dog could n't bark.

And round it we went, and thro' it, but never a murmur, a breath —
It was all of it fair as life, it was all of it quiet as death,   20
And we hated the beautiful isle, for whenever we strove to speak
Our voices were thinner and fainter than any flittermouse-shriek;
And the men that were mighty of tongue and could raise such a battle-
    cry
That a hundred who heard it would rush on a thousand lances and
    die —
O, they to be dumb'd by the charm! — so fluster'd with anger were they
They almost fell on each other; but after we sail'd away.

IV

And we came to the Isle of Shouting; we landed, a score of wild birds
Cried from the topmost summit with human voices and words.
Once in an hour they cried, and whenever their voices peal'd
The steer fell down at the plow and the harvest died from the field,   30
And the men dropt dead in the valleys and half of the cattle went lame,
And the roof sank in on the hearth, and the dwelling broke into flame;
And the shouting of these wild birds ran into the hearts of my crew,
Till they shouted along with the shouting and seized one another and
    slew.
But I drew them the one from the other; I saw that we could not stay,
And we left the dead to the birds, and we sail'd with our wounded
    away.

V

And we came to the Isle of Flowers; their breath met us out on the seas,
For the Spring and the middle Summer sat each on the lap of the
    breeze;
And the red passion-flower to the cliffs, and the dark-blue clematis,
    clung,
And starr'd with a myriad blossom the long convolvulus hung;   40
And the topmost spire of the mountain was lilies in lieu of snow,
And the lilies like glaciers winded down, running out below
Thro' the fire of the tulip and poppy, the blaze of gorse, and the blush
Of millions of roses that sprang without leaf or a thorn from the bush;
And the whole isle-side flashing down from the peak without ever a tree
Swept like a torrent of gems from the sky to the blue of the sea.
And we roll'd upon capes of crocus and vaunted our kith and our kin,
And we wallow'd in beds of lilies, and chanted the triumph of Finn,
Till each like a golden image was pollen'd from head to feet
And each was as dry as a cricket, with thirst in the middle-day heat.
Blossom and blossom, and promise of blossom, but never a fruit!   51
And we hated the Flowering Isle, as we hated the isle that was mute,
And we tore up the flowers by the million and flung them in bight and
    bay,
And we left but a naked rock, and in anger we sail'd away.

VI

And we came to the Isle of Fruits; all round from the cliffs and the
  capes,
Purple or amber, dangled a hundred fathom of grapes,
And the warm melon lay like a little sun on the tawny sand,
And the fig ran up from the beach and rioted over the land,
And the mountain arose like a jewell'd throne thro' the fragrant air,
Glowing with all-color'd plums and with golden masses of pear,   60
And the crimson and scarlet of berries that flamed upon bine and vine,
But in every berry and fruit was the poisonous pleasure of wine;
And the peak of the mountain was apples, the hugest that ever were
  seen,
And they prest, as they grew, on each other, with hardly a leaflet
  between,
And all of them redder than rosiest health or than utterest shame,
And setting, when Even descended, the very sunset aflame.
And we stay'd three days, and we gorged and we madden'd, till every
  one drew
His sword on his fellow to slay him, and ever they struck and they slew;
And myself, I had eaten but sparely, and fought till I sunder'd the fray,
Then I bade them remember my father's death, and we sail'd away. 70

VII

And we came to the Isle of Fire; we were lured by the light from afar,
For the peak sent up one league of fire to the Northern Star;
Lured by the glare and the blare, but scarcely could stand upright,
For the whole isle shudder'd and shook like a man in a mortal affright.
We were giddy besides with the fruits we had gorged, and so crazed
  that at last
There were some leap'd into the fire; and away we sail'd, and we past
Over that undersea isle, where the water is clearer than air.
Down we look'd — what a garden! O bliss, what a Paradise there!
Towers of a happier time, low down in a rainbow deep
Silent palaces, quiet fields of eternal sleep!   80
And three of the gentlest and best of my people, whate'er I could say,
Plunged head-down in the sea, and the Paradise trembled away.

VIII

And we came to the Bounteous Isle, where the heavens lean low on the
  land,
And ever at dawn from the cloud glitter'd o'er us a sun-bright hand,
Then it open'd and dropt at the side of each man, as he rose from his
  rest,
Bread enough for his need till the laborless day dipt under the west;
And we wander'd about it and thro' it. O, never was time so good!

And we sang of the triumphs of Finn, and the boast of our ancient
blood,
And we gazed at the wandering wave as we sat by the gurgle of
springs, 89
And we chanted the songs of the Bards and the glories of fairy kings.
But at length we began to be weary, to sigh, and to stretch and yawn,
Till we hated the Bounteous Isle and the sun-bright hand of the dawn,
For there was not an enemy near, but the whole green isle was our own,
And we took to playing at ball, and we took to throwing the stone,
And we took to playing at battle, but that was a perilous play,
For the passion of battle was in us, we slew and we sail'd away.

IX

And we came to the Isle of Witches and heard their musical cry —
"Come to us, O, come, come!" in the stormy red of a sky
Dashing the fires and the shadows of dawn on the beautiful shapes,
For a wild witch naked as heaven stood on each of the loftiest capes,
And a hundred ranged on the rock like white sea-birds in a row, 101
And a hundred gamboll'd and pranced on the wrecks in the sand below,
And a hundred splash'd from the ledges, and bosom'd the burst of the
spray;
But I knew we should fall on each other, and hastily sail'd away.

X

And we came in an evil time to the Isle of the Double Towers,
One was of smooth-cut stone, one carved all over with flowers,
But an earthquake always moved in the hollows under the dells,
And they shock'd on each other and butted each other with clashing of
bells, 108
And the daws flew out of the towers and jangled and wrangled in vain,
And the clash and boom of the bells rang into the heart and the brain,
Till the passion of battle was on us, and all took sides with the towers,
There were some for the clean-cut stone, there were more for the carven
flowers,
And the wrathful thunder of God peal'd over us all the day,
For the one half slew the other, and after we sail'd away.

XI

And we came to the Isle of a Saint who had sail'd with Saint Brendan
of yore,
He had lived ever since on the isle and his winters were fifteen score,
And his voice was low as from other worlds, and his eyes were sweet,
And his white hair sank to his heels, and his white beard fell to his feet,
And he spake to me: "O Maeldune, let be this purpose of thine!
Remember the words of the Lord when he told us, 'Vengeance is mine!'

His fathers have slain thy fathers in war or in single strife,　　121
Thy fathers have slain his fathers, each taken a life for a life,
Thy father had slain his father, how long shall the murder last?
Go back to the Isle of Finn and suffer the Past to be Past."
And we kiss'd the fringe of his beard, and we pray'd as we heard him
　　pray,
And the holy man he assoil'd us, and sadly we sail'd away.

XII

And we came to the isle we were blown from, and there on the shore
　　was he,
The man that had slain my father. I saw him and let him be.
O, weary was I of the travel, the trouble, the strife, and the sin,
When I landed again with a tithe of my men, on the Isle of Finn!　130
1880*

BATTLE OF BRUNANBURH

(A translation from the Anglo-Saxon, first printed in 1880, with the
following prefatory note: "Constantinus, King of the Scots, after
having sworn allegiance to Athelstan, allied himself with the Danes
of Ireland under Anlaf, and invading England, was defeated by
Athelstan and his brother Edmund with great slaughter at Brunanburh in the year 937.")

I

[1] ATHELSTAN King,
Lord among Earls,
Bracelet-bestower and
Baron of Barons,
He with his brother,
Edmund Atheling,
Gaining a lifelong
Glory in battle,
Slew with the sword-edge
There by Brunanburh,　　　　　　　　　　　　　　10
Brake the shield-wall,
Hew'd the linden-wood,[2]

[1] I have more or less availed myself of my son's prose translation of this
poem in the "Contemporary Review" (November, 1876). [All the footnotes
are Tennyson's.]
[2] Shields of lindenwood.

Hack'd the battle-shield,
Sons of Edward with hammer'd brands.

II

Theirs was a greatness
Got from their grandsires —
Theirs that so often in
Strife with their enemies
Struck for their hoards and their hearts and their homes.

III

Bow'd the spoiler,   20
Bent the Scotsman,
Fell the ship-crews
Doom'd to the death.
All the field with blood of the fighters
Flow'd, from when first the great
Sun-star of morning-tide,
Lamp of the Lord God
Lord everlasting,
Glode over earth till the glorious creature
Sank to his setting.   30

IV

There lay many a man
Marr'd by the javelin,
Men of the Northland
Shot over shield.
There was the Scotsman
Weary of war.

V

We the West-Saxons,
Long as the daylight
Lasted, in companies
Troubled the track of the host that we hated;   40
Grimly with swords that were sharp from the grindstone,
Fiercely we hack'd at the flyers before us.

VI

Mighty the Mercian,
Hard was his hand-play,
Sparing not any of
Those that with Anlaf,
Warriors over the

Weltering waters
Borne in the bark's-bosom,
Drew to this island — 50
Doom'd to the death.

VII

Five young kings put asleep by the sword-stroke,
Seven strong earls of the army of Anlaf
Fell on the war-field, numberless numbers,
Shipmen and Scotsmen.

VIII

Then the Norse leader —
Dire was his need of it,
Few were his following —
Fled to his war-ship;
Fleeted his vessel to sea with the king in it, 60
Saving his life on the fallow flood.

IX

Also the crafty one,
Constantinus,
Crept to his North again,
Hoar-headed hero!

X

Slender warrant had
He to be proud of
The welcome of war-knives —
He that was reft of his
Folk and his friends that had 70
Fallen in conflict,
Leaving his son too
Lost in the carnage,
Mangled to morsels,
A youngster in war!

XI

Slender reason had
He to be glad of
The clash of the war-glaive —
Traitor and trickster
And spurner of treaties — 80
He nor had Anlaf
With armies so broken

A reason for bragging
That they had the better
In perils of battle
On places of slaughter —
The struggle of standards,
The rush of the javelins,
The crash of the charges,[3]
The wielding of weapons —   90
The play that they play'd with
The children of Edward.

XII

Then with their nail'd prows
Parted the Norsemen, a
Blood-redden'd relic of
Javelins over
The jarring breaker, the deep-sea billow,
Shaping their way toward Dyflen [4] again,
Shamed in their souls.

XIII

Also the brethren,   100
King and Atheling,
Each in his glory,
Went to his own in his own West-Saxon-land,
Glad of the war.

XIV

Many a carcase they left to be carrion,
Many a livid one, many a sallow-skin —
Left for the white-tail'd eagle to tear it, and
Left for the horny-nibb'd raven to rend it, and
Gave to the garbaging war-hawk to gorge it, and
That gray beast, the wolf of the weald.   110

XV

Never had huger
Slaughter of heroes
Slain by the sword-edge —
Such as old writers
Have writ of in histories —
Hapt in this isle, since
Up from the East hither
Saxon and Angle from

[3] Lit. "the gathering of men."   [4] Dublin.

Over the broad billow
Broke into Britain with   120
Haughty war-workers who
Harried the Welshman, when
Earls that were lured by the
Hunger of glory gat
Hold of the land.

1880

RIZPAH

17 —

I

WAILING, wailing, wailing, the wind over land and sea —
And Willy's voice in the wind, "O mother, come out to me!"
Why should he call me to-night, when he knows that I cannot go?
For the downs are as bright as day, and the full moon stares at the
    snow.

II

We should be seen, my dear; they would spy us out of the town.
The loud black nights for us, and the storm rushing over the down,
When I cannot see my own hand, but am led by the creak of the
    chain,
And grovel and grope for my son till I find myself drenched with the
    rain.

III

Anything fallen again? nay — what was there left to fall?
I have taken them home, I have number'd the bones, I have hidden
    them all.   10
What am I saying? and what are *you*? do you come as a spy?
Falls? what falls? who knows? As the tree falls so must it lie.

IV

Who let her in? how long has she been? you — what have you heard?
Why did you sit so quiet? you never have spoken a word.
O — to pray with me — yes — a lady — none of their spies —
But the night has crept into my heart, and begun to darken my eyes.

V

Ah — you, that have lived so soft, what should *you* know of the night,
The blast and the burning shame and the bitter frost and the fright?

I have done it, while you were asleep — you were only made for the
    day.
I have gather'd my baby together — and now you may go your
    way.   20

VI

Nay — for it 's kind of you, madam, to sit by an old dying wife.
But say nothing hard of my boy, I have only an hour of life.
I kiss'd my boy in the prison, before he went out to die.
"They dared me to do it," he said, and he never has told me a lie.
I whipt him for robbing an orchard once when he was but a child —
"The farmer dared me to do it," he said; he was always so wild —
And idle — and could n't be idle — my Willy — he never could rest.
The King should have made him a soldier, he would have been one of
    his best.

VII

But he lived with a lot of wild mates, and they never would let him
    be good;
They swore that he dare not rob the mail, and he swore that he
    would;   30
And he took no life, but he took one purse, and when all was done
He flung it among his fellows — "I 'll none of it," said my son.

VIII

I came into court to the judge and the lawyers. I told them my tale,
God's own truth — but they kill'd him, they kill'd him for robbing the
    mail.
They hang'd him in chains for a show — we had always borne a good
    name —
To be hang'd for a thief — and then put away — is n't that enough
    shame?
Dust to dust — low down — let us hide! but they set him so high
That all the ships of the world could stare at him, passing by.
God 'ill pardon the hell-black raven and horrible fowls of the air,
But not the black heart of the lawyer who kill'd him and hang'd him
    there.   40

IX

And the jailer forced me away. I had bid him my last good-bye;
They had fasten'd the door of his cell. "O mother!" I heard him cry.
I could n't get back tho' I tried, he had something further to say,
And now I never shall know it. The jailer forced me away.

X

Then since I could n't but hear that cry of my boy that was dead,
They seized me and shut me up: they fasten'd me down on my bed.

"Mother, O mother!" — he call'd in the dark to me year after year —
They beat me for that, they beat me — you know that I could n't but
 hear;
And then at the last they found I had grown so stupid and still
They let me abroad again — but the creatures had worked their
 will.   50

XI

Flesh of my flesh was gone, but bone of my bone was left —
I stole them all from the lawyers — and you, will you call it a theft? —
My baby, the bones that had suck'd me, the bones that had laughed
 and had cried —
Theirs? O, no! they are mine — not theirs — they had moved in my
 side.

XII

Do you think I was scared by the bones? I kiss'd 'em, I buried 'em
 all —
I can't dig deep, I am old — in the night by the churchyard wall.
My Willy 'ill rise up whole when the trumpet of judgment 'ill sound,
But I charge you never to say that I laid him in holy ground.

XIII

They would scratch him up — they would hang him again on the
 cursed tree.
Sin? O, yes, we are sinners, I know — let all that be,   60
And read me a Bible verse of the Lord's goodwill toward men —
"Full of compassion and mercy, the Lord" — let me hear it again;
"Full of compassion and mercy — long-suffering." Yes, O, yes!
For the lawyer is born but to murder — the Saviour lives but to bless.
He 'll never put on the black cap except for the worst of the worst,
And the first may be last — I have heard it in church — and the last
 may be first.
Suffering — O, long-suffering — yes, as the Lord must know,
Year after year in the mist and the wind and the shower and the snow.

XIV

Heard, have you? what? they have told you he never repented his sin.
How do they know it? are *they* his mother? are *you* of his kin? 70
Heard! have you ever heard, when the storm on the downs began,
The wind that 'ill wail like a child and the sea that 'ill moan like a man?

XV

Election, Election, and Reprobation — it 's all very well.
But I go to-night to my boy, and I shall not find him in hell.

For I cared so much for my boy that the Lord has look'd into my care,
And He means me I'm sure to be happy with Willy, I know not where.

XVI

And if *he* be lost — but to save *my* soul, that is all your desire —
Do you think that I care for *my* soul if my boy be gone to the fire?
I have been with God in the dark — go, go, you may leave me alone —
You never have borne a child — you are just as hard as a stone.   80

XVII

Madam, I beg your pardon! I think that you mean to be kind,
But I cannot hear what you say for my Willy's voice in the wind —
The snow and the sky so bright — he used but to call in the dark,
And he calls to me now from the church and not from the gibbet —
        for hark!
Nay — you can hear it yourself — it is coming — shaking the walls —
Willy — the moon 's in a cloud —— Good-night. I am going. He calls.
1880*

"FRATER AVE ATQUE VALE"

Row us out from Desenzano, to your Sirmione row!
So they row'd, and there we landed — "O venusta Sirmio!"
There to me thro' all the groves of olive in the summer glow.
There beneath the Roman ruin where the purple flowers grow,
Came that "Ave atque Vale" of the Poet's hopeless woe,
Tenderest of Roman poets nineteen hundred years ago,
"Frater Ave atque Vale" — as we wander'd to and fro
Gazing at the Lydian laughter of the Garda Lake below
Sweet Catullus's all-but-island, olive-silvery Sirmio!

1880 (1883)*

TO VIRGIL

WRITTEN AT THE REQUEST OF THE MANTUANS
FOR THE NINETEENTH CENTENARY OF VIRGIL'S DEATH

I

Roman Virgil, thou that singest
        Ilion's lofty temples robed in fire,

Ilion falling, Rome arising,
    wars, and filial faith, and Dido's pyre;

II

Landscape-lover, lord of language
    more than he that sang the "Works and Days,"
All the chosen coin of fancy
    flashing out from many a golden phrase;

III

Thou that singest wheat and woodland,
    tilth and vineyard, hive and horse and herd;
All the charm of all the Muses
    often flowering in a lonely word;

IV

Poet of the happy Tityrus
    piping underneath his beechen bowers;
Poet of the poet-satyr
    whom the laughing shepherd bound with flowers;

V

Chanter of the Pollio, glorying
    in the blissful years again to be,
Summers of the snakeless meadow,
    unlaborious earth and oarless sea;   10

VI

Thou that seest Universal
    Nature moved by Universal Mind;
Thou majestic in thy sadness
    at the doubtful doom of human kind;

VII

Light among the vanish'd ages;
    star that gildest yet this phantom shore;
Golden branch amid the shadows,
    kings and realms that pass to rise no more;

VIII

Now thy Forum roars no longer,
    fallen every purple Cæsar's dome —
Tho' thine ocean-roll of rhythm
    sound forever of Imperial Rome —

IX

Now the Rome of slaves hath perish'd,
    and the Rome of freemen holds her place,
I, from out the Northern Island
    sunder'd once from all the human race,

X

I salute thee, Mantovano,
    I that loved thee since my day began,
Wielder of the stateliest measure
    ever moulded by the lips of man.   20
1882°

TIRESIAS

TO E. FITZGERALD

OLD FITZ, who from your suburb grange,
    Where once I tarried for a while,
Glance at the wheeling orb of change,
    And greet it with a kindly smile;
Whom yet I see as there you sit
    Beneath your sheltering garden-tree,
And watch your doves about you flit,
    And plant on shoulder, hand, and knee,
Or on your head their rosy feet,
    As if they knew your diet spares   10
Whatever moved in that full sheet
    Let down to Peter at his prayers;
Who live on milk and meal and grass;
    And once for ten long weeks I tried
Your table of Pythagoras,
    And seem'd at first "a thing enskied,"
As Shakespeare has it, airy-light
    To float above the ways of men,
Then fell from that half-spiritual height
    Chill'd, till I tasted flesh again   20
One night when earth was winter-black,
    And all the heavens flash'd in frost;
And on me, half-asleep, came back
    That wholesome heat the blood had lost,
And set me climbing icy capes
    And glaciers, over which there roll'd

To meet me long-arm'd vines with grapes
    Of Eshcol hugeness; for the cold
Without, and warmth within me, wrought
    To mould the dream; but none can say   30
That Lenten fare makes Lenten thought
    Who reads your golden Eastern lay,
Than which I know no version done
    In English more divinely well;
A planet equal to the sun
    Which cast it, that large infidel
Your Omar; and your Omar drew
    Full-handed plaudits from our best
In modern letters, and from two,
    Old friends outvaluing all the rest,   40
Two voices heard on earth no more;
    But we old friends are still alive,
And I am nearing seventy-four,
    While you have touch'd at seventy-five,
And so I send a birthday line
    Of greeting; and my son, who dipt
In some forgotten book of mine
    With sallow scraps of manuscript,
And dating many a year ago,
    Has hit on this, which you will take,   50
My Fitz, and welcome, as I know,
    Less for its own than for the sake
Of one recalling gracious times,
    When, in our younger London days,
You found some merit in my rhymes,
    And I more pleasure in your praise.

TIRESIAS

I wish I were as in the years of old,
While yet the blessed daylight made itself
Ruddy thro' both the roofs of sight, and woke
These eyes, now dull, but then so keen to seek
The meanings ambush'd under all they saw,
The flight of birds, the flame of sacrifice,
What omens may foreshadow fate to man
And woman, and the secret of the Gods.
    My son, the Gods, despite of human prayer,
Are slower to forgive than human kings.   10
The great God Arês burns in anger still

Against the guiltless heirs of him from Tyre,
Our Cadmus, out of whom thou art, who found
Beside the springs of Dircê, smote, and still'd
Thro' all its folds the multitudinous beast,
The dragon, which our trembling fathers call'd
The God's own son.

              A tale, that told to me,
When but thine age, by age as winter-white
As mine is now, amazed, but made me yearn
For larger glimpses of that more than man   20
Which rolls the heavens, and lifts and lays the deep,
Yet loves and hates with mortal hates and loves,
And moves unseen among the ways of men.

    Then, in my wanderings all the lands that lie
Subjected to the Heliconian ridge
Have heard this footstep fall, altho' my wont
Was more to scale the highest of the heights
With some strange hope to see the nearer God.

    One naked peak — the sister of the Sun
Would climb from out the dark, and linger there   30
To silver all the valleys with her shafts —
There once, but long ago, five-fold thy term
Of years, I lay; the winds were dead for heat;
The noonday crag made the hand burn; and sick
For shadow — not one bush was near — I rose,
Following a torrent till its myriad falls
Found silence in the hollows underneath.

    There in a secret olive-glade I saw
Pallas Athene climbing from the bath
In anger; yet one glittering foot disturb'd   40
The lucid well; one snowy knee was prest
Against the margin flowers; a dreadful light
Came from her golden hair, her golden helm
And all her golden armor on the grass,
And from her virgin breast, and virgin eyes
Remaining fixt on mine, till mine grew dark
For ever, and I heard a voice that said,
"Henceforth be blind, for thou hast seen too much,
And speak the truth that no man may believe."

    Son, in the hidden world of sight that lives   50
Behind this darkness, I behold her still,
Beyond all work of those who carve the stone,
Beyond all dreams of Godlike womanhood,
Ineffable beauty, out of whom, at a glance,
And as it were, perforce, upon me flash'd

The power of prophesying — but to me
No power — so chain'd and coupled with the curse
Of blindness and their unbelief who heard
And heard not, when I spake of famine, plague,
Shrine-shattering earthquake, fire, flood, thunderbolt,   60
And angers of the Gods for evil done
And expiation lack'd — no power on Fate
Theirs, or mine own! for when the crowd would roar
For blood, for war, whose issue was their doom,
To cast wise words among the multitude
Was flinging fruit to lions; nor, in hours
Of civil outbreak, when I knew the twain
Would each waste each, and bring on both the yoke
Of stronger states, was mine the voice to curb
The madness of our cities and their kings.   70
    Who ever turn'd upon his heel to hear
My warning that the tyranny of one
Was prelude to the tyranny of all?
My counsel that the tyranny of all
Led backward to the tyranny of one?
    This power hath work'd no good to aught that lives
And these blind hands were useless in their wars.
O, therefore, that the unfulfill'd desire,
The grief for ever born from griefs to be,
The boundless yearning of the prophet's heart —   80
Could *that* stand forth, and like a statue, rear'd
To some great citizen, win all praise from all
Who past it, saying, "That was he!"
                        In vain!
Virtue must shape itself in deed, and those
Whom weakness or necessity have cramp'd
Within themselves, immerging, each, his urn
In his own well, draws solace as he may.
    Menœceus, thou hast eyes, and I can hear
Too plainly what full tides of onset sap
Our seven high gates, and what a weight of war   90
Rides on those ringing axles! jingle of bits,
Shouts, arrows, tramp of the horn-footed horse
That grind the glebe to powder! Stony showers
Of that ear-stunning hail of Arês crash
Along the sounding walls. Above, below,
Shock after shock, the song-built towers and gates
Reel, bruised and butted with the shuddering
War-thunder of iron rams; and from within
The city comes a murmur void of joy,

Lest she be taken captive — maidens, wives,   100
And mothers with their babblers of the dawn,
And oldest age in shadow from the night,
Falling about their shrines before their Gods,
And wailing, "Save us."
              And they wail to thee!
These eyeless eyes, that cannot see thine own,
See this, that only in thy virtue lies
The saving of our Thebes; for, yesternight,
To me, the great God Arês, whose one bliss
Is war and human sacrifice — himself
Blood-red from battle, spear and helmet tipt   110
With stormy light as on a mast at sea,
Stood out before a darkness, crying, "Thebes,
Thy Thebes shall fall and perish, for I loathe
The seed of Cadmus — yet if one of these
By his own hand — if one of these — "
                    My son,
No sound is breathed so potent to coerce,
And to conciliate, as their names who dare
For that sweet mother land which gave them birth
Nobly to do, nobly to die. Their names,
Graven on memorial columns, are a song   120
Heard in the future; few, but more than wall
And rampart, their examples reach a hand
Far thro' all years, and everywhere they meet
And kindle generous purpose, and the strength
To mould it into action pure as theirs.
  Fairer thy fate than mine, if life's best end
Be to end well! and thou refusing this,
Unvenerable will thy memory be
While men shall move the lips; but if thou dare —
Thou, one of these, the race of Cadmus — then   130
No stone is fitted in yon marble girth
Whose echo shall not tongue thy glorious doom,
Nor in this pavement but shall ring thy name
To every hoof that clangs it, and the springs
Of Dircê laving yonder battle-plain,
Heard from the roofs by night, will murmur thee
To thine own Thebes, while Thebes thro' thee shall stand
Firm-based with all her Gods.
               The Dragon's cave
Half hid, they tell me, now in flowing vines —
Where once he dwelt and whence he roll'd himself   140
At dead of night — thou knowest, and that smooth rock

Before it, altar-fashion'd, where of late
The woman-breasted Sphinx, with wings drawn back,
Folded her lion paws, and look'd to Thebes.
There blanch the bones of whom she slew, and these
Mixt with her own, because the fierce beast found
A wiser than herself, and dash'd herself
Dead in her rage; but thou art wise enough,
Tho' young, to love thy wiser, blunt the curse
Of Pallas, bear, and tho' I speak the truth   150
Believe I speak it, let thine own hand strike
Thy youthful pulses into rest and quench
The red God's anger, fearing not to plunge
Thy torch of life in darkness, rather — thou
Rejoicing that the sun, the moon, the stars
Send no such light upon the ways of men
As one great deed.
          Thither, my son, and there
Thou, that hast never known the embrace of love,
Offer thy maiden life.
            This useless hand!
I felt one warm tear fall upon it. Gone!   160
He will achieve his greatness.
             But for me,
I would that I were gather'd to my rest,
And mingled with the famous kings of old,
On whom about their ocean-islets flash
The faces of the Gods — the wise man's word,
Here trampled by the populace underfoot,
There crown'd with worship — and these eyes will find
The men I knew, and watch the chariot whirl
About the goal again, and hunters race
The shadowy lion, and the warrior-kings,   170
In height and prowess more than human, strive
Again for glory, while the golden lyre
Is ever sounding in heroic ears
Heroic hymns, and every way the vales
Wind, clouded with the grateful incense-fume
Of those who mix all odor to the Gods
On one far height in one far-shining fire.

"One height and one far-shining fire!"
   And while I fancied that my friend
For this brief idyll would require   180

A less diffuse and opulent end,
And would defend his judgment well,
   If I should deem it over nice —
The tolling of his funeral bell
   Broke on my Pagan Paradise,
And mixt the dream of classic times,
   And all the phantoms of the dream,
With present grief, and made the rhymes,
   That miss'd his living welcome, seem
Like would-be guests an hour too late,   190
   Who down the highway moving on
With easy laughter find the gate
   Is bolted, and the master gone.
Gone into darkness, that full light
   Of friendship! past, in sleep, away
By night, into the deeper night!
   The deeper night? A clearer day
Than our poor twilight dawn on earth —
   If night, what barren toil to be!
What life, so maim'd by night, were worth   200
   Our living out? Not mine to me
Remembering all the golden hours
   Now silent, and so many dead,
And him the last; and laying flowers,
   This wreath, above his honor'd head,
And praying that, when I from hence
   Shall fade with him into the unknown,
My close of earth's experience
   May prove as peaceful as his own.

1883 (1885)*

THE ANCIENT SAGE

A THOUSAND summers ere the time of Christ,
From out his ancient city came a Seer
Whom one that loved and honor'd him, and yet
Was no disciple, richly garb'd, but worn
From wasteful living, follow'd — in his hand
A scroll of verse — till that old man before
A cavern whence an affluent fountain pour'd
From darkness into daylight, turn'd and spoke:

   "This wealth of waters might but seem to draw
From yon dark cave, but, son, the source is higher,   10

Yon summit half-a-league in air — and higher
The cloud that hides it — higher still the heavens
Whereby the cloud was moulded, and whereout
The cloud descended. Force is from the heights.
I am wearied of our city, son, and go
To spend my one last year among the hills.
What hast thou there? Some death-song for the Ghouls
To make their banquet relish? let me read.

     " 'How far thro' all the bloom and brake
         That nightingale is heard!   20
     What power but the bird's could make
         This music in the bird?
     How summer-bright are yonder skies,
         And earth as fair in hue!
     And yet what sign of aught that lies
         Behind the green and blue?
     But man to-day is fancy's fool
         As man hath ever been.
     The nameless Power, or Powers that rule
         Were never heard or seen.'   30

If thou wouldst hear the Nameless, and wilt dive
Into the temple-cave of thine own self,
There, brooding by the central altar, thou
Mayst haply learn the Nameless hath a voice,
By which thou wilt abide, if thou be wise,
As if thou knewest, tho' thou canst not know;
For Knowledge is the swallow on the lake
That sees and stirs the surface-shadow there
But never yet hath dipt into the abysm,
The abysm of all abysms, beneath, within   40
The blue of sky and sea, the green of earth,
And in the million-millionth of a grain
Which cleft and cleft again for evermore,
And ever vanishing, never vanishes,
To me, my son, more mystic than myself,
Or even than the Nameless is to me.
    "And when thou sendest thy free soul thro' heaven,
Nor understandest bound nor boundlessness,
Thou seest the Nameless of the hundred names.
    "And if the Nameless should withdraw from all   50
Thy frailty counts most real, all thy world
Might vanish like thy shadow in the dark.

" 'And since — from when this earth began —
    The Nameless never came
  Among us, never spake with man,
    And never named the Name' —

Thou canst not prove the Nameless, O my son,
Nor canst thou prove the world thou movest in,
Thou canst not prove that thou art body alone,
Nor canst thou prove that thou art spirit alone,   60
Nor canst thou prove that thou art both in one.
Thou canst not prove thou art immortal, no,
Nor yet that thou art mortal — nay, my son,
Thou canst not prove that I, who speak with thee,
Am not thyself in converse with thyself,
For nothing worthy proving can be proven,
Nor yet disproven. Wherefore thou be wise,
Cleave ever to the sunnier side of doubt,
And cling to Faith beyond the forms of Faith!
She reels not in the storm of warring words,   70
She brightens at the clash of 'Yes' and 'No,'
She sees the best that glimmers thro' the worst,
She feels the sun is hid but for a night,
She spies the summer thro' the winter bud,
She tastes the fruit before the blossom falls,
She hears the lark within the songless egg,
She finds the fountain where they wail'd 'Mirage!'

    " 'What Power? aught akin to Mind,
      The mind in me and you?
    Or power as of the Gods gone blind   80
      Who see not what they do?'

But some in yonder city hold, my son,
That none but gods could build this house of ours,
So beautiful, vast, various, so beyond
All work of man, yet, like all work of man,
A beauty with defect — till That which knows,
And is not known, but felt thro' what we feel
Within ourselves is highest, shall descend
On this half-deed, and shape it at the last
According to the Highest in the Highest.   90

    " 'What Power but the Years that make
      And break the vase of clay,
    And stir the sleeping earth, and wake
      The bloom that fades away?

What rulers but the Days and Hours
    That cancel weal with woe,
And wind the front of youth with flowers,
    And cap our age with snow?'

The days and hours are ever glancing by,
And seem to flicker past thro' sun and shade,   100
Or short, or long, as Pleasure leads, or Pain,
But with the Nameless is nor day nor hour;
Tho' we, thin minds, who creep from thought to thought,
Break into 'Thens' and 'Whens' the Eternal Now —
This double seeming of the single world! —
My words are like the babblings in a dream
Of nightmare, when the babblings break the dream.
But thou be wise in this dream-world of ours,
Nor take thy dial for thy deity,
But make the passing shadow serve thy will.   110

    " 'The years that made the stripling wise
        Undo their work again,
    And leave him, blind of heart and eyes,
        The last and least of men;
    Who clings to earth, and once would dare
        Hell-heat or Arctic cold,
    And now one breath of cooler air
        Would loose him from his hold.
    His winter chills him to the root,
        He withers marrow and mind;   120
    The kernel of the shrivell'd fruit
        Is jutting thro' the rind;
    The tiger spasms tear his chest,
        The palsy wags his head;
    The wife, the sons, who love him best
        Would fain that he were dead;
    The griefs by which he once was wrung
        Were never worth the while' —

Who knows? or whether this earth-narrow life
Be yet but yolk, and forming in the shell?   130

    " 'The shaft of scorn that once had stung
        But wakes a dotard smile.'

The placid gleam of sunset after storm!

    " 'The statesman's brain that sway'd the past
        Is feebler than his knees;

The passive sailor wrecks at last
   In ever-silent seas;
The warrior hath forgot his arms,
   The learned all his lore;
The changing market frets or charms   140
   The merchant's hope no more:
The prophet's beacon burn'd in vain,
   And now is lost in cloud;
The plowman passes, bent with pain,
   To mix with what he plow'd;
The poet whom his age would quote
   As heir of endless fame —
He knows not even the book he wrote,
   Not even his own name.
For man has overlived his day,   150
   And, darkening in the light,
Scarce feels the senses break away
   To mix with ancient Night.'

The shell must break before the bird can fly.

   " 'The years that when my youth began
      Had set the lily and rose
   By all my ways where'er they ran,
      Have ended mortal foes;
   My rose of love for ever gone,
      My lily of truth and trust —   160
   They made her lily and rose in one,
      And changed her into dust.
   O rose-tree planted in my grief,
      And growing on her tomb,
   Her dust is greening in your leaf,
      Her blood is in your bloom
   O slender lily waving there,
      And laughing back the light,
   In vain you tell me "Earth is fair"
      When all is dark as night.'   170

My son, the world is dark with griefs and graves,
So dark that men cry out against the heavens.
Who knows but that the darkness is in man?
The doors of Night may be the gates of Light;
For wert thou born or blind or deaf, and then
Suddenly heal'd, how wouldst thou glory in all
The splendors and the voices of the world!
And we, the poor earth's dying race, and yet
No phantoms, watching from a phantom shore

Await the last and largest sense to make   180
The phantom walls of this illusion fade,
And show us that the world is wholly fair.

   " 'But vain the tears for darken'd years
     As laughter over wine,
   And vain the laughter as the tears,
     O brother, mine or thine,
   For all that laugh, and all that weep
     And all that breathe are one
   Slight ripple on the boundless deep
     That moves, and all is gone.'   190

But that one ripple on the boundless deep
Feels that the deep is boundless, and itself
For ever changing form, but evermore
One with the boundless motion of the deep.

   " 'Yet wine and laughter, friends! and set
     The lamps alight, and call
   For golden music, and forget
     The darkness of the pall.'

If utter darkness closed the day, my son —
But earth's dark forehead flings athwart the heavens   200
Her shadow crown'd with stars — and yonder — out
To northward — some that never set, but pass
From sight and night to lose themselves in day.
I hate the black negation of the bier,
And wish the dead, as happier than ourselves
And higher, having climb'd one step beyond
Our village miseries, might be borne in white
To burial or to burning, hymn'd from hence
With songs in praise of death, and crown'd with flowers!

   " 'O worms and maggots of to-day   210
     Without their hope of wings!'

But louder than thy rhyme the silent Word
Of that world-prophet in the heart of man.

   " 'Tho' some have gleams, or so they say,
     Of more than mortal things.'

To-day? but what of yesterday? for oft
On me, when boy, there came what then I call'd,

Who knew no books and no philosophies,
In my boy-phrase, 'The Passion of the Past.'
The first gray streak of earliest summer-dawn,   220
The last long stripe of waning crimson gloom,
As if the late and early were but one —
A height, a broken grange, a grove, a flower
Had murmurs, 'Lost and gone, and lost and gone!'
A breath, a whisper — some divine farewell —
Desolate sweetness — far and far away —
What had he loved, what had he lost, the boy?
I know not, and I speak of what has been.

    "And more, my son! for more than once when I
Sat all alone, revolving in myself   230
The word that is the symbol of myself,
The mortal limit of the Self was loosed,
And past into the Nameless, as a cloud
Melts into heaven. I touch'd my limbs, the limbs
Were strange, not mine — and yet no shade of doubt,
But utter clearness, and thro' loss of self
The gain of such large life as match'd with ours
Were sun to spark — unshadowable in words,
Themselves but shadows of a shadow-world.

    "'And idle gleams will come and go,   240
      But still the clouds remain;'

The clouds themselves are children of the Sun.

    "'And Night and Shadow rule below
      When only Day should reign.'

And Day and Night are children of the Sun,
And idle gleams to thee are light to me.
Some say, the Light was father of the Night,
And some, the Night was father of the Light,
No night, no day! — I touch thy world again —
No ill, no good! such counter-terms, my son,   250
Are border-races, holding each its own
By endless war. But night enough is there
In yon dark city. Get thee back; and since
The key to that weird casket, which for thee
But holds a skull, is neither thine nor mine,
But in the hand of what is more than man,
Or in man's hand when man is more than man,
Let be thy wail, and help thy fellow-men,

And make thy gold thy vassal, not thy king,
And fling free alms into the beggar's bowl,   260
And send the day into the darken'd heart;
Nor list for guerdon in the voice of men,
A dying echo from a falling wall;
Nor care — for Hunger hath the evil eye —
To vex the noon with fiery gems, or fold
Thy presence in the silk of sumptuous looms;
Nor roll thy viands on a luscious tongue,
Nor drown thyself with flies in honeyed wine;
Nor thou be rageful, like a handled bee,
And lose thy life by usage of thy sting;   270
Nor harm an adder thro' the lust for harm,
Nor make a snail's horn shrink for wantonness.
And more — think well! Do-well will follow thought,
And in the fatal sequence of this world
An evil thought may soil thy children's blood;
But curb the beast would cast thee in the mire,
And leave the hot swamp of voluptuousness,
A cloud between the Nameless and thyself,
And lay thine uphill shoulder to the wheel,
And climb the Mount of Blessing, whence, if thou   280
Look higher, then — perchance — thou mayest — beyond
A hundred ever-rising mountain lines,
And past the range of Night and Shadow — see
The high-heaven dawn of more than mortal day
Strike on the Mount of Vision!
                    So, farewell."

1885*

POETS AND THEIR BIBLIOGRAPHIES

OLD poets foster'd under friendlier skies,
    Old Virgil who would write ten lines, they say,
    At dawn, and lavish all the golden day
To make them wealthier in his readers' eyes;
And you, old popular Horace, you the wise
    Adviser of the nine-years-ponder'd lay,
    And you, that wear a wreath of sweeter bay,
Catullus, whose dead songster never dies;
If, glancing downward on the kindly sphere
    That once had roll'd you round and round the sun,   10

You see your Art still shrined in human shelves,
You should be jubilant that you flourish'd here
    Before the Love of Letters, overdone,
Had swampt the sacred poets with themselves.

1885

VASTNESS

I

MANY a hearth upon our dark globe sighs after many a vanish'd face,
Many a planet by many a sun may roll with the dust of a vanish'd race.

II

Raving politics, never at rest — as this poor earth's pale history runs, —
What is it all but a trouble of ants in the gleam of a million million of
    suns?

III

Lies upon this side, lies upon that side, truthless violence mourn'd by
    the wise,
Thousands of voices drowning his own in a popular torrent of lies upon
    lies;

IV

Stately purposes, valor in battle, glorious annals of army and fleet,
Death for the right cause, death for the wrong cause, trumpets of vic-
    tory, groans of defeat;

V

Innocence seethed in her mother's milk, and Charity setting the martyr
    aflame;
Thraldom who walks with the banner of Freedom, and recks not to
    ruin a realm in her name.   10

VI

Faith at her zenith, or all but lost in the gloom of doubts that darken
    the schools;
Craft with a bunch of all-heal in her hand, follow'd up by her vassal
    legion of fools;

VII

Trade flying over a thousand seas with her spice and her vintage, her
    silk and her corn;
Desolate offing, sailorless harbors, famishing populace, wharves forlorn;

VIII

Star of the morning, Hope in the sunrise; gloom of the evening, Life
at a close;
Pleasure who flaunts on her wide downway with her flying robe and
her poison'd rose;

IX

Pain, that has crawl'd from the corpse of Pleasure, a worm which
writhes all day, and at night
Stirs up again in the heart of the sleeper, and stings him back to the
curse of the light;

X

Wealth with his wines and his wedded harlots; honest Poverty, bare
to the bone;   19
Opulent Avarice, lean as Poverty; Flattery gilding the rift in a throne;

XI

Fame blowing out from her golden trumpet a jubilant challenge to
Time and to Fate;
Slander, her shadow, sowing the nettle on all the laurell'd graves of the
great;

XII

Love for the maiden, crown'd with marriage, no regrets for aught that
has been,
Household happiness, gracious children, debtless competence, golden
mean;

XIII

National hatreds of whole generations, and pigmy spites of the village
spire;
Vows that will last to the last death-ruckle, and vows that are snapt in
a moment of fire;

XIV

He that has lived for the lust of the minute, and died in the doing it,
flesh wthout mind;
He that has nail'd all flesh to the Cross, till Self died out in the love of
his kind;

XV

Spring and Summer and Autumn and Winter, and all these old revolutions of earth;
All new-old revolutions of Empire — change of the tide — what is all
of it worth?   30

XVI

What the philosophies, all the sciences, poesy, varying voices of prayer,
All that is noblest, all that is basest, all that is filthy with all that is fair?

XVII

What is it all, if we all of us end but in being our own corpse-coffins at
    last?
Swallow'd in Vastness, lost in Silence, drown'd in the deeps of a mean-
    ingless Past?

XVIII

What but a murmur of gnats in the gloom, or a moment's anger of bees
    in their hive? —

.   .   .   .

Peace, let it be! for I loved him, and love him for ever: the dead are
    not dead but alive.

1885

From

LOCKSLEY HALL SIXTY YEARS AFTER

Gone the cry of "Forward, Forward," lost within a growing gloom;
Lost, or only heard in silence from the silence of a tomb.

Half the marvels of my morning, triumphs over time and space,
Staled by frequence, shrunk by usage into commonest commonplace!

"Forward" rang the voices then, and of the many mine was one.
Let us hush this cry of "Forward" till ten thousand years have gone. . . .

———

Chaos, Cosmos! Cosmos, Chaos! once again the sickening game;
Freedom, free to slay herself, and dying while they shout her name. . . .

———

Bring the old dark ages back without the faith, without the hope,
Break the State, the Church, the Throne, and roll their ruins down the
    slope.

Authors — essayist, atheist, novelist, realist, rhymester, play your part,
Paint the mortal shame of nature with the living hues of art.

Rip your brothers' vices open, strip your own foul passions bare;
Down with Reticence, down with Reverence — forward — naked —
    let them stare.

Feed the budding rose of boyhood with the drainage of your sewer;
Send the drain into the fountain, lest the stream should issue pure.

Set the maiden fancies wallowing in the troughs of Zolaism, —
Forward, forward, ay, and backward, downward too into the abysm!

Do your best to charm the worst, to lower the rising race of men;
Have we risen from out the beast, then back into the beast again? . . .

Is there evil but on earth? or pain in every peopled sphere?
Well, be grateful for the sounding watchword "Evolution" here,

Evolution ever climbing after some ideal good,
And Reversion ever dragging Evolution in the mud.

What are men that He should heed us? cried the king of sacred song;
Insects of an hour, that hourly work their brother insect wrong,

While the silent heavens roll, and suns along their fiery way,
All their planets whirling round them, flash a million miles a day.

Many an æon moulded earth before her highest, man, was born,
Many an æon too may pass when earth is manless and forlorn,

Earth so huge, and yet so bounded — pools of salt, and plots of land —
Shallow skin of green and azure — chains of mountain, grains of sand!

Only That which made us meant us to be mightier by and by,
Set the sphere of all the boundless heavens within the human eye,

Sent the shadow of Himself, the boundless, thro' the human soul;
Boundless inward in the atom, boundless outward in the Whole. . . .

Is it well that while we range with Science, glorying in the Time,
City children soak and blacken soul and sense in city slime?

There among the glooming alleys Progress halts on palsied feet,
Crime and hunger cast our maidens by the thousand on the street.

There the master scrimps his haggard sempstress of her daily bread,
There a single sordid attic holds the living and the dead.

There the smouldering fire of fever creeps across the rotted floor,
And the crowded couch of incest in the warrens of the poor. . . .
1886°

DEMETER AND PERSEPHONE

(IN ENNA)

FAINT as a climate-changing bird that flies
All night across the darkness, and at dawn
Falls on the threshold of her native land,
And can no more, thou camest, O my child,
Led upward by the God of ghosts and dreams,
Who laid thee at Eleusis, dazed and dumb
With passing thro' at once from state to state,
Until I brought thee hither, that the day,
When here thy hands let fall the gather'd flower,
Might break thro' clouded memories once again   10
On thy lost self. A sudden nightingale
Saw thee, and flash'd into a frolic of song
And welcome; and a gleam as of the moon,
When first she peers along the tremulous deep,
Fled wavering o'er thy face, and chased away
That shadow of a likeness to the king
Of shadows, thy dark mate. Persephone!
Queen of the dead no more — my child! Thine eyes
Again were human-godlike, and the Sun
Burst from a swimming fleece of winter gray,   20
And robed thee in his day from head to feet —
"Mother!" and I was folded in thine arms.

Child, those imperial, disimpassion'd eyes
Awed even me at first, thy mother — eyes
That oft had seen the serpent-wanded power
Draw downward into Hades with his drift
Of flickering spectres, lighted from below
By the red race of fiery Phlegethon;
But when before have Gods or men beheld
The Life that had descended re-arise,   30

And lighted from above him by the Sun?
So mighty was the mother's childless cry,
A cry that rang thro' Hades, Earth, and Heaven!

    So in this pleasant vale we stand again,
The field of Enna, now once more ablaze
With flowers that brighten as thy footstep falls,
All flowers — but for one black blur of earth
Left by that closing chasm, thro' which the car
Of dark Aïdoneus rising rapt thee hence.
And here, my child, tho' folded in thine arms,   **40**
I feel the deathless heart of motherhood
Within me shudder, lest the naked glebe
Should yawn once more into the gulf, and thence
The shrilly whinnyings of the team of Hell,
Ascending, pierce the glad and songful air,
And all at once their arch'd necks, midnight-maned,
Jet upward thro' the midday blossom. No!
For, see, thy foot has touch'd it; all the space
Of blank earth-baldness clothes itself afresh,
And breaks into the crocus-purple hour   **50**
That saw thee vanish.

                Child, when thou wert gone,
I envied human wives, and nested birds,
Yea, the cubb'd lioness; went in search of thee
Thro' many a palace, many a cot, and gave
Thy breast to ailing infants in the night,
And set the mother waking in a maze
To find her sick one whole; and forth again
Among the wail of midnight winds, and cried,
"Where is my loved one? Wherefore do ye wail?"
And out from all the night an answer shrill'd,   **60**
"We know not, and we know not why we wail."
I climb'd on all the cliffs of all the seas,
And ask'd the waves that moan about the world,
"Where? do ye make your moaning for my child?"
And round from all the world the voices came,
"We know not, and we know not why we moan."
"Where?" and I stared from every eagle-peak,
I thridded the black heart of all the woods,
I peer'd thro' tomb and cave, and in the storms
Of autumn swept across the city, and heard   **70**
The murmur of their temples chanting me,
Me, me, the desolate mother! "Where?" — and turn'd,

And fled by many a waste, forlorn of man,
And grieved for man thro' all my grief for thee, —
The jungle rooted in his shatter'd hearth,
The serpent coil'd about his broken shaft,
The scorpion crawling over naked skulls; —
I saw the tiger in the ruin'd fane
Spring from his fallen God, but trace of thee
I saw not; and far on, and, following out   80
A league of labyrinthine darkness, came
On three gray heads beneath a gleaming rift.
"Where?" and I heard one voice from all the three,
"We know not, for we spin the lives of men,
And not of Gods, and know not why we spin!
There is a Fate beyond us." Nothing knew.

    Last as the likeness of a dying man,
Without his knowledge, from him flits to warn
A far-off friendship that he comes no more,
So he, the God of dreams, who heard my cry,   90
Drew from thyself the likeness of thyself
Without thy knowledge, and thy shadow past
Before me, crying, "The Bright one in the highest
Is brother of the Dark one in the lowest,
And Bright and Dark have sworn that I, the child
Of thee, the great Earth-Mother, thee, the Power
That lifts her buried life from gloom to bloom,
Should be for ever and for evermore
The Bride of Darkness."

             So the Shadow wail'd.
Then I, Earth-Goddess, cursed the Gods of heaven.   100
I would not mingle with their feasts; to me
Their nectar smack'd of hemlock on the lips,
Their rich ambrosia tasted aconite.
That man, that only lives and loves an hour,
Seem'd nobler than their hard eternities.
My quick tears kill'd the flower, my ravings hush'd
The bird, and lost in utter grief I fail'd
To send my life thro' olive-yard and vine
And golden-grain, my gift to helpless man.
Rain-rotten died the wheat, the barley-spears   110
Were hollow-husk'd, the leaf fell, and the Sun,
Pale at my grief, drew down before his time
Sickening, and Ætna kept her winter snow.

Then He, the brother of this Darkness, He
Who still is highest, glancing from his height
On earth a fruitless fallow, when he miss'd
The wonted steam of sacrifice, the praise
And prayer of men, decreed that thou shouldst dwell
For nine white moons of each whole year with me,
Three dark ones in the shadow with thy king.   120

Once more the reaper in the gleam of dawn
Will see me by the landmark far away,
Blessing his field, or seated in the dusk
Of even, by the lonely threshing-floor,
Rejoicing in the harvest and the grange.

Yet I, Earth-Goddess, am but ill-content
With them who still are highest. Those gray heads,
What meant they by their "Fate beyond the Fates"
But younger kindlier Gods to bear us down,
As we bore down the Gods before us? Gods,   130
To quench, not hurl the thunderbolt, to stay,
Not spread the plague, the famine; Gods indeed,
To send the noon into the night and break
The sunless halls of Hades into Heaven?
Till thy dark lord accept and love the Sun,
And all the Shadow die into the Light,
When thou shalt dwell the whole bright year with me,
And souls of men, who grew beyond their race,
And made themselves as Gods against the fear
Of Death and Hell; and thou that hast from men,   140
As Queen of Death, that worship which is Fear,
Henceforth, as having risen from out the dead,
Shalt ever send thy life along with mine
From buried grain thro' springing blade, and bless
Their garner'd autumn also, reap with me,
Earth-mother, in the harvest hymns of Earth
The worship which is Love, and see no more
The Stone, the Wheel, the dimly-glimmering lawns
Of that Elysium, all the hateful fires
Of torment, and the shadowy warrior glide   150
Along the silent field of Asphodel.

1887 (1889) *

THE OAK

LIVE thy Life,
    Young and old,
Like yon oak,
Bright in spring,
    Living gold;

Summer-rich
    Then; and then
Autumn-changed,
Soberer-hued
    Gold again.   10

All his leaves
    Fallen at length,
Look, he stands,
Trunk and bough,
    Naked strength.
1889

PARNASSUS

Exegi monumentum . . .
Quod non . . .
Possit diruere . . .
                  . . . innumerabilis
Annorum series et fuga temporum.
                       HORACE.

I

WHAT be those crown'd forms high over the sacred fountain?
Bards, that the mighty Muses have raised to the heights of the mountain,
And over the flight of the Ages! O Goddesses, help me up thither!
Lightning may shrivel the laurel of Cæsar, but mine would not wither.
Steep is the mountain, but you, will help me to overcome it,
And stand with my head in the zenith, and roll my voice from the summit,
Sounding for ever and ever thro' Earth and her listening nations,
And mixt with the great sphere-music of stars and of constellations.

II

What be those two shapes high over the sacred fountain,
Taller than all the Muses, and huger than all the mountain?   10
On those two known peaks they stand ever spreading and heightening;
Poet, that evergreen laurel is blasted by more than lightning!
Look, in their deep double shadow the crown'd ones all disappearing!
Sing like a bird and be happy, nor hope for a deathless hearing!
"Sounding for ever and ever?" pass on! the sight confuses —
These are Astronomy and Geology, terrible Muses!

III

If the lips were touch'd with fire from off a pure Pierian altar,
Tho' their music here be mortal need the singer greatly care?
Other songs for other worlds! the fire within him would not falter;
Let the golden Iliad vanish, Homer here is Homer there.   20
1889*

MERLIN AND THE GLEAM

I

O YOUNG Mariner,
You from the haven
Under the sea-cliff,
You that are watching
The gray Magician
With eyes of wonder,
I am Merlin,
And *I* am dying,
I am Merlin
Who follow the Gleam.   10

II

Mighty the Wizard
Who found me at sunrise
Sleeping, and woke me
And learn'd me Magic!
Great the Master,
And sweet the Magic,
When over the valley,
In early summers,
Over the mountain,
On human faces,   20
And all around me,

Moving to melody,
Floated the Gleam.

III

Once at the croak of a Raven who crost it
A barbarous people,
Blind to the magic
And deaf to the melody,
Snarl'd at and cursed me,
A demon vext me,
The light retreated,   30
The landskip darken'd,
The melody deaden'd,
The Master whisper'd,
"Follow the Gleam."

IV

Then to the melody,
Over a wilderness
Gliding, and glancing at
Elf of the woodland,
Gnome of the cavern,
Griffin and Giant,   40
And dancing of Fairies
In desolate hollows,
And wraiths of the mountain,
And rolling of dragons
By warble of water,
Or cataract music
Of falling torrents,
Flitted the Gleam.

V

Down from the mountain
And over the level,   50
And streaming and shining on
Silent river,
Silvery willow,
Pasture and plowland,
Innocent maidens,
Garrulous children,
Homestead and harvest,
Reaper and gleaner,
And rough-ruddy faces
Of lowly labor,   60
Slided the Gleam —

VI

Then, with a melody
Stronger and statelier,
Led me at length
To the city and palace
Of Arthur the King;
Touch'd at the golden
Cross of the churches,
Flash'd on the tournament,
Flicker'd and bicker'd   70
From helmet to helmet,
And last on the forehead
Of Arthur the blameless
Rested the Gleam.

VII

Clouds and darkness
Closed upon Camelot;
Arthur had vanish'd
I knew not whither,
The king who loved me,
And cannot die;   80
For out of the darkness
Silent and slowly
The Gleam, that had waned to a wintry glimmer
On icy fallow
And faded forest,
Drew to the valley
Named of the shadow,
And slowly brightening
Out of the glimmer,
And slowly moving again to a melody   90
Yearningly tender,
Fell on the shadow,
No longer a shadow,
But clothed with the Gleam.

VIII

And broader and brighter
The Gleam flying onward,
Wed to the melody,
Sang thro' the world;
And slower and fainter,
Old and weary,   100
But eager to follow,

I saw, whenever
In passing it glanced upon
Hamlet or city,
That under the Crosses
The dead man's garden,
The mortal hillock,
Woud break into blossom;
And so to the land's
Last limit I came —   110
And can no longer,
But die rejoicing,
For thro' the Magic
Of Him the Mighty,
Who taught me in childhood,
There on the border
Of boundless Ocean,
And all but in Heaven
Hovers the Gleam.

IX

Not of the sunlight,   120
Not of the moonlight,
Not of the starlight!
O young Mariner,
Down to the haven,
Call your companions,
Launch your vessel
And crowd your canvas,
And, ere it vanishes
Over the margin,
After it, follow it,   130
Follow the Gleam.

1889*

FAR — FAR — AWAY

(FOR MUSIC)

WHAT sight so lured him thro' the fields he knew
As where earth's green stole into heaven's own hue,
                         Far — far — away?

What sound was dearest in his native dells?
The mellow lin-lan-lone of evening bells
                         Far — far — away.

What vague world-whisper, mystic pain or joy,
Thro' those three words would haunt him when a boy,
>> Far — far — away?

A whisper from his dawn of life? a breath   10
From some fair dawn beyond the doors of death
>> Far — far — away?

Far, far, how far? from o'er the gates of birth,
The faint horizons, all the bounds of earth,
>> Far — far — away?

What charm in words, a charm no words could give?
O dying words, can Music make you live
>> Far — far — away?

1889

JUNE BRACKEN AND HEATHER

TO ———

THERE on the top of the down,
The wild heather round me and over me June's high blue,
When I look'd at the bracken so bright and the heather so brown,
I thought to myself I would offer this book to you,
This, and my love together,
To you that are seventy-seven,
With a faith as clear as the heights of the June-blue heaven,
And a fancy as summer-new
As the green of the bracken amid the gloom of the heather.

1892*

THE DEATH OF ŒNONE

ŒNONE sat within the cave from out
Whose ivy-matted mouth she used to gaze
Down at the Troad; but the goodly view
Was now one blank, and all the serpent vines
Which on the touch of heavenly feet had risen,
And gliding thro' the branches overbower'd

The naked Three, were wither'd long ago,
And thro' the sunless winter morning-mist
In silence wept upon the flowerless earth.
    And while she stared at those dead cords that ran   10
Dark thro' the mist, and linking tree to tree,
But once were gayer than a dawning sky
With many a pendent bell and fragrant star,
Her Past became her Present, and she saw
Him, climbing toward her with the golden fruit,
Him, happy to be chosen Judge of Gods,
Her husband in the flush of youth and dawn,
Paris, himself as beauteous as a God.
    Anon from out the long ravine below,
She heard a wailing cry, that seem'd at first   20
Thin as the batlike shrillings of the Dead
When driven to Hades, but, in coming near,
Across the downward thunder of the brook
Sounded "Œnone"; and on a sudden he,
Paris, no longer beauteous as a God,
Struck by a poison'd arrow in the fight,
Lame, crooked, reeling, livid, thro' the mist
Rose, like the wraith of his dead self, and moan'd:
    "Œnone, *my* Œnone, while we dwelt
Together in this valley — happy then —   30
Too happy had I died within thine arms,
Before the feud of Gods had marr'd our peace,
And sunder'd each from each. I am dying now
Pierced by a poison'd dart. Save me. Thou knowest,
Taught by some God, whatever herb or balm
May clear the blood from poison, and thy fame
Is blown thro' all the Troad, and to thee
The shepherd brings his adder-bitten lamb,
The wounded warrior climbs from Troy to thee.
My life and death are in thy hand. The Gods   40
Avenge on stony hearts a fruitless prayer
For pity. Let me owe my life to thee.
I wrought thee bitter wrong, but thou forgive,
Forget it. Man is but the slave of Fate.
Œnone, by thy love which once was mine,
Help, heal me. I am poison'd to the heart."
"And I to mine," she said. "Adulterer,
Go back to thine adulteress and die!"
    He groan'd, he turn'd, and in the mist at once
Became a shadow, sank and disappear'd,   50
But, ere the mountain rolls into the plain,

Fell headlong dead; and of the shepherds one
Their oldest, and the same who first had found
Paris, a naked babe, among the woods
Of Ida, following lighted on him there,
And shouted, and the shepherds heard and came.

    One raised the Prince, one sleek'd the squalid hair,
One kiss'd his hand, another closed his eyes,
And then, remembering the gay playmate rear'd
Among them, and forgetful of the man,   60
Whose crime had half unpeopled Ilion, these
All that day long labour'd, hewing the pines,
And built their shepherd-prince a funeral pile;
And, while the star of eve was drawing light
From the dead sun, kindled the pyre, and all
Stood round it, hush'd, or calling on his name.

    But when the white fog vanish'd like a ghost
Before the day, and every topmost pine
Spired into bluest heaven, still in her cave,
Amazed, and ever seeming stared upon   70
By ghastlier than the Gorgon head, a face, —
His face deform'd by lurid blotch and blain —
There, like a creature frozen to the heart
Beyond all hope of warmth, Œnone sat
Not moving, till in front of that ravine
Which drowsed in gloom, self-darken'd from the west,
The sunset blazed along the wall of Troy.

    Then her head sank, she slept, and thro' her dream
A ghostly murmur floated, "Come to me,
Œnone! I can wrong thee now no more,   80
Œnone, my Œnone," and the dream
Wail'd in her, when she woke beneath the stars.

    What star could burn so low? not Ilion yet.
What light was there? She rose and slowly down,
By the long torrent's ever-deepen'd roar,
Paced, following, as in a trance, the silent cry.
She waked a bird of prey that scream'd and past;
She roused a snake that hissing writhed away;
A panther sprang across her path, she heard
The shriek of some lost life among the pines,   90
But when she gain'd the broader vale, and saw
The ring of faces redden'd by the flames
Enfolding the dark body which had lain
Of old in her embrace, paused — and then ask'd
Falteringly, "Who lies on yonder pyre?"
But every man was mute for reverence.

Then moving quickly forward till the heat
Smote on her brow, she lifted up a voice
Of shrill command, "Who burns upon the pyre?"
Whereon their oldest and their boldest said,   100
"He, whom thou wouldst not heal!" and all at once
The morning light of happy marriage broke
Thro' all the clouded years of widowhood,
And muffling up her comely head, and crying
"Husband!" she leapt upon the funeral pile,
And mixt herself with *him* and past in fire.
1892*

From AKBAR'S DREAM

HYMN

I

Once again thou flamest heavenward, once again we see thee rise.
Every morning is thy birthday gladdening human hearts and eyes.
  Every morning here we greet it, bowing lowly down before thee,
Thee the Godlike, thee the changeless in thine ever-changing skies.

II

Shadow-maker, shadow-slayer, arrowing light from clime to clime,
Hear thy myriad laureates hail thee monarch in their woodland rhyme.
  Warble bird, and open flower, and, men, below the dome of azure
Kneel adoring Him the Timeless in the flame that measures Time!
1892*

POETS AND CRITICS

This thing, that thing is the rage,
Helter-skelter runs the age;
Minds on this round earth of ours
Vary like the leaves and flowers,
    Fashion'd after certain laws;
Sing thou low or loud or sweet,
All at all points thou canst not meet,
    Some will pass and some will pause.

What is true at last will tell:
Few at first will place thee well;   10

Some too low would have thee shine,
Some too high — no fault of thine —
   Hold thine own, and work thy will!
Year will graze the heel of year,
But seldom comes the poet here,
   And the Critic's rarer still.

1892

THE SILENT VOICES

When the dumb Hour, clothed in black,
Brings the Dreams about my bed,
Call me not so often back,
Silent Voices of the dead,
Toward the lowland ways behind me,
And the sunlight that is gone!
Call me rather, silent voices,
Forward to the starry track
Glimmering up the heights beyond me
On, and always on!

1892

CROSSING THE BAR

SUNSET and evening star,
   And one clear call for me!
And may there be no moaning of the bar,
   When I put out to sea,

But such a tide as moving seems asleep,
   Too full for sound and foam,
When that which drew from out the boundless deep
   Turns again home.

Twilight and evening bell,
   And after that the dark!   10
And may there be no sadness of farewell,
   When I embark;

For tho' from out our bourne of Time and Place
   The flood may bear me far,
I hope to see my Pilot face to face
   When I have crost the bar.

1889*

NOTES

ARMAGEDDON (page 1), a long fragmentary dream-vision, was first
published in 1931 by Sir Charles Tennyson, who ascribes it to "the
poet's fifteenth or sixteenth year." Tennyson drew freely on his manuscript, especially on the lines here reprinted, in composing his
Cambridge Prize Poem "Timbuctoo" (1829), which likewise describes
a "mystical" experience.

ODE TO MEMORY (page 3) appeared in 1830 with the subtitle "Written very Early in Life." Though clearly derivative in style, the piece is
remarkable for its first-hand descriptive detail, its evocation of the
Lincolnshire landscape, the garden at Somersby, and the sea at Mable-
thorpe. Memory, here the sense of an immediate past, already serves
as a guide to the world of the aesthetic imagination.

THE MYSTIC (page 6), suppressed after its appearance in 1830, may be
compared with the more personal "Armageddon," which is similarly
concerned with the intimations of eternity and implies a like detachment from life in society.

SUPPOSED CONFESSIONS OF A SECOND-RATE SENSITIVE MIND
(page 8) in 1830, "Supposed . . . Mind not in Unity with Itself" —
despite its half-ironic, half-apologetic title, remains an intensely personal poem, an early foreshadowing of the intellectual doubt of *In
Memoriam*.

THE KRAKEN (page 13): The kraken was a semi-mythical Norwegian
sea-monster of which Tennyson may have read as a child in an old
travel-book but which he here regards as an apocalyptic beast.

RECOLLECTIONS OF THE ARABIAN NIGHTS (page 14) describes
an aesthetic dream voyage to the pavilion of Haroun al Raschid, the
great eighth-century Caliph of Bagdad, poet, scholar, and patron of
the arts. It is reminiscent in decor of some of the exotic pieces in
Poems by Two Brothers.

THE SLEEPING BEAUTY (page 20) appeared in substantially this form
as a descriptive lyric in the 1830 volume. In 1842 it became the third
section of "The Day-Dream," a complete and rather elaborate rendering of the fairy-tale.

A CHARACTER (page 21): Sunderland, the ablest debater in the Cambridge Union, has been identified as the original of this portrait. Tennyson here sees him as the type or "character" of the intellectual
dilettante or self-pleased aesthete.

SIR LAUNCELOT AND QUEEN GUINEVERE (page 24) is Tennyson's earliest extant poem on an Arthurian subject, written (according to the *Memoir*) "partly if not wholly . . . in 1830." Unlike the complex passionate Queen of the *Idylls*, Guinevere is here all innocence and beauty, and Lancelot is hardly to be blamed for succumbing to her charm.

THE LADY OF SHALOTT (page 25), much revised after first publication in 1832, is a carefully wrought allegory of art and life, suggested (according to Palgrave) by "an Italian romance upon the Donna di Scalotta." The Lady reappears as "the lily maid of Astolat" in "Lancelot and Elaine" (1859).

ŒNONE (page 32), likewise much altered between 1832 and 1842, is the earliest of Tennyson's great classical idyls. As an "idyl" it translates its epic material into "a little picture." Œnone, the nymph of Mount Ida whom Paris deserted for Helen of Troy ("the Greek woman" of l. 257), remembers her lost lover and particularly the occasion of his momentous "choice." But Œnone's unreasoning passion parallels that of Paris, who rejects the wisdom of Pallas (l. 135 f.); and the end of the poem makes it clear that her private doom is but an image of the destruction of Troy itself. Aphrodite (ll. 170–178), or Venus, was worshipped in Idalium (hence "Idalian") and Paphos (hence "Paphian"), cities of Cyprus.

TO —— WITH THE FOLLOWING POEM (page 38): These lines were apparently addressed to Richard Trench, one of the Cambridge Apostles, later Archbishop of Dublin, an able scholar and a writer of moralistic verse. Trench it was who reminded the poet, "Tennyson, we cannot live in art."

THE PALACE OF ART (page 39), much revised after first publication, is, as the introduction suggests, "a sort of allegory" of selfish art and human love. A few of its many allusions may be glossed: St. Cecily (l. 99), St. Cecilia, patron saint of music, said to have invented the organ; Uther's son (105), King Arthur, carried at death to the paradisal isle of Avalon (107); Ausonian king (111), Numa Pompilius, in legend the second king of Rome, taught by the nymph Egeria; Cama (115), Hindu god of love; Europa (117), Phoenician princess carried off by Zeus disguised as a bull; Ganymede (121), Trojan boy borne to Olympus by Zeus as an eagle to become cupbearer to the gods; Ionian father (137), Homer; Verulam (163), Francis Bacon, Baron Verulam; Memnon (171), Theban statue reputed to issue music when struck by the morning light; "Mene, mene" (227), the writing on the wall of Belshazzar's palace (see Daniel 5:5–26).

THE HESPERIDES (page 47), suppressed after its appearance in 1832, is Tennyson's warmest celebration of a "pure" art. The Hesperides, daughters of Evening in Greek myth, were guardians, assisted by the dragon Ladon, of a sacred tree bearing golden apples. Hanno (l. 2) was an actual explorer of ancient Carthage; the introduction describes his travels along the African coast.

THE LOTOS-EATERS (page 50), another poem greatly revised for republication in 1842, was suggested by a passage in the *Odyssey*, which describes the discovery by Ulysses (the *he* of l. 1) and his men of lotos-land on the North African coast and of the lotos bloom, a sort of "tranquilizer" that brings dreamful ease. The "island home" (l. 44) is Ithaca. Contrast the mood of the Choric Song with that of "Ulysses" (p. 66).

A DREAM OF FAIR WOMEN (page 55) is a dream-vision in the tradition of Chaucer and the medieval poets. The women who pass across the dream are Helen of Troy (l. 85 f.); Iphigenia (100 f.), daughter of Agamemnon, the Greek commander against the Trojans, sacrificed to Artemis before the departure of her father's forces; Cleopatra (127 f.), who commanded the passion of Mark Antony but who could not beguile Octavius Caesar (139, 155); Jephthah's daughter (178 f.), sacrificed to fulfil her father's rash vow (see Judges 11:30–40); and Rosamond Clifford (249 f.), mistress of Henry II, allegedly murdered by Eleanor of Aquitaine. Fulvia (259) was Mark Antony's Roman wife. She who clasped her father's head (266) was Margaret Roper, daughter of Sir Thomas More. The queen who saved her poisoned husband (269–272) was Eleanor of Castile, wife of Edward I.

TO —— (page 63) was almost certainly addressed to Arthur Hallam.

TO CHRISTOPHER NORTH (page 63): "North," whose real name was John Wilson, had reviewed Tennyson's 1830 volume in *Blackwood's Edinburgh Magazine* for May, 1832; his criticism had freely mingled "blame and praise."

TO J. S. (page 64) is an elegy addressed to James Spedding on the death of his brother Edward. James, an Apostle and one of Tennyson's closest Cambridge friends, was to distinguish himself as editor of the works of Bacon.

ULYSSES (page 66), written in 1833 soon after Hallam's death, expresses Tennyson's "feeling about the need of going forward." The poem derives in idea from Ulysses' description of his last voyage in Dante's *Inferno* (Canto XXVI); but whereas Dante condemns the Greek's curiosity and presumption, Tennyson exalts the eternally restless aspiration.

TITHONUS (page 68) was written at least in rough form at about the same time as "Ulysses," to which it stands as a sort of complement. In Greek myth Tithonus of Troy, loved by Eos, goddess of the Dawn, was granted immortality but not eternal youth; oppressed by age, he was ultimately turned into a grasshopper. Compare Swift's mordant treatment of the Struldbrugs in *Gulliver's Travels*, who like Tithonus must live on forever, a fearful burden to themselves.

THE TWO VOICES (page 70), called in manuscript "The Thoughts of a Suicide," was written in the troubled months immediately following Hallam's death. "I was so utterly miserable," Tennyson explained, "a burden to myself and to my family, that I said, 'Is life worth anything?' "

ST. AGNES' EVE (page 89): According to a medieval legend (the basis of Keats' "Eve of St. Agnes"), a young girl following a prescribed ritual might expect to envision her future husband on January 20, the eve of the martyrdom of St. Agnes. In Tennyson's poem, a young nun has a vision of the Heavenly Bridegroom.

MOVE EASTWARD, HAPPY EARTH (page 90) was apparently written in 1836 on the occasion of Charles Tennyson Turner's marriage, at which time Tennyson seems first to have declared his own love for Emily Sellwood, sister of the bride.

A FAREWELL (page 90) seems to have been written in 1837 at the time of the family's removal from Somersby and to be addressed to the brook near the vicarage.

THE EPIC (page 91) and AUDLEY COURT (page 93) belong to the series Tennyson later called the "English Idyls"; both are designed as genre pictures of early-Victorian rural society. "The Epic" serves as a modern frame for the heroic "Morte d' Arthur" and thus as an apology for the resort to epical subject matter.

LOVE AND DUTY (page 95), we may assume, relates to the breaking in 1840 of Tennyson's engagement to Emily Sellwood.

WILL WATERPROOF'S LYRICAL MONOLOGUE (page 97): "The Cock," where these verses were made, was Tennyson's favorite London tavern in the late 1830's.

LOCKSLEY HALL (page 104) should be read as a dramatic monologue. Though the speaker in his sensitivity resembles Tennyson and in his violence Tennyson's brother Frederick, he is less significant as an individual than as a spokesman of early-Victorian ideas and emotions.

AMPHION (page 117): In Greek myth Amphion was so accomplished a harper that his music lifted building stones into place. Tennyson assigns to him a power over the whole life of nature.

THE NEW TIMON AND THE POETS (page 119): Edward Bulwer-Lytton, remembering Shakespeare's angry man, Timon of Athens, in 1845 published *The New Timon*, a satire on his own age and its literary life, in the course of which he accused Tennyson of "outbabying Wordsworth and outglittering Keates [*sic*]." In reply Tennyson wrote the present piece, a devastating attack on Bulwer's flagrant dandyism, which without his permission was sent by a friend to *Punch*.

TO —— AFTER READING A LIFE AND LETTERS (page 121) seems to have been addressed to Charles Tennyson Turner, the poet's brother, who had largely abandoned poetry for the life of a country clergyman. The literary biography was possibly Richard Monckton Milnes's *Life, Letters and Literary Remains of John Keats* (1848).

THE PRINCESS (page 123), as its subtitle suggests, is a "medley" both of styles and themes. Though the mock-heroic verse with which the story of Princess Ida begins has a true comic gusto, Tennyson brings the piece to a wholly serious, a too earnest close, which, as the Conclusion predicts, may satisfy neither the mockers nor the realists. The great blank-verse lyrics appeared in the first edition (1847); the intercalary songs, all in rhyme, were included in 1850; and the passages describing the "weird seizures" of the Prince were added in 1851. The poem supports as well as burlesques the cause of feminism; but the larger conflict, as in "The Palace of Art," is the struggle between art and nature, and the resolution is best suggested by the beautifully wrought mountain-idyl, "Come Down, O Maid."

IN MEMORIAM (page 178), as Professor Whitehead observes in *Science and the Modern World,* belongs among such intellectual landmarks as *Paradise Lost* and Pope's *Essay on Man,* insofar as "it exactly expressed the character of its period." More clearly indeed than any other Victorian poem, it reflects the impact on a quick sensibility of the wondrous and alarming new philosophies which called into question the great traditions of a humanistic culture. From the Prologue to the marriage song with which it concludes, it seeks repeatedly to relate its private emotions to the general doubt, fear, and tentative hope engendered by the new science of the nineteenth century, especially by the geology of Lyell, the astronomy of Herschel, and the biology of the pre-Darwinians. What value and permanence, it asks, can the individual spirit retain in a world of ageless time and infinite space and unending evolutionary change? It thus spoke with special cogency to the generation of 1850, when it was first published; and its speculations on the nature and condition of man have a considerable relevance to our own time. But the poem must be approached and estimated as poetry, and its generalities must be seen first of all in the context of its particular "action" or drama. *In Memoriam* is, of course, an elegy rather than a religious epic or a didactic essay. It is a deeply personal tribute to Arthur Henry Hallam (1811–1833), who for his last five years was Tennyson's closest friend and confidant and whose influence persisted throughout Tennyson's life. Hallam had been the most animated young man among the Cambridge Apostles; and his college friends, some of them later scholars and statesmen of high distinction, had been uniformly impressed by his qualities of mind and character. Tennyson as elegist is fully aware of the loss suffered by society in Hallam's death; yet he feels a much more personal bereavement in that Hallam had been his constant companion, more understanding of his moods than his own brothers, and, as fiancé of his sister Emily, was soon actually to have joined the Tennyson family circle.

The lyrics that constitute the poem, scattered through Tennyson's notebooks like entries in a diary, were written over some sixteen years from the receipt of the death news in October, 1833, to the writing of the Prologue in 1849, when they were arranged in the present sequence. The "action" and the progress of the emotion, "the way of the soul," are dated or marked off by the parallel Christmas poems: XXX, Christmas of 1833, at the close of the period from Hallam's death in Vienna to the return of his body to England and its burial; LXXVIII, presumably Christmas of 1834; and CV, Christmas of 1837, just after the removal of the Tennysons from Somersby. The epilogue, dated "thrice three years" from the "dark day" of Hallam's death, concerns the marriage of Cecilia Tennyson to Edmund Lushington, the friend to whom LXXXV is also addressed. *In Memoriam* is packed with references not only to such private affairs but also to Tennyson's readings in the Bible, the classics, and modern literature; and a good many of its allusions require a rather detailed glossing. Of the several attempts to elucidate the poem as a whole, the most useful remains A. C. Bradley's *Commentary* (1901), which will supply a copious though still incomplete supplement to my necessarily meager notes below.

I: The singer to one clear harp seems to be Goethe.

VII: The dark house is the Hallam residence at 67 Wimpole Street in London.

IX–XVII: These sections describe the passage of the ship bringing Hallam's body to England. The "thou" addressed is the ship.

XVIII: This section describes the burial at Clevedon by the Bristol Channel. The "pure hands" are the local farmers who acted as pallbearers. The second last stanza alludes to the mode of resuscitation used by Elisha (see II Kings 4:32–37).

XIX: Hallam who died at Vienna, on the Danube, was buried near the Severn River. The Wye as a tributary of the Severn is partly tidal.

XXIII: Like several other sections, this one draws on the traditions of the pastoral elegy — hence the references to Pan as god of nature, the Argive (or Greek) hills, and Arcadia, the home of the shepherd-poets.

XXXIII: The "thou" addressed is any theological liberal who may feel his broadened faith superior to a more literal creed.

XXXVII: Urania is the muse of Astronomy, hence of Heavenly Poetry, and Melpomene is the muse of Tragedy or (as here) of Elegy. Parnassus is the Greek mountain abode of all the muses.

LII: The "sinless years" describe Christ's earthly life.

LVI: This section, one of the most significant in the intellectual argument of the poem, foreshadows the work of Darwin, but it was written, we are told, even before the appearance of Chambers's *Vestiges of Creation* (1844). It is probably indebted to Lyell's *Geology*.

LVII: This is a dirge addressed perhaps to Emily Tennyson, who had been Hallam's fiancée.

LXVII: The "broad water" is the Severn River.

LXXI: The first stanza refers to the visit made by Tennyson and Hallam to the French Pyrenees in the summer of 1830.

LXXII: The "dim dawn" is September 15, 1834, the first anniversary of Hallam's death. As in the conventional pastoral elegy, nature is here depicted as suffering a sympathetic death.

LXXIX: This section is addressed to Tennyson's favorite brother, Charles Tennyson Turner.

LXXXV: This section is addressed to Edmund Lushington, Professor of Greek at Glasgow.

LXXXVII: The "reverend walls" are the walls of Trinity at Cambridge.

LXXXVIII: The "wild bird" is the nightingale.

LXXXIX: Hallam, having left the Inner Temple where he was studying law, visits Somersby.

XCV: This section, the climax of the poem, describes a family gathering on the lawn at Somersby and then a solitary mystical experience, which brings reassurance of the infinite life.

XCVI: The last stanza alludes to the revelation of the law to Moses on Mount Sinai and the lawless worship of the golden calf by the Israelites (see Exodus 19:16–25 and 32:1–6).

XCVIII: The "you" is Charles Tennyson Turner setting off on his honeymoon and planning to visit the Rhine valley (where Tennyson had been with Hallam in 1832) and Vienna (where Hallam died).

XCIX: This marks another anniversary of Hallam's death; *cf*. sec. LXXII.

C–CIII: These sections concern the removal of the Tennysons from Somersby to High Beech near London.

CIII: According to Tennyson the maidens of the allegorical dream are both the muses and the highest human attributes that may endure beyond earthly life. The river is life; the sea, eternity. Anakim are powerful giants, the sons of Anak (see Numbers 13:33).

CVII: Hallam's birthday was February 1.

CXIV: Pallas Athena, Greek goddess of wisdom, sprang from the brain of Zeus.

CXX: "Paul" is the Apostle, who fought with beasts (see I Corinthians 15:32).

CXXI: This section, greatly admired by Gerard Manley Hopkins, correlates the twin aspects of Venus, the planet of love: Hesper, the evening star (hence a death symbol), and Phosphor, the morning star (token of life and renewal).

CXXVII: The second stanza, Tennyson explained, refers to the barricades of Paris during the revolution of 1830.

The epilogue addressed to Lushington (*cf.* sec. LXXXV) is an epithalamium, for which Tennyson found precedent in the traditions of the pastoral elegy. The eighth stanza alludes to the stars that shook Jupiter's approval of the marriage of Thetis and Peleus.

DE PROFUNDIS (page 260) was written, or at least begun, in August, 1852, on the birth of Hallam, the poet's elder son. The title means "from the depths" or (as in l. 1) "out of the deep."

ODE ON THE DEATH OF THE DUKE OF WELLINGTON (page 262): As Poet Laureate, Tennyson here commemorates a great public event, the funeral of the hero of Waterloo, at St. Paul's Cathedral on November 18, 1852. The "Mighty Seaman" (l. 83) is Lord Nelson, the greatest British naval leader during the Napoleonic wars, killed at Trafalgar in 1805.

TO E. L. ON HIS TRAVELS IN GREECE (page 269) is addressed to Edward Lear, author of inspired nonsense and master of the limerick, known also in his own time for several illustrated travel-books, especially his *Landscape-Painter in Albania and Illyria* (1851), to which Tennyson here alludes.

THE DAISY (page 270) is addressed by Tennyson in Edinburgh to his wife at home, recalling their belated honeymoon in Italy during the summer of 1851. A fine example of the verse letter, it is also an exercise in an original meter, involving an extra syllable in the last line of each stanza. The "Lari Maxume" (l. 76) is "Larius the Greatest," Virgil's name in the *Georgics* for Lake Como. The "Lariano" (78) is a small lake boat.

TO THE REV. F. D. MAURICE (page 273): Before Tennyson's time at Cambridge, Maurice had been leader of the "Apostles"; in the 1850's he was the strongest force behind the Christian Socialist movement and, though a devout churchman, was frequently charged with heterodoxy. The poet here in his best Horatian style invites him to visit Farringford on the Isle of Wight, where he may see his godson Hallam Tennyson and discuss among friends the condition of England and the war in Crimea.

THE CHARGE OF THE LIGHT BRIGADE (page 274), circulated in this final version among the soldiers in Crimea, commemorates the disastrous charge against the Russian batteries at Balaclava (October 25, 1854), occasioned (according to *The Times'* report which Tennyson read) by "some hideous blunder" of the commanding officer. For a spirited modern account of the engagement, see Cecil Woodham-Smith's *The Reason Why*.

MAUD (page 277), Tennyson's favorite poem for reading aloud, was developed from the lyric "O that 't were possible," which had appeared (with some significant differences) in *The Tribute* for 1837. As a "monodrama," in which the varying moods of a single character replace the various persons of a drama, *Maud* was designed as "the history of a morbid poetic soul under the blighting influence of a recklessly speculative age." Though at pains to dissociate himself from the morbidity and madness, Tennyson seems to endorse much of his hero's indictment of a materialistic society. As the poem begins, Maud, promised to the hero even before her birth, returns with her brother and father from long residence abroad — presumably to marry the "new-made lord" (Part I, l. 332). She is forbidden to speak to the hero, whose father had been ruined by a speculation which enriched her father. Nevertheless, they do meet and pledge themselves to each other. When Maud's brother intervenes, the hero kills him in a duel, escapes to Brittany, and suffers an attack of insanity. Maud apparently dies (off-stage) of a broken heart; but her "ghastly Wraith" (Part II, l. 32) haunts the hero until "the dreary phantom" (Part III, l. 36) is exorcised by his losing himself in a larger cause, a concerted social action, the war in Crimea. In Part I, Timour (l. 46) is Tamerlane, the brutal Asian conqueror of the fourteenth century. Isis (144) is the Egyptian goddess, a veiled statue of whom stood at Saïs. Poland (147) was partitioned in 1846, and Hungary was defeated in its revolt from Austria in 1849. The "broad-brimmed" hat (370) as worn by the Quakers may perhaps identify John Bright, a political leader opposed to England's role in the Crimean war. "Gorgonized" (464) means turned to stone as by the petrifying aspect of Medusa. Of line 651 Tennyson remarked, "This is the central idea, the holy power of Love." In Part II, Lamech (96) is the Biblical character (Genesis 4:23) who lamented having killed a young man. The references of ll. 290–291 may seem obscure: "him" is Maud's brother, the "wolf" is her father. The Norwegian "rat" (296) that came to England in the eighteenth century was brought, said the Jacobites, by George I from Hanover in 1714. In Part III, the "Lion" (14) is Leo, a northern constellation.

IN THE VALLEY OF CAUTERETZ (page 314), written on Tennyson's return in the summer of 1861 to Cauteretz in the French Pyrenees, recalls his first visit to the valley with Arthur Hallam thirty-one (not thirty-two, as in the poem) years earlier.

HELEN'S TOWER (page 314), written in 1861, though later somewhat revised for publication, was inscribed on a tower erected by Lord Dufferin on his Irish estate as a memorial to his mother, Helen, Countess of Gifford. The fourth line refers to birthday verses once made by Lady Gifford for her son and now engraved on the tower.

MILTON (page 314) is an experiment in imitation of the Greek Alcaic measure, according to the fixed pattern of which each stanza consists of two lines of eleven syllables followed by one of nine and one of ten syllables. As in all classical "quantitative" verse, a heavy stress must fall on each long vowel and each short one followed by two consonantal sounds, whereas in standard English "qualitative" verse the heavy stress falls on the accented syllables.

ENOCH ARDEN (page 318), once the most popular of Tennyson's poems, translated into many languages, had its origin in a story told to the poet by the Pre-Raphaelite sculptor Thomas Woolner. The often labored simplicity of the piece and its many touches of sentimental "realism" have but little appeal to most modern readers, who in any case look to prose fiction rather than to verse for narratives of domesticity.

NORTHERN FARMER (OLD STYLE) (page 340), a dramatic monologue in Lincolnshire dialect, presents an old farm-bailiff (or land-agent) who, though dying, insists, against his doctor's orders, upon having his customary pint of ale. The reader many find some of the following glosses a helpful supplement to Tennyson's footnotes: line 1, "Where hast thou been . . . me lying here alone"; 2, "Nurse, thou art no good of a nurse"; 3, "I may not have any more ale"; 5, *a,* he; 11, "he told me my sins, and his tithe was due"; 13, "Learned he may be"; 14, "he brought up against me . . . about Bessy's child"; 16, *raäte,* poor-law tax; 23, "In any case, I supported him"; 27, *summun,* i.e., David (Psalms 116:11, "I said in my haste, All men are liars"); 28, *stubbed,* cleared for farming; 30, *boggle,* ghost; 32, *raäved an' rembled,* plowed up and threw away; 33, "It was the gamekeeper's (ghost), for they found him there lying on his face"; 35, Noaks or Thimbleby had shot him; 36, *soize,* assizes, court trial; 37, "Do but . . . "; 40, *yows,* ewes; 41, *nobbut,* only; 42, *ta-year,* this year; 46, "I am not one who sows . . . "; 49, "He might have taken old Jones who hasn't a half-penny worth of sense"; 52, *cauve,* calve; 54, *sewer-loy,* surely; 58, "that quite baffles me"; 61, "kettle of steam," the new steam thresher; 62, "worrying and annoying the . . . fields"; 66, "Doctor's a teetoaler, and he's always telling the same old story"; 67, *floy,* fly.

NORTHERN FARMER (NEW STYLE) (page 342) presents an independent land holder conscious of his "proputty" as he gives advice to his son Sam on the subject of marriage. The dialect continues: line 5, "a crow to pluck," an argument to settle, a bone to pick; 14, "scores of girls"; 24, "a lass that has nothing"; 27, *nobbut,* only; 28, *ligs,* lies; *shere,* shire, county; 30, "he hasn't got rid of them (the debts) yet"; 31, *grip,* ditch; 38, *burn,* born; 41, *esh,* ash; 52, "But he struggled and worked himself to death"; 55, *brig,* bridge.

LUCRETIUS (page 344), both an appreciation and an implicit judgment of the Roman philosopher (c. 99–55 B.C.), is rich in images and ideas drawn from his great poem *De Rerum Natura* ("On the Nature of Things"). Tennyson pictures Lucretius (under the influence of a love potion administered by his wife Lucilia), disgusted that sensuality has betrayed the life of reason and convinced that suicide alone will provide release. The teacher (l. 13) is Epicurus, also referred to as "My master" (116). The "Cadmean teeth" (50) are the teeth of the dragon slain by Cadmus of Thebes, from which sprang armed warriors. The "mulberry-faced Dictator" (54) is Sulla (or Sylla), who after a tyrannic rule (82–79 B.C.) retired to a dissolute old age, attended by his courtesans, the "Hetairai" (52). Lucretius celebrated Venus in the "procemium" (70), the introduction, to his poem. He now calls upon her to restrain Mavors (82), Mars, from further bloodshed in Rome; yet the Venus he entreats is not the amorist who seduced Anchises the Trojan (88), made love to Adonis (90), and attracted young Paris (91), but the Venus, the Cyprian (Kypris, 95), whom he Lucretius once took to symbolize the generative power of nature. The Sicilian (93) is Empedocles, who invoked Calliope, the muse of epic poetry. The *De Rerum Natura* was dedicated to C. Memmius Gemellus (*cf.* 119). Ovid tells how King Numa seized the gods Picus and Faunus (182) to extort from them some divine secrets. In lines 235–240 Lucretius recalls the heroic Lucretia who, ravished by Tarquin (Collatine) committed suicide; her example served to stimulate resistance to the Tarquins, which led to the establishment of the Roman Republic, now threatened, as Lucretius sees, with final collapse.

IN THE GARDEN AT SWAINSTON (page 352): Swainston on the Isle of Wight near Tennyson's Farringford was the home of Sir John Simeon, one of Tennyson's closest friends. This lyric, written in the week of Sir John's funeral, places him beside the two dead men dearest to the poet's memory, Arthur Hallam and Harry Lushington.

IDYLLS OF THE KING (page 353), Tennyson's most ambitious work, occupied his attention at intervals from the writing of the "Morte d'Arthur" in 1833 till the final ordering of the twelve parts fifty-five years later. Four "Idylls" (the word so spelled to distinguish the poem from the "English Idyls") appeared in 1859 centered on the theme of true love and false: "Enid" (finally divided as "The Marriage of Geraint" and "Geraint and Enid"), "Vivien" (later "Merlin and Vivien"), "Elaine" ("Lancelot and Elaine"), and "Guinevere." Except for "Enid," drawn from the Welsh *Mabinogian,* all of these pieces and the seven other "Idylls" were derived primarily from Malory's *Morte d'Arthur,* though Tennyson felt free to supplement Malory with other sources, to make original additions, and in general to adapt his materials to his own designs. His central purpose became apparent with the publication in 1869 of "The Coming of Arthur," "Pelleas and Ettarre," "The Holy Grail," and "The Passing of Arthur" (this last incorporating his early "Morte d'Arthur"); he would trace through narrative and description the rise and decline of a goodly fellowship and suggest through symbol and allegory the values on which the health of any good society must depend. To complete his pattern he wrote "Gareth and Lynette" (1872), a study of innocence and young idealism, to stand near the beginning of the sequence; "Balin and Balan" (1885), a tale of evil commingling with good, to come near the middle; and "The Last Tournament" (1871), a dark and bitter parallel to the tragedy of Lancelot and Guinevere, to be placed near the end. Both "The Coming of Arthur" and the epilogue "To the Queen" (1872) intimate the moral intention of the whole and its relevance to a modern world.

THE COMING OF ARTHUR (page 353): The "three fair queens" (l. 275) may represent Faith, Hope, and Charity, though Tennyson preferred to explain them as larger and more elusive symbols, "three Graces" and "the noblest of women"; they reappear in

"The Passing of Arthur" (l. 366). The Lady of the Lake (282) represents the Church. Urim (298) refers to certain objects, probably jewels, valued as symbols of revelation by the Hebrew high priests (see Exodus 28:30).

MERLIN AND VIVIEN (page 365): Broceliande (l. 2) is in Brittany. The "gray cricket" (108) is the minstrel (9); Vivien habitually resorts to an animal imagery — *cf.* "reckling" (707), the weakest puppy in a litter, hence a weakling infant. Merlin (471 f.) uses heraldic terms; "dexter chief" describes the upper corner of a shield against the bearer's right side.

THE HOLY GRAIL (page 388): In the middle ages the Grail was either the cup from which Christ drank at the Last Supper or the dish in which Joseph of Arimathea caught the blood of Christ on the cross; Tennyson combines the two legends. "Aromat" (48) is a poetic variation of Arimathea. The Siege Perilous (172) is the chair designed by Merlin to test the character of men; Tennyson said that it represented the "spiritual imagination." Taliessin (300) is a renowned Welsh bard of the sixth century. The wyvern and the griffin (350) are grotesque heraldic animals with great wings. The "paynims" (661), or pagans, as survivors of the Druids, worshipped or held tribal rites in stone circles like those at Stonehenge. While the knights are off on the Grail quest, the city (713–717) has suffered neglect and the proud heraldic animals carved on its walls and and roof-eaves have fallen in the dust. Cana (759) was the scene of Christ's first miracle, the changing of the water into wine (see John 2:1–10).

PELLEAS AND ETTARRE (page 410): Far from being the knight of perfect courtesy as in older tradition, Gawain here appears as a self-seeking opportunist whose betrayal of chivalry is but one more indication of a failing ethic in Arthur's society. The young Gareth of the second Idyll is rewarded for his innocence and idealism; the young Pelleas here is completely disillusioned. In line 421 "lurdane" means stupid and lazy.

THE LAST TOURNAMENT (page 425), one of the most skillfully executed of the Idylls, is a grim and "unromantic" reworking of the romance of Tristram and Isolt. The "carcanet" (l. 6) won by Tristram is a necklace. "Vail'd" (50) means lowered, not veiled. To "caracole" (206) in horsemanship is to make half-turns to right and left. The "daintier namesake" (265) of Isolt is Isolt of the White Hands, Tristram's wife left behind in Brittany. The "Paynim harper" (322) is Orpheus. In hunting, "slot and fewmets" (371) are footprints and droppings. Alioth and Alcor (479) are stars in the Great Bear. Line 481 refers to the Moabites who saw water as red as blood (see II Kings 3:22). "Roky" (501) means foggy. A "levin-brand" (611) is a flash of lightning.

GUINEVERE (page 443) draws but little from any source apart from Tennyson's own imagination. The "housel" and "shrift" (l. 147) are the Eucharist and confession. Bude and Bos (289) are areas of Cornwall. The "Pendragonship" (594) was the headship of the Britons, whose emblem was the Dragon. To "vail" (657) is to lower.

THE PASSING OF ARTHUR (page 460) expands the "Morte d'Arthur" of the 1842 volume by adding an introduction (ll. 1–169) and a conclusion (ll. 441–469); so ably has Tennyson fused the old and the new verses that no shift in style is apparent. "Lief" (248) means beloved. The "streamer of the northern morn" (307) is the northern lights, and the "isles of winter" (308) are icebergs. The three queens (366) appear in "The Coming of Arthur" (l. 275).

TO THE QUEEN (page 471): The "rememberable day" (l. 3) was the occasion of the public appearance of Victoria and her son Edward, Prince of Wales, in February, 1872, on the recovery of the latter from typhoid fever. The "thunderless lightnings . . . under sea" (12) are cabled messages from abroad. The "true North" (14) is the newly confederated Dominion of Canada. Hougoumont (20) was the castle occupied by the British as a key position at the battle of Waterloo. The "one" (35) is Albert, Prince Consort, to whom Tennyson dedicated the *Idylls*. Geoffrey (42) is Geoffrey of Monmouth, the twelfth-century author of a history of Britain, who set down many of the Arthurian legends; Malleor is, of course, Sir Thomas Malory, author of *Morte d'Arthur* (1470).

SIR JOHN FRANKLIN (page 474): Since Tennyson's wife was Sir John Franklin's niece, the poet felt a special concern with the fate of the great Arctic explorer who had perished — it was learned after long years of search — in 1847 in his effort to survey the far north of Canada and possibly to reach the North Pole.

THE REVENGE (page 474): In 1591 Sir Richard Grenville, who some years earlier had led a colonizing mission to America, was given command of *The Revenge* in a small fleet under Lord Thomas Howard assigned to the Azores to waylay Spanish cargo-vessels returning from the West Indies. Though Spain sent fifty-three warships against Howard's sixteen, Grenville refused to flee until he had taken all his sick men aboard *The Revenge*. Then only did he attempt to drive through the encircling Spanish fleet. He was finally forced to surrender but not before he had fiercely fought off the enemy for fifteen hours, had lost all but twenty of his men, and had himself received mortal wounds.

PREFATORY POEM TO MY BROTHER'S SONNETS (page 478) was written as a tribute to Tennyson's brother Charles (1808–1879) and used as preface to the collected sonnets (1880).

THE VOYAGE OF MAELDUNE (page 479) was based, we are told, on the story of Maildune as it appears in P. W. Joyce's *Old Celtic Romances* (1879), but most of the details are of Tennyson's own invention. Finn (l. 48), father of Ossian, was the greatest legendary chieftain of Erin. St. Brandon (115), sailor saint of sixth-century Ireland, is reputed to have reached the North American continent on his voyages. Stanza X is said to symbolize the disputes between Protestants and Roman Catholics.

RIZPAH (page 487): The Biblical Rizpah (II Samuel 21:8–11) stood guard over the bones of her sons hanged by the Gibeonites. The English mother who here, as she lies dying, tells her story to a visiting evangelical charity-worker, has secretly gathered and buried the bones of her son from the gibbet where he was hanged, according to eighteenth-century law, for robbing a mail coach.

"FRATER AVE ATQUE VALE" (page 490), written on Tennyson's visit in the summer of 1880 to Lake Garda where Catullus had once main-tained his country-house, is a beautifully cadenced tribute to the Roman lyrist, rich in its echoes and translations from the Latin, warm in its original response to both the landscape and the poet. The title, "Brother, hail and farewell," from Catullus' elegiac lines to his brother, had a particular significance to Tennyson as he remembered the recent death of his own brother Charles. Desenzano is a town on Lake Garda about three miles from Sirmione, the "lovely Sirmio" — "O venusta Sirmio" — of Catullus, the peninsula ("all-but-island") where he lived.

TO VIRGIL (page 490): Virgil (70–19 B.C.), to whom Tennyson all his life felt a strong personal affinity as artist, was the foremost of the Latin poets. A native of rural Mantua — hence Mantovano (stanza X) — he was much concerned with a country subject matter, as in the *Georgics* (alluded to in III) and the pastoral *Eclogues* (*cf.* reference in IV to the shepherd Tityrus). Yet he is first of all remem-bered for his epic of great cities, the *Aeneid* (I) in which he achieved his prophetic view of the course of human civilization (VI, VII). The author of *Works and Days* (II) was the Greek poet Hesiod. Pollio (V) was Virgil's patron.

TIRESIAS (page 492), though begun at about the time of "Ulysses," was not completed till fifty years later. The dedication to Edward Fitz Gerald, translator of Omar Khayyám's *Rubáiyát* and one of Tennyson's oldest friends, was written shortly before Fitz Gerald's death in June of 1883 and the concluding lines (178–209) soon afterwards. (Fitz, as the introduction intimates, was a teetotaler and a vegetarian, a "Pythagorean"; Tennyson, on the other hand, when following the diet, craved meat and had dreams of "Eshcol" grapes, the winy fruit of Canaan). Tiresias, stricken blind in his far-off youth when he looked on Athena in her bath (38–49) and given the gift of prophecy with-out the power of compelling men to believe his word, here tells the young Menœceus what he must do to save Thebes from destruction. Menœceus, son of Creon, was of the race of Cadmus (13), who incurred the wrath of Ares (Mars) by slaying the dragon guarding the sacred springs of Dirce. Thebes had been "song-built" (96) to the music of Amphion's harp. The reference in l. 147 is to Oedipus who solved the riddle of the Sphinx. Tiresias becomes Tennyson's image of disillusioned age alienated from all social vanities and devoted to eternal values.

THE ANCIENT SAGE (page 498), the fullest statement of Tennyson's lifelong mystical experience and his late idealistic philosophy, assigns its argument to an aged prophet, a figure suggested by the poet's reading of Lao-tse, the saintly seer of China in the seventh century B.C. The young man's scroll from which the sage recites supplies the matter of a debate somewhat reminiscent in movement of "The Two Voices."

LOCKSLEY HALL SIXTY YEARS AFTER (page 508), published forty-four years after the first "Locksley Hall," continues the melodramatic story. The speaker, now eighty years old, has long been reconciled to Amy and her husband, but he is now violently opposed to Judith, the fiancée of his grandson. What concerns us more, however, than the narrative is the disillusioned commentary on nineteenth-century life and literature, some of which appears in the stanzas here reprinted. The opinions, though expressed with some hysteria, often run parallel to Tennyson's own.

DEMETER AND PERSEPHONE (page 510): In the Greek vegetation myth Demeter, goddess of the earth, neglected to foster the harvest when she learned that her daughter Persephone had been carried off by Aïdoneus (or Dis) to become his queen of Hades. Lest the life of nature die, Zeus — the "He" of Tennyson's poem (l. 115) — arranged to return Persephone to Demeter for nine months of each year, though she was to pass the remainder — the winter — in the under-world. In the present monologue Demeter speaks just as Persephone on a visit to earth awakens at Eleusis, a town near Athens where Demeter was worshipped. The god of ghosts (5) is Hermes. Phlegethon (28) is the infernal river of fire. In l. 148 the stone (of Sisyphus) and the wheel (of Ixion) represent the torments of Hades. Demeter's final vision of love (126 f.) is intended as an anticipation of Christian charity.

PARNASSUS (page 514): The epigraph from Horace, loosely paraphrased in stanza I, means: "I have completed myself a monument which the passage of uncounted years cannot destroy." Parnassus was the sacred mount of poetry which the Muses helped great bards to ascend. Tennyson sees the terrible modern muses, Astronomy and Geology, the concepts of infinite space and endless time, mocking all the pride and aspiration of human beings. He concludes, however, that the true Pierian inspiration is valid at all times and in all places.

MERLIN AND THE GLEAM (page 515), designed as a poetic auto-biography, traces in broad outline the course of Tennyson's develop-ment. The Gleam is "the higher poetic imagination." The Raven of stanza III may represent the hostility of the early reviewers or possibly the opposition of Tennyson's grandfather. There follow references to the "Romantic" pieces of 1842, the domestic idyls and then (VI) the *Idylls of the King*. Stanza VII, misplaced by poetic license, alludes to the death of Arthur Hallam (now equated with King Arthur) and the writing of *In Memoriam*. Finally comes the ultimate acceptance, the period of faith and idealism (VIII).

JUNE BRACKEN AND HEATHER (page 519), addressed to Tennyson's wife, stood as dedication to his last volume, *The Death of Œnone, Akbar's Dream and Other Poems*.

THE DEATH OF ŒNONE (page 519): See "Œnone" (page 32, above).
Years after her desertion by Paris, Œnone obtains the revenge she has
predicted ("Œnone," l. 253); able if she will to heal him of a wound
from the poisoned arrow of Philoctetes, she chooses to see him die.
Then as his body lies on the funeral pyre, she leaps into the flames to
join him in death. The Gorgon (l. 71) in Greek myth was a hideous
female monster, the sight of whose head could turn the beholder to
stone.

AKBAR'S DREAM (page 522): Akbar the Great, emperor of Hindustan
from 1556 to 1605, practiced a broad religious toleration in the belief
that truth lay in the best of all creeds. Tennyson pictures him dreaming of a temple for the new faith, the threats to its continuance and
at last the acceptance by all men of an an enlightened religion. The
Hymn to the Sun (here reprinted) concludes the dream.

CROSSING THE BAR (page 523), though written and published in 1889,
was, according to Tennyson's own wish, to be placed "at the end of
all editions" of his poems.

INDEX OF TITLES

RIVERSIDE EDITIONS

* In preparation